Museum Administration

AMERICAN ASSOCIATION FOR STATE AND LOCAL HISTORY BOOK SERIES

ABOUT THE SERIES

The American Association for State and Local History Book Series publishes technical and professional information for those who practice and support history, and addresses issues critical to the field of state and local history. To submit a proposal or manuscript to the series, please request proposal guidelines from AASLH headquarters: AASLH Book Series, 1717 Church St., Nashville, Tennessee 37203. Telephone: (615) 320-3203. Fax: (615) 327-9013. Web site: www.aaslh.org.

ABOUT THE ORGANIZATION

The American Association for State and Local History (AASLH) is a nonprofit educational organization dedicated to advancing knowledge, understanding, and appreciation of local history in the United States and Canada. In addition to sponsorship of this book series, the Association publishes the periodical *History News*, a newsletter, technical leaflets and reports, and other materials; confers prizes and awards in recognition of outstanding achievement in the field; and supports a broad education program and other activities designed to help members work more effectively. To join the organization, contact: Membership Director, AASLH, 1717 Church St., Nashville, Tennessee 37203.

Museum Administration

An Introduction

Hugh H. Genoways
and
Lynne M. Ireland

A Division of Rowman & Littlefield Publishers, Inc.
Walnut Creek • Lanham • New York • Toronto • Oxford

ALTAMIRA PRESS
A Division of Rowman & Littlefield Publishers, Inc.
1630 North Main Street, #367
Walnut Creek, CA 94596
www.altamirapress.com

Rowman & Littlefield Publishers, Inc.
A Member of the Rowman & Littlefield Publishing Group
4501 Forbes Boulevard, Suite 200
Lanham, MD 20706

PO Box 317
Oxford
OX2 9RU, UK

British Library Cataloguing in Publication Information Available

Library of Congress Cataloging-in-Publication Data

Genoways, Hugh H.
Museum administration : an introduction / Hugh H. Genoways and Lynne M. Ireland.
p. cm.—(American Association for State and Local History book series)
Includes bibliographical references and index.
ISBN 0-7591-0293-7 (alk. paper)—ISBN 0-7591-0294-5 (pbk. : alk. paper)
1. Museums—Management. 2. Museums—United States—Management.
I. Ireland, Lynne M., 1953– II. Title. III. Series.

AM121.G465 2003 ISBN: 978-0-7591-0294-1
069′.068—dc21 2003002004

Printed in the United States of America

∞™ The paper used in this publication meets the minimum requirements of American National Standard for Information Sciences—Permanence of Paper for Printed Library Materials, ANSI/NISO Z39.48-1992.

CONTENTS

PREFACE

A leader is best
When people barely know he exists,
When his work is done, his aim fulfilled,
They will say:
We did it ourselves.

—Lao-Tzu, sixth-century B.C. Taoist poet

The best executive is the one who has sense enough to pick good men to do what he wants done, and the self-restraint enough to keep from meddling with them while they do it.

—Theodore Roosevelt, twenty-sixth President of the United States, 1901–1909

Details are not my thing. You wouldn't expect the captain of a ship to go down and fix the boiler, would you?

—Jesse "The Body" Ventura, Governor of Minnesota, 2001

Although these quotes give excellent insight into the leadership that administrators must provide to their organizations, they do not describe the complexity that administrators in museums will encounter. Indeed, museum administrators will find themselves in a position, unless they work for a few of the largest museums in the country, where they need to fulfill many roles because there may be no one else to do the job. They may well need to go and "fix the boiler" or else expect to be cold. And after fixing the boiler, they may well need to scrub the toilet prior to reading a budget report, calming a stressed-out volunteer, and giving a personal tour to a potential donor. We hope this book will give students and those taking on new administrative duties some of the knowledge they will need to meet these challenges.

This book is the outgrowth of our teaching a course in museum administration and management in the Museum Studies Program at the University of Nebraska-Lincoln each year since 1991. It has been prepared partly as a textbook for use in similar courses, but we also believe it will be useful to individual readers who are interested in increasing their knowledge of museum administration as they grow in their professional careers.

Throughout this book material has been set aside in special boxes to enhance the understanding of the subject being covered. Many boxes highlight practical knowledge gleaned from relevant sources. Additionally, three types of boxes contain materials that give the reader special insight into or opportunity for applying the concepts discussed in the text.

Case Reviews are brief summaries of real situations that have occurred in museum-related organizations and that pertain to particular topics under consideration. These offer insight into how real-life scenarios develop and evolve, devolve, and are eventually resolved.

Case Studies are fictitious situations presented for the reader to analyze and resolve. Readers looking for the "correct" answers to the case studies will be disappointed. We use case studies as the basis of class discussions, and we tell our students the "correct" answers are those that they can concisely state and defend. Many issues with which museum administrators must deal, and the appropriate responses to them, will depend upon the circumstances under which they arise. No answer will work in every situation. We want our readers to learn to think analytically, to develop their basic administrative philosophy, and to be able to state the issues and their proposed courses of action succinctly.

Exercises, as their title implies, will provide readers an opportunity to practice preparing documents, statements, and policies they will need in administrative positions.

The unifying theme and activity throughout this book and our course is a project to plan a new museum (Box P.1) and to prepare all of the documents and policies the institution would need to operate. This book is arranged in the general order in which we would expect the documents to be prepared, beginning with a mission statement and bylaws and ending with a code of professional conduct. The final three chapters (13–15)

Box P.1

Exercise: Museum Plan

As a member of a group, plan a museum of a predesignated type (art, history, anthropology, natural science). Your museum has an annual budget of $650,000 and has just been given a newly renovated structure of 40,000 square feet, all at ground level. Your plan should include at least the elements listed below.

For those using this book as a textbook, this is a semester-long project. For those readers who are using this book individually or as a member of a small group of staff, follow along with this exercise as you read through the book. Try your hand at writing these documents as examples to use as models at a later time. Or use this list of documents and the information in the following chapters to create these documents for your institution.

mission statement and symbol
bylaws
strategic plan
budget (benefits are 24.32 percent of salaries)
personnel policies
collection policies
public program policies
multicultural statement
staffing
marketing plan
floor plan
development plan
code of professional museum conduct (two-page limit)

The total document should not exceed fifty pages, double-spaced, typed. You will find the book *Organizing Your Museum: The Essentials*, edited by Sara Dubberly, particularly useful in this project.

discuss legal and philosophical issues that all museum administrators need to consider.

The semester-long planning project in our course is always done in small groups of four to seven people. It is so organized because we believe that the ability to function in small groups or teams is critical to successful work in the museum environment. Observing the functioning of these groups has been fascinating. All have successfully completed the assigned task, but in many cases the experience has been very uncomfortable. Our educational system does not promote and recognize team or group achievement; rather, notice and "glory" go to the individual whose performance is exemplary. This is not a good background for museum work. Today's museum staffers must be willing to submerge their desire for personal recognition in the effort to attain recognition and success for the institution. We urge anyone using this book as a text to emphasize the team approach in every aspect of coursework and professional work. Students need the experience and all of us have more to learn about effective work in groups.

Acknowledgments

We wish to extend our gratitude to Merlin P. Lawson, Dean of Graduate Studies, University of Nebraska-Lincoln, for long-term and continuing support of the Museum Studies Program. We deeply appreciate the support of Lawrence Sommer, Director of the Nebraska State Historical Society, throughout this project and for arranging release time for Lynne Ireland for the final preparation of the manuscript. The excellent editorial work of Deborah B. Eisloeffel significantly improved the manuscript for this book. Angie Fox, Technical Artist, University of Nebraska State Museum, prepared the organizational charts that appear in chapter 3. Whitney Bruhn checked facts and index entries.

Our thanks also go to the students who have taken our course in museum administration and management. They have aided this project in countless ways, including serving as guinea pigs for testing of this manuscript as it developed. They also assisted with literature searches, research, writing, discussions, and fact checking. We are grateful to each of them: Carolyn Albracht, Patty Amgwert, Mary Anne Andrei, Deborah Arenz, Leann Arndt, Steve Arnold, Julie Ashby, Eric Bachenberg, Kelli Bacon, Marcia Baker, Sandra Barnum, David Barrett, Laura (Barss) Mooney, Shannon Beatty, Gwen Bedient, Kristin Bergquist, James Bert, Zachary Beverage, David Bingell, Lorraine Blahnik-Leak, Renee Boen, William Bomar, René Botts, Courtney Bradsby, Laurie Bragg, Peterson Brink, Barbara (Burke) Brockley, William Bush, Judy Buss, Melissa Calderwood, Ruth Callahan, Jeffrey Cannon, Natalie Carlsson, Laura Casey, Vicki Pike Clarke, Aimee Clem, Nathan Collins, Rebecca Copple, Jennifer Cook, Gregory Cox, Erin Crombach, Mary Cruse, Susan Curtis, Mark Daniels, Sarah Davis, Paula Doe, Sonya Dollins-Colton, the late Dianne Draeger, William N. Duly, David Dyer, Cyndi Edwards, Sara

(Emmons) Lamb, Michael Florer, Julienne Foster, Susan Foutz, Saundra Frerichs, Debra Garden, Margaret Genoways, Sarah Gleason, Amanda Goudy, Matthew Goyer, Amy Greving, Judith Gustafson, Sharon Gustafson, Belinda Hall, Guy Hanley, the late William Hansen, Marin Hanson, Michelle Amina Harm, Erin Hauser, Jennifer Hiechel, Mary Frances Hill, Pam (Sept) Hill, Tommy Lee Hill, Pam (Correll) Howard, Shelley Howe, Julie Hutchinson, Celia Ison, Patricia Jacques, Karen Janovy, Jeffrey Johns, Christopher Johnson, Lana Koepke Johnson, Jason Jurgena, Yunju Kim, Dean Knudsen, Jill Koelling, Teresa Kreutzer, Michael Lacome, Mandy Langfald, Jennifer Laughlin, Tracy Lauritzen Wright, Michael Lebens, Yonghun Lee, Sylvia Lee-Nguyen, Shannon Liedell, Jong-Deock Lim, Grace Linden, Mara Linsky, Cybele Londono, Margaret Lyman, Margaret Macdonald, Kathy (Maloney) Partee, Brian Mancuso, Lillian Martens, Josephine Martins, Ron Marvin, Pam (Maurer) Cuttlers, Jeffrey McConkey, Patricia McElyea, Holly (Trimper) McEntee, Stephanie (Mestl) Polk, Mary-Jo Miller, Tadashi Mizusaki, Amber Mohr, Thomas Mooney, Kevin Moriarty, Raney Morrison, Jill Mulligan, Warner Myers, Clint Neuguth, Emily Nimsakont, Nao Nomura, Erica Nordmeier, Faith Norwood, Lisa Nun, Kevin Obrist, Samantha Pawley, Kristy Peterson, Lois Peterson, Steve Pettit, Carolyn Pirnat, Sarah Polak, Tina Nicole Maria Popson, Gail DeBuse Potter, Fred Poyner IV, Vonnda Pulscher, Eloise Ramirez, Rachel Rarick, Shirley Ray, F. James Remar, Keely Rennie, Karin Roberts, Zachary Roehrs, Diane Rogness, Russell Ronspies, Margaret Merlyn Ropp, Nancy Russell, DiAnna Schenck, Carrie Schneider, Sara (Scott) Sudbeck, Kirsten Seifikar, Susie Severson, Megan Sharp, Susan Shore, Angela Simon, Samuel Sinner, Roxanne Smith, Janneken Smucker, Susan Soriente, John Stepp, Elizabeth Schirber Stinson, Jessica Carlat Stoner, Stacey Stonum, Susan Stout, Janelle (Strandberg) Aieta, Carrie (Streeter) Jackson, Pui Siu Sun, Judy Sweeney, Rachel Swetland, Jennifer Taylor, Kristen Thimijan, Joel Thoreson, Michele Tilley, Jeff Tolin, April Tollison-Kleinfeldt, Jennifer Torres, Dana Twersky, Ina Van Der Veen, Rena Vannoy, Alison Van Wagner, Luis Vasquez, Terry Vidal, Elizabeth Villa, Brian Volkmer, Theodore Volkmer, Karen Wagner, Kathy (Wakeley) Wachter-Heinle, Ruth Anne Walker, Carolyn Wallingford, Deborah Wallis, Stacey Walsh, Jennifer Wiggins, Beth Wilkins, Bart Wilsey, Diane Wilson, Nelle Woods, Melissa Woodson, Linda Wruck, Jenny Yearous, Soon-Bong Yoon, Courtney Yilk, and Michael Zaidman.

CHAPTER ONE
INTRODUCTION

Who Wants to Be a Museum Administrator?

Each year as we start our course in Museum Administration and Management, we ask our students: "Who wants to be a museum administrator when you graduate?" Most years we get two or three students to raise their hands. In over ten years of teaching, we do not recall more than a third of the class claiming museum administration to be their ambition. This paltry response causes us to opine that the museums of this country are going to be really clean, because the bulk of these students must be destined for the broom-pushing squad. Of all the staff members of museums, in our experience it's only the lowliest custodian who does not have administrative and managerial responsibilities.

Anyone seeking a professional position within a museum must expect that a certain amount of time will be devoted to administrative duties. Even the smallest project will involve a plan of work, the assignment of someone to do it, and a budget to pay for it. The manager of that project will be expected to see the work done, done well, on time, and within the confines of the allotted budget. The office manager procuring and maintaining supplies for use by the staff; the staff artist determining the need for and then purchasing and monitoring use of materials for museum exhibitions; the registrar negotiating a loan; the educator scheduling volunteer docents—all are functioning as administrators.

This book, therefore, is not just for museum directors or department heads but for all members of the museum staff who have administrative duties. (To our way of thinking, that's just about everybody.) Although originally conceived as a textbook for students taking a course in museum administration as part of a graduate degree program in museum studies, we believe this book will also be especially appropriate for museum staff members who are just entering the museum profession or who are moving ahead in their careers and taking on more administrative responsibilities.

Yes, that is correct! If you see yourself "moving ahead" or "moving up" in your museum career, you can expect your administrative duties to increase, along with the amount of time you devote to these responsibilities. Anyone entering the museum profession (or for that matter any profession) should expect a career filled with ever increasing administrative duties. It is important to study and to improve administrative skills, as well as museum knowledge, throughout our careers. Many people reach a plateau in their professional development beyond which they are not able to succeed; most often this involves some failure in administrative responsibilities because the person has not adequately developed the skills the position requires.

Although written centuries before museums developed as the institutions we know today, Chaucer's observation is apt: "The life so short, the craft so long to learn." We hope this book will serve as a starting point for a long life of learning about how to make museums work.

What Is Administration?

"Administration" comes from the Latin *administrare,* "to serve." "Manage" has as its root the word *manus* or "hand." It seems fitting to us that administration and management are fundamentally "hands-on" words, because making things happen is what administration and management are all about. To administer is "to have charge of, to direct and control the use of, to exert control over,"[1] and it is this responsibility and authority that make administration satisfying, worthwhile, and even fun. Museum administrators make choices, developing and executing plans so that museum collections can be preserved and museum visitors can have compelling experiences with the artifacts and specimens from those collections—a far cry from the mere paper pushing that gives administration a bad name.

That's not to say that putting things down on paper isn't important. In fact, the preparation of plans and documents is a major component of the museum administrators' purview. Creation of a mission statement and a strategic plan is the most vital; these two documents define the museum's niche in both the not-for-profit and the museum worlds and determine how these roles will be filled. Other guiding documents that must be written (or reviewed and revised if already in existence) and then implemented include:

- bylaws
- articles of incorporation
- organizational chart
- budget
- policies related to collections management, personnel, facilities, and public programs
- development, marketing, and public relations plans
- code of professional conduct

Administration of the organization requires skill in conflict management, interpersonal relations, budget management and monitoring, and staff supervision and evaluation. Managers must also set legal and ethical standards and maintain involvement in the museum profession. Certainly all of these issues are very important, but we would place budget management and staff evaluations at the top of our lists. Financially sound museums are the only ones that have the opportunity to fulfill their stated missions. Financial stability is no accident; it results from active budget management. Effective staff evaluation ensures the maximum utility of the museum's most important asset, the time and skills of its staff. The most innovative and exceptional mission statement and strategic plan come to naught if the financial and human resources are not managed well.

What Webster's definition of administration does not address are the critical elements of leadership and vision, but these are qualities museum administrators, particularly directors, are expected to embody. They are difficult attributes to define and instill, partly because our notions of what leadership is and how it should be exercised are shifting. Leadership is no longer perceived as the solitary province of the person "in charge"; rather it is exhibited by every staff member who has the ability to institute change, and does so, however minor that change might be. Similarly, we cite as visionary institutions that have found new mechanisms for community involvement and ownership, over those that have merely realized some particular project. Another meaning of administration's Latin root *ministere* is "to serve"; visionary leadership in museums in the twenty-first century is revealed by an institution-wide commitment to this fundamental meaning.

One way to move the discussion of leadership and vision from the ethereal to the concrete is the strategic planning process. If this process is done in a "bottom-up" fashion, with a broad representation of the museum's staff, board, supporters, and audience, this group of stakeholders can develop a common vision for the museum. This shared vision gives the museum administrator an agreed-upon direction in which to lead and informs the activity of museum administrators throughout the organization.

What Is a Museum?

The American Association of Museums (AAM) defines a museum as "an organized and permanent nonprofit institution, essentially educational or esthetic in purpose, with professional staff, which owns and utilizes tangible objects, cares for them, and exhibits them to the public on some regular schedule."[2] Institutional activities, such as education, collection, preservation, and exhibition, are based on objects. In addition, the AAM recognizes as museums certain types of institutions that do not collect (for example, art centers, children's museums, nature centers, planetariums, and science and technology centers), because they exhibit objects and use them for educational purposes, even if they do not hold collections permanently.

Collecting institutions can be broadly divided into those that hold nonliving collections and those that maintain living ones. Although the AAM does not list archives among the types of museums holding nonliving collections, our definition of museums does include archives because they make and preserve collections, use them for educational purposes, and on occasion will exhibit them. Many "museums" hold significant archival collections as well.

Expanding technology is raising new questions about what constitutes a collection and whether "objects" can exist solely in electronic form. All museum professionals should determine how they believe museums should be defined and why. Consider the case review "What's in a Name" and draw your own conclusions.

Box 1.1

Case Review: What's in a Name?

The American Association of Museums' (AAM's) definition of museums has been extended to include noncollecting organizations, such as nature centers and science centers. This was done in the belief that the primary characteristic of the modern museum is its educational function: using objects in hands-on, active, or inquiry-based programs.

If noncollecting museums can fall under the AAM definition, why can't the name "museum" be extended to include nonexhibiting institutions as well? If "education using objects" is the most important issue, why is "exhibits open to the public on a regular basis" a critical defining characteristic? Can museums be educational without exhibits?

Some types of "museums" are excluded under the AAM definition already, and there will be new challenges to the limits of this definition in the future. We already are seeing virtual museums, which exist only in cyberspace, appearing on the World Wide Web. Do these institutions have "collections"? Do cyberspace images qualify as exhibits? They are certainly available to the public on a regular basis. Should these museums be included under the AAM definition? Many are definitely intended to educate the public.

Some university-based natural history museums have major collections of specimens and artifacts, but they are not included under the AAM definition of museums, and they are not able to compete for funds from the federally funded Institute of Museum and Library Services (IMLS) because they do not have exhibits that are open to the public on a regular basis. However, they use their specimens for educational purposes in a variety of other ways. Research based on studies of these collections is published, adding to the total body of knowledge of humankind. This new knowledge informs a wide variety of educational programs, including the programs of other museums. The specimens and artifacts are used in classroom and laboratory education, which is hands-on, active, formal education at the undergraduate or graduate levels. These museums also provide educational opportunities through tours of the collections; furthermore, staff answer inquiries from the public, write popular and semipopular articles and books, and present public lectures. Why are museums such as the Museum of Southwestern Biology at the University of New Mexico, the Texas Cooperative Wildlife Collections at Texas A&M University, and the Museum of Vertebrate Zoology at the University of California-Berkeley not included under the AAM definition and eligible for funding from IMLS? Do you think exhibition of collections on a regular basis should be the critical factor in determining eligibility?

How do you think "museum" should be defined?

Virtual museums:

http://www.diegorivera.com/index.html	The Virtual Diego Rivera Web Museum, accessed December 16, 2002
http://www.foodmuseum.com/	The Food Museum, accessed December 16, 2002
http://2k.si.edu/	The Virtual Smithsonian, accessed December 16, 2002

Box 1.1 (continued)

University museums:

http://www.unm.edu/~museum/	Museum of Southwestern Biology, University of New Mexico, accessed December 16, 2002
http://wfscnet.tamu.edu/tcwc/tcwc.htm	Texas Cooperative Wildlife Collections, Texas A&M University, accessed December 16, 2002
http://www.ip.berkeley.edu/mvz/	Museum of Vertebrate Zoology, University of California, Berkeley, accessed December 16, 2002

Types of Museums

Museums holding nonliving collections can be divided into categories based upon such criteria as users, disciplinary areas, parent organizations, and governance structure. Children's museums are defined primarily by their principal users—children. Disciplinary divisions identify art, anthropology, history, natural history, or science museums and historic sites and houses. Many museums are classified as *general museums* because of the breadth of their collections and programs, whereas others are considered *specialty museums* because of their narrow focus on particular topics, for instance, halls of fame and sports, automobile, and technology museums. Institutions with living collections that are considered museums include aquariums, arboretums, botanical gardens, and zoos (see box 1.2, near the end of this chapter, for a more complete list).

Many museums are operated by a variety of government entities, including federal, state, county, and city units. Universities and colleges operate another large group of museums. Some museums are operated by for-profit companies, usually through a nonprofit subdivision. Another large group of museums is operated by parent not-for-profit societies and organizations. Museums operated by historical and zoological societies fall in this category. Finally, museums may be operated as nonprofit organizations by free-standing, often self-perpetuating boards of trustees.

In reading museum literature, one will often see references to "public" museums or "private" museums. These terms are sometimes mistakenly thought to refer to the funding sources for museums, but in reality they distinguish the type of governance of the museum and the parent organization, if there is one. Public museums are under the control of public or governmental entities, such as federal or state agencies, public universities, county government, or city parks departments. Private museums are under the control of private boards or private companies. Generally, public museums receive the majority of their funding from public sources—for example, federal, state, or county budgets. Private museums generally receive the majority of their funds from private sources, such as corporations, endowment returns, and individual contributions. Yet public museums may receive some funds from endowment returns or funds raised from private individuals, and private museums may receive public funds from government grants or direct budgetary allocations from a governmental entity. Finally, both public and private museums can earn income from entrance fees, museum stores, educational programs, and many other sources.

Regardless of category, almost all museums exist for some public purpose. Although their use is somewhat confusing, the terms "public" and "private" will be encountered commonly in museum literature.

The Museum Profession

Although we talk about "the museum profession," there is no uniform concurrence that such a beast exists. The controversy extends back at least as far as the 1930s. Alexander Ruthven, museum director at the University of Michigan, wrote in 1931, "A museum man is a professional zoologist, botanist, geologist, archaeologist, business man, teacher, editor, taxidermist, or some other kind of specialist, working in a museum and having a knowledge of methods of gathering, preserving, demonstrating, and otherwise using data which should be saved. He cannot be a professional museum man, for his institution can only serve the world through the efforts of specialists, in particular fields of knowledge."[3] Albert Parr,[4] director of the American Museum of Natural History, echoed these same ideas in the 1950s and 1960s.

Laurence Coleman, writing in *The Museum in America* in 1939, countered this idea, arguing that museum work was a discipline of its own.[5] Later, Edward Alexander also supported this idea in his 1979 *Museums in*

Motion: "The paramount essence of the museum profession is a common cause and goals."[6] As recently as 1988, Stephen Weil questioned the existence of a museum profession: "Some believe that American museum workers have already succeeded in achieving this status. Others doubt that they ever can. . . . I think that almost everybody, however, would agree that many important improvements in American museums themselves have come about as a by-product of this struggle by museum workers to gain professional identification."[7] Victor Danilov, after citing the pundits above, concluded in 1994, "Museum work may or may not be looked upon as a profession, depending upon one's interpretation, but there appears to be little doubt that many aspects of museum work are professional in nature and require specialized training and experience."[8]

We believe that there is a museum profession and that this profession initially can be identified by its adherence to a common set of values as described by Mary Anne Andrei and Hugh Genoways[9] and more fully discussed in chapter 10. We agree that there is a diverse range of specialists who work in museums and reflect equally diverse backgrounds and training. But if we use the standards that define a profession in conjunction with these common values the shape and existence of the museum profession become obvious.[10]

Eileen Hoffman, in Danilov's book, suggests several standards that define a profession. The first is "intellectual activities after long, specialized education and training."[11] Everyone would agree that museum work is essentially intellectual, but is there uniformity of training? There is an ever-expanding number of museum studies and related academic programs, providing long, specialized education for an increasing number of the people entering the museum profession. Some individuals still take a discipline-based route into the museum profession and adhere to the common values of their particular specialization; they just happen to be performing their work in a museum environment. Thus we conclude that not all people working in museums (even some who have been employed by museums for long periods of time) are members of the profession.

Hoffman's second criterion is that the work of a profession is service-oriented and not for personal gain. This is the essence of museum work and clearly the basis for the common values of the museum profession. The third marker of a profession is that it "sets its own standards, adopts a code of ethics, and has a strong closely-knit professional organization."[12]

The activities of the American Association of Museums surely have set the standards for the profession through accreditation of museums and by establishing the criteria for museum studies programs. The AAM has established a code of ethics (although we believe it would be more aptly called a code of professional conduct), and the common values we will discuss in chapter 10 represent a set of professional ethics.

We concur with the conclusion that "such controversy notwithstanding, a professional structure is now in place with national and international representation, numbering thousands of institutions and individuals who communicate regularly among themselves through publications and programs, and it has resulted in a de facto profession."[13] The museum profession may be in its early years of development, but it is well established, and there will be no return to pre-professional days.

Museum Studies Programs

"Museum studies" refers to academic programs designed to prepare students for professional positions within museums. Many were developed based upon the recommendations of the Professional Practices Committee of the AAM in 1983.[14] In their broadest definition, museum studies programs may include applied history, arts management, conservation, decorative arts, historical administration, historic preservation, nonprofit management, public administration, public affairs, public history, and public horticulture. Most museum studies programs offer master of arts (M.A.) or master of science (M.S.) degrees, although there are at least six institutions in the United States that offer programs at the baccalaureate level. There are no doctoral-level programs in museum studies, but there are some in the associated areas of public history and arts administration. Some institutions offer only a few courses in museum studies, while others provide minors in museum studies as part of a degree in a subject-matter discipline. Another option is one of several certificate programs. These are generally one or two years in length and are usually taken in conjunction with, or following, another graduate degree.

The survey of training programs conducted by the AAM in 1998 listed just over 180 academic programs offering some type of museum studies training. The 1999 *Guide to Museum Studies and Training in the United States* lists over 50 graduate degree-granting academic programs in museum studies. These programs have had their detractors, who believe there is no substitute for experience. In the past, the primary path into the museum profession was not academic; individuals with disciplinary expertise would be hired by museums and allowed "to work their way up through the organization," learning the profession as they progressed in their careers. This system has developed some excellent professionals. The prime benefit we think museum studies programs offer is to greatly reduce the time needed to learn the basics of the museum profession—typically eight to ten years of on-the-job learning down to approximately two years in a program. Of course classroom work cannot replace real-world experience, which academic programs help provide by requiring three- to six-month museum internships for their students.

Museum historian Edward Alexander notes the roots of museum studies programs extend back as far as 1908–1910, when three programs were initiated. Sarah Stevenson started a high school diploma program at the Philadelphia Museum of Art to prepare students for work in art museums. At the Farnsworth Museum at Wellesley College, Myrtilla Avery started a course combining museum and art library skills. At the University of Iowa, Professor Homer Dill began a program that resulted in a minor in museum studies to go with a four-year degree in natural science. This program included taxidermy, exhibit techniques, freehand drawing, and modeling. Of these three programs, only the one at the University of Iowa survives today.[15]

John Cotton Dana and Paul J. Sachs started two famous early museum training programs. Dana's at the Newark Museum provided a year of apprenticeship for groups of postbaccalaureate students who were given lectures in addition to work in various programs within the museum. Sachs's one-year graduate program at Harvard University combined course work in museum studies and art history with experience at the Fogg Art Museum.[16]

Following World War II and through the 1960s, museum studies programs developed slowly, but the 1970s saw explosive growth in new programs, mirroring the eruption of new museums nationwide. The majority of today's academic training programs in museum studies had their origins between 1970 and 1979. New programs have continued to appear, indicating a bright future for this developing academic field and auguring a continuing and expanding need for trained museum professionals.

Public History Programs

Some museum professionals receive training through public history programs. The Public History Resource Center website suggests that public historians, "as opposed to academic Historians, work with and for the general public. They work in archives, museums, public policy organizations, historical societies, and in media. . . . The purpose of a public historian is to collect, preserve, and disseminate information on the past. Public Historians use such tools as photographs, oral histories, museum exhibitions, and multimedia to address a wide variety of historical issues and to present those issues to a non-academic audience."

Many individuals looking to enter the field of public history pursue a graduate degree and can choose from, at last count, more than sixty graduate programs in the United States. A graduate degree in public history (or museum studies) can be a great asset when entering the museum field. In *Public History, An Introduction*, D. B. Mock observes, "Even in the small historical museum, an undergraduate degree is virtually essential, and more and more beginning professionals are coming to the field with master's or doctoral degrees in history or a related academic specialty."[17] Public history programs "have prepared students well for careers whether in museum, archives, records management, or other fields closely allied to the historical discipline," D. C. Dolan concludes.[18]

The National Council on Public History, located in Indianapolis, Indiana, "works to advance the professionalism of public history and to advocate enhanced public and governmental support for historical programs." It maintains a website, publishes *The Public Historian* quarterly journal and the quarterly *Public History News,* sponsors an annual conference, and serves as a clearinghouse of information on public history programs and courses, including publishing *A Guide to Graduate Programs in Public History.*

Archival Management Programs

The Society of American Archivists (SAA) has approved a curriculum for a Master of Archival Studies (MAS). While no institutions seem to have adopted the full program, a number of colleges and universities are providing archival academic training. The traditional route to obtain training in archival management has been through master of library science programs. The SAA website[19] lists fifteen such programs, including those at the Catholic University of America, Dominican University, Long Island University, Pratt Institute, Rutgers University, St. John's University, University of Albany, University of Kentucky, University of Maryland, University of Pittsburgh, University of South Carolina, University of Southern Mississippi, University of Texas at Austin, University of Wisconsin-Milwaukee, and Wayne State University.

The SAA website lists sixteen additional academic programs that offer degrees or course work in archival management and administration. These programs offer certificates and minors or majors with M.A., M.S., and Ph.D. degrees through such departments as history, public history, and information science. An interestingly diverse program in this group is the M.A. in Archival, Museum, and Editing Studies at Duquesne University. Adams and Ritzenthaler[20] list twenty other academic programs that offer course work in archival studies, including museum studies, public history, preservation studies, and historic administration programs. The Graduate Program in Museum Studies at the University of Nebraska-Lincoln, for example, offers a specialization in archival management within the M.A. and M.S. degrees it awards.

Museum Associations

When you enter the museum profession, you are joining a group that has national and international members. Museum workers have formed professional associations to share their ideas and further their mutual interests. In the United States, the primary professional museum association is the American Association of Museums, located in Washington, D.C. The AAM holds annual meetings and publishes the magazine *Museum News,* covering current issues in the profession; *Aviso,* a newsletter that carries notices, career opportunities, and service advertisements; specific "how-to" guides and research results through its Technical Information Service; and books on museum issues. The AAM advocates for national issues that further the interests of museums and museum professionals and offers continuing education through its workshop series. The association's Accreditation Commission[21] sets "the gold standard" and grants accreditation to museums that meet its rigorous criteria. The Association also supports six regional museum associations:

Southeastern Museums Conference (SEMC) (Alabama, Arkansas, Florida, Georgia, Kentucky, Louisiana, Mississippi, North Carolina, South Carolina, Tennessee, Virginia, West Virginia)
Mid-Atlantic Association of Museums (MAAM) (District of Columbia, Delaware, Maryland, New Jersey, New York, Pennsylvania)
Association of Midwest Museums (AMM) (Illinois, Indiana, Iowa, Michigan, Minnesota, Missouri, Ohio, Wisconsin)
Mountain-Plains Museums Association (MPMA) (Colorado, Kansas, Montana, Nebraska, New Mexico, North Dakota, Oklahoma, South Dakota, Texas, Wyoming)
New England Museums Association (NEMA) (Connecticut, Maine, Massachusetts, New Hampshire, Rhode Island, Vermont)
Western Museums Association (WMA) (Alaska, Arizona, California, Hawaii, Idaho, Nevada, Oregon, Utah, Washington)

These associations hold annual meetings and produce newsletters with job notices and technical information. The regional associations also sponsor professional development workshops.

Nearly every state has its own state museum association. Their programs vary greatly, but they all offer an excellent opportunity for new museum professionals to become involved in the museum community. The National Association of State Museum Associations (NASMA) website lists contacts for state organizations, many of which maintain their own web presence.

Twelve Standing Professional Committees carry out many of the activities of the AAM:

Museum Management Committee
Committee on Audience Research and Evaluation
Committee on Museum Professional Training
Curators Committee
Development and Membership
Committee on Education
Media and Technology

Museum Association Security Committee
National Association for Museum Exhibition (NAME)
Public Relations and Marketing
Registrar Committee
Small Museum Administrators[22]

As their names indicate, the committees focus on museum occupations and professional activities. These committees offer an excellent opportunity for new professionals to be involved in "the museum business."

The Council of Affiliates of the AAM is a group of more than two dozen other museum associations, generally representing more specialized groups of museums and interests. Members of the Council range from the American Association for Museum Volunteers and the Council of American Jewish Museums to the International Museum Theatre Alliance and the Museum Store Association.[23] Professional staff members working in these areas will find advantages in joining the appropriate associations.

The American Association for State and Local History (AASLH) is another very important museum-related organization. This not-for-profit professional organization of individuals and institutions is dedicated to the "promotion of effort and activity in the fields of state, provincial and local history in the United States and Canada." Based in Nashville, Tennessee, AASLH encourages the highest-quality expressions of state and local history through publications, exhibits, public programs, and professional development activities. The AASLH publishes *History News,* a quarterly magazine that includes practical how-to information and in-depth professional articles; *Dispatch,* a monthly newsletter that reports on training programs, exhibitions, publications, and career opportunities; and *Technical Leaflets,* practical instructional guides for museum tasks from constructing exhibit mounts to the proper storage of photographs and documents. The organization also publishes books of interest to the profession in partnership with AltaMira Press. AASLH offers quality workshops at sites around the country, holds annual meetings, and operates the Video Lending Library, which provides informational and training videos.

Institutions with living collections are represented by two major organizations in North America. Established in 1924, the American Zoo and

Aquarium Association (AZA) is dedicated to the advancement of zoos and aquariums in the Americas and strives for higher levels of professionalism among facilities and for those working in zoos and aquariums. AZA has adopted conservation of the world's wildlife and its habitats as its highest priority. Accreditation of institutions was enacted on a voluntary basis in 1972; today, all institutional members must be accredited by the AZA. In addition, members pledge to follow the Code of Professional Ethics that was adopted in 1976. AZA offices in Silver Spring, Maryland, provide a monthly newsletter, *Communiqué,* as well as brochures designed to support the conservation goals of its members.

The American Association of Botanical Gardens and Arboreta (AABGA), based in Pennsylvania, is the professional association for public gardens in North America. It publishes a monthly newsletter and the quarterly journal *The Public Garden,* and sponsors regional and national conferences each year.

The Society of American Archivists (SAA) is the oldest (founded in 1936) and largest national professional association for archivists. The Society publishes a semiannual journal, *American Archivist;* a bimonthly newsletter, *Archival Outlook;* and books on a variety of archival topics. It sponsors an annual meeting, workshops, and continuing education opportunities.

The International Council of Museums (ICOM), based in Paris, France, represents the international museum profession. ICOM publishes *Museum International* and has working groups that focus on museum careers. The ICOM and the AAM have a joint committee to conduct business of mutual interest; regional and national museum associations in every part of the globe partner similarly with ICOM.[24]

It's Only an Introduction

As our definitions, issues, and resources listed here illustrate, everyone entering the world of museum administration is becoming part of a complex profession. So even with more than a dozen chapters, this text can be only an introduction. You will recognize after a quick glance at the topics covered that each of them has been the subject of hundreds, and in many cases thousands, of books. Marketing, public relations, accounting, budgeting, personnel management, interpersonal relations, and the law—

these are the focus of entire professions. People devote whole careers to understanding and contributing to each of these fields. So it is inevitable that our discussions here are merely "introductions" to the many topics museum administration touches in some way.

What does the inclusion of all of the disparate subjects in this text mean? In order to function effectively in their positions, museum administrators need to develop basic skills in all these areas. "Jack-of-all-trades, but a master of none" may be an apt description of many neophyte museum administrators, but we believe that if you read this book, work the exercises, and discuss the case studies and case reviews, you should have most of the baseline skills necessary to function as a museum administrator. You will have entered the "novice class."

To move closer to "master of some," you should read most or all of the references and additional works listed. Familiarity with these resources, when coupled with actual museum experience, will enable you to pass from "novice" in administration to the intermediate level.

Besides basic mastery of the facts and concepts of these professional areas, museum administrators, particularly museum directors, must set ethical standards and must be capable of giving the museum a vision and displaying leadership. How does one become a visionary and a leader? These are intangible qualities, and while we can discuss techniques for making a vision reality or exercising leadership, we are not certain that any book can teach these attributes. Experience is the great teacher.

At least ten years of administrative experience, in our view, is needed to reach the level of "expert" in museum administration, and several of these years should be served as a museum director (or major department head in larger institutions). What's so challenging about museum administrative positions that such a long preparation and contemplation period is needed for mastery? We believe these positions, especially directorships of medium and large museums, are some of the most complex jobs in the not-for-profit sector.

One of the greatest challenges faced by museum administrators is matching expectations with resources. The director, and in turn the middle managers in the museum, will be faced with the sizable and sometimes contradictory expectations of the board, the staff, and the public. Given the skills of the staff and the funds provided by the board, which probably were raised from the community, are there enough resources to meet all the expectations? Is there a shared vision of what these resources will produce?

It is the responsibility of the director and other museum managers to plan, organize, and bring to bear all of the skills of the staff to accomplish the task, whatever it may be. Many museum tasks require teamwork among groups of staff. According to David Fleming, Director of Tyne and Wear Museums in the United Kingdom, "Team building is among the key leadership tasks. The essence of team building is establishing a balance of skills and competencies; agreeing on common aims; and fostering creative discussion."[25] Individual egos and the need for individual recognition must be put aside so that the success of the team and the museum becomes the ultimate goal. Teamwork is not easy under the best of circumstances and is even more difficult under the pressures of understaffing, funding shortages, and tight time schedules.

These circumstances, combined with the high and possibly conflicting expectations of museum constituents, make museum positions quite stressful, especially for managers and directors. The "burn-out" rate is fairly high, and the average length of service of a museum director in a position is less than four years. Given the long lead time needed to make many museum projects reality, such turnover creates considerable instability. Stress is hazardous when you do not deal with it openly and constructively[26]; skills in stress management must be added to all the other skills museum administrators need to learn. "We must be aware of the inherent dangers and develop our own stress management programs."[27]

Continuing education is also a fact of life for museum administrators and can be obtained through such programs as the Museum Management Institute held at the University of California-Berkeley and supported by the Getty Leadership Institute; the Museum Management Program held annually at the University of Colorado in Boulder; the Seminar for Historical Administration; the American Law Institute-American Bar Association's annual "Legal Problems in Museum Administration" course; or the Campbell Center in Mt. Carroll, Illinois, among others. National organizations regularly sponsor workshops and seminars on administration topics. Not only do these programs provide continuing study, but they allow for contemplation and discussions with professional colleagues, and they provide an important opportunity to recharge batteries run low by the challenges of museum administration.

Box 1.2

Museums by Categories Listed in the *Official Museum Directory, 2002*

- Art
  - Art Museums and Galleries
  - Arts and Crafts Museums
  - China, Glass, and Silver Museums
  - Civic Art and Cultural Centers
  - Decorative Arts Museums
  - Folk Art Museums
  - Textile Museums
- Children's Museums
- College and University Museums
- Company Museums
- General Museums
- History
  - Historic Houses and Historic Buildings
  - Historic Sites
  - Historical and Preservation Societies
  - Historical Society Museums
  - Maritime and Naval Museums and Historic Ships
  - Military Museums
  - Preservation Projects
- Nature Centers
- Park Museums and Visitor Centers
- Science
  - Aeronautics and Space Museums
  - Anthropology and Ethnology Museums
  - Aquariums, Marine Museums, and Oceanariums
  - Arboretums
  - Archaeology Museums and Archaeological Sites
  - Aviaries and Ornithology Museums
  - Botanic and Aquatic Gardens, Conservatories, and Horticulture Societies
  - Entomology Museums
  - Geology, Mineralogy, and Paleontology Museums
  - Herbariums
  - Herpetology Museums
  - Medical, Dental, Health, Pharmacological, Apothecary, and Psychiatry Museums
  - Natural History and Natural Science Museums
  - Planetariums, Observatories, and Astronomy Museums
  - Science Museums and Centers
  - Wildlife Refuges and Bird Sanctuaries
  - Zoos

Box 1.2 (continued)

Specialized

Agriculture Museums	Logging and Lumber Museums
Antiques Museums	Mappariums
Architecture Museums	Mining Museums
Audiovisual and Film Museums	Money and Numismatics Museums
Circus Museums	Musical Instruments Museums
Comedy Museums	Philatelic Museums
Communications Museums	Photography Museums
Costume Museums	Religious Museums
Crime Museums	Scouting Museums
Culturally Specific Museums	Sports Museums
Electricity Museums	Technology Museums
Fire-Fighting Museums	Theatre Museums
Forestry Museums	Toy and Doll Museums
Furniture Museums	Transportation Museums
Gun Museums	Typography Museums
Hobby Museums	Village Museums
Horological Museums	Wax Museums
Industrial Museums	Whaling Museums
Lapidary Arts Museums	Woodcarving Museums

Now Who Wants to Be an Administrator?

We've described the challenges facing museum administrators and the wide range of knowledge and experience museum workers need, but we've also offered a sampling of resources available to help museum professionals acquire the mental equipment to respond effectively to our changing museum environment. Museum work right now is as filled with promise as it is fraught with problems. No matter what position you hold in a museum, you will be expected to perform some administrative duties, and every day you work in a museum will present another set of opportunities to make something happen.

Museum administration may sound pretty deadly, but take it from us—in our combined forty years of experience in museum administration we have been aggravated, consternated, exhilarated, frustrated, and stimulated, but we have never been bored. Perhaps that's because at the base of it all, beneath the budgets and the charts and the legalities, is our belief in the power of objects to affect the people who interact with them. This remarkable relationship between people and the objects in which they find meaning is the reason museums exist, and it is made possible by effective museum administration.

Notes

1. Webster's II.
2. Alexander 1979, 5.
3. Danilov 1994, 26.
4. Parr 1960, 1964.
5. Coleman 1939, 418.
6. Alexander 1979, 233.
7. Weil 1988, 31.
8. Danilov 1994, 15.
9. Andrei and Genoways 1997, 6–12.
10. Danilov 1994, 12.
11. Ibid.
12. Ibid.
13. Hein 2000, 41.
14. Professional Practices Committee of the American Association of Museums 1983.
15. Alexander 1997.
16. Alexander 1997, 212.
17. Dolan 1986, 247.
18. Mock 1986, 401.
19. http://www.archivists.org/.
20. Adams and Ritzenthaler 1999.
21. Taylor 1990.
22. AAM 2000, A-14–15.
23. AAM 2000, A-18–21.
24. AAM 2000, A-34–36.
25. Fleming 1999, 98.
26. Janes 1999, 23.
27. Janes 1999, 22.

CHAPTER TWO
IN THE BEGINNING

The missions of museums include collecting and preserving all manner of human-made artifacts and natural specimens (living and nonliving), as well as exhibiting, interpreting, and educating in order to expand our knowledge about ourselves, our society, and our world. It is the aim of museums to be a resource for humankind and to foster an informed appreciation of our diverse world. It is also the goal of museums to preserve this heritage for posterity.[1] Today's many types of museums, although diverse in their individual missions, have in common a commitment to education and public service.

The establishment of a new museum is a complex process requiring a clear sense of purpose on the one hand and compliance with state and federal regulations on the other. The organizers and promoters of a new museum must take time for careful planning because decisions made in the initial stages will determine the future operations of the museum and the success of its programs and activities. The most important first steps in establishing a new museum include developing a well-defined mission statement, writing bylaws, drafting articles of incorporation, and applying to the Internal Revenue Service for tax-exempt status.

Mission Statement

The mission statement should serve as a touchstone for the institution's staff and the board, suggests Will Hendricks, director of Historic Travellers' Rest in Nashville, Tennessee.[2] It may consist of a simple, one-line description, or it may be expanded to cover the institution's goals, purpose, and scope of collections. Many funding agencies, including the Institute of Museum and Library Services, evaluate museums on the effectiveness with which they fulfill their mission. A mission statement can prove useful not only in defining a museum but also in guiding marketing, publicity, and fund-raising. The statement may be printed on museum publications—from letterhead and business cards to brochures and catalogs—or it may become part of advertising—appearing, for example, as a bottom line on publicity materials.[3] A museum's mission becomes its words to live by, benefiting the organization by focusing and inspiring employees, board, and visitors.

As Gail Anderson, writing for the American Association of Museums, correctly observes, a museum must create a well-written statement that conveys the primary purpose of the institution not only to the staff and board, but also to the public.[4] "The mission of a nonprofit organization is more difficult to define than that of a for-profit entity." The mission of a for-profit organization is centered on "profitability, thus the criteria for success include the bottom line, return on investment, sales, profit margins, and market share," and these are calculated easily. In a nonprofit institution, the mission is focused on education and public service, which are more difficult to define and more challenging to measure.[5] For example, how can a museum, which educates the public through exhibits, evaluate its success? A museum may count its number of visitors, but the amount or quality of learning is not so easily quantified.

Development of a successful mission statement depends on creating text that is broad enough to cover the many possible activities in which a museum may wish to engage. This is crucial because laws obligate the board of the museum to limit its activities to those in the mission statement. The mission statement should be both a broad expression of purpose and a guide for the museum in regard to programs, services, and activities. Although it is necessary to file the statement of purpose with the museum's incorporation papers, this document can be amended by a legal procedure. Thus, a museum's mission statement is not etched in stone and can be reviewed and revised if necessary.[6]

The responsibility for developing a museum's mission statement resides with the board and usually the director or executive officer. These leaders may choose to inform staff members of the intent to create or revise the mission statement and invite their input.[7] While the board ultimately has final approval of the mission statement, it is valuable to include input from staff to help clarify the assumptions and desires of those most involved in the museum.

There is no "proper" length for a mission statement, but it should be clear and concise. In some institutions, the mission statements are contained in a single sentence or phrase, for example[8]:

> A:shiwi A:wan Museum and Heritage Center is an eco-museum dedicated to honoring, cultivating and nurturing the dynamic process of Zuni culture.

Some museums create a short mission statement followed by a more detailed statement that contains various points for the institution to follow. An example of this kind of statement reads:

> The Nebraska State Historical Society safeguards Nebraska's past and makes it accessible in ways that enrich present and future generations.

This statement is supplemented by a longer, more explanatory description of the institution's goals, objectives, and strategies:

> The Nebraska State Historical Society is the primary institution with responsibility to collect, preserve, research, and interpret artifacts, documents, and published materials related to Nebraska's heritage. The Society, as an agency of state government, shall hold, as a trustee for the state, all of the Society's current and future collections and shall have all the authority granted to it by law.

Other museums have a single longer statement:

> The Smithsonian's Anacostia Museum is a national resource devoted to the identification, documentation, protection, and interpretation of the African American experience in Washington, D.C., the nation's capital, and the "Upper South," a region including Virginia, Maryland, North Carolina, South Carolina, and northern Georgia. The Anacostia Museum will also examine contemporary social issues (e.g., housing, transportation, health care) and their impact upon the African American communities in the region. The museum is also committed to the collection, protection, and interpretation of contemporary popular culture and its articulation and manifestation in the African American population.[9]

While length and format may differ from museum to museum, it is imperative that the contents of the statement follow several guidelines. First, the mission statement must be free of jargon or verbosity because it will be read not only by the museum's personnel but also by the general public.[10] If the public cannot fully understand and relate to the museum's mission, the mission statement has failed. According to Marie Malaro,[11] working for the Smithsonian Institution, the mission must also be written so that it sets forth this basic information:

- the purpose of the museum
- the present scope and uses of the museum's collections
- the more immediate goals of the museum

Most importantly, the mission should be capable of being realized. A museum is guaranteed to fail if its mission statement cannot be understood, followed, or fulfilled.

The mission statement also directly affects how the institution is managed. By setting the priorities for the museum, the mission statement can put the organization on the track for success. The mission statement becomes the most important starting point for a museum and must be made visible and obvious through public programs. The statement drives a museum by directly spelling out the purpose with guidelines and goals. Only through careful creation and constant evaluation of its mission statement can a museum survive.

Bylaws

"Bylaws are the significant written rules by which a museum is governed,"[12] notes Kim Zeitlin, senior partner in the Washington, D.C., law firm of Zeitlin and Buonasera. A museum's tax-exempt status may depend on the bylaws to satisfy legal requirements related to the museum's internal management. The bylaws define, in procedural detail, the roles and responsibilities of the board of trustees, officers, members, and staff. This document must cover all aspects of the museum's activities in the broadest sense.

Bylaws take on added importance during disputes about the way a

Box 2.1

Case Study: We Are on a Mission

You have just been appointed the assistant director for operations and programs of the International Museum of Primitive Art in Laredo, Texas. The museum was founded in 1989 with a major donation of primitive art from Niger, Nigeria, and Benin and an endowment of $10 million bequeathed to the City of Laredo. The anonymous donors were presumably from the Laredo area but gave no guidance for the direction of their generous gift. The city has set up the museum as a separate nonprofit organization with a board composed of the mayor, two city council members, four private citizens appointed by the mayor and serving four-year alternating terms, and the mayor of Nuevo Laredo as an *ex officio* member. The staff of the museum is now fifteen people and is anticipated to grow to twenty-five by the year 2006.

On your first day at work, the director presents you with a stack of documents, including budgets, acquisition policy, collection policy, strategic plan, exhibit schedule, annual schedule of educational programs, and code of professional conduct. On the top of the stack is the museum's mission statement, adopted by the board in 1991. You pick up the statement and read:

Mission

> The mission of the International Museum of Primitive Art is to collect, exhibit, and present programming concerning primitive art from around the world, with special emphasis on West Africa, Mexico, and Thailand. The Museum will promote interest in and knowledge of primitive art through traveling major exhibits throughout the U.S., Canada, and Mexico; loans of art to private citizens and businesses in the Greater Laredo area; and the production of videos and films about primitive art and artists. The Museum will further promote primitive art by holding at least one event annually that brings artists who produce primitive art to the Museum.

You spend the remainder of the week reading the other documents. Finally, on Friday, you read through the budget. You are shocked to see that the museum has had a budget deficit of over $150,000 for the past three years and that money was withdrawn from the principal of the endowment to cover the deficit. The board has capitalized the collections to cover the funds withdrawn from the endowment.

On Friday afternoon, you are meeting with Director Andy Smiley and Assistant Director for Collections and Traveling Exhibits Joe Kool. You aren't five minutes into the meeting when you blurt out, "Do you know that we have been running a budget deficit for the past three years?" Director Smiley replies calmly: "Oh, yes, but that will take care of itself when we get things really rolling around here." "But we are using up the principal of our endowment," you respond in a slightly elevated voice. "We will be putting it back as the money starts to roll in," says Director Smiley with a knowing nod to Joe Kool. "I have reviewed the budgets," you say, "and clearly our largest expenses have been for travel and purchase of collections. In fact, they have far exceeded the amount of our deficit each year. Can't we cut back in those areas?"

Box 2.1 (continued)

Mr. Smiley replies with a slightly irritated tone in his voice: "Well, we must collect to carry out our mission. Joe and his wife Reel, our curator of collections, have been traveling to West Africa each year to collect. They usually spend only about eight weeks, that is all they can stand. It is difficult work, you know. It is clear that our donors expected us to continue to build and fill out our West African collection, so we have made that a prime goal of our mission and strategic plan. Board member Councilwoman Mary Mutton has business interests in Thailand and elsewhere in Southeast Asia. She has been willing to collect for us, so it seemed only appropriate that we pay her expenses. You know Southeast Asians are the fastest growing segment of tourists coming to the U.S., so the board decided that it was important to include collecting primitive art from Thailand in our mission. We wanted to get started collecting this art before some large metropolitan art museum beats us. And of course we had to send two-person film crews with each of these parties to fulfill part of our educational mission." Exasperated, you shout out, "To hell with the mission statement! Mission statements can always be changed, but you can never get back endowment funds that you have spent."

Director Smiley, showing his keen insight into staff management, responds, "Well, why don't you rewrite our mission statement so that it better suits our resources. Bring it in at 10 A.M. on Tuesday so that we can review it. We have a board meeting on Thursday. I will introduce you, and you can present your ideas for revising our mission statement." Smiley and Kool give each other knowing smiles and slight nods.

1. Revise the mission statement.
2. How will your new mission statement better serve the International Museum of Primitive Art?
3. How will your new mission statement help cut the budget deficit that your museum is experiencing?
4. What other museum documents and policies should be examined in light of the museum's budget deficit?
5. What resistance to changing the mission statement do you expect to have from the staff? Director? Board?
6. How will you defend your belief that the museum's mission statement must be changed?

museum is carrying out its mission and in disagreements among board members about proper governance procedure. Conflicts—such as dissatisfied board members attempting to gain control of the board or a group from outside the organization mounting a legal challenge to the museum—may be resolved by consulting the formal procedures and the rights and powers of trustees and members outlined in the bylaws. Well-written bylaws, when adhered to, will ensure board decisions are fair and will provide protection against legal challenges.

The bylaws document[13] should begin with a title, for example, "Bylaws of the Museum of the ________." The sections of the bylaws are typically titled "Articles" and numbered with Roman numerals.[14]

Article I should include the official name of the museum and its location, including city, county, and state. If there is a governing or parent organization, its name should also be listed.

Article II should include the purpose of the museum, expressed in terms of its mission, including mandates, goals, and objectives.

Article III should outline the composition of the board of trustees, board of directors, or other governing authority for the museum, including the number to be chosen and the qualifications for membership. The number of board members will depend on the museum's size and nature. The bylaws also should define terms of office for board members and nomination and selection or election procedures. The board may be self-perpetuating, appointed by the parent organization, elected from the membership of the organization, or consist of both appointed and elected members. Museums often stagger terms of office by grouping board members together in classes. The bylaws also should account for the first few years of the museum's existence, when, for example, one-third of the board would be elected for a one-year term, one-third for a two-year term, and one-third for a three-year term. Some bylaws may also limit the number of terms any single trustee can serve, whereas others may not let board members serve consecutive terms.

Article III should also detail the responsibilities of board members. According to Lord and Lord,[15] in *The Manual of Museum Management*, boards are expected to perform certain duties:

1. ensure the continuity of the museum's mission, mandate, and purposes
2. act as an advocate in the community for public involvement in the museum
3. provide for the present and long-term security and preservation of the collection, and the safety of staff and visitors, at a level consistent with the museum's mission and mandate
4. ensure that the museum serves as wide a public as possible

5. ensure that the museum undertakes research to create and disseminate accurate and objective knowledge relevant to its collection
6. review and approve policies consistent with the museum's mission and mandate, and monitor staff implementation of these policies
7. plan for the future of the museum, including reviewing and approving a corporate plan (or strategic plan or business plan) that identifies the museum's goals and ways to attain them and monitor implementation of the plan
8. ensure the financial stability of the museum, through reviewing, approving, and monitoring budgets and financial reports; arranging for regular audits; investing the museum's financial assets wisely; and raising funds as required to allow the museum to meet its current and future financial responsibilities
9. recruit and negotiate a contract with the museum's director, evaluate his or her performance, and terminate his or her employment if necessary
10. ensure that the museum has adequate staff to undertake all museum functions

Article III also should specify the number of board meetings per year. It may specify the time, day, and place they will be held and the number of members necessary to constitute a quorum for the transaction of business. A provision concerning filling vacancies on the board is also necessary. Whether appointed by the board president or elected by the board, persons filling vacancies usually serve only until the original term expires.

Most boards appoint their members to committees so that the board can work on a wide range of issues simultaneously. Standing committees address ongoing activities fundamental to the purpose and programs of the museum. Chairpersons of standing committees are appointed by the president and should be a member of the board of trustees. Committee members are most often recruited from among the museum membership and are not necessarily board members. Here is a list of typical standing committees:

- Executive
- Nominating
- Finance and Fund Raising
- Planning
- Membership
- Public Programming
- Public and Media Relations
- Museum Store Operations
- Budget Development
- Bylaws
- Multicultural Advisory

A statement that *ad hoc* committees[16] will be formed as needed also may be included.

Article IV should include a description of the general responsibilities of professional staff, especially the executive director's functions, duties, and limitations. The executive director should be in charge of the museum's management and administration, subject only to direction from the board of trustees and state laws. Care should be exercised to ensure that a change in job description for staff does not require a change of bylaws.

Article V should define the power and duties of officers of the board. The president should be the chief executive officer and should preside at all meetings of the museum membership, the board of trustees, and the executive committee. The president also is responsible for making an annual report to the secretary of state as required by law. The president usually appoints all committee chairpersons and committee members authorized by the board of trustees. The president is also a nonvoting member of all committees. In the absence of the president, the vice president should perform the duties of the president. The vice president should assist the president in the general supervision of the museum and the future planning by the museum. The secretary should attend and keep minutes of all meetings and should conduct routine correspondence for the board. The treasurer should be responsible for all funds of the museum and/or membership organization. The treasurer should collect membership fees or other dues of the museum membership organization, keep a full and accurate account of receipts and expenditures, and make disbursements as directed by the board of trustees. In larger museums, the treasurer's duties in most cases will relate primarily to the membership organization, and the museum's operations will be handled by paid staff, such as a business manager. In smaller museums, the treasurer may handle the funds of the membership organization as well as those from museum operations. The treasurer annually arranges for, and presents to the board, an audit of all funds.

Article VI may describe the various classes of membership. Because a museum is a public institution, its membership should be open to all persons, businesses, and organizations that support the mission of the museum and are willing to pay the prescribed dues. Typical membership categories may include individual, family, patron, affiliate organization, corporate, benefactor, and honorary life. Some museums offer their members voting rights as long as they are in good standing. The bylaws should not be so specific that they list the actual amount of dues, because any raise in rates would require a change in bylaws. Instead, the bylaws should state that the board will determine the scale and amount of membership dues at the annual meeting of the museum.

Article VII should describe any financial provisions for the museum. It should define the fiscal year and may also assign authority to sign checks, transfer funds, enter contracts, and accept gifts and donations. It should furthermore detail financial reporting requirements and budget preparations.

Article VIII determines the parliamentary authority by which the board meetings will be governed. In most cases, the authority used for governing meetings is the most current edition of *Robert's Rules of Order.*[17] These rules should be used in all cases in which they are applicable and in which they are not inconsistent with state statutes, the bylaws, or any special rules the museum may adopt.

Article IX should provide for the amendment of the bylaws. It should determine the number of members needed to amend the bylaws. Proposed changes in the bylaws should be approved by the board of trustees and distributed to the membership in writing at least twenty-one days prior to the meeting at which the amendments will be considered.

Article X should provide for the potential dissolution of the museum. The bylaws may determine the number of members necessary to dissolve the museum (usually at least two-thirds of the membership). Article X also needs to state where any remaining property, whether real or personal, should be donated. The museum, after donating its collections, would be considered dissolved and its corporate status terminated.

Articles of Incorporation

The articles of incorporation and the bylaws are the museum's two governing documents. The bylaws define a system of internal law and government, and the articles of incorporation establish the relationship between the museum as a nonprofit corporation and the state in which it operates. The articles of incorporation also establish the museum's legal existence as a nonprofit organization, authorize its perpetual operation, specify its 501(c)(3) federal tax status (which must be granted by the Internal Revenue Service), declare its right to hold property and receive gifts, and make provisions for the museum's assets in the event of dissolution. Regulations regarding articles of incorporation are different from state to state. Nonprofit corporations must be founded on, and adhere strictly to, the prescribed legal regulations or statutes in their state of incorporation.

All states have laws governing incorporation; many require steps similar to those followed in Nebraska:

1. Obtain a Federal Identification (ID) Number from the Internal Revenue Service (SS-4 form)
2. Draft Articles of Incorporation
3. File Articles of Incorporation with the Corporate Division of the Secretary of State along with payment of fees (in 2002, ten dollars plus five dollars per page)
4. Publish a Notice of Incorporation in a legal, local newspaper for three successive weeks
5. File Affidavits of Publication with the Secretary of State
6. Purchase a corporate seal, hold organizational meeting, develop and adopt bylaws, and elect officers

7. Establish a corporate checking account. It is necessary to have a Federal ID Number, a corporate seal, and a corporate resolution authorizing a checking account. This resolution should be passed at the first board meeting.[18]

Many states have standard "certificate of incorporation" or "articles of incorporation" forms, but in some, the incorporators of an organization must draft their own legal documents. These articles of incorporation must be filed with the Secretary of State by incorporators who are the chief organizers or promoters of the museum. An attorney could be helpful when preparing and filing the articles of incorporation, drafting bylaws, and paying fees. If a lawyer helps substantially, he or she may be listed as an incorporator.

State statutes will outline the information required in the articles of incorporation, which will be similar to what the State of Nebraska requires:[19]

1. The title or heading of the document (e.g., "Articles of Incorporation")
2. A corporate name for the organization (name of the museum)
3. A statement of the nonprofit nature of the organization. It should include one of the following statements:
   (i) This corporation is a public benefit corporation;
   (ii) This corporation is a mutual benefit corporation; or
   (iii) This corporation is a religious corporation.
4. The street address for the corporate office or principal place of activity, and the name of its initial registered agent at that office, for service of processes
5. The name and street address of each incorporator
6. A statement of whether or not the corporation will have members
7. Provisions not inconsistent with law regarding the distribution of assets on dissolution
8. Signatures of each incorporator and every board of trustees member listed in the articles
9. Consent or approval from the Secretary of State's office

The most common organizational structure for museums is the nonprofit corporation. Not all museum organizations go to the trouble to incorporate, obtain a Federal ID Number, and apply to the Internal Revenue Service (IRS) for tax-exempt status, despite the benefits. The corporate structure not only establishes a framework within which the museum operates; it also offers financial stability and limited tax liability.[20]

IRS Status

As an incorporated entity, a museum can apply for nonprofit status and thereby obtain certain benefits. The organization must complete the appropriate paperwork and be granted 501(c)(3) status by the IRS. Museums that are a unit of state or local government, including an educational institution such as a college or university, will derive similar benefits from the IRS status 170(c)(1) possessed by their parent institution.[21]

Marie Malaro[22] provides an excellent discussion of IRS regulations and how to comply with them in order to receive 501(c)(3) status. First, an institution must have a public service mission. An institution also must be organized as a not-for-profit or charitable corporation. The term "charitable" is used in its generally accepted legal sense by the IRS and includes the advancement of education or science and the erection or maintenance of public buildings or monuments, under which museums qualify. The articles of incorporation of an institution must limit the organization's purposes to one or more of the exempt purposes set forth by the IRS in section 501(c)(3) of the tax code.[23]

In addition, the assets of the organization must be permanently dedicated to an exempt purpose. Thus, should the institution dissolve, its assets must be distributed for an exempt purpose or to the federal, state, or local government for a public purpose. While state law may dictate that the assets must be distributed to an exempt entity, the IRS recommends writing the provision into the articles of incorporation because the organization's application for nonprofit status will be processed more rapidly.

To achieve nonprofit status with the IRS, an institution, in its governing structures, must preclude self-interest or private financial gain. The IRS states that for an organization to qualify for 501(c)(3), "no part of the net earnings will inure to the benefit of the organization's private shareholders or individuals."[24]

A museum granted section 501(c)(3) status also must not produce propaganda or otherwise attempt to influence legislation as a substantial part of its activities. The museum is barred from any political activities and may not participate in or intervene in any political campaign on behalf of, or in opposition to, any candidate for public office.[25]

Museums with a 501(c)(3) status are eligible to receive tax-deductible contributions. These contributions benefit not only the institution but also the donor, who receives a tax deduction. The rules governing tax-deductible contributions apply most specifically to the donor, and an organization is not responsible for reporting contribution information to the IRS on behalf of a donor. Except in the case of a quid pro quo contribution, the donor must request and obtain written acknowledgment of the donation from the organization. Although there is no prescribed format for written acknowledgment, the museum must provide sufficient information to substantiate the amount of the contribution. In the case of donation of objects or artifacts, museums must encourage donors to secure an independent third-party appraisal of the fair market value of the object or artifact. This value may then be submitted by the donor to the IRS to substantiate the tax deduction. The IRS requires a receipt for gifts valued over $250.[26]

A written disclosure statement to donors of a quid pro quo contribution in excess of $75 is required of the organization. For example, if a donor gives a museum $100 and receives tickets for a special exhibition valued at $40, the donor has made a quid pro quo contribution. The charitable contribution portion of the payment is $60. Even though the part of the payment available for deduction does not exceed $75, a disclosure statement must be filed because the donor's payment (quid pro quo contribution) exceeds $75. According to the IRS, the required written statement must:

1. Inform the donor that the amount of the contribution that is deductible for federal income tax purposes is limited to the excess of any money (and the value of any property other than money) contributed by the donor over the value of goods or services provided by the organization.
2. Provide the donor with a good faith estimate of the value of the goods or service that the donor received.

In order to retain its 501(c)(3) status, a museum organization will be required to file IRS forms 990, 990EZ, or 990-PF and pay any unrelated business income tax.[27]

Conclusion

In reality, a museum professional rarely will be faced with the challenging task of building a museum from its beginning. More common than starting a museum from scratch is reforming and reorganizing an existing museum that has lacked administrative leadership. No matter the circumstance, anyone seeking a professional museum position must expect a certain amount of time to be devoted to administrative duties and, therefore, should understand the mechanisms and significance of the mission statement, bylaws, articles of incorporation, and IRS nonprofit status.

A museum is not a special entity in the eyes of the law and, therefore, has legal requirements to fulfill. Following the steps outlined in this chapter can be a complicated and tedious process; however, each new museum does not need to reinvent the wheel. Numerous resources are available to guide a museum professional through the process. Many of the resources are listed in the readings for this chapter and are available from professional organizations such as the American Association of Museums and American Association for State and Local History.

With a well-defined mission statement, a set of bylaws, articles of incorporation, and tax-exempt status from the Internal Revenue Service, a museum is at the end of its beginning. With this solid organizational foundation, the museum can move forward to build the programs, collections, and facilities that fulfill its mission. It is ready to get to work.

Box 2.2

The Case of the "Purloined" Documents

Susie Jay has just completed her degree in museum studies and has accepted a position as the first paid director of the Moose Antler City Historical Society. Moose Antler is a town of 25,000 located in the northern United States near the Canadian border. The Moose Antler City Historical Society was founded in 1959, has a collection of 30,000 objects, and has just built a new museum building. Susie is expected to catalog the collection, prepare exhibits, and plan and present educational programs. The collections have accumulated primarily through donations from members of the local community. The building was paid for with contributions from local citizens, fund-raising activities, and grants from two private foundations, resulting in a total of $230,000. The board has done amazing work in planning and executing the fund drive, recording donations, and sending letters confirming all donations.

Ms. Jay attacks her new job with all the energy of a recent graduate hoping to make an impression and do her best for the future of the museum. A letter arrives from the Forest Foundation, one of the donors to the fund-raising effort. The foundation staff is completing its annual report and needs a copy of the Historical Society's IRS status statement. Ms. Jay, knowing the importance of the request and wanting to respond in a timely manner, goes to the files to make a copy of the IRS document, but it is not there.

Susie calls Jack Pine, longtime treasurer of the Historical Society, believing that he will have the document in question, but Jack is vague. When Susie mentions 990 forms and quid pro quo contribution letters for the members, Jack seems even vaguer. Susie closes this conversation. Guessing that Jack may be suffering a bit of old-age-memory loss, Susie calls the society's new president, Fannie Foxx. Mrs. Foxx is the wife of the Moose Antler bank president and is the immediate past president of the Moose Antler Junior League. Susie's conversation with Fannie is even more confusing and ends with Fannie saying, "Well, Susie, just leave this to Jack and me, and we will take care of it." With relief, Susie goes back to planning the museum's opening exhibit.

Two weeks later Susie receives a call from Mary Mink at the Forest Foundation. Mary seems a little irritated and firmly requests the IRS status document, making the point that the foundation auditor is coming in a week, and this document is needed. Susie makes a lame excuse and promises to have it in tomorrow's mail. Susie is now in a panic. She calls her closest friend on the board, Sugar Maples, who served as the chair of the fund-raising campaign. Sugar has been very open and supportive of Susie. Sugar is puzzled by Susie's request and professes no knowledge of an IRS status form, has never heard of a 990 form or a quid pro quo letter, and asks a lot of questions about the importance of these documents. Sugar calls Fannie, and the conversation lasts about fifteen minutes. Sugar returns to report that Fannie has confessed that no one has ever seen an IRS status form and that Jack has never filed a 990 form. Fannie suspects that the Historical Society has neither been incorporated nor received IRS 501(c)(3) status.

Box 2.2 (continued)

What are Susie's responsibilities in this situation?
What are the board's responsibilities?
How can Susie determine if the Historical Society has been incorporated? Received IRS 501(c)(3) status?
If the museum is not incorporated, what documents will Susie need to work with the board to write?
What procedures should Susie and the board follow to get the 501(c)(3) IRS status?

Notes

1. Kavanagh 1994.
2. Hendricks 1990.
3. Hoagland 1994.
4. Anderson 1998.
5. Wolf 1990.
6. Ibid.
7. Hoagland 1994.
8. Anderson 1998, 33.
9. Ibid.
10. Hoagland 1994.
11. Malaro 1998.
12. Zeitlin 1996, 1.
13. Modified from Nichols 1989.
14. Robert and Evans 1990, 559–592.
15. Lord and Lord 1997, 19.
16. *Ad hoc* committees are temporary committees that exist to address a particular question or issue.
17. Robert and Evans 1990.
18. Nebraska Department of Economic Development, "Information on Nonprofit Incorporation in Nebraska," available at http://63.239.54.223/npincorp.html.
19. Pepperl 1997.
20. Nichols 1989.
21. IRS 2001.
22. Malaro 1998.
23. IRS 2001.
24. Ibid.
25. Ibid.
26. Malaro 1998.
27. IRS 2001.

CHAPTER THREE
THE WORKING MUSEUM

The working museum is about *people.* Although museums exist to collect, preserve, and interpret things, it is the staff (whether paid or volunteer) that is the museum's most valuable asset. This disparate group of talents will fulfill the museum's mission and provide its programs. Administrators, accountants, artisans, exhibit designers, discipline-area experts, conservators, collection managers, educators, housekeepers, administrative assistants, salespersons, groundskeepers, maintenance staff, secretaries, docents, and many others must be integrated into a functional unit that is capable of accomplishing complex tasks. Museum administrators will find working with their staffs to be the most challenging, frustrating, and rewarding part of their jobs. This chapter explores how the staff of a museum interacts and how that interaction can be managed to keep the museum working smoothly.

Organization

A simple chart on a piece of paper might not seem something of value, but when that chart outlines the organization of the museum staff, it can be extremely useful. An organizational diagram gives staff members a quick visual reference for understanding where they fit in relationship to everyone else in the museum. The organizational chart is a road map that outlines routes and connections; the system it describes can be an impediment or an enhancement to the flow of museum work, depending on how that operational structure has been designed. Robert Janes, director of the Glenbow Museum, in Calgary, Alberta, Canada, and his staff reviewed potential organizational structures while considering their museum's needs. Janes's discussion in *Museums and the Paradox of Change*[1] provides a useful analysis for any museum considering reworking its internal staff organization.

In the most common type of internal organization in museums, a board of trustees tops the *hierarchy,* with the director of the museum immediately below it. The remainder of the staff is arranged in branches representing the various divisions and programs within the museum. Collections, public programs, and administration frequently comprise the major branches, represented by blocks on the hierarchical organizational chart. All branches ultimately converge at the position of the director, who serves as the fulcrum point between board and staff. Hierarchical structures have been criticized for encouraging top-down decision making and categorical thinking about staff and resources. Many of the challenges facing museums require responses from multiple areas of expertise, whereas individual branches of the hierarchy tend to act as separate entities. Staff members are reluctant to cross over to work for other units within the museum because they are concerned that their supervisors will not reward their efforts. These problems have led museums and other organizations to investigate other types of internal organization.[2]

Horizontal management structure is an alternative to "corporate hierarchy." It tries to "flatten the pyramid," generally accomplished by removing middle managers. This strategy moves decision making to lower levels within the organization, where the work is accomplished, and is said to "empower" the staff by making more of them responsible for outcomes. One problem with this organizational structure is what to do with the middle managers. In the for-profit sector, they are generally dismissed, or "downsized," an action not ordinarily taken in nonprofits. In museums, many of the middle managers are also curators who are subject-area specialists. These are staff members whose knowledge museums can ill afford to lose.

Matrix management is seen as a marriage of the hierarchy structure and a more horizontal, empowered approach. An outgrowth of the 1960s aerospace industry, matrix management was created for complex, multidisciplinary projects in which the resources and expertise of a single hierarchical division would be insufficient to accomplish the task. Instead of a flat, two-dimensional pyramid, the organizational structure of matrix management is best visualized as a "three-dimensional tic-tac-toe board."[3] Major functions—collections, administration, and public programs in our example—form the major facets of the cube and intersect to accomplish tasks. Major projects, such as exhibitions, require involvement of person-

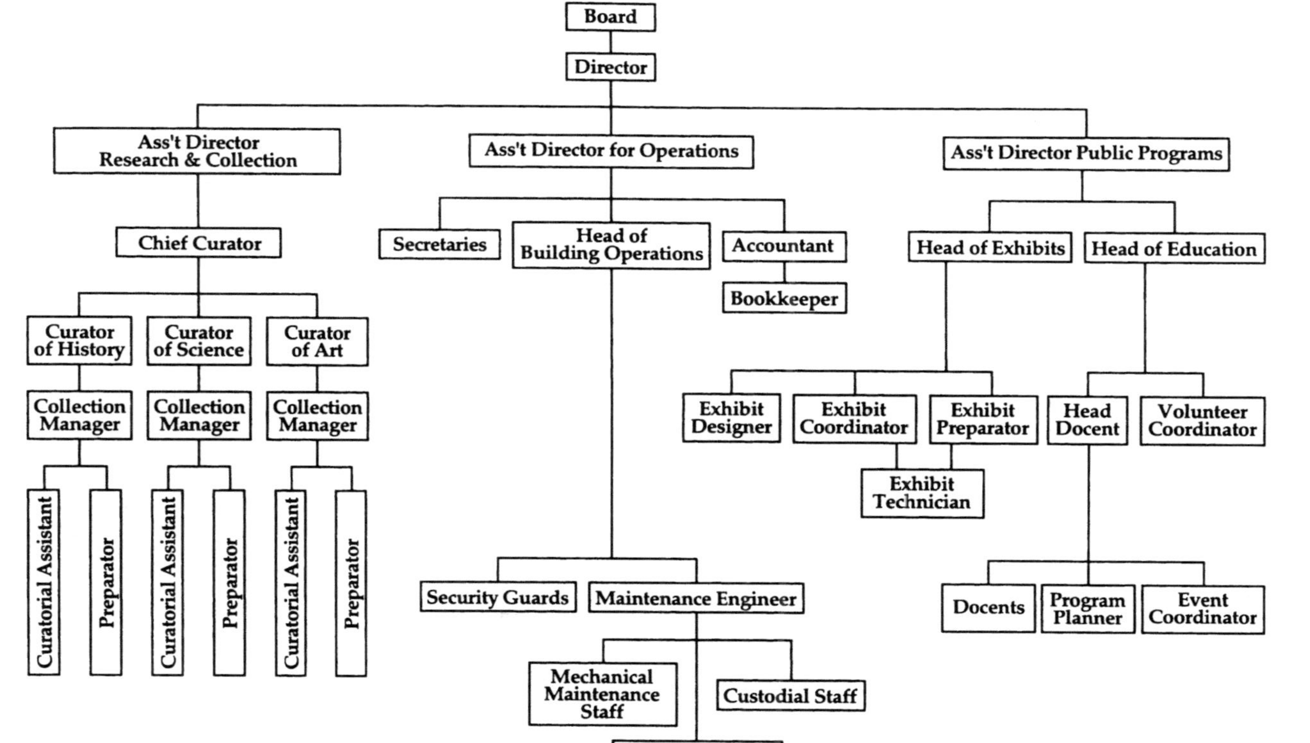

Figure 3.1 Hierarchical organizational chart. This is the traditional internal organization of most museums and other nonprofit institutions. Note that only three positions report directly to the director. At least seven of the positions could be classified as middle management.

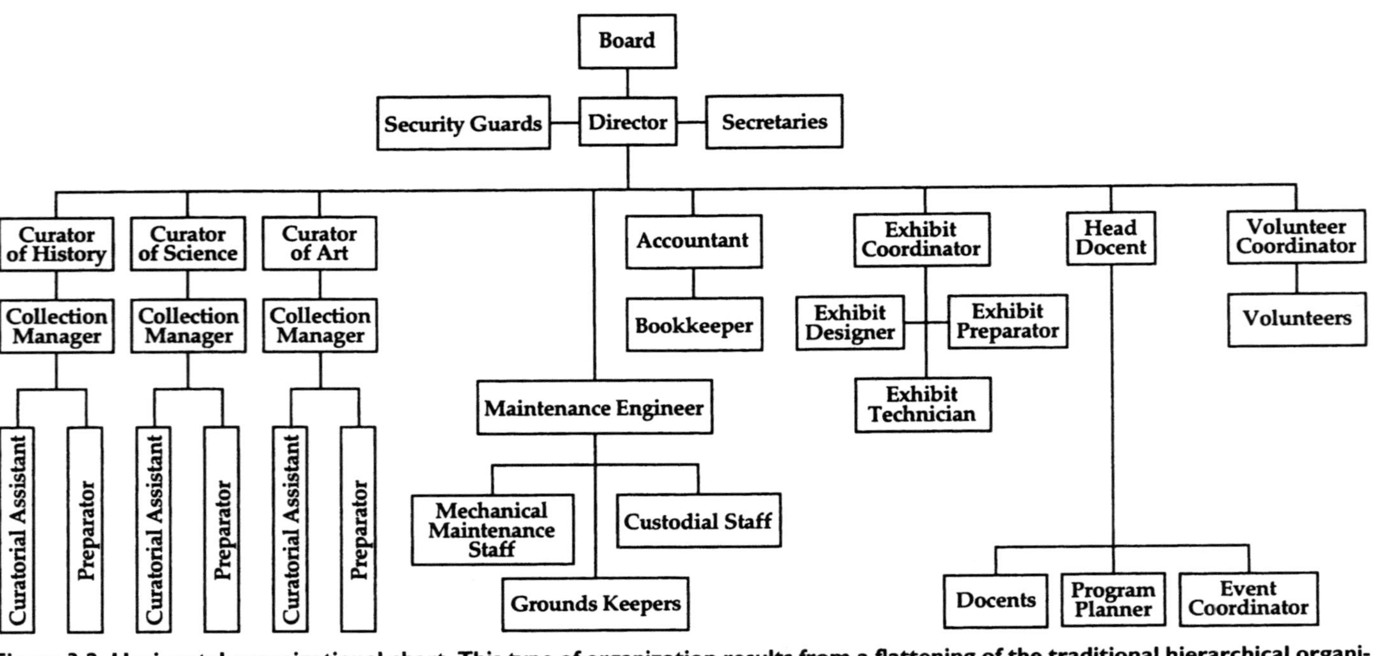

Figure 3.2 Horizontal organizational chart. This type of organization results from a flattening of the traditional hierarchical organization. The primary difference is that middle management positions have been deleted, and now ten positions report directly to the director.

nel from all facets: the curators, registrars, and conservators of the collections division; the designers, educators, marketers, and publishers of the public programs division; and the finance, visitor service, maintenance, and security representatives of the administration division.[4] Teamwork, obviously, is key.

This teamwork has to extend to those in supervisory roles as well. Most often, matrix management is applied to specific tasks and coexists with a more traditional hierarchical structure. Workers find themselves answerable to both their functional supervisor and the manager of the special project. This "two-or-more-bosses system" can produce conflicts over both human and financial resources. Good strategic planning that involves all the museum's functional groups and results in a shared vision of institutional aims and priorities can be invaluable in preventing such conflicts.

Advantages of the matrix management system, particularly when it is used as an adjunct to a more traditional structure, include decentralization of authority and responsibility, giving more staff the chance to gain experience in decision making and supervisory roles; a high level of motivation and visibility for staff members participating in the special project; and the opportunity for staff to grow in communication and negotiation skills. These advantages also can be the downside: traditional lines of authority and ultimate responsibility are removed, so forward progress can be stymied; high expectations can create counterproductive pressure; and pressure can result in poor communication, refusal to come to consensus, and ultimately, no decision. The complexity of reporting and supervision can be another problem. An uncomfortable staff, uncertain about priorities, supervision, and evaluation, will work less efficiently. Clear museum-wide expectations about special projects and traditional functions can help ensure employee effectiveness and a successful outcome.

Although they may not call it matrix management, many museums, like many for-profit organizations, have developed a team approach to complex, multifaceted creative endeavors. The Kellogg Project administered by the Field Museum of Natural History from 1985 to 1995 trained staff from a variety of museums in team building, especially for the production of exhibits. Properly managed, this team structure can result in more effective exhibitions and public programs that combine curatorial, educational, and design elements in ways that enrich the audience's expe-

Person	Administration of Museum Programs	Curation of Art Collection	Curation of Science Collection	Curation of History Collection	Planning New Art Exhibit	Planning New History Exhibit	Design Art Exhibit	Design History Exhibit	Planning New Science Education Program	Delivering Education Programs	Volunteer Coordinator	Security	Budget Management	Museum Maintenance	Moving Science Collection
Director	+	−	−	−	+	+	−	−	−	−	−	+	+	+	−
Staff #1	+	+	−	−	+	−	+	−	−	−	−	−	+	−	+
Staff #2	−	+	−	−	−	−	−	−	−	−	−	−	−	+	+
Staff #3	+	−	+	−	−	−	−	−	+	−	−	−	+	−	+
Staff #4	−	−	+	−	−	−	−	−	+	−	−	−	−	+	+
Staff #5	+	−	−	+	−	+	−	+	−	−	−	−	+	−	+
Staff #6	−	−	−	+	−	−	−	−	−	−	−	−	−	+	+
Staff #7	+	−	−	−	+	+	+	+	−	−	−	−	+	−	−
Staff #8	−	−	−	−	+	+	+	+	−	−	−	−	−	−	−
Staff #9	+	−	−	−	+	+	−	−	+	+	+	−	+	+	−
Staff #10	−	−	−	−	+	−	−	−	+	+	−	−	−	−	−
Staff #11	−	−	−	−	−	+	−	−	−	+	−	−	−	+	−
Staff #12	−	−	−	−	−	−	−	−	+	−	+	−	−	+	−
Staff #13	−	−	−	−	+	+	−	−	−	−	−	−	+	−	−
Staff #14	−	−	−	−	−	−	−	−	−	−	−	+	−	−	−
Staff #15	−	−	−	−	−	−	−	−	−	−	−	−	−	+	−

Figure 3.3 Matrix organizational chart. In organizations using this type of internal organization, most positions do not need to be identified by job titles. Work is assigned by the tasks to be completed and by the skills of the staff members. Teams of staff members come together to perform tasks and then dissolve to reform into other teams. These teams (and concurrently the organizational chart) could change often, even on a daily basis. The matrix is open at the right and at the bottom so that new tasks and new staff members can be added.

rience. Internally, team structures can produce the benefits—flattened hierarchy, decentralized decision making, and personal growth of staff members—matrix management claims.

Regardless of the rubric under which it functions, the team should have a clearly defined role or mission to be successful, and the responsibilities of the team as a whole and of individual team members should be well understood. The team leader should be carefully selected and given all the necessary administrative support. Teams have been and remain a very successful management structure for museums, particularly for public programs and exhibit development and production; many museums have produced award-winning results with teamwork. Teams have not been as commonly used in the research areas of museums, but they have been organized for short periods on special projects such as relocating collections.

The *work process* model organizes the museum around major work processes conducted by the museum, such as collection management, research, education, exhibition, and publications. Multidisciplinary teams are formed around these work processes, with staff members assigned to a particular team. In this model, borrowed from business, executives would delegate to the lower levels, resulting in semiautonomous work units. To further reduce territoriality, administrators would become members of a work process team. This model is designed to facilitate action and risk taking and to support learning and active experimentation. Where employees would report when not engaged in a major project is just one of the challenges of this system and may explain why few museums have adopted it.[5]

In the *shamrock* model, proposed by organizational analyst Charles Handy,[6] work is performed by three core groups, or three leaves of the shamrock. The first leaf is the professional core of the museum, incorporating those staff members without whose subject area and organizational knowledge the museum would cease to function. The second leaf contains outside contractors who can perform tasks more efficiently (and thus at a lower cost) than could professional staff. Many times these contractors will be small, for-profit businesses hired to perform specialized tasks that are cyclical or associated with projects that recur only at long intervals. The third leaf, or core group, consists of part-time and temporary staff members. These people may be added to the museum staff for major or special projects such as mounting a new permanent exhibit or a major fundraising campaign. As these activities are completed, the staff may again be reduced to the professional core represented by the first leaf. A modified form of this organizational model was adopted by the Glenbow Museum. Challenges included learning to work with contractors, who were compensated and whose work was evaluated on the basis of a given end product rather than receiving an hourly wage and day-to-day supervision. Glenbow has continued to evolve and now uses "multiple structures" including formal hierarchy, cross-functional and project teams, and individual experts.[7]

New museums will need to decide which of these internal organizational structural models they wish to adopt. This decision should be based upon the size of the museum and its strategic plan and take into account its goals and philosophy. "Many organizational theorists insist that structure should follow strategy."[8] A structure well suited to a small county history museum will not likely serve a large urban art museum equally well. It will be worth the museum's time to consider these issues carefully because the internal organization of the museum can either enhance or inhibit the museum's ability to fulfill its mission. Museums that have been in existence for some time but want to find ways of working more effectively for greater outcomes may wish to reconsider their organizational structures. In our experience, creating a structure in which multidisciplinary teams can function to address complex tasks as an adjunct to a more traditional management hierarchy gives museums both flexibility and a secure base.

Board-Director-Staff Interactions

No matter what its internal structure, every corporation operates under a board of directors or trustees. In the nonprofit sector these board members are volunteers. Expectations placed on them will vary depending on the size and nature of the organization they govern, and the expectations may change with time and the development of the organization. One thing remains constant: trustees are expected to conduct the business of the organization in such a way as to uphold the public trust. Nonprofit organizations are allowed special legal status predicated on their operation for the public good. The governing board is a human organization with

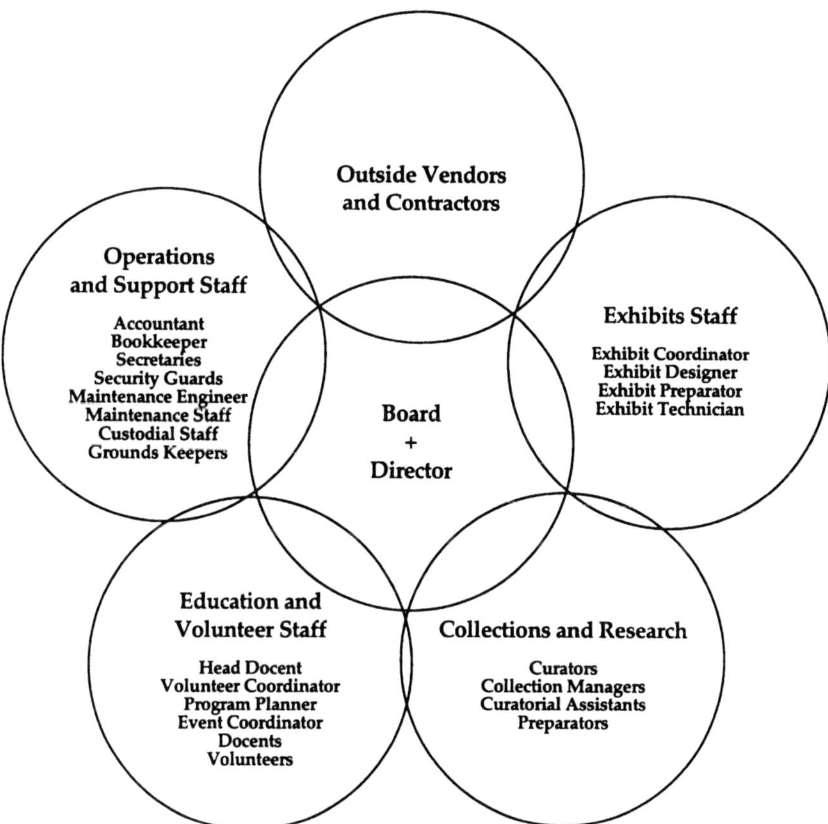

Figure 3.4 Shamrock organizational chart. This type of organization places emphasis on teams performing the needed tasks, but it is designed to bring some stability and structure to the teams and provides a flexible home base for staff members.

great personal and joint responsibility and accountability. Each board member is a steward of a vital, philanthropic public trust.[9] Board members are ultimately responsible for ensuring this trust is uncompromised, which is one reason many nonprofits refer to their board members as "trustees" rather than "directors." "Trustees" serves as a constant, subtle reminder of the nature of the service board members are entrusted to perform.

The framework within which the organization governs and manages itself is usually three-legged; the board delegates some of its authority and responsibility to an executive director, who in turn shares this power and obligation with the museum staff. All three legs must move in coordination to fulfill the museum's mission and meet the needs of its constituencies. (If the organization is a public institution, subject to control by municipal, county, state, or federal entities, another leg may exist. Discussion here is limited to the interaction of board members, the executive director, and the museum staff. Many of the same dynamics and strategies are applicable to organizations where governmental officials may exercise some control.)

A clear definition of roles and responsibilities of board members, the executive director, and staff is critical in the creation and maintenance of an effectively run museum. Misunderstanding of or refusal to observe these necessarily different roles is at the root of many internal museum conflicts. Fortunately, good advice abounds outlining the duties trustees, executive directors, and staff must fulfill, and there's plenty of work to go around!

Trustee responsibilities are similar for most nonprofit organizations, but because museums serve as repositories of our cultural heritage, museum trustees fulfill certain singular duties.

Integrity and an open mind are essential to trustees as they perform their two main roles—fiduciary and supportive.[10] Ensuring that the financial resources exist to allow the museum to fulfill its mission and setting policies that support the executive director and staff in doing so are primary among trustees' chores. The overriding fiduciary responsibility of the nonprofit board is the duty to act for the good of others. The board can best serve the museum by focusing on the strategic issues that will most affect the future of the museum, and it should also constantly work to strengthen its own effectiveness.[11] Strategic planning requires a continual assessment of the external and internal environments of the museum by the trustees. They must coordinate discussions about the mission and related strategies, provide final approval, and then evaluate the extent to which the museum's mission and goals are accomplished.[12]

Regardless of the organizational structure chosen by the museum, the board maintains the position of ultimate authority and responsibility. The board hires the executive director to assist in carrying out policies and developing the programs it mandates; the executive director serves at the pleasure of the board. "In the broadest sense, the responsibilities can be split with the understanding that the trustees establish policy and the

Box 3.1

Responsibilities of Board Members

Responsibilities common to all nonprofit board members:

Attend board meetings and participate actively in committee work
Define the mission of the organization and participate in strategic planning
Approve selection, compensation, regular evaluation, and dismissal of the chief executive
Approve and oversee adherence to the annual budget, as well as control investment policies and the management of reserve funds
Oversee and evaluate programs of the organization, support the staff of the organization, and advocate the organization to the public
Personally contribute financially to the organization and identify, cultivate, and solicit prospective donors
Ensure that the board maintains effective organization and fulfills its governance responsibilities

Source: *Welcome to the board: Your guide to effective participation* by F. Howe. San Francisco: Jossey-Bass, Inc. 1995.

Additional responsibilities specific to museum board members include:

Ensure the continuity of the museum's mission, mandate, and purposes
Provide for the present and long-term security and preservation of the collection
Ensure that the museum serves a broad public audience
Ensure that the museum undertakes research to create and disseminate accurate and objective knowledge relevant to its collection
Review and approve policies consistent with the museum's mission and mandate, and monitor staff implementation of these policies
Ensure that the museum has adequate staff to fulfill its mission

Source: *The manual of museum management* by B. Lord and G. D. Lord. Walnut Creek, CA: AltaMira Press, 1997.

director oversees operations," notes longtime museum director Helmuth Naumer.[13]

The extent to which the board and the director achieve this separation will vary from entity to entity and will depend on the size and life cycle of the organization. At the start, the board is more likely to dominate because the resources the trustees bring to the organization are extremely critical. Early on the executive director may be the only paid staff member, requiring board members to assume active roles. In the midlife of an organization, the board may again be pushed into dominance to deal with events such as an identity crisis, a consolidation, a merger, or a major expansion. Despite the changing roles that trustees, the executive director, or staff members may play during times of organizational change, respect for communication channels and the hierarchy of the structure must be maintained. The more effective and accurate the communication among the three "legs," the more likely it is that whatever changes unfold will be accommodated smoothly.

"Board-staff relationships" usually refers to the interaction between the board and the executive director because the staff generally has limited direct contact and less influence with board members. The executive director of a museum or nonprofit occupies a unique role vis-à-vis the board, which functions as "the boss." Although the director serves at the pleasure of and is answerable to the board, she can exercise considerable influence over it. The trustees' information about and understanding of the organization and its operations will largely come from the director, who also will set agendas, lead the strategic planning process, and participate in most committee work. The director is ethically and legally obliged to provide accurate and concise information about the museum's programs in a form accessible to the board. Information must be timely and relevant to decision making.

Extensive literature and surveys conclude that the interaction between the executive director and the board president is the most important factor in board-staff relationships. The key to creating balance in board and museum staff actions is a positive relationship between these two leaders, based on trust and honesty.[14] Such a relationship requires clear, written descriptions of the responsibilities of the executive director and the president and a mutual respect between these individuals. The two must also recognize when they should defer to the larger board for a final decision.

Board members bring a variety of values with them to their service; their economic, technological, social, political, legal, religious, ethical, aesthetic, and cultural outlooks will be determined, in part, by their respective backgrounds and experiences. One board member's frames of reference may be in conflict with those of another, and since these frames of reference influence the objectives and strategies that individual board members will consider, conflicts can affect the board's work processes, product, and policies. The policies set forth by the board govern the daily activities of the director and staff, and while it is the executive director's vision that determines precisely how the organization moves forward, the philosophical values of the board will necessarily influence the vision of the executive director.[15] A director's success is directly related to his understanding of the board and its values. Becoming acquainted with board members as individuals and learning more about their particular beliefs will help both the director and the board president develop strategies for minimizing potential conflicts of values and keeping board members' "eyes on the prize."

Another challenge in board-staff dynamics stems from the "democratization" of museums, which began in the 1980s in North America with the inclusion on boards of members from previously under- or unrepresented groups. Diversity brings important new perspectives to boards and allows them to more fully serve their constituents and fulfill their missions. It can also exacerbate differences in values and lead to tensions within boards, which may have been previously dominated by people of a particular gender, race, or economic background.[16] Directors can find themselves caught in the middle of board misunderstandings. Again, the executive director and board president, working together, can encourage focus on the museum's mission. Creating a shared vision of what the museum can accomplish helps board members look at their obvious differences as rich assets for the organization.

Providing leadership to the board and taking responsibility for supporting and facilitating the board's work are hallmarks of the most effective museum directors.[17] This "board-centered leadership" is achieved through actions and attitudes as described in box 3.2.

Rather than take full control of the organization, the executive director should work to ensure that the board fulfills its public, organizational, and legal roles. Such an approach is consistent with ethical and legal strictures and enhances organizational effectiveness. Giving board members specific assignments, tasks, and functions energizes board members to fulfill their obligations and responsibilities in a positive and constructive manner.[18]

Yet it's a peculiar relationship in which the executive director, as the board's employee, essentially gives marching orders to "the boss." The delicate balance between the functions of any board and the executive director produces a constant state of tension, but this tension should be

Box 3.2

Executive Director Behaviors for Board-Centered Leadership

Facilitating interaction in board relationships
Showing consideration and respect toward board members
Envisioning change and innovation for the organization with the board
Providing useful and helpful information to the board
Initiating and maintaining structure for the board
Promoting board accomplishments and productivity

Source: "Executive leadership" by D. Heimovics and R. D. Herman. In *The Jossey-Bass handbook of nonprofit leadership and management*, ed. R. D. Herman, 137–153. San Francisco: Jossey-Bass, Inc., 1994.

distinguished from conflict, which can undermine the health of the organization. The very nature of a nonprofit organization, which brings together individuals of varied backgrounds, can lead to conflict in many areas. While the executive director may be responsible for enabling the board to work more effectively, the board plays a major role in maintaining an environment of healthy disagreement and keeping conflicts impersonal. Extensive dialogue and examination of responsibilities are precursors to growth in a board-executive relationship.[19] Once again, the board president can play a critical role. The executive director is wise to remain sensitive to the potential of the board and to frequently express thanks to these volunteers. Equally, the board members should respect the executive director's expertise and institutional knowledge because board members require those qualities to make informed, intelligent decisions. Once the board has hired the executive director, it should support that individual unless substantive cause to revoke that support arises.

Many organizations employ a "partnership" or "team" approach to the executive-board relationship, which is more appropriate than a superior-subordinate approach. The executive director typically has greater expertise in and identification with the museum, while the board retains legal and hierarchical superiority. Thus these two roles are not exactly equal, but they are each dependent on the other.

Measuring the success of the executive director and staff in carrying out board plans and policies is not as easy in the museum world as it is in the corporate. The financial bottom line is rarely the most accurate indicator, and for some board members accustomed to the hard data of the corporate sector, the intangibility of museum products and the perceived abstruseness of the goals can be unnerving. This difference can cause tension between and frustration for board members and the executive director. Increasingly, museums are under pressure to compile performance measurement data that record not only outputs (e.g., 14,864 school children given tours of the museum), but outcomes (43 percent of these children showed an increased understanding of the exhibit subject; see chapter 12 for a discussion of outcome-based evaluation). Whatever system is used, providing board members with appropriate figures in concise reports can hclp bridge this evaluation gap.

While much emphasis is placed on the relationship between the executive director and the board, the museum staff members also influence this relationship because they are the ones putting into action the policies and programs established by the board. Staff should have input into policy formulation because they are the ones most knowledgeable about day-to-day operations and the implementation and effectiveness of existing policies.[20] The board should solicit, via the director, staff counsel about policies relating to their areas of expertise. The director provides the forum in which staff may evaluate current policies and programs and offer suggestions for improvement or change. The director then can determine the most effective way to convey staff input accurately to the appropriate board members so they can make more-informed decisions regarding policy and programming. All parties should be respectful of the board-director-staff hierarchical structure in order to ensure accurate and effective communication. The executive director is the vital link in this communications process.

Museum staff members are accountable not only to the director and the board but also to the professional community of which each is a part. The professional communities of curators, historians, archivists, and other professionals each have their own standards and ideology, and these professional guidelines may conflict with the standards and ideologies that board members bring to the organization. To lessen or alleviate conflict, everyone should help foster an atmosphere of mutual respect for each person's qualifications and contributions. The board of directors must set the tone and share it with the staff via the executive director.

A word of caution is needed about the changing roles of staff and board members. Increasing professionalism in the nonprofit sector sometimes leads to staff-oriented organizations.[21] Too great a reliance on the staff's professional expertise can create a "yes-board" (or a "rubber stamp" board), which concedes to the staff on nearly every issue. On the other end of the spectrum is the board that discounts the expertise of director and staff and does not share responsibility with the executive director or listen to staff input. This in turn undermines staff effectiveness and can result in a loss of purpose. Either development signals a lack of trust among the three parties and failure to acknowledge their mutual reliance.[22]

Although it is not uncommon for trustees to experience confusion regarding the boundaries between their responsibilities and those of the staff, a board that insists on participation in operational matters signals an underlying problem. Regular involvement by board members in personnel matters reflects a management deficiency, such as a lack of internal policies and practices for staff. Constant trustee involvement in administrative issues also indicates weak or ineffective administration, or a loss of confidence in the executive director's leadership. However, such actions also could be motivated by the misguided zeal of individual members of the board who interpret their responsibility as running the organization rather than ensuring that the organization is well run. Analyzing the situation based on the suggestions for board-centered leadership (box 3.2) may give clues to solving board overinvolvement. For example, "providing useful and helpful information to the board" should not include the level of detail communicated among staff involved in day-to-day operations. Emphasizing the structure that exists for board involvement and recognizing appropriate board accomplishments and productivity may help curb excessive board involvement.

"The process of working with governing board members is part of the art of human relations," in which one must apply "diverse skills to accomplish joint goals," according to philanthropy consultant Arthur Frantzreb.[23] The varied and complex relationships that exist in the administration and management of a nonprofit museum can potentially lead to conflict and ultimately jeopardize the purpose or programs of the museum. All persons involved with the museum should be given a detailed description of their responsibilities and duties and understand the roles and obligations of board, director, and staff. At every turn, it is important for each to respect the authority, abilities, and contributions of the others. This essential mutual respect builds trust, and without trust, communication lines break down. Communication—honest, efficient, and accurate—is at the crux of this complex interaction.

Tools to assist in creating and nurturing effective boards are available and useful. Guides to board relations for nonprofit organizations in general may be helpful, but the resources of the Museum Trustees Association (MTA) are particularly aimed at the unique dynamics of museum leadership. This nonprofit organization, founded in 1986, addresses major issues, such as strategy, policy, ethics, inclusion, sustainability, and stewardship, faced by the over 75,000 museum trustees in the United States. The association, based in Washington, D.C., can be reached at www.mta-hq.org.

A more sophisticated understanding of the board-staff dynamic develops when museum staff members assume the role of board member for other organizations. We encourage our students and staff to become involved in nonprofit organizations, such as social service agencies, student groups, or regional or state museum associations, where they can fill roles of board members. Their expectations of what trustees should know, do, and attend to change once they have looked at issues from the boardroom vantage point.

The challenge of leadership in the nonprofit organization is integrating the realms of mission, resource acquisition, and strategy and seeing that the decisions and actions in one realm are consistent with and mutually reinforce those in the others.[24] An equal challenge is fostering an environment that integrates the functions, energy, and contributions of trustees, executive director, and staff so that their efforts are consistent and mutually reinforcing as they strive to fulfill the museum's mission.

Does Anyone Want This Job?

Changing Expectations for Museum Professionals

Diminished funding and simultaneously heightened expectations for museums mean a new breed of museum professional is needed to meet the challenges of the rapidly evolving museum world. Instead of searching for the candidate with the best academic credentials, museum boards in the United States are now searching for persons who can assess critically, reason, communicate, persuade, listen, facilitate, challenge, inspire, and exercise vision, as well as show practical experience in such areas as long-term planning, human resource development, finance, marketing, the law, computers, professional standards, research methodology, collections care and management, presentation and interpretation, and security and facilities management.[25] And let's not forget the board-director balancing act we have just discussed. This description is quite a mouthful; some might suggest it could be restated succinctly as the ability to walk on water.

If these are the standards for museum directors, the expectations for other museum staff are not much lower. The reality is, of course, that few candidates or current museum employees will have all, or even most, of these abilities. How could they? The wide range of background and expertise needed in the current museum environment exceeds any one human's capacity.

In recognition of this, many museums have taken a page from the corporate notebook and have turned over complex and important tasks to small groups. Developing a new exhibition, reconfiguring the museum website, creating a long-range conservation plan, publishing a catalog, and designing a new outcome-based education program are examples of projects likely to be assigned to a museum work group. Although there are many jokes about incompetent and ineffectual committees and their lousy work products, many administrators have discovered that a well-selected small group, given appropriate resources and authority, will produce a higher quality product than any one person can.

Financial pressures for many museums have increased, and strategies for reducing operating costs have sometimes included decreases in staffing. An effective small group process can enable a shrinking staff to realize the fullest potential of its time, talents, and energy.

Dynamics of Small Groups

Museum professionals face some of their most difficult challenges as members of small groups. These groups will be responsible for making most of the decisions and implementing policies within the museum setting. Even if the small group is only a minor element of a larger committee, the same dynamics apply. Museum tasks can be complex, confusing, and inherently fraught with conflicts (for example, the curator's desire to protect and preserve artifacts versus the educator's interest in providing maximum accessibility). Strained budgets, tight deadlines, and high internal and external expectations can create an institutional atmosphere so tense that clear thinking and good decision making become difficult. It is essential, for the benefit of not only those directly involved but the museum's constituencies as well, to improve these processes and to spur more efficient and productive interaction while maintaining a healthy psychological balance within the group.

Selection is the key first step. What skills and depth of knowledge will be required for the project—from commencement to completion? Who on the museum staff could provide solid input for the required tasks? These are often obvious choices, particularly in smaller organizations, where the number of staff with expertise in a given area is limited.

A tougher question may be "who is available?" Time constraints will have an effect on group interaction. A team member under extreme pressure from higher priority items may find it difficult to commit to other projects that have lesser status on his agenda. On the other hand, a member who is given a high-priority group task but also has several lower priority items simmering on a back burner may be unable to concentrate adequately on the task, bringing tension into the group and thus slowing progress toward the designated goal.

Achieving a uniformly high degree of commitment among all group members is a fantasy, but accurate workload information can help eliminate common problems. Supervisors are key people to involve in team selection; common courtesy demands early, clear communication about plans, which may affect someone else's workload, activities, or intentions. Supervisors consulted before the team is selected may be able to assist in rescheduling priorities or reassigning tasks. Supervisors who hear about the project after the fact are much less likely to be cooperative.

Who will lead the group? The person with the most hierarchical authority, such as a supervisor or manager, might not always be the best choice. Giving lower-ranking staffers the chance to facilitate a team can create an important learning and esteem-building experience and allow them to sharpen their skills as leaders while at the same time affording administrators a chance to step outside their usual role. A manager's subject-area expertise or creativity may suggest a role different from that dictated by the organizational hierarchy.

There may be resistance to assigning group leadership to someone other than the person highest up on the institutional food chain. Some staff members may decline the opportunity because they are accustomed to being led and being led is easier than being in the forefront.[26] Simultaneously, people who are accustomed to being in positions of authority may have difficulty allowing other people to call the shots. Potential resistance is an important consideration when appointing the group leader.

Another consideration is the role the group leader will play: leader? facilitator? convener? arbiter of unresolved issues? The role will depend on the task the group is assigned. The head of the emergency response team, for example, will need to be what's called "an authoritarian facilitator"; in an urgent situation, this person must make decisions quickly, and those choices must be accepted by the group members if disaster is to be averted. For nonemergency tasks, a democratic facilitator, who seeks the maximum amount of participation and involvement from the group in making decisions, may be most effective. And in circumstances where the expertise and commitment to the task are equal, simply getting the group together may suffice.[27]

Some observers feel that a group leader functions "within a group in helping that group to grow and to work productively" and that "no sharp distinction can be made between leadership and membership roles."[28] Yet in most cases some differentiation is inevitable; the leader is ultimately responsible for motivating and guiding the group in the appropriate direction (keeping everyone on track or focused) and for the eventual outcome or production of the group. Perhaps the ideal leader is both a "task specialist," who is goal oriented, and a "social-emotional specialist," who is concerned about the satisfaction of group members and about giving emotional rewards. The leader's focus should be on both production and people.[29]

Regardless of their place in the organization, the people chosen to lead groups must be given sufficient authority and resources to accomplish the task assigned. If final decision making rests outside the team, or if its work is to be submitted elsewhere for editorial comment, input, or final approval, that fact should be made clear at the outset.

What about group size? For typical museum projects, the group varies from three to ten members, depending on the expertise required. Five has been suggested as the optimal number of members to ensure effective discussion and participation;[30] certainly the complexity of group interaction and team building expands significantly as group numbers grow.

It is up to the facilitator-leader, in cooperation with other group members, to determine who will play which roles and to maximize the positive aspects of each role for the benefit of the group and the project as a whole. Certain personality types may have difficulties working together, although a skilled facilitator frequently will be able to steer the group toward the desired goals despite the personalities involved.

Hundreds of volumes have been written about personality types, mechanisms for identifying and assessing them, methods of integrating various types in the workplace, and suggestions for managing conflicting types. Many of these analyses are extraordinarily complex; others divide people into simplistic categories (e.g., leaders and followers, task-oriented vs. social-oriented).[31] Some museum managers and staff have found participating in assessments—of personality, learning styles, work approaches—to be a useful step toward increased self-awareness and understanding of others. Some groups use assessments as an initial team-building exercise. The motivation for such investigations is to create an environment of understanding where people can work effectively with one another.

Our experience has been that personality assessment can sometimes lead to typecasting. "Jessica will be perfect for this group; she's such a ______." "Of course Matt's slowing things down; he's a typical ______." Many of us fall into the all-too-human tendency to attribute behavior we do not like to negative personality traits. It's much easier to do this than to actually analyze the dynamic of the situation in question. Often it is the situation, more than personality, that influences behavior.[32] We all behave differently around our bosses, our mothers, our constituents, our colleagues, our best friends, our mates. Consider, too, the number of times there is a significant difference between what we intend and what the impact of our behavior actually is. Few of us want others to draw conclusions about us as persons and the "type" we are, so it's important to avoid typecasting.

Nevertheless, the selection process should include some discussion of the individual personalities and the social context of the group. These items should be considered along with skills and time constraints in order to preclude serious conflicts and to enhance the efficiency of the group.[33]

Several variables can influence group effectiveness and final team output, either negatively or positively. A very important, yet most unpredictable, variable is how much member effort is brought to bear on the assigned task. If individuals feel they will receive personal satisfaction or achieve personal goals while working within the group, their individual effort will increase accordingly. Coordination among members so that their efforts are not wasted or duplicated is critical to maintaining a high level of commitment to the task, but good coordination becomes increasingly difficult as the number of group members increases, and productivity can drop. In addition to completing the task assigned, the members must address its actual coordination—how are we going to do this?[34]

Researchers found that the creativity of final products increased when teams considered a number of performance strategies early on. Doing it "the way we've always done it" or reworking an older strategy is common, if less conducive to creativity. Most groups gave planning activities a low priority even though the group members realized that planning was an important part of completing their task. (Almost all of us would rather "just do it" than talk about how we could best go about it.)

The skills and knowledge of the group members may also have a big impact on the interaction of a group. Who knows how much about what and the degree of significance that knowledge plays in completing the task will obviously affect both the workings of the team and its product.[35] Selecting team members with necessary and complementary skills sets and knowledge can help create the balance required to accomplish the task in question and set the stage for development of an effective team.

Building a Team

What's in a name? We have used the terms "group" and "team" interchangeably in this discussion, but "team" implies a level of affiliation and shared purpose greater than that of a mere "group." In a team, individual strengths and differences are recognized and valued as part of the common belief that all individual contributions are critical for success. Ideally, teams are synergistic—what they produce in concert is greater than the mere sum of the individual parts.[36]

But how is such a team created? More is needed than just the admonition to "work together." Team dynamics in the workplace as well as the sports arena have been the subject of countless publications. We offer here a sampling of analyses you may find helpful in your own creation of, participation in, or leadership of groups and teams.

Perhaps "a rose is a rose is a rose," but not all groups are created equal. David W. Johnson and Roger T. Johnson[37] cite four group categories that may result from putting people together (see box 3.3).

Clearly not every group will function as a high-performance entity. Members will be affected "by a number of dynamics that impair their effectiveness, such as group immaturity, uncritically and quickly accepting members' dominant response, social loafing, free-riding, and groupthink."[38] Depending on the makeup of the group, it may be impossible to overcome some of these problems and mold the individuals into a high-performance team.

If a group of strangers is to become a cooperative team, the members must develop an idea of *positive interdependence* and see the whole organization instead of the individual. Positive interdependence occurs when the separate members see themselves as an indispensable part of the group and realize that without each person's help, the whole organization will

Box 3.3

Types of Groups

Pseudogroups—This is a group in name only, populated by people who have no intention of working together. Their behavior is poorly coordinated and the production of this group is extremely low and unreliable.

Traditional groups—Members of this group will share information to complete their task, but continue to accomplish their work on an individual basis. They do not have the cohesion to work together and are still rewarded on an individual basis.

Cooperative groups—This group truly strives to work together and promote each group member's success. They support each member's effort and provide feedback on their effectiveness as an entity.

High-performance groups—A highly motivated group that outperforms all expectations and goals that were set for the members.

Source: "Cooperative learning and social interdependence theory" by D. W. Johnson and R. T. Johnson. In *Theory and research on small groups*, ed. R. S. Tindale et al. New York: Plenum Press, 1998.

fail at its task. "Group members have to know that they . . . have two responsibilities: to maximize their own productivity, and to maximize the productivity of all other group members."[39]

Some believe team building to be an evolutionary process and that team interactions, like other human relationships, change over time (see box 3.4). Whether teams move to a more refined level of interaction depends on a number of factors, not the least of which is trust.

A Matter of Trust

"Trust" is a term that has come up again and again in our descriptions of the dynamics of the working museum. Trust is the foundation of relationships, both inside and outside the museum, yet it's not often explicitly addressed. Trust, or the lack thereof, has a critical role to play in determin-

Box 3.4

Stages of Team Development

Membership—The initial stages, in which no one member is certain what to expect from the others, what roles will be played by whom, how much to invest in the group, who will be compatible. Input is superficial and polite.

Subgroup—Members start to identify who has similar views and common interests, and these people band together, supporting each other's ideas, viewing other subgroups as "too"—verbose, biased, naïve, narrow, practical, abstract. Progress is minimal because no one expects the other subgroups will collaborate.

Confrontation—Out of frustration with the inability to engage vigorously the issues to be addressed, the subgroups engage in struggles for control of the team's destiny. Coalitions fight with other coalitions over issues of power and status, but people say what they really think.

Individual differentiation—Members develop an understanding of what their individual jobs are, what to expect of one another, and what the team can do, lessening the need for subgroup alliances. Work is parceled out efficiently, but there's limited collective action. The team's goals are reasonably accepted, and most members want the work to get done.

Shared responsibility—Individual uniqueness and collective effort are both valued. Members keep each other informed, trust one another to act, fight hard and fair over issue-based disagreements, support and confront each other, and are truly dedicated to the team's overarching goal.

Source: *Managing for excellence* by D. Bradford and A. Cohen. New York: John Wiley & Sons, 1984.

ing whether or not the museum actually works. Creating an environment in which trust flourishes is critical for success, whether museum staff are working as individuals or as part of groups or teams.

Dennis and Michelle Reina assess the role of trust and the result of its betrayal in the workings of organizations. They describe three important types of trust:

> Contractual trust, "the trust of character," implies that there is an understanding that we will do what we say we will. It forms the basis of most interactions in the workplace. Employees and leaders both have a strong need to have confidence in each other's intentions, consistency, and reliability.
> Communication trust, "the trust of disclosure," is the willingness to share information, tell the truth, admit mistakes, maintain confidentiality, and speak with good purpose.
> Competence trust, "the trust of capability," assumes that people have the ability to do what is needed and the capacity to interact effectively with others. Narrowly speaking, it means being able to rely on someone to complete a specific task properly.[40]

Cultivating trust is key to developing effective teams and productive work environments. Certain attitudes and actions can help such trust to grow (see box 3.5).

Interpersonal Relations

What is required in museum groups is utterly simple—expressing one's ideas clearly and unambiguously and being able to listen, hear, and respond to other people's ideas. So simple, yet somehow so difficult to achieve. Part of the challenge stems from an emphasis on the assigned task—spending the great bulk of our team time concentrating on what needs to be done and very little on how best to go about doing it. Group members may make widely divergent assumptions about how the group will conduct itself—what the rules of the game are. Even when groups have established a common understanding of how they intend to function, taking time out for a "checkup" may remind members of the expectations for group interaction as well as identify areas where they need to improve (see box 3.6).

Box 3.5

Behaviors That Foster Trust in Teams

Contractual Trust

Manage expectations and establish boundaries. At the outset team members have a strong need to know what is expected of them and what they may expect in return. Explicit expectations are stated clearly and understood requirements define team boundaries, roles, and responsibilities. The purpose of and expectations for the team, when clearly established, allow team members to align toward the same objectives.

Honor agreements. Working agreements make explicit how team members would like to work together. Many groups have ground rules or team charters that govern team member behavior at meetings and elsewhere. How will decisions be made? Is it OK to miss a meeting occasionally to handle other obligations? Is it OK to say, "I don't know?" Once the group agrees how it intends to operate, trust is built each time a team member honors the agreement.

Encourage mutually serving intentions. Teams that jointly support each other in being successful are more successful. Hidden agendas break down trust.

Communication Trust

Share information. When team members share information, it contributes to learning of individuals, as well as the team.

Tell the truth. When team members do not tell the truth they betray the very principle of teamwork. There is greater risk in being dishonest than in being honest. When team members are not forthright in their communication, they engage in a form of collusion. Truth goes underground, trust declines, and team performance suffers.

Admit mistakes. High-trust teams have regular checkpoints to monitor their progress, and leaders can set the tone by providing safe opportunities for people to admit their mistakes. Errors can be viewed as learning opportunities from which value is derived.

Maintain confidentiality. Information shared in confidence should not be shared with others. What is said within the team confines should stay there, unless the information is clearly for publication.

Speak with good purpose. Team members who speak constructively and affirmatively and stand up for each other build trust. Support and praise for one another builds results. Frustrations and disappointments are inevitable; the choice is whether they are aired within the team or voiced through gossip and backbiting.

Competence Trust

Respect people's knowledge, skills, and abilities. Regarding people as competent increases their capacity to acquire new skills. Discounting and disrespecting others' expertise creates an environment in which trust is minimal and few ideas are expressed.

Box 3.5 (continued)

Involve others and seek their input. Share information, exchange ideas, and brainstorm solutions as part of day-to-day work as a way to built trust and the total team performance.

Help people learn skills. Acknowledging people's competencies expands their willingness to learn and take risks. Identifying skills they want to learn may enable team members to teach each other.

Source: *Trust and betrayal in the workplace: Building effective relationships in your organization* by D. S. and M. L. Reina. Williston, VT: Barrett-Koehler Publishers, Inc., 1999.

Box 3.6

How Are We Doing?

How are members expressing themselves? Are some aggressive? Non-participatory? Are they saying what they mean?

How well do members listen to each other?

How do members respond to each other? Are they critical of others' ideas, concerned for self? Do they ignore each other?

How democratic is the communication pattern? Is everybody contributing? Do people address each other, is all the communication directed at one person? Do some people get listened to more than others?

Is the group moving towards achieving its purpose? What is the content? Is it relevant? Is it task-oriented or maintenance-oriented?

Is the leadership style appropriate to the task? What style is being displayed? How is the group responding to the leadership style? Are members eagerly participating? Is there high or low commitment to activities and ideas? Is there a lack of enthusiasm, resisting of ideas, holding back on contributing?

What is the climate of the group? Are the people pleased to be there? Do they start out by greeting each other and showing interest in each other before getting down to the particular business of that meeting?

Is there a clear sense of cohesion and cooperation?

How clearly are the goals understood and accepted? Are the goals still appropriate? Are they still clearly understood, or do group members need a reminder? Are group members still committed to each other and to their purpose?

Source: *Making groups work: Rethinking practice* by J. Benjamin, J. Bessant, and R. Watts. St. Leonards, Australia: Allen & Unwin, 1997.

To strengthen staff members' performance in groups as well as their interaction with the public, some museums offer staff interpersonal skills training. We use interpersonal skills every time we interact with each other, but very few of us can reasonably claim that we need no help in this area. Some training uses role playing to give group members a chance to "practice" certain scenarios and deal with stressful situations prior to real-world interaction. The pressure is less in a mock situation, and role playing allows people to get to know each other's way of thinking, as well as how they might be approached on particular topics in real-life situations. Instigating practice sessions that are "personalized" to the institution may also forestall future pressures by allowing potential conflicts to be discussed prior to a crisis. Doing so may save time and stress in the long run. An exhibits team, for example, could improvise its response to a significant donor demanding last-minute changes.

This kind of skills training need not be expensive or hugely time consuming. Facilitators specializing in interpersonal effectiveness may be available within the nonprofit community at little or no cost to your organization; independent consultants may be persuaded to offer services to your museum *pro bono* or for a reduced fee.

The Decision-Making Process

A common complaint about group or team work is that "nothing ever gets decided." This is often the result of an ambiguous or undetermined process for making decisions. Who decides? The team leader? The group as a whole? Will the majority rule, or will the group have to reach consensus? Although today consensus may be the preferred decision-making process, sometimes democracy is the chosen method. No group will ever become fully democratic, but it can be democratic to the degree that it demonstrates five qualities: (1) "group" power, the recognition and acceptance of the group's authority to make decisions; (2) inclusiveness; (3) commitment to the democratic process; (4) a feeling of shared experience and respect for individuality and competence of each group member; and (5) constructive deliberation in the form of judicious argument, critical listening, and earnest decision making.[41]

A small group also may opt for a consensus strategy. This process has been used in political circles for many years and is a hand-me-down from the Religious Society of Friends (Quakers), which has used this method in conducting its business for over three centuries (see box 3.7).

Box 3.7

The Processes of Democratic and Consensus Decision Making

Majority Vote Group Decisions

Members make proposals in the form of motions. The motions are discussed. Votes are taken. If four out of seven members agree, the vote is carried.

Members try to convince the majority of the value of their proposals.

All remarks are addressed to the chair (not directly to other group members).

The chair does not argue for or against any motion. His or her task is to ensure orderly discussion procedures.

The secretary records the majority decisions as they are made.

Consensus Group Decisions

Members express opinions on the issue. Issues are discussed until solutions are found which incorporate all points of view or are satisfying to all members.

Members try to formulate solutions that will achieve consensus (all agree).

All remarks are addressed to the group as a whole with the permission of the coordinator (not directly to other group members).

The coordinator does not argue for or against any solution. He or she helps the group reach consensus by formulating proposals that may be acceptable to all members. (the sense of the meeting.)

The recorder records proposals that appear to represent consensus and reads them to the group so that group members can confirm agreement or modify the proposals.

Source: *Democracy in small groups: Participation, decision making and communications* by J. W. Gastil. Philadelphia: New Society, 1993.

While it has been suggested that there are several advantages to the consensus method of decision making, it is important to note that some groups will be focused more on reaching a decision than the actual quality of the decision. Regardless of which decision-making strategy is chosen, team members need a shared understanding of how the group will make its choices.

Conflict Management

Despite the best of intentions and group processes, conflict in the museum is inevitable. Managing conflict is as important for museum managers as it is for any other business or organization leaders. Conflict left unaddressed can lead to a seriously impaired working environment for both those directly involved and those on the sidelines. But a certain amount of conflict, managed effectively, can actually increase organizational effectiveness, according to management analyst M. A. Rahim. He suggests four levels of conflict may be evidenced in the workplace—intrapersonal, interpersonal, intragroup, and intergroup.[42] Museum managers likely will spend most of their energy attending to interpersonal conflicts but may well be called upon to arbitrate intragroup troubles and may have to respond to intergroup disharmony. Sources of conflict may include differing goals, beliefs, attitudes, or ideas.

Investigators who have studied conflict management have noted that often conflict is perceived instead of real. The concentration of the staff is against each other instead of on the goal or mission of the organization, and differences instead of similarities are emphasized. Each person involved in the conflict takes on the problem singly instead of as a team, and the resolutions developed are beneficial not to the museum but only to the individual. The challenge for administrators comes in helping staff understand the sources of perceived conflicts and in keeping the focus on the greater good for the museum.

A. J. Friedman identifies three factors as contributing to museum conflicts[43]:

Hierarchy

Organizational structure can lead to competition and eventual conflict. The greater the difference in the level of authority, the greater the potential for conflict to arise. People who work in areas like education, public programs, and exhibits in traditional museums tend to have, or feel they have, an inferior rank (and therefore lower budgets with which to work) compared with those who work with collections or are involved in research. This perceived pecking order polarizes departments, which lessens the amount of contact they have with each other and ultimately hurts the whole organization in its attempt to fulfill its mission.

Conflict of Interest

Sometimes departments within an organization end up having vastly different goals, and this situation can lead to disputes among departments if the differences foster competition. Typically, public-oriented departments and those with collections care or research concerns perceive themselves to be in opposition.[44] Some of the functions of these departments are contradictory by nature; for instance, exhibiting an item may impede the goal of preserving it. If policies are not clearly laid out or if limited budgets cause scarce resources, competition levels will rise among departments and may prompt stereotyping and an "us against them" attitude.

Overdependency

Situations may arise in which one department becomes heavily dependent on another for the resources needed to carry out its function or reach its goal. Each decision of the less dependent department can have a direct or indirect impact on the dependent one and be a source of resentment if the needs and realities of the lesser department are not kept in mind. For example, a publications department that relies on graphic designers from the museum exhibition department may be frustrated if its design needs get lost in the shuffle of exhibition design projects.

Whatever the source of conflict, typical responses include avoidance, competition, accommodation, compromise, problem solving, and collaboration. Avoidance and competition are the responses most likely to contribute to declining morale, although a period of short-term avoidance may be advantageous for disagreeing parties when it allows time for them to regain their composure and think through all of the issues and circumstances that are causing the conflict.[45]

Accommodation is often the response if one party to the conflict is subordinate to the other. Most of the time a manager will try to accommodate the wishes of the director, president, board member, or other superior. Some studies on manager-subordinate conflicts suggest, however, the subordinates may take on avoidance, competition, or problem-solving strategies.

Problem solving through compromise and collaboration is the most effective response to conflict. Compromise is most typical when the discord is between people at the same level, and a compromise solution will often be sought by coworkers. Despite good intentions, competitive emotions are much more likely to surface in turmoil between equals than in supervisor-subordinate conflict, so managers may play a useful role in facilitating problem solving.[46]

In a win-win scenario, the problem is seen as external to the people involved. The conflict is managed as "opposing parties collaborate to seek a higher quality solution that meets their mutual needs while preserving their relationship."[47] A well-developed problem-solving process that allows for cooperative decision making can help turn conflict into solvable problems.

Manifestations of excessive conflict within a museum can be the presence of frequent interpersonal conflict, high employee illness and absentee rates, depression, lethargy, work slowdowns, increased grumbling and rumormongering, and scapegoating. These troubles can lead to lower output, more errors, high levels of agitation, and perhaps even secret meetings on the part of subordinate employees. All of this discontent can then bring on higher employee turnover and time spent interviewing prospective employees and training new ones rather than achieving the museum's goals.

The best way to manage conflict is to conscientiously work to create an environment in which positive interaction can flourish. A commitment to respect for differences and open communication, as well as to the museum's mission, shared by *all* the people who make up the museum, from the board and executive director through managers and staff, can help foster such a climate. Specialists in a museum—administrators, designers, curators, conservators, educators, collection managers—"must work closely together as they collect, preserve, and interpret their collections."[48] Self-directed work teams that are dedicated to their jobs have the best chance of success.[49]

Managers serve their own, as well as the museum's, best interests by listening to their employees, paying attention to expressions of dissatisfaction, and responding to staff suggestions for improvements.[50] A museum that promotes a structured style of conflict management, which uses cooperation within self-directed work teams and good, open communication, can help keep conflicts to a minimum and produce positive results from those that do arise.

Conclusion

It is people who make a museum work, and people who work together in a productive manner create the most effective museum. The multifaceted talents of the staff are the museum's most valuable assets. Each person on the staff is a unique individual with distinct needs, emotions, and personality traits. Today's museum administrators need to possess sensitivity to individuals and identify the resources and challenges they will bring to the larger group.

Working effectively with groups and within groups is critical to the success of any museum professional and to the success of any museum. The board members, director, and staff can work together to create mechanisms through which the museum's mission can be fulfilled, and both the museum's constituents and those doing the museum's work directly will benefit. Organizational structures can help or hinder the museum at work, but more telling are the factors of shared vision; clear, open, honest communication; cooperative spirit; and trust. These elements have a far greater impact on what the museum, through its governing body and workers, is able to accomplish than any organizational method.

A working museum is made up of team players. Each person will work as part of many groups, and the dynamics of group interaction are important to understand in order to maximize productivity. Museum professionals will face some of their most difficult challenges as members of the small groups that will be responsible for making many of the decisions and implementing policies within the museum. A shared commitment to respecting differences and maintaining communication, as well as to carrying out the museum's mission, is essential to creating a functional, working museum.

An effective organizational structure, well-defined roles for board, director, and staff, and capable teams, when combined in an atmosphere of communication, cooperation, and trust, can create a museum that really *works.*

Notes

1. Janes 1997.
2. Chell 1987, 159.
3. Benedetto 1985, 2.
4. Lord and Lord 1997, 33.
5. Janes 1997, 50.
6. Handy 1989.

7. Janes 1997, 243.
8. Kotler and Kotler 1998, 94.
9. Frantzreb 1989, 73.
10. Howe 1995, 5.
11. Axelrod 1994, 120, 131.
12. Hay 1990, 154.
13. Naumer 1977, 31.
14. Duca 1996, 4.
15. Hay 1990, 155.
16. Dickenson 1994.
17. Heimovics and Herman 1994, 141–142.
18. Frantzreb 1989, 74.
19. Duca 1996, 93–98.
20. Axelrod 1994, 131.
21. Duca 1996, 97.
22. Axelrod 1994, 131.
23. Frantzreb 1989, 75.
24. Heimovics and Herman 1994, 144.
25. Tolles 1991.
26. Gastil 1993.
27. Benjamin et al. 1997, 122.
28. Benne and Sheats 1970, 133–142.
29. Hare 1982, 124.
30. Ibid., 146.
31. Ibid., 138.
32. Bradford and Cohen 1984, 148.
33. Nemiroff and King 1975, 4.
34. Hackman and Morris 1983, 334.
35. Dubrin 1997, 161.
36. Ibid., 184.
37. Johnson and Johnson 1998.
38. Ibid.
39. Ibid., 25.
40. Reina and Reina 1999.
41. Gastil 1993.
42. Rahim 2000.
43. Friedman 1991, 38.
44. McLean 1993, 46.
45. Rahim 1992, 29.

46. Ibid.
47. Katz and Lawyer 1985, 117.
48. Kane 1991, 48.
49. Dubrin 1997, 100.
50. Lundin and Lundin 1995.

CHAPTER FOUR
STRATEGIC PLANNING

Many museums spend precious time and resources chasing a vague dream of professionalism and mission fulfillment. They try to do everything at once, only to be left feeling unfulfilled when their well-intentioned efforts do not accomplish all that staff and board members had hoped. Such museums do not have a clear vision, a set of common goals shared among staff, board, and constituents that focuses their day-to-day work efforts. They do not have a strategic plan. All museums need strategic planning, and it should be an active, ongoing process rather than one that occurs every few years without future use or reference.[1]

What Is Strategic Planning?

Strategic planning is "a disciplined effort to produce fundamental decisions and actions that shape and guide what an organization is, what it does, and why it does it," notes John Bryson,[2] professor of planning and public affairs at the University of Minnesota. It is "a process that defines goals and then provides strategies to achieve them," observes Keith Curtis,[3] professor of health administration and policy at the University of Oklahoma. He believes strategic planning can create a shared sense of organizational identity. When finished, a strategic plan creates general goals with specific objectives, delegates responsibility, establishes deadlines and a system of evaluation, and facilitates daily decision making.[4]

Strategic planning also forces the board and staff to look at external forces and to establish goals to meet the needs of the museum's audience and stakeholders. Strategic planning forces museum staff, board, and constituents to evaluate the museum's mission, revise the mission to be consistent with community needs, and develop action plans to fulfill that mission, while taking into consideration available resources.[5]

CHAPTER 4

Arguments for Strategic Planning

In addition to focusing a museum's energies toward success, a strategic plan

- makes the most of limited resources
- reduces the length and number of meetings
- invests "stakeholders" in the success of the museum
- provides tools to measure effectiveness
- improves public relations
- improves access to funding by establishing clear connections between community needs and the museum's efforts
- gives volunteers more satisfying involvement
- establishes organizational priorities
- serves as a basis for staff evaluation
- reduces crisis management
- encourages decision making with an eye to the future
- improves museum output
- eases decision making under changing circumstances
- builds teamwork
- increases efficiency
- increases outside political support
- identifies areas requiring improvement or change
- defines available resources
- instills staff commitment to the museum and guides daily performance
- eases recruitment of new board members

- eases recruitment of prospective and repeat financial donations.[6]

A successful organization is one that has a clear understanding of mandates; an established, well-communicated, and inspiring mission; effectively managed resources to fulfill its mission; a clear communication network; strategic organization; and effective and competent leadership. A strategic plan is a critical lens through which activities can be focused, leading to this success.[7]

Ultimately, strategic planning should increase board and management support for, and commitment to, the museum. It can be time consuming, but it can also save time by increasing efficiency.[8] Museum size does not matter; even volunteer-operated museums need to focus on success. Facilitators and books can help inexperienced museums with strategic planning, and although strategic planning is theoretical, it also includes action plans to make the theories realities. Strategic planning sometimes is opposed by key stakeholders who fear a favorite program will be eliminated. This may happen, but strategic planning will help stakeholders to see that certain programs offer the best advantage to further the museum's mission, and strategic planning will ensure that these programs, and the museum itself, succeed.[9]

Bryson and Alston argue in their book *Creating and Implementing Your Strategic Plan* that a museum in crisis or major transition (that is, the building just burned down or a new director is being sought) should deal with the issues at hand and postpone strategic planning until a later date. These events do not *eliminate* the need for planning; they only affect its timing. Even crises will require planning.[10] A museum experiencing a major financial crisis, for example, might want to consider a modified version of strategic planning and develop a plan focusing on that situation. Finally, if the board and management of a museum will not commit to developing a strategic plan, it should not be undertaken. A lack of commitment should raise a general concern about the success of the museum and may signal the time to replace such a board or staff.

Some of the symptoms of a museum that needs a strategic plan are listed in box 4.1. A museum experiencing any of these symptoms is operating below optimal level, and strategic planning should be seriously considered.

Box 4.1

Symptoms of an Organization in Need of a Strategic Plan

- The board is unable to make decisions.
- The board delays decision making due to lack of participation.
- A large board is dominated by a minority.
- Volunteers and donations are dwindling.
- There are internal power struggles.
- The audience is dissatisfied.
- There are problems due to unclear roles.
- Crisis management prevails.
- Meetings are long with poor attendance.
- Good ideas are not being implemented.
- Agendas ramble.
- The museum focuses on many unrelated projects.
- People do not follow through on commitments.
- The museum cannot attract outside money.
- It is difficult to quantify and communicate progress.

Source: "Strategic planning for nonprofit organizations" by M. Smiley. *National Trust for Historic Preservation Information Series* 66:1–24, 1992.

Basic Strategic Planning Processes

The process of strategic planning can be simple or complex. Authors have defined it variously with from four to ten steps. Box 4.2 offers five ways of viewing the strategic planning process.

Although they use different terminology, all of these strategic planning processes are virtually the same. They direct museum strategic planners to clarify their mission and values, identify the external and internal forces that influence their activities, identify specifics to fulfill their mission, formulate action plans and responsibility centered on achieving goal objectives, and evaluate their success in achieving these goals. Presented here is a modified version of Bryson and Alston's[11] process, incorporating elements from the other authors.

Step 1: Initiate and Agree on Process

Some basic agreements are needed prior to beginning the strategic planning process. First, the museum board, staff, and volunteers should

Box 4.2

Phases of a Strategic Plan

***From Management Goal Setting to Organizational Results,* by K. Curtis**

1. Environmental scan
2. Strategy Formulation
3. Execution
4. Control and Evaluation

***Creating and Implementing Your Strategic Plan,* by J. M. Bryson and F. K. Alston**

1. Initiate and agree on strategic planning process
2. Clarify organizational mandates
3. Identify and understand stakeholders, develop and refine mission
4. Assess the environment to identify Strengths, Weaknesses, Opportunities, and Threats
5. Identify and frame strategic issues
6. Formulate strategies to manage strategic issues
7. Review and adopt the strategic plan
8. Establish an effective organizational vision for the future
9. Develop an effective implementation process
10. Reassess strategies and strategic planning process

***Handbook of Strategic Planning,* by J. R. Gardner, R. Rochlin, and H. W. A. Sweeny (eds.)**

1. External analysis
2. Internal analysis
3. Strategic direction setting
4. Definition of base and contingency plans
5. Policy/Strategy/Program implementation
6. Performance evaluation

***Strategic Long Range Planning,* by R. Simerly**

1. Establish goals providing direction for museum
2. Establish necessary objectives to reach goals
3. Assign individuals to carry out each objective
4. Set deadlines for completing each objective
5. Decide how to evaluate success of reaching each objective
6. Establish system of checks and balances to determine difficulties in reaching objectives
7. Revise objectives and deadlines when necessary

Box 4.2 (continued)

***Strategic Planning for Nonprofit Organizations,* by M. Smiley**

1. Assessment
2. Long-range planning
3. Short-range planning
4. Implementation
5. Evaluation

be supportive and ready to participate. This broad sponsorship keeps the process from becoming one person's or group's project. Lack of inclusion is a common reason planning fails.[12] If possible, so as to build internal support and a sense of ownership, top decision makers, middle management, and front-line personnel all should be involved in the process.[13]

Once broad support is achieved, a strategic planning committee of effective policy makers should be formed. It is imperative that staff, the "doers," be involved in all aspects of strategic planning to ensure their commitment to accomplishing the goals outlined by the plan. It also is wise to include representatives of constituent groups to ensure that the strategic planning process is not overly internalized and that outside factors always are represented. This step will help the museum develop new stakeholders and enhance the commitment of existing stakeholders. It can be interesting to have a representative or two from groups that do not use the museum or that the museum wishes to target in the future. An outside facilitator should be considered for an organization's first attempt at strategic planning or for a museum with a limited number of staff. Even if strategic planning is a common event for a museum, an outside facilitator may still be used to ensure that the process is unbiased, nonthreatening, and nonjudgmental.[14]

Once the strategic planning committee is formed, it should establish why the strategic planning effort is needed now, what steps will be included in the process, who will be responsible for carrying out the steps, and deadlines and guidelines for reports. The committee also should determine what resources are needed for the process, if they are available, and where they can be obtained.[15] At this point, the committee should determine how long the planning process should take, and it should plan the time and place for periodic retreats. Periodic retreats are advised as they allow the committee to refocus and regroup away from the museum and daily pressures. The museum director or board president should not preside over the retreats or any brainstorming sessions in order to avoid "groupthink" (a group's inclination to agree with the desires of the executive officer[16]), which would devalue the planning process. The strategic planning effort should take place over six to twelve months to allow time for adequate information gathering and to avoid rushing the process.

Step 2: Identify Organizational Mandates

Organizational mandates are the "musts" a museum faces, usually dictated by external forces. These mandates may be laws, guidelines imposed by funders, budgets, or societal expectations. In the process of strategic planning and possible mission restructuring, the museum must have a clear understanding of what it is expected and required to do. After the mandates have been compiled, they should be clearly listed and distributed to all committee members and then referred to regularly to ensure compliance.[17]

Step 3: Identify and Understand Stakeholders and Develop Mission

A museum should identify its stakeholders and understand what they want or expect from the museum. A stakeholder is any person or group that can place a claim on the museum's resources and products. This may include members, employees, board members, teachers, civic leaders, granting or funding organizations, cooperating organizations, competing organizations, the media, visitors, and others. Each museum will have a different set of stakeholders depending on its situation.

Once stakeholders have been identified, it is important to identify their needs and the criteria they use to assess the museum's performance. This is vital because the success of the museum depends on the support of stakeholders. The strategic planning committee can identify internal stakeholder needs and criteria, and it also can brainstorm criteria it believes external stakeholders are using; however, direct stakeholder surveys provide much more detailed, accurate, and worthwhile information.

If external stakeholder (constituent) representatives have been included on the strategic planning committee, they could be surveyed, or they could assist with survey development. This analysis will ascertain stakeholder needs and criteria as well as stakeholder perceptions of current operations and suggestions for future changes. A list of museum needs that stakeholders meet also should be compiled. This list will help clarify the important roles stakeholders play in the success of the museum, and it should further convince committee members of the importance of stakeholder satisfaction.

Addressing the mission is an especially important part of strategic planning. As the museum's statement of purpose (see chapter 2), the mission should guide the direction and activities of the museum. Ultimately, everything a museum does should relate to its mission.[18] It is important to develop or revise the mission statement early in the strategic planning process because the plan guides the activities of the museum toward mission fulfillment.[19] Values and purpose, not projects or campaigns, drive the museum to success over time.[20]

Using the mandates and stakeholder needs as a guiding force, the committee members should write individual mission statements that answer the following questions[21]: Who are we? What and whose needs do we fill? How do we fill those needs? What are our core values? Why are we unique? After finishing individual mission statements, members come together and coalesce them into one mission statement that can be accepted. If the museum already had a mission statement, the new one can be compared with the original and be used to modify or replace it.[22]

Step 4: Internal and External Assessments

Strategic planning often fails because it is based on incomplete information. This fourth step in the strategic planning process is commonly called a SWOT analysis. A SWOT analysis evaluates internal **S**trengths and **W**eaknesses and external **O**pportunities and **T**hreats. The objective of any museum should be to take advantage of strengths and opportunities and minimize weaknesses and threats.[23]

Internal Analysis

Internal strengths and weaknesses are identified by evaluating resources, present strategies, and performance. According to Burkhart and Reuss,[24] there are four basic components of an internal analysis:

1. Board assessment
2. Staff assessment
3. Volunteer assessment
4. Statistical review of finances and output

Board Assessment—The role of a museum board is to advance the museum in the community; provide guidance and expertise in policy, fiscal, and legal issues; raise public awareness; and raise funds for museum efforts. The board assessment should give the strategic planning committee a well-rounded understanding of board commitment, areas where board responsibility is unclear, personal agendas of members, and board perceptions of how the museum is operating now and should operate in the future. It should illuminate board weaknesses and strengths and identify areas where the board can enhance museum operations. As part of a board assessment, members should be asked why they are on the board, whether they have other affiliations that affect their board service, if they have had personal experiences with the museum that were not board-related, and what their personal goals for the museum are.[25]

Staff and Volunteer Assessments—The role of museum staff members is to carry out board policy, supervise and manage museum activities, operate the facilities, manage and recruit volunteers, and handle public relations. The volunteers help the staff perform their functions, and in some museums they serve as staff. Volunteers are generally community members and can be strong advocates for the museum. The staff and volunteer assessment should concentrate on determining staff and volunteer work satisfaction. This includes whether they feel adequate resources are available for work to be accomplished, staff and volunteer goals for the museum, whether staff and volunteers perceive the museum as a valuable resource, and whether they feel the museum is living up to its mission and potential. This assessment can help determine what is causing staff weaknesses and identify staff strengths, thus allowing plans to be made to minimize the former and capitalize on the latter.[26]

Statistical Review of Finances and Output—This can be compiled from financial documents and should show actual, budgeted, and variance amounts. Output can be determined from attendance records, public response to programs and exhibits, and any other relevant statistical data. Comparison with other museums of similar size is a vital part of an internal assessment. This step also should look at any previously established goals to see whether or not they were met, and at the museum's market penetration—the size of the potential client base measured against the served client base.[27]

External Analysis

This type of analysis requires that the strategic planning committee view the museum in relation to the external environment. It should analyze three major forces that affect the museum operations—trends (political, economic, social, and technological), audience, and competitors and collaborators. Trends can be analyzed through research and data compilation. Surveys of audiences, competitors, and collaborators can be done to examine how the activities of these forces can and will affect the museum.[28]

Board members or committee members from constituent groups should be part of this analysis of external forces and their impact on the museum. These committee members probably work outside the museum and may be better able to identify how external forces relate to the museum. It also may behoove the strategic planning committee to consider the external environment before the internal environment because doing so will focus further strategic planning efforts on fulfilling the needs of external key stakeholders. Burkhart and Reuss stress the importance of this assessment.[29]

> Perhaps no other part of the strategic planning process is as vital to the nonprofit organization's long-term success as the external assessment. If the external assessment is accomplished openly, objectively, and thoroughly, it will provide a well-crafted vision of the marketplace and the environmental factors that affect the organization.

Step 5: Identify Strategic Issues

A strategic issue is a fundamental policy choice determined by a museum's mandates, mission, values, product, audience, financing, and management. Look to internal and external stakeholder perceptions and suggestions for common themes and relate these to the museum's mandates and mission, and to the SWOT analysis. This will help identify the issues that the museum needs to address.[30] To determine if an issue is strategic, define the consequences if the issue is not addressed; if there are no consequences, the issue is not strategic. There are three kinds of strategic issues: 1) those where no action is required but the issue must be monitored; 2) those that can be handled as part of the regular strategic planning cycle; and 3) those that require immediate response.[31]

Once they are identified, list the strategic issues in priority order. This list should contain a description of the issue, a discussion of the factors that make the issue strategic, and a discussion of the consequences if the issue is not addressed. Turn the issues into opportunities, compare these opportunities with the mission, and, if consistent, prepare to work on them. Ranking the issues enables the museum to focus on the most critical.

Step 6: Review and Adopt Strategic Issues

Before starting the next step in the strategic planning process, review again what strategic issues should be pursued. Involvement of many people in the planning process can create a hodgepodge of inconsistent and contradictory ideas. Refining the many ideas through a process that respects and builds on needs prevents lack of focus.[32] The final list should be formally adopted by the strategic planning committee.

Step 7: Formulate Strategies (Action or Work Plans) to Manage Strategic Issues

Strategic issues can be converted into goals for the museum to pursue. It has been suggested that the number of goals be limited to eight because more inhibits a shared vision.[33] Small museums with limited staff and resources may want to limit their goals to three over a five-year period. Develop goals that guide the museum's actions toward mission fulfillment. It is during this step that the strategic planning committee establishes the action plans (strategies) that will guide policies, programs, actions, decisions, and resource allocations to facilitate reaching goals made clear by strategic issues.[34]

Goals should be prioritized by cross-checking them with the museum's mission. Development of an action plan (objectives) should define the goals, build on strengths and opportunities, and minimize threats and weaknesses.[35] Action plans will detail tasks, assign responsibility for each task, and specify time frames for task completion. Action plans should be achievable, measurable, flexible, and understandable. These goals and action plans will determine the course of the museum for the time period of the strategic plan.[36]

Once an action plan is agreed upon, it is important to determine what resources will be needed to carry it out. Will it be necessary to add, redistribute, or reduce resources? For museums with limited resources, the cost and effort needed to achieve each increment of the plan should be determined.[37] The increments should be ranked in priority order, and the board should decide what part or parts of the plan it is willing to or can afford to implement. In reality, action plans can help facilitate budgeting and fundraising activities. Each task will have financial implications, and knowing when the task will take place helps the museum analyze the cash flow of the program.[38]

Step 8: Establish a Vision for the Future of the Museum

Vision embraces values that never change in the service of a long-range purpose; it inspires commitment and focuses action. According to Curtis,[39] "an organization must have a long-term vision, especially when it is dealing in crisis or ad hoc situations." This process serves as an inspirational tool to all those involved in the development or implementation of the strategic plan. Here the committee paints a picture of what the museum will look like when it implements its strategic plan and achieves its full potential. This "vision of success" should include the museum's mission, strategic issues, established goals, action plans, performance criteria, decision-making rules, and ethical standards. Once the vision of success is formulated, it should be communicated to the entire museum organization.[40]

Step 9: Evaluation and Reassessment

If a detailed work plan has been established, it should be relatively easy to evaluate whether the strategic plan is working successfully. Evaluations should be done on a regular basis, approximately every year, to establish which goals have been met, if new ones should be undertaken, if some should be scrapped, or if plans should be reworked. Evaluation should not be overlooked, because funders use evaluation to inform their funding decisions.[41]

Implementation

When the strategic planning committee has completed its work, the plan should be submitted to the museum staff members, the "doers," for their approval. This is a critical step because staff involvement is key to implementation of the plan. Finally, the plan must be approved by the board—the "deciders."[42] The board, as the governing body for the museum, must fully support the document because it will direct the museum for the next three to five years. The goal of the strategic plan is to translate vision into specific, annual operational plans.

When the plan has been accepted by the board—the goals, action plan, and work plan have been set—whose responsibility is it to see that the strategic plan is successfully implemented? More strategic plans fail at this point than at any other time in this long and time-consuming process. The director of the museum must be the person who is responsible for implementing the strategic plan. The director sits in a pivotal position between the board and the staff. The director must work with the board to obtain the resources necessary for implementation. The board must approve the annual budgets that allocate resources. The director should be reporting progress on the plan to the board on a regular basis and keeping the board's focus on this document.

The director has the responsibility to see that appropriate portions of the plan are placed in the performance expectations of direct report managers for the coming year. The director must be certain these managers incorporate portions of the plan in the expectations for staff members reporting to them. The fulfillment of these expectations must become a major portion of the annual evaluation of all of the museum's staff. In subsequent years, as the staff sets expectations for the coming year, appropriate portions of the plan must be incorporated. It is the director who must be certain that staff members who fulfill their expectations are rewarded and that the evaluation process occurs on at least an annual basis. Well-implemented plans achieve the desired results on time, and with few unintended side effects. The secret of good implementation is simple—it requires commitment from all who are needed to carry it out.

Box 4.3

Exercise: Strategic Planning

Obtain a copy of your museum's strategic plan or the plan for a museum with which you are familiar. Be certain that you have permission to obtain a copy of the document. Study the strategic plan carefully and answer the questions posed below.

1. Does the strategic plan follow one of the models discussed in this chapter? Is it a combination of several of these models?
2. Does the plan have an executive summary? Does the summary effectively present the overall plan?
3. Is the museum's mission statement a guiding principle for the strategic plan?
4. Are the museum's mandates identified?
5. Were internal and external assessments conducted? Are the results included in the strategic plan?
6. Are strategic issues identified? Are the strategic issues put in priority order?
7. Are stakeholders identified? Are stakeholders involved in the planning process?
8. Are nonuser target audiences identified? Are representatives of nonuser target audiences involved in the planning process?
9. Is there an action plan? Is it appropriately detailed? If not, what details should be added?
10. Is a plan in place for the implementation of the strategic plan?
11. Is a "vision of success" included in the strategic plan?
12. Is a process in place to evaluate progress on the implementation of the strategic plan?
13. Is the director's role in implementing the strategic plan well defined?
14. Is a mechanism identified for incorporating the action plan into the annual goals and evaluation of staff members?
15. Is a process in place to update the strategic plan on a regular basis?
16. What is the strongest section of the plan?
17. What is the weakest section of the plan? Rewrite this section to bring it to the level of the stronger sections.
18. Was the plan prepared through a bottom-up or a top-down process?

Conclusion

The final product of the strategic planning process should be a document that can be distributed widely to staff, board, strategic planning committee members, potential funders, and other interested parties. This document should include a two-page executive summary, the museum's mission statement, the external assessment results, the internal assessment results, the defined strategic issues or goals, the objectives or work plan to achieve the goals, and a conclusion discussing implementation. This may all seem like an extraordinary amount of effort and planning, but those museums that engage in strategic planning and follow through with implementation will be better managed museums—museums that attract and keep dedicated staff, obtain necessary resources, and provide recognized value to their constituents. The document that has just been completed—the museum's strategic plan—is second in importance only to the museum's mission statement.

Notes

1. Smiley 1992; Burkhart and Reuss 1993.
2. Bryson 1988.
3. Curtis 1994.
4. Bryson and Alston 1996.
5. Burkhart and Reuss 1993.
6. Smiley 1992.
7. Bryson and Alston 1996.
8. Smiley 1992.
9. McHugh 1980; Bryson and Alston 1996.
10. Bryson and Alston 1996.
11. Ibid.
12. Phillips 1995.
13. Simerly 1985.
14. Bryson 1988; Bryson and Alston 1996.
15. Bryson and Alston 1996.
16. Curtis 1994, 77.
17. Bryson 1988; Bryson and Alston 1996.
18. Burkhart and Reuss 1993.
19. Bryson 1988; Curtis 1994.
20. Phillips 1995.
21. Bryson 1988.
22. Bryson 1988; Burkhart and Reuss 1993.
23. Bryson and Alston 1996.
24. Burkhart and Reuss 1993.
25. Ibid.
26. Ibid.
27. Ibid.

28. Bryson 1988.
29. Burkhart and Reuss 1993.
30. Bryson 1988.
31. Bryson and Alston 1996.
32. Phillips 1995, 10.
33. Curtis 1994.
34. Smiley 1992.
35. Ibid.
36. Burkhart and Reuss 1993.
37. Ibid.
38. McHugh 1980.
39. Curtis 1994.
40. Bryson and Alston 1996.
41. Burkhart and Reuss 1993.
42. Phillips 1995.

CHAPTER FIVE
BUDGETS AND ACCOUNTING

Mention the word "budget" to museum staff members and a resounding sigh of resignation echoes through the halls. For most, number crunching does not rank high on the list of exciting museum duties. Although they may not look forward to this fiscal activity, most museum staff will admit that the budgeting process is crucial to fulfilling the museum's mission. Without the proper allocation of resources, museums cannot operate in the present, much less preserve their collections in perpetuity. Serving the needs of stakeholders and fulfilling the mission are ultimately a question of the bottom line; if the financial wherewithal is missing, the museum cannot succeed, however brilliant its intent.

Nowhere is the old adage "knowledge is power" more true than in the budgetary arena. Many museum professionals avoid the budget process like they would an infestation of carpet beetles. But understanding where the money comes from, where it goes, and the cost of doing museum business can enable staff to be actively involved in controlling their own destinies. Accounting systems can provide access to information critical to making the best choices about the museum's precious financial resources.

Budgetary Terminology

Ensuring the financial well-being of the museum has become a growing concern for museum administrators and staff. Familiarity with some budgetary and accounting terminology is key, so let's define our terms. First, the *budget* is a basic plan with costs attached, and the *annual budget* puts monetary values on the year's short- and long-term planned goals. This annual budget may often comprise two principal parts: the *operating budget* and the *capital budget.* The operating budget includes the revenues and expenditures for the museum's day-to-day collections care, public programming, and basic operation of the museum building and site. The *capital budget* contains the amount retained for planned big-ticket investment in equipment and systems, as well as development of the museum's site or buildings via renovation, relocation, new construction, or renewal of exhibits.[1]

The budget system for nonprofits works effectively only with the addition of a partner, the *accounting system.* These two systems are interdependent; their interaction provides greater protection for and control over the revenue and resources of the institution. Once an annual budget is adopted, the accounting system serves as the basis for budget control. Monthly statements allow monitoring of actual expenditures in comparison with projections. This monitoring enables administrators to compare current year income and outgo with that of previous years.[2]

Types of Funds

Many museums base their budgeting and accounting systems on the principles of fund accounting. *Funds* are used to separate revenue and resources within an organization for certain activities and objectives.[3] An easy way of visualizing funds is as separate "pots" or "piggy banks" of money.

The *general fund* (which may also be called the "current" or "operating" fund) holds the money used, at the museum's discretion, to provide activities related to the organization's primary mission.

Capital funds are designated for the purchase of fixed assets, such as equipment and buildings. This fund may also be called the "fixed asset" or "plant" fund in some organizations.[4]

A *restricted fund* designates revenue or investment income earned from revenue that must be spent according to stipulations placed on the income by a donor or a governing body. Another fund, the *debt fund,* denotes money set aside to retire debts, such as bond issues or mortgages.[5]

Acquisition funds refer to the amount reserved for the purchase of objects for the collection or for expenses associated with acquisitions (such as shipping, insurance, and appraisal).

Endowment funds are donated monies that are invested; the income from unrestricted endowment funds may be used for operations or other legitimate purposes, whereas earnings from restricted endowment funds are earmarked for specific aims, such as acquisitions, exhibits, or seminars.[6] The *endowment principal* is that portion of the fund that remains invested and untouched and continues to earn income. Only the interest or other income earned from the principal should be expended for appropriate purposes.

Accounting Terms

Assets are items of monetary value that are owned or controlled by the museum. Assets can include cash, buildings, land, permanent equipment, accounts receivable (money owed to the museum), endowments, and inventory. Because museums hold their collections in perpetuity, they have staunchly refused to consider the collections "assets."

Liabilities are any monies owed to other parties, and would include accounts and notes payable, salaries, and benefits. To determine a *fund balance,* liabilities are subtracted from assets.

Museum budgets also rely on *grant projects* supported by government or foundation funds that often require separate accounting.[7] *Direct costs* are the actual expenses incurred in carrying out the activities proposed under the grant. Salaries, benefits, equipment, rentals, travel, expendable supplies, and operating expenses are direct costs. *Indirect costs* are the costs that the institution will incur from adding the grant activities to its programs. Heating and lighting of the building where the activities will be conducted, accounting costs, maintenance of the building, and housekeeping are examples.[8]

A myriad of resources, including the works we cite, offer more extensive definitions of budget and accounting terminology. Be sure to familiarize yourself with the terms used in the museum where you work and what they designate.

The Budget Cycle

A budget is a detailed and quantified plan for reaching organizational goals expressed in monetary or fiscal terms. Museums often develop their budgets in categories correlated to the funds they use in their accounting—the operating budget for the day-to-day operation of the museum (based on the operating fund) and the capital budget for planned capital expenditures (to be paid out of the capital fund), for example.[9]

Budget cycles begin with budget development. In order to develop a budget, museums must engage in program planning. Here is where the museum's strategic plan serves as an invaluable budget tool, outlining the institution's highest priorities. Needs assessments and feasibility studies can help staff determine what it is the museum will do; costs are then estimated for those programs. The challenge comes as proposed costs are then matched to funds available. It's a rare museum that has sufficient funds to go around.

The simple allocation of money is not effective budgeting; a clear understanding of the museum's mission, organizational goals, and available resources is essential in the budget-development process. The strategic plan ensures that the uses of revenues are appropriate while expenses are kept reasonable.[10] The budget is a valuable tool for administering and integrating programs. The development process can shed light on conflicting goals or interests within museum departments and can aid in coordinating these issues. The budget serves as a means of communication between the various levels within the museum and announces to all staff members the institution's objectives, plans, and directives. Including staff in budget development can generate enthusiasm for museum goals, as well as an increased understanding of the costs of doing business.

The continuing operation of the museum is based on its ability to identify its goals and needs, which are communicated through the budgetary process in order to secure the funding required. Disclosure of the planned budget will give the staff information to use to evaluate the museum's financial prospects and assess forecasted financial figures, and will help the museum in achieving its objectives.

Once the budget has been submitted to the board for acceptance[11] and approved, the budget cycle turns to the fiscal management stage, when anticipated costs are determined, internal funds are allocated, restricted accounts are established, financial transactions are recorded, and operations are monitored. The planned budget can be used as a control device and measuring stick by which the museum's performance can be assessed and its course set for succeeding years.

The last stage of the budget cycle involves end-of-the-year financial statements, a financial audit, and cost and program analyses. Although it may seem ironic, museum budgets that yield a surplus of revenues when implemented demonstrate a "lack of achievement rather than good management" if the funds could have been better utilized to improve public programs, salaries, exhibits, collections management, or other aspects of museum operation.[12]

It is imperative that the museum director, in consultation with the board, establish a calendar to stipulate the beginning and ending time frames for each of these stages in the budget cycle, as well as to identify who is responsible for these particular activities during the fiscal year.[13]

The Fiscal Year

The fiscal year serves to place all financial transactions within a time frame for the purposes of financial management and record keeping. The beginning and ending for the fiscal year should be determined in consideration of: 1) the museum's program year so that activities are reflected in one fiscal year rather than being split between two; 2) the museum's more inactive period within the year so that financial reckoning and audits put less strain on staff; and 3) the fiscal year of the primary funding source for the organization.[14] Many states and universities have fiscal years that run from July 1 to June 30. The fiscal year for the federal government is October 1 to September 30. Some organizations choose a fiscal year that corresponds to the calendar year—January 1 to December 31. The fiscal year is set in the bylaws of the organization; any changes in the calendar will necessitate bylaws amendments as well.

Once the fiscal year is in place, budget preparation can begin. As a financial plan for the museum, the budget estimates the revenues and expenses for the coming year. Revenues and expenses are subdivided into specific categories, with each containing dollar estimates. Traditionally, there are two formats for the expense portion of the operating budget. The *line-item budget* focuses on the objects of spending, such as salaries and supplies. The newer approach, known as the program budget or PPBS (planning, programming, budgeting system), lists the programs and program elements for which the funds will be spent.[15] With the PPBS system, resources are allocated to each activity based upon the planned output of each program. This makes it easier to communicate costs associated with particular programs and to analyze benefits or results from each, which can be an advantage not only for keeping board and staff well informed, but in communicating needs and outcomes to potential funders and the public. Boxes 5.1 and 5.2 show examples of each budget format.

Preparing the Budget

Who is responsible for the budgetary process? Ultimately, the board of trustees has final financial responsibility for the museum and for setting long-range goals and program priorities.[16] But budgeting should grow from the staff level; any person who will have the responsibility for carrying out an activity also should have responsibility for the budgetary planning related to it.[17]

Typically, the museum director will work with a finance committee established by the board to develop and monitor the budget. The finance committee may include staff and resource people with fiduciary expertise who may not be board members. The museum director and board can prepare a budget successfully by following these steps:

Identify goals—Before any numbers can be generated for the budget, the museum board and staff must assess their organization's activities,

Box 5.1

Example of Line-Item Museum Budget

This budget shows expenses by type. It lists operating expenses, but does not tie them to specific programs or outcomes. The majority of the budget will support staff salaries, but information on what those staff will do will have to be communicated via other written material, for example.

REVENUE		EXPENSES	
Admissions & memberships	$135,000	Salaries	$232,000
Gift shop	$ 43,800	Facilities	$ 65,000
Corporate sponsors	$ 70,000	Promotions	$ 24,500
Grants	$ 52,000	Program costs	$ 11,800
Contributions	$ 91,500	Exhibit supplies	$ 4,500
		Office and other	$ 54,500
TOTAL	$392,300	TOTAL	$392,300

Box 5.2

Example of a Program Budget

This budget outlines expenses by program. It lists expenses for particular activities but does not break down the amount of staff time, facilities costs, and materials that go into a particular program.

REVENUE		EXPENSES	
Admissions & memberships	$135,000	Traveling exhibit	$ 50,000
Gift shop	$ 43,800	Outreach kits	$ 25,500
Corporate sponsors	$ 70,000	Degas exhibit	$ 80,800
Grants	$ 52,000	Imperial China exhibit	$120,000
Contributions	$ 91,500	Permanent collection	$ 70,000
		Docent training	$ 5,000
		Security training	$ 2,000
		Lecture series	$ 9,000
		General admission	$ 10,000
		Membership	$ 20,000
TOTAL	$392,300	TOTAL	$392,300

mission, and programs. Staff and board work together as a team to identify long-range strategic and short-term plans, as well as the core activities for the museum within the next year. Activities that could be accomplished if money were unlimited also can be included at this preliminary stage in order to identify all possibilities for fund allocation.[18]

Approximate cost—The activities identified should be assigned an approximated cost. In order not to underbudget for the coming year, budget planners should estimate costs on the high side or establish a ten percent contingency fund. Budget planners must factor in administrative costs for programs and activities; adding new programs adds costs for staff, office space, and equipment. One approach is to review the museum's budgets from previous years and add a percentage increment for inflation and other factors to create a new figure for the coming year. "Zero-based budgeting," in contrast, assumes nothing and starts from zero, adding on expenses for programs identified in the strategic plan. In such a scenario, every facet of the museum program is reconsidered. Regardless of the approach used, planners must consider changes in salaries and workload, possible efficiencies and economies, and the needs of the museum's audience as well as the future social, political, economic, and cultural environments.[19]

Allocate resources—The income expected to be generated from the program activities should be considered along with the museum's other revenue sources. As a general rule, all income should be underestimated by at least ten percent; however, the museum's past history should be reviewed as a reference in generating these figures. Consideration has to be given to whether future revenue generation will be in the form of unrestricted funds (such as admissions, memberships, museum store sales, and general donations) or as restricted funds (grants and other income given with special conditions for its use).[20]

Unrestricted income can be allocated to cover administrative costs and for all programs and activities listed within the budget. Restricted income should be allocated to the program or activity specifically stipulated. Distinctions also can be made between "hard" and "soft" money in order to allocate resources appropriately. Hard money, or guaranteed income, such as interest income from an endowment, should be committed to long-term strategic goals within the budget. Soft money, or money from unguaranteed sources such as store sales or grants, is more appropriately applied to shorter-term projects.[21]

Compare and set priorities—In order to balance the budget, museum program activities must be evaluated and compared to determine their cost effectiveness. At this stage in the process, some activities may have to be delayed or sacrificed if revenues do not meet expenses. To help in determining which activities must be delayed or sacrificed and which will be implemented, the administrative staff and board return again to the mission and strategic plan to ensure that the budget will meet the organization's goals and continue to fulfill its purpose.[22]

Adjust and balance—Once priorities have been set, the budget is adjusted and balanced by reallocating estimated revenue. This balanced budget, however, will become unbalanced if unexpected expenses in the future cause revenues to fall short. In theory, overstating expenses and underestimating revenues during the budget planning process will make up for minor discrepancies, and a balance can be maintained as the budget is implemented.[23]

Submit for board approval—Once the budget figures have been developed, the board will review and approve the budget. At this time, the board will officially set the financial limitations for the museum staff. By approving the budget, the board has stated its commitment to finding the means to meet the expenses; therefore, the budget must be feasible and not based on the wishful thinking of board members or museum staff.[24]

Evaluate and amend—The final stage of the budget process involves the continual monitoring and amending of the budget to fit the revenues and expenses as they develop during the year. It is almost certain the budget will be changed during the fiscal year; a degree of flexibility must be allowed by the board and the director to tailor the budget to financial situations as they arise.

This process is not limited to one-year budget development but can be applied to budgets planned several years in advance. Museum exhibitions often take several years to develop; long-term budgeting allows for their cost to be spread over a longer period of time in order to raise and commit funds to the project. This form of long-range budget planning is critical to successful strategic planning for museums. It involves the use of historical budgetary figures, the current year's budget, and the projected budget. With these data, trends are analyzed and projections are made for future budgets. Typically, projections are made for the next three to four years, and both conservative and optimistic figures are generated. Visualizing future budgets serves as an ongoing management tool that allows the board and staff to evaluate the budget in new or changing circumstances. Budget development, management, and planning ensure that the museum is fulfilling its mission and strategic plans[25] and its obligation to serve the public.

Budget Management

Financial failure! This phrase strikes fear in museum professionals as they prepare budgets and consider their institutions' future. In the 1990s, financial mismanagement at the New York Historical Society (see box 5.4) affected staff, directors, and trustees as well the community, creating years of tension and fear of closure.[26] Optimism and expansion fueled by economic boom times look imprudent once the bubble bursts. What can a museum do to protect itself? The creation and maintenance of a budgeting system is key to carrying out museum programs in the present and to ensuring the likelihood of operating into the future.

Monitoring the Budget

Is monitoring the budget really all that critical to the overall success and fulfillment of goals in a nonprofit museum? Yes! Unfortunately, many museums fail to recognize that budget management plays a vital role in maintaining the financial health and future of their organizations. As funding options for museums grow increasingly scarce, museums must attract public attention and revenue by demonstrating that resources are used efficiently and effectively. The benefits produced by an institution must be sufficient to justify the costs of producing those benefits. Monitoring the budget demonstrates an ongoing commitment to efficient fulfillment of mission.[27]

"Making the budget system work requires a specific management program to process and control the revenue and income receipts as well as the budget expenditures," advises administration professor C. William Garner.[28] How do managers institute this budget control? While the details may appear tedious, the establishment of such a program is crucial. Several key internal controls are critical (see box 5.3).

Box 5.3

Hallmarks of a Good Budget Management Program

Adequately trained employees with distinct channels of authority
Separation of duties among employees
Receipt and disbursement of funds, transaction authorization, and record keeping involve at least two people
Proper authorization procedures
Appropriate documentation
Thorough record-keeping for all expenditures: purchase orders, receipts, invoices
Cross-checking
Independent auditing

Source: *Accounting and budgeting in public and nonprofit organizations: A manager's guide* by C. W. Garner. San Francisco: Jossey-Bass, Inc., 1991.

Budget Management Involves Everyone

The budget management process relies on both the museum's governing body and its staff. The roles they play depend on the size, structure, and income sources of the nonprofit. Those who plan the museum's finances should spell out roles and responsibilities through written policies and procedures, which should be kept up to date and be completely understood by those involved.

The *trustees* play a vital role in the process. "The board can help secure the museum's future survival by budgetary planning and sound financial projection," notes Alan Ullberg, former general counsel for the Smithsonian.[29] Long-range strategic planning and other financial planning, initiated by the board, serve as a means of balancing anticipated resources against future financial needs. The creation of a detailed five-year plan, with revisions each year based on current fiscal numbers, is essential to a museum's financial future. Trustees also have an important interest in the museum's annual budget, because the board is ultimately responsible for the allocation of the museum's resources. Trustees cannot abdicate this responsibility by simply accepting the director's proposed budget without a critical evaluation. The board, in addition to its role of authorizing and overseeing expenditures, needs to provide policies and guidelines to help measure the impact of the budget, positive or negative.[30] The board's finance committee is often charged to work with the director and to evaluate changes during the fiscal year and adjust when making new projections to avoid potentially dangerous errors.

The *executive director* (or director or chief executive officer) also figures into the equation of budget management. In a sustained, year-round effort, the CEO typically arranges any early strategic planning sessions with the trustees. The director should prepare recommendations to guide budget development, ensure that the budget schedule deadlines are met, review the draft budgets, and make resource allocation decisions. Once the budget receives board approval, the director moves to the monitoring stage with the assistance of the *chief financial officer*, provided one is on staff. The director works to communicate the results of financial observations and corrective actions to the trustees and seeks the board's input and approval for the necessary fiscal or program changes. The CFO, who bears the day-to-day responsibilities of coordinating budget development, implementation, and monitoring, prepares and analyzes reports on budgeted versus actual income and expenses for the museum's fiscal management and for board use. The CFO must also oversee any corrective actions, such as reallocations or cuts.[31]

The museum's *program* or *division managers* (curators, collection managers, educators, and so forth) provide specialized knowledge of the current program needs and costs and the impacts caused by any reduction or expansion of their program's operations. Managers develop draft budgets for their programs and divisions. As the budget is carried out, the managers are best qualified to participate in monitoring and to submit to the director resource allocation decisions or recommended changes in activities to meet the budgeted expense or income targets. Once the board, the director, and the CFO approve the budget, the program or division managers inform the staff about any budget or operational changes. Managers review regular financial reports created by the CFO, scrutinize income and expenses, and help determine and carry out corrective changes.[32]

Other possible participants in the process include the *clerical support staff,* whose responsibilities may include preparing documents and materials throughout the budgeting process. In small museums, one or two people may perform all the tasks associated with budget management; the director and support staff may divide the functions of the CFO.[33]

Consultants and *outside specialists,* such as independent auditors and accountants, architects, engineers, bond counsel, and program area specialists, also figure in budget development and monitoring. Selected clients and volunteers may be needed to provide ideas for improving the budget. Specialized analysis may require the assistance of the *information systems department,* if there is one, or the museum's computer specialist.[34]

Management of the budget never ends with the approval by the board. Instead, the budgeting process is yearlong, involving people at every level in the institution, from the board to the director and chief financial officer to the department level. Each employee, by virtue of the paycheck received and the materials consumed in performance of the job, is a direct participant in the museum's budget management. Providing all museum staff with an understanding of the fiscal realities of the institution can help ensure that expenditures are made wisely and resources utilized with maximum effectiveness.[35]

Tools of Measurement for Budget Management

An audit is an inspection of an organization's accounting and budgeting operations and is a useful tool for budget managers. Just as important, an independent, or external, audit strengthens the museum's credibility as a public trust, protects its tax-exempt status, satisfies granting agencies, and assists board and staff in fulfilling legal fiduciary requirements.[36]

The audit addresses three basic issues—equity, efficiency, and effectiveness. Equity refers to the equitable distribution of expenditures and services among the institution's different budget units and programs. Efficiency designates the measure of work that was accomplished in relation to how much it cost. Effectiveness refers to the measure of the quality of the services provided and the benefits obtained.[37]

To conduct an external audit, a neutral third-party accountant inspects the museum's accounting and budgeting operations at the close of the fiscal year. The accountant's report makes recommendations on any inconsistencies found in the inspection.[38]

Internal audits supplement the work of the external audit reports. The board's finance committee or department staff provides the internal audit. These audits may be conducted at periodic intervals and take a random look at the museum's accounting forms, payment authorization policies, inventory records, financial statements, or petty cash receipts. In addition, internal audits could review the outcomes of museum programs in relation to the quality of services being provided and the amount of allocated resources required. Both the external and internal audits provide valuable recommendations; the director and the board must determine the most useful response to these suggestions.[39]

An essential principle for management of nonprofits is that "money must come in, before it can go out."[40] Cash flow projections and planning are useful budget-monitoring tools to ensure this is the case. The term *cash flow* designates the relationship between the amount of cash a museum actually has available in the bank during a given period and the amount it needs to pay the bills during the same period. Effective cash flow management requires ongoing attention, not a reactive response once cash flow problems develop. Cash flow projections predict when cash will be received by the museum each month and then compare cash expected with anticipated cash expenditures. The board and top management must then identify any projected periods of negative cash flow and plan specific actions to avoid such shortfalls so that programs and services may continue without interruption.[41]

Negative cash flow problems typically occur when the museum receives its income later than it is needed. A negative situation would occur, for example, in the case of "after-the-fact funding," in which some grants or contracts reimburse the museum only after specific services have been rendered. Nevertheless, the nonprofit has to pay for staff, office space, equipment and supplies, and other needed resources in advance. Monthly cash flow projections that focus on the anticipated timing of cash receipts and disbursements, supplemented by regular financial reports, help highlight times when cash flow problems are likely to occur or when cash would be available for investment. The board and the museum's financial managers and director must plan far enough in advance of potential problems to allow for action to offset the risky negative cash flow. Possible solutions include postponing major purchases, new staff hires, or wage increases.[42]

Another solution for budget managers is short-term borrowing. Incurring debt should be considered with great caution; this seductive short-term solution can have long-term repercussions. More than one museum has found itself barely able to generate sufficient income to pay heavy debt interest, much less the principal owed.[43]

Computers and Budget Management

Good budget management relies on the accurate and complete analysis of as much fiscal data as possible. Producing data manually can be hugely time-consuming. Computer technology increases productivity and reduces errors. Many software packages are available for museum use that link the database functions essential for budgeting and the accounting function of the spreadsheet. Networked computers can allow museum departments to quickly ascertain budget category balances and speed the business office's processing of expenditure requests. Computers are just as valuable, if not more so, in small museums where staff time is very limited.[44]

Budget Management in Practice

Museums and other nonprofit organizations walk a delicate balance in budget management. As part of their mission of public service, nonprofits can and do make money. However, the profit must be directed toward the public purpose for which the organization was established, held in reserve, or given to another organization with a stated public purpose. Museums, as not-for-profit or charitable corporations, must avoid even the appearance of any personal or private financial gain.

Budget surpluses for museums may appear to potential donors not as good financial management but rather as complacency or a lack of ambition for program development. In addition, many museums operate under a *balanced budget constraint,* in which future funding cuts will occur if there is a surplus at the end of the fiscal year. If circumstances make a large surplus unavoidable, the nonprofit board may designate such surpluses as *funds functioning as endowment.*[45] In less stable financial times, the board can "undesignate" part of the quasi-endowment's funds to increase unrestricted cash reserves.

Financial Statements and Reports

A variety of internal reports may be used by museums to monitor their budgets, but the Federal Accounting Standards Board (FASB) has designated the following standardized formal financial statements for nonprofits:

Balance Sheet (Statement of Financial Position), which summarizes assets, liabilities, and fund balance at the end of a reporting period.

Income Statement (Statement of Revenues and Expenses), a report of the amount of change in net assets for the period.

Statement of Cash Flows, which provides information about cash receipts and cash payments during a period.[46]

The information provided on these statements is important for external audits and for filing the tax-exempt nonprofit's annual return (Form 990) with the Internal Revenue Service (IRS). The financial statements help trustees and the director to determine whether the organization has a surplus or deficit or has experienced any unusually large expenditures or revenues.[47] This information is crucial in order for the nonprofit to engage in useful long- and short-term financial and strategic planning. Large deficits, of course, signify an institution in substantial trouble, with closure and dispersal of the collections a looming threat.

Cutting the Budget

Budgetary overruns or revenue shortfalls often tempt museums and other nonprofits to take extreme action in cutting costs and raising revenues. But an analysis of the institution's overall financial condition and the long-term effects of short-term solutions needs to be made before deciding what action to take. The museum's mission should not become defined through budget cuts. Still, cutting costs has a more predictable impact on the museum's financial condition than increasing revenues.[48]

Making cuts is a particularly difficult process for many museums because their single largest expenditure is salaries. If seventy percent or more of the budget supports wages and benefits for employees, it becomes next to impossible to effect significant costs savings without eliminating positions. A natural tendency is to make across-the-board reductions so that every department feels some of the pain, but a more strategic view suggests preserving the museum's core services and eliminating those programs that are less central, less well received, or unprofitable. Issues of quality should be viewed with the same consideration as issues of revenues or costs. It will be difficult to retain current members, much less attract new ones, if public service is allowed to slip.[49]

In examining ways to increase revenue, budget managers should remember that more revenues can mean more costs. An increase in membership dues, for example, may result in a net revenue gain of zero if increased services are offered to make the dues hike more palatable. Adding income-producing programs increases net revenues only if additional staff are not required to carry out those programs. A revenue-expense analysis will help the museum make effective choices.

Warning signs that retrenchment may be necessary may include a five percent decline in members or paid admissions for two consecutive years; administrative staff growth that is twenty percent greater than increases in other staff; a decline in gifts and donations for two years or a decrease in the percentage of gifts and donations in the operating budget for three or more years; and a decrease in surrounding area employment or business activity for two years.[50] These indicators do not necessarily signal impending disaster, but they are reasons to examine finances very closely.

Budget cutting is as complex as budget building, and it too should involve participation of both board and staff in a honest assessment of circumstances and options. Political and marketing skills are needed just as much as financial expertise in order to preserve organizational morale and create mechanisms not only for survival but for future growth. The New-York Historical Society's experience amplifies the need to consider the impact of budget cuts on internal and external audiences and to initiate changes in a way that reinforces the museum's image as a humane institution with a future (see box 5.4).

Accounting

Budget management requires both a day-to-day approach and a long view. The critical data for this management are provided by the accounting system. Accounting is essentially an information system that records, classifies, and summarizes business activity. The rules that govern how accountants measure, process, and communicate financial information are called Generally Accepted Accounting Principles (GAAP). Until recently, there had not been a set of generally accepted accounting principles for nonprofit organizations. During the past few years, the American Institute of Certified Public Accountants (AICPA) and the Financial Accounting Standards Board (FASB) have set standards for preparing financial statements "designed to communicate . . . the manner in which resources of [nonprofit] organizations have been used to carry out the organization's objectives."[51]

Accounting Methods

Adequate accounting procedures and records are essential for the museum to manage monies received wisely and in accordance with its charitable purposes. There are two basic types of accounting systems—accrual and cash.

The *accrual accounting* system details revenues when they are received and expenses when they are committed. In the accrual system, funds that have been committed are *encumbered*, and they show on the books as having been spent, even if the money has not been paid out. The benefit of this system is that it gives managers a clear view of the balance available for operating at any one point in time.

Box 5.4

Case Review: The New-York Historical Society

Holly Hotchner, a former senior manager and museum director at the New-York Historical Society, shares the consequences of her museum's financial management choices in "Life on a Fiscal Precipice." During her eleven years at the society, she served under five CEOs, several restructurings, and changes of board chairs, presidents, and directors, and she was the only senior manager to weather both of the organization's "near-bankruptcies." By February 3, 1993, the board voted to close the institution. In January of that year, the galleries had been closed and the staff severely cut. A once thriving organization, the New-York Historical Society cut the remaining staff of seventy-five to a mere thirty-five. Headlines screamed about the inevitable closure of the New York "Hysterical" Society and the end for "New York's Attic."

How could such a financial disaster occur? Several factors contributed to the near destruction of the New-York Historical Society, which remains in operation today. Despite valiant fundraising, the $22 million raised was not for day-to-day operations but largely for programs, exhibitions, and specific collections projects, which "often increased the operating budget and put more strain on an already overworked staff." The endowment received little attention or funds. During this time, the value of the Society's endowment dropped 27 percent, administrative costs jumped by 40 percent of the operating budget, and the Society continued to operate with a deficit of nearly $2 million per year. The endowment continued to diminish. By October 1992, cash flow projections indicated that the Society could not remain open through January of 1993. Earlier near bankruptcies came back to haunt an organization operating on the brink of financial disaster for many years. While the institution eventually survived, via a combination of one-time deaccessioning, which raised serious ethical questions, and public funding, it became infamous as an example of financial mismanagement and dereliction of board duty.

Source: "Life on a Fiscal Precipice" by H. Hotchner. In *Institutional trauma: Major change in museums and its effect on staff,* ed. E. H. Gurian, 135–155. Washington, D.C.: American Association of Museums, 1995.

Cash accounting records transactions at the time they occur; revenue is noted when it is received, and expenses are recorded when they are paid out. Dollars that have been committed to ordered materials or services not yet received are not reflected, nor is income owed but not yet received. The administrator must keep in mind that X dollars have been promised to Y, and therefore are not available to pay for Z. The benefit of this system is that it is simple, much like a personal checking account, and it reflects funds that are on hand at any one time.

Modified accrual accounting combines the ability to encumber funds and reserve them for expected expenditures with the simplicity of the cash system's recording of income and outgo at the time transactions take place. Whether the accounting is done on the cash, accrual, or modified accrual basis is not as critical as that it be done accurately, regularly, and with timely production of subsequent regular reports.

The board of trustees must do all in its power to protect the financial well-being of the museum. An accountant should advise the director and the board of practices that can be adopted for daily museum use and control, such as requiring two people to be involved in documentation of payments and check writing.[52]

Regardless of the basis of accounting, museums will use a double entry process based on an algebraic formula: Assets = Liabilities + Fund Balance. (Some of us find this equation easier to grasp if it is stated a little differently: Assets − Liabilities = Fund Balance.) Simply put, the equation means that what the museum owns (assets) is equal to what it owes (liabilities) plus the fund balance. Debits and credits are used to record changes in revenue, income, and expenses. For ease in recording and tracking information about specific transactions, specific account numbers are assigned to designate types of expenditures or income. A chart of accounts is the master list which serves as the key and explains the types of transactions, which are identified by a particular account number.[53]

The accounting system provides managers with critical monthly statements that outline the museum's current financial status. This information allows managers to make adjustments in implementing the planned budget, such as initiating or deferring purchases, delaying hiring of temporary staff, and so on, depending on the fiscal picture.

Monthly budget status reports compare budgeted amounts with monthly expenditures and year-to-date totals. Many accounting software systems also calculate percentage of time elapsed and percentage of budget expended, a useful measure for tracking expenditures like permanent salaries, which vary little from month to month.[54] Not all museum expenditures or income is regular; extra staff may be required during high visitation seasons, and admissions income may fluctuate due to weather or time of year. In such cases, data from prior fiscal years also may be included on these reports for comparative purposes so that managers can

Box 5.5

Case Review: Chart of Accounts

A clearly articulated chart of accounts helps differentiate and track expenses. Excerpts from a public museum's chart of accounts illustrate the range of expenditures incorporated under each account name.

4100 Personal Services—expenses related to permanent and temporary employees
4101 Permanent Salaries—payroll for permanent staff members
4200 Operating Expenses—directly related to a program's primary service activities
4211 Postage Expense—cost of U.S. postal services, including postage meter expense, box rental, stamps
4212 Communications Expense—costs for telephone or other telecommunications services or facilities, including basic telephone service, switchboards and other telephone equipment, tolls, data modems, telephone control lines, Western Union TWX, Telex or other data communications message services
4213 Freight Expense—transportation costs for parcels and shipments via parcel, shipping, and freight companies
4214 Data Processing Service—costs of data processing and word processing services, except for consulting fees
4215 Publications and Printing—expenses incurred in publishing reports and legal notices, advertising, duplication and copying services, book binding, picture framing, film processing, photographic services, etc.
4221 Other Contractual Service—Consulting fees, costs of services performed under contract by individuals or group
4235 Data Processing Software License Service Fees—fees for upgrading software or maintenance of software packages
4261 Repair and Maintenance, Buildings and Other Structures—maintenance, minor repair, and inspection fees for buildings and structures including equipment attached to the building such as furnaces, boilers, etc.
4800 Capital Outlay—expenditures that result in the acquisition of or addition to fixed assets. Fixed assets are resources of a long-term character owned or held by the government and may include:
4841 Office Equipment
4856 Hardware—data processing—purchase of electronic data processing equipment, including central processing units, peripheral equipment and terminals
4857 Software—data processing—purchases of computer software or licenses, including operation systems, special purpose systems, and application systems
4886 Household/Institutional Equipment—purchase of food service, janitorial, and household and institutional equipment and furniture
4881 Photography/Media Equipment—purchase of projectors, screen, cameras, darkroom equipment, multilith machines and presses

Source: Nebraska State Historical Society, 2001.

see patterns over time. (See box 5.6 for an excerpt from a sample budget status report.)

The general ledger itemizes specific expenditures paid out and revenue generated. Access to this level of detail allows the manager to ascertain whether a particular vendor has been paid, how much income a given program has been generating, whether a grant payment has been received, and so on. (See box 5.7 for an excerpt from a sample general ledger.)

The Necessity of Number Crunching

Accounting is a very effective means of accomplishing financial record keeping for museums. Accounting practices and procedures may be slightly more casual or formal, depending on the size and complexity of the organization and on whether most accounting is done internally or externally. Regardless of the size of the nonprofit, accounting practices are valuable aids in decision making and in communicating fiscal information.

Conclusion

While the terms and steps involved in the budgetary process are many and complex, it is worth the time it takes to fully understand the flow of money and how it is accounted for in a nonprofit organization. The easiest way to become familiar with budgeting and accounting systems is to jump in and start dealing with numbers. By looking at actual printouts and addressing real situations, you will find the process becomes clearer.

All museums, large and small, need to have policies and procedures in place that guarantee the budget, once prepared, is followed. The board is ultimately responsible for ensuring that the adopted budget is realistic and that it is carried out. However, this does not absolve the museum staff from involvement. Budgeting affects every department and every program in every museum. In an environment where funding is less than abundant, responsible staff will stick to the budget developed through the museum's process. While most staff did not join the museum profession purely for the joy of budgeting and accounting, it will be to their and the museum's benefit to spend time and energy attending to financial processes. Without sound fiscal practices, the museum's future (as well as the staff's) is endangered.

Box 5.6

Excerpt from a Monthly Budget Status Report

Budget Status Report as of 08/31/2000 Pct. of Time Elapsed = 17.26

Expenditures	Budgeted Amount	Current Month	Year-to-Date	Pct. of Budget	Variance
4111 Permanent Salaries-Wages	$467,485.00	52,673.88	87,445.56	18.71	380,039.44
4131 Retirement Plans Expense	32,353.00	3,758.27	6,185.18	19.12	26,167.82
4132 OASDI Expense	33,899.00	3,893.66	6,427.02	18.96	27,471.98
4134 Life & Accident Insurance Expense	325.00	26.46	52.92	16.28	272.08
4135 Health Insurance Expense	61,464.00	4,636.02	9,047.45	14.72	52,416.55
4144 Employee Assistance Program	201.00				201.00
4211 Postage Expense	8,500.00	434.39	856.83	10.08	7,643.17
4212 Communication Expense	7,000.00	559.56	1,114.95	15.93	5,885.05
4215 Publication & Printing Expense	12,010.00	205.57	1,569.82	13.07	10,440.18
4311 Office Supplies Expense	7,795.00	646.45	1,940.63	24.90	5,854.37
4483 Workers Comp Premiums	1,100.00	2469.48	1,459.27	132.66	(359.27)
4100 Personal Services	$595,727.00	64,988.29	109,158.13	18.32	486,568.87
4200 Operating Account Total	93,727.00	6,107.40	12,214.46	13.03	81,512.54
4700 Travel Account Total	10,300.00	1,689.16	2,436.09	23.65	7,863.91
4800 Capital Outlay Account Total	7,700.00				7,700.00
Expenditures Total	707,454.00	691,46.93	123,808.68	17.5	561,767.60

Summary of Expenditures by Fund Type	Budgeted Amount	Current Month	Year-to-Date	Pct. of Budget	Variance
1000 General Fund	606,394.00	69,146.93	120,901.04	19.94	463,615.24
2000 Cash Fund	101,060.00		2,907.64	2.88	98,152.36
Expenditures Total	707,454.00	69,146.93	123,808.68	17.5	561,767.60

Clues to Deciphering Budget Status Report

Note date of report and percent of time elapsed. This will tell you when the fiscal year began, in this case, July 1.

Read column heads to ascertain what column numbers designate and whether numbers indicate dollars, percentages, or other measures.

Box 5.6 (continued)

Comparing percentages of budget expended year-to-date with percentage of time elapsed is one way of tracking expenditures. Be aware that not all expenses occur on a regular basis; seasonal spending decreases or increases can cause a false sense of security or panic. Ideally your budget report would include the previous year's history, providing a ready comparison for determining whether increased or decreased expenditures are typical.

Parentheses indicate negative numbers, meaning overspent accounts, where actual expenses exceed budgeted amounts.

Most reports will include summary lines, which group related accounts together. In this case, all accounts related to employee salaries and benefits are lumped together for easy reference under "Personal Services Account Total."

Blanks indicate no activity in the particular account. In some reports this lack of activity might be reflected by zeros or dashes (———).

In fund accounting systems, reports may indicate which fund or "pot" expenditures have been made from.

Revenue sources and amounts will be included in most reports, although they are not excerpted here.

Source: Adapted from Nebraska State Historical Society, 2001.

Budget management provides one of the major keys to an institution's failure or success. Museums face a world of increased competition for public and private funds. Developing and monitoring an annual budget in support of the organization's "mission-driven" focus bolsters the museum's chances for financial stability and security. Budget failure or success determines the future for the museum director as well. Budget management requires sufficient planning and development, staff involvement, and continual monitoring aided by tools of monthly reports and annual audits to ensure that the doors will remain open and services will be provided to the community.

The finest collections, best-designed facilities and programs, and most talented staff in the world cannot ensure the financial stability of the museum. Financial mismanagement, as some museums have learned, may very possibly cause the institution to close its doors. Without a solid economic foundation, maintained by careful budget planning and accurate accounting, the museum's physical and human assets are in jeopardy. Understanding the museum's financial processes empowers staff to

Box 5.7

Excerpts from Monthly General Ledger Report

General Ledger as of 8/31/2000

Account	Trans Date	Payee/Explanation	Current Month	Year-to-Date
4111	8/11/2000	Payroll B16	64,988.29	109,158.13
4211	8/17/2000	All Needs Computer & Mailing	434.39	856.83
4212	8/28/2000	DAS Communications	559.56	1,114.95
4215	8/23/2000	Snapper's Camera	205.57	801.21
4311	8/14/2000	Information Technology Solutions	404.80	
4311	8/18/2000	WF Office Equipment		
4311	8/23/2000	Laser Blazers, Inc.	178.00	
		Detail account 4311 total	646.65	1058.58
4483		Balance Forward		1459.27
Revenue				
7111	8/03/2000	Admissions for week of 7/26	693.75	35,782.00
7211	8/09/2000	MF Producer Services		
	8/17/2000	Educational Telecommunications	475.69	
	8/21/2000	Houghton Mifflin	1000.00	
		Detail account 7211 total	1568.96	11,152.64

Clues to Deciphering General Ledger Reports

General ledgers function somewhat like a "checkbook," showing the date an amount was paid, the amount, the payee, and the amount paid from that account to date. The report breaks down the lump sums listed as paid out of particular accounts in the monthly status report. (Compare three transactions paid from account 4311 on this general ledger report to the amount listed under that account on the budget status report in Box 5.6.)

"Balance Forward" denotes accounts in which there was no activity in the reporting period.

General ledger reports also list specific amounts of revenue and their sources (income from museum admissions, sales of photographs or other reproductions of collections materials, etc.).

Source: Adapted from Nebraska State Historical Society, 2001.

Box 5.8

Case Study: If You Can't Take the Heat . . .

At the beginning of the year 2000, it all looked so good. The economy was booming, unemployment was next to nonexistent, and the zoo was opening two new grant-funded exhibits (including endangered mole rats that were so ugly they were cute). Sure, gas prices were climbing, but all the better to keep folks close to home, attending local favorites.

Then it rained—for the entire month of June. The first of July dawned bright. And hot. And every day it got hotter. Plants wilted; staff sweated; visitors crabbed.

So here you are at the end of August. Gross attendance figures are down 7 percent. When the budget was set a year ago, everyone overlooked the school board's decision to start classes a week earlier than usual, so "the season" has turned out to be shorter than in previous years. And that's not all. When it gets over ninety-five degrees, the pony rides have to be shut down to protect the animals. No ponies, no ticket sales. When it's sweltering, nobody wants to eat any of the big-ticket pizza and sandwich items from the ZooChew. And last year's stuffed animal craze that had visitors beating down the zoo store door is passe this year. So earned income is down.

But costs are up. Triple-digit temperatures mean big air-conditioning bills. After the June monsoon, water bills skyrocketed as gardeners struggled to keep the botanical specimens alive in the dry heat. Hot times or cold, the critters have to be fed.

Still, it's not all over. Although the outdoor exhibits close after Labor Day, two big events at Halloween and before Christmas are always moneymakers. But how to make it to November?

As you sit at your desk, numbers swimming before your eyes, there's a knock at the door. Your education department head, Bea Smart, sticks her head in, eyes glowing, and says, "I've just come from a preview of our new computer interactive. It's fabulous! It will be great to premiere it at ZooBoo in October! The designers have 'comped' us thousands of dollars' worth of service on this, so once we pay them the $3,000 for the hardware, it's ours!"

Suddenly your nagging headache starts to pound, so you excuse yourself and walk down the hall toward the drinking fountain, pain reliever in hand. You pass Trevor Temp, your hardest-working seasonal employee, who says, "I know you're really busy, but I just have to tell you this is the best summer job I've ever had. And it's especially great that it doesn't end at Labor Day. The fall quarter at the community college doesn't start 'til October, and since I can work here 'til then, I'm going to finally have enough money to pay tuition!"

You swallow hard, then plunk down heavily at your desk, piled high with invoices and budget reports. Even though there's a few dollars more in income than costs at the moment, once the regular season ends, there won't be enough income to keep up with costs. What to do? Defer buying the new interactive, which would risk lower attendance (and income) at the big fall event? Cut temporary staff early? Reduce rations for the animals? Confess to the board you underestimated (or overestimated, which is it?)? Ask to borrow from the endowment principal until times improve?

Using the figures below, assess the zoo's current financial status and its prospects. Where are the real problems? What are they? How bad are they?

Box 5.8 (continued)

Create a plan to balance the budget. How much will the zoo need to earn and cut in order to balance the budget? What additional information do you wish you had access to? What conclusions can you draw about the kind of financial reporting you need?

EXPENSES	Budgeted	YTD Projected	YTD Actual	Variance
Salaries-permanent	310,355	205,464	205,464	104,891
Salaries-seasonal	50,000	42,500	42,500	7,500
Payroll taxes	27,045	18,969	18,969	8,076
Animal food	28,000	18,666	18,666	9,334
Advertising	4,000	3,200	3,400	600
Dues/subscriptions/fees	1,000	650	650	350
Electricity	20,000	16,000	20,000	0
Equipment	3,500	500	500	3,000
Fund-raising	10,000	8,000	8,000	2,000
Insurance-general	40,000	26,666	26,666	13,334
Insurance-group/med	18,000	12,000	12,000	6,000
Natural gas	8,000	5,600	5,600	2,400
Office supplies	3,000	2,400	2,400	600
Plants	2,500	2,000	2,500	0
Postage	12,000	7,200	8,500	3,500
Professional serv.	2,000	2,000	2,000	0
Printing	12,000	9,000	9,000	3,000
Repairs/maintenance	10,000	7,500	7,500	2,500
Sanitation	12,000	10,500	10,500	1,500
Special events	2,000	500	500	500
Staff development	1,000	0	0	1,000
Supplies	14,000	12,000	12,000	2,000
Store	4,000	3,800	3,800	200
Telephone	13,000	9,000	9,000	4,000
Train repairs/supplies	1,000	800	950	50
Travel	1,000	500	0	1,000
Vehicle expense	4,500	3,850	3,800	700
Vending expense	800	725	800	0
Vet services	10,000	8,300	8,300	1,700
Water	34,000	28,900	33,000	1,000
TOTAL	658,700	467,190	476,965	180,735

Box 5.8 (continued)

INCOME-operations	Budgeted	YTD Projected	YTD Actual	Variance
Membership dues	315,000	283,500	253,655	61,345
Gate admission	115,000	103,500	91,255	23,745
Adopt-an-animal	2,000	1,800	1,800	200
Education	15,000	13,500	10,555	4,445
Fountain donations	3,000	2,850	1,975	1,025
Food service	8,000	7,200	6,120	1,880
Fund raising	30,000	27,000	20,000	10,000
Pellet machines	7,000	6,300	4,670	2,330
Pony rides	21,000	18,900	13,065	7,935
Railway	80,000	72,000	54,800	25,200
Rental	14,000	12,600	8,000	6,000
Special events	10,000	6,000	5,000	5,000
Store	8,000	7,200	5,590	2,410
Vending	700	630	590	110
TOTAL Operating Income	628,700	562,980	477,075	151,625
OTHER INCOME				
Interest from endowment	20,000			
Contributions-misc.	10,000			
Total other	30,000			
TOTAL INCOME	658,700			

actively participate in wise use of its resources and ultimately its survival and success.

Notes

1. Lord and Lord 1997, 159.
2. Garner 1991, 112.
3. Maddox 1999, 64.
4. Dalsimer 1996, 6.
5. Garner 1991, 32.
6. Lord and Lord 1997, 159.
7. Ibid.
8. Anthony and Herzlinger 1980, 11.
9. Ibid., 326.

10. Wolf 1999, 187.
11. Maddox 1999, 27–44.
12. Anthony and Herzlinger 1980, 187.
13. Vinter and Kish 1984, 27–28.
14. Wolf 1999, 176–77.
15. Anthony and Herzlinger 1980, 303.
16. Ullberg and Ullberg 1981, 21; Wolf 1999, 187.
17. Powell 1980, 3.
18. Wolf 1999, 187–188.
19. Ibid., 188–189.
20. Ibid., 191–192.
21. Anthony and Herzlinger 1980, 335.
22. Wolf 1999, 193–194.
23. Ibid., 194–196.
24. Ibid., 196.
25. Ibid., 196–200.
26. Hotchner 1995, 135–155.
27. Garner 1991, 89.
28. Ibid., 91.
29. Ullberg and Ullberg 1981, 13.
30. Wolf 1999, 53.
31. Dropkin and LaTouche 1998, 12.
32. Ibid., 12–13.
33. Ibid., 13.
34. Ibid.
35. Powell 1980, 18.
36. Garner 1991, 226.
37. Ibid., 226–227.
38. Ibid., 228.
39. Ullberg and Ullberg 1981, 26–27.
40. Chapo 2000.
41. Dropkin and LaTouche 1998, 89.
42. Ibid., 90.
43. Ibid., 91.
44. Garner 1991, 1–2; Sheeran 1992, 16, 19.
45. Wolf 1999, 186.
46. Phelan 1994, 68–72.
47. Wolf, 1999, 215.
48. Chabotar 1991.

49. Ibid.
50. Ibid.
51. Phelan 1994, 67.
52. Wolf 1999, 229.
53. Garner 1991, 130–132.
54. Wolf 1999, 230.

CHAPTER SIX
DEVELOPMENT

Money, money, money. Nonprofit organizations are consumed with the pursuit of the green. Not because they want to be, but because they have to be in order to survive, flourish, and provide programming for their constituencies. Museums, like other nonprofit organizations, must be continually aware of the costs of every day and every project and must be concerned with where to find the money to cover those costs. Every dollar counts.

Development is the important process of making sure those dollars are there, of constantly analyzing and planning for current and future fiscal needs. It is an aptly named endeavor; to develop means "to realize the potentialities of; to aid in the growth of; to cause to unfold, expand, or grow gradually; to acquire gradually." Development is an ongoing effort that relies on a variety of strategies and a long-term view. And while the end result of development is money, development is really about relationships with people. It is individual people who make the decision to become a member, attend a special event, contribute to a campaign, or write a will. And it is groups of people who decide which grants to fund. So successful development activity requires the involvement of individuals (e.g., the director, development officer, or board members) who are as personable as they are financially savvy.

Development addresses three principal monetary needs:

Annual Needs—the funding required for a museum's yearly programming and daily operations

Capital Needs—new buildings, renovations, and repairs a museum anticipates it will require in the next ten to fifteen years to continue to develop its programming and to serve its constituency

Endowment Needs—a fund sufficiently large to generate enough interest to provide a steady source of operating support to offset fluctuations in donations and grants; a secondary source of income

Museums should create an overall approach to meet each area of need. In *The Art of Raising Money,* William J. Smith compares this comprehensive program to a three-legged stool. "Each leg is essential if the stool is to stand and if it is to have stability."[1] The first step in accurately assessing and planning for the needs of a museum is to create a development plan.

The Development Plan

A development plan is a strategy for raising funds. According to Lord and Lord, the purpose of a development plan is "to identify opportunities for fund-raising, develop a fund-raising plan, and train staff and volunteers in implementing the plan."[2] A development plan can be created for annual giving, membership, capital campaign, endowment funds, or specific programs, or it may encompass all the emphases a museum is planning to pursue. A development plan should be consistent with the goals of a museum's strategic plan; it starts where the strategic plan ends by mapping out how a museum will raise funds in each of the identified areas. The scope of the development plan depends on the needs of the museum and the scope of the fund-raising campaign. Together the strategic plan and the development plan help a museum determine and achieve its fund-raising priorities.

Careful analysis and decision making that address the essential elements will produce a comprehensive development plan. The eight plan elements listed in box 6.1 are typical categories; they will vary depending on the particular museum and its needs.

Regardless of the goal amount or the funding source being pursued, the benefits of creating a development plan outweigh the costs. Generating funds has become more sophisticated and requires careful planning and analysis. Understanding fund-raising principles enables a museum to target different funding sources (donations, grants, and earned income) effectively. Many efforts have failed because of inadequate understanding or planning. The planning process allows the people involved to examine all the factors from different perspectives and gain full knowledge of the

Box 6.1

Elements of an Effective Development Plan

Designating a development officer and identifying organizational structure and guidelines for fund-raising personnel and volunteers
Determining the fund-raising campaign goal
Reviewing the museum's fund-raising activities
Researching potential donors
Identifying fund-raising methods and preparing campaign materials
Recruiting and training campaign personnel
Creating an implementation plan, budget, and manual
Determining how the fund-raising effort will be monitored and evaluated

Source: "The museum planning process" by B. Lord and G.D. Lord. In *Organizing your museum: The essentials*, ed. S. Dubberly, 37–41. Washington, DC: American Association of Museums, 2001.

goal of the fund-raising effort, their responsibilities, how the campaign will be operated, and the schedule.

Fund-Raising

Fund-raising is the process whereby an organization generates funds from individuals, businesses, foundations, or government. According to master fund-raiser Henry Rosso, a fund-raising campaign has five phases: analysis, planning, execution, control, and evaluation. *Analysis* is the process of examining all the factors that affect a fund-raising campaign. In the *planning* process, identified factors are considered to determine what must be accomplished and to outline the strategies to do so. In *execution* of the plan, the development officer ensures the campaign stays on schedule and moves toward the anticipated final result. Ongoing evaluation allows the development officer to track progress and *control* strategies, determining whether they should be changed or continued based on the current responses of contributors, staff, and volunteers. A final analysis and *evaluation* identify the success (or lack thereof) of strategies and methods. Lessons learned will be useful for planning future fund-raising campaigns.[3]

The Annual Campaign

The annual campaign is a museum's effort to raise funds for daily operating and programming needs. The challenge for annual campaigns is to encourage donors to contribute; since donors know they are going to be asked to give every year and possibly to increase their pledges, their gifts often reach certain levels and plateau or increase only moderately.

Generating funds is the principal objective of an annual campaign, but nonmonetary benefits may also accrue, such as:

- building and expanding a donor base for the museum
- establishing patterns of giving to the museum
- informing and involving the constituency in a way that bonds it to the museum
- using the donor base as a source of information to identify potential large donors[4]

An annual campaign should be an ongoing, full-time process in that the staff and board should be continually scanning for possible gift opportunities. Some museums concentrate their solicitations within a certain time period; toward the end of the calendar year, donors may be anticipating their tax liabilities and therefore may be looking for tax benefits associated with contributions. An annual campaign also can be a powerful advocacy tool, with the pattern of giving serving as tangible evidence of constituent and corporate support.

The Capital Campaign

A capital campaign is an intensive fund-raising effort to generate a substantial sum of money to meet the capital needs of a museum, such as constructing new buildings, remodeling existing buildings, or installing new and expensive technology. Capital campaign goals tend to be large, and time lines usually range from eighteen months to three to five years, depending on the campaign complexities.[5] Capital campaigns generally receive a positive response from donors because the results are highly visible.

Feasibility studies help determine whether a museum is prepared to conduct a capital campaign and assess the likelihood of success. Significant questions are posed in such a study (see box 6.2); if most cannot be answered affirmatively, the questions serve as a guide to action necessary in order for the campaign to become feasible.

Box 6.2

Is a Capital Campaign Feasible?

Strategic plan—Does the museum have a three- or five-year strategic plan approved by the board? Are staff and board members committed to dedicating their fund-raising efforts to meet the financial needs?
Strong case—Does the museum have a compelling mission and a cogent argument for its needs?
Well-defined constituency—Do the people, organizations, and companies who benefit and affect the organization support the campaign? Are they willing to contribute toward it?
Community awareness—Is the museum's status in the broader community positive? Is the community aware and appreciative of the efforts of the organization? Are relationships established with businesses, foundations, and corporations? Is the level of their support sufficient to meet the needs of the campaign?
Ongoing prospect research—Is there a subcommittee or staff member who will identify potential sources of large gifts throughout the fund-raising effort?
Good communication—Have communication channels been established allowing information to be relayed to and received from the constituency? How will the museum report and update the constituency on the progress of the campaign?
Potential for large gifts—Does the museum have a donor base such that five to ten percent of the donors can give fifty to sixty percent of the campaign goal?
Leadership—Are visible, well-connected supporters willing to head the effort? Are staff able, available and experienced?

Source: *Achieving excellence in fund raising* by H. A. Rosso and Associates, 94–97. San Francisco: Jossey-Bass, Inc., 1991.

Accurate budget numbers are critical to effective planning for the financial support of a capital project. The budget should be specific enough to provide essential figures but not require detailed examination. It is important to identify major cost items such as the cost of the building project, architect fees, campaign and management expenses, and debt service. Accurate and reasonable figures are essential in winning donor confidence; contributors find it easier to support a project that appears to be a good value.

Capital campaign pledges are generally payable over a period of three to five years. The longer the payment period, the more time contributors have to be generous (and enjoy whatever tax advantages may accrue). Payments may be more manageable over a longer period of time. Museums must be aware of the nature and time frame of incoming pledges when planning the capital expenditures.

The Endowment Campaign

The object of the endowment campaign is to create a sizable principal, which then produces a return that can be drawn upon to supplement the general operating budget or support a specific purpose of the organization. The income from the endowment may be used to sustain a museum so it is not solely dependent on the success of ongoing fund-raising efforts.

Some endowments are established or added to by gifts of cash assets presented to the museum during the donor's lifetime; others are created through a planned giving program, which is oriented to a larger gift and comes primarily from the estate of the donor. Cash assets may take the form of stock certificates, real estate, insurance, or a gift of personal property. The principal benefit of the gift is not available until some future date, when the gift "matures" (the donors or their designees die), or at the end of a specific term. Planned gifts enable donors to gain both the satisfaction of contributing to an organization and the tax benefits. Depending on the planned giving option used, the donors or heirs may reduce their income, capital gains, gift, or estate taxes.

Multiple planned giving options are available to benefit both donor and museum (see box 6.3). A full-fledged planned giving program involves complex legal and financial transactions. Museums initiating such programs may find it best to begin with the simplest approach, the development of bequests, and then gradually utilize a wider range of planned giving methods.

Building endowment funds can be an ongoing operation. Donors should be continually sought for contributions to address the growth and increased cost of operating the organization. Endowment funds provide a steady source of annual income. However, an endowment fund is not as liquid as other sources, since only the income generated from the principal is available for use, and there may be donor-specified restrictions for fund use. To supplement this stream of income, museums should actively raise funds for daily operating needs.

Box 6.3

Instruments for Planned Giving

A variety of options exist for donors and museums, including

Bequests—The donors make provisions in their wills for the museum to receive a gift of money or assets upon their deaths. The gift can be small or large and may or may not be designated for certain uses.

Pooled-income fund—The donor's gift is invested in the museum's pooled-income fund, also known as the museum's trust fund. The donor receives a yearly income from the fund based on her share of the fund's net earnings, similar to a mutual fund. When the donor or her designee dies, the value of the gift is available for use by the museum.

Charitable gift annuity—This is a contract between the donor and the museum. The museum promises to pay the donor a predetermined amount annually, in exchange for the gift.

Charitable remainder unitrust—The donor irrevocably transfers money, stock certificates, or property to the museum. The trustee pays the donor or his designee an income for life or for a period of years determined when the assets are transferred. The donor or his designee receives an annual income in payments based on a fixed percentage (not less than five percent) of the fair market value of the trust assets. This means the income will vary each year. Upon the death of the donor, the asset belongs to the museum.

Charitable remainder annuity trust—The donor irrevocably transfers a principal sum of money which is invested by the museum. The donor or her designee receives annual payment of a fixed-dollar amount. The annual payments must be at least five percent of the initial net market value of the contributed principal. Upon the death of the donor or her designee the asset belongs to the museum.

Charitable lead trust—The income from the trust property is directed to the museum for a predetermined period of years. At the end of the predetermined period the trust reverts back to the donor or his/her designee.

Source: *Achieving excellence in fund raising* by H. A. Rosso and Associates, 97–98. San Francisco: Jossey-Bass, Inc., 1991.

Where Does the Money Come From?

In 2001, a total of $212 billion was contributed to nonprofit organizations according to *Giving USA 2001*.[6] Individuals were the largest donor group, contributing $160.72 billion or 75.8 percent of the total. Foundations were a distant second, contributing a total of $25.90 billion, 12.2 percent of the total; bequests followed, with contributions of $16.33 billion, 7.7 percent of the total; and corporations came in last, contributing

$9.05 billion, 4.3 percent of the total. The dynamics of giving are different for each of these funding sources.

Individual Donors

Individual donors give from the heart. While their donations may be advantageous to their pocketbooks by lessening their tax burdens, most donors give to what they believe in.

Individual donors give, but they also expect to get something back.[7] It is difficult to guess whether a particular donor is motivated by enhanced social status or a sense of solidarity with other givers or a feeling of moral obligation, or simply the desire to get rid of the gift solicitor, but regardless of the impetus, most donors share certain expectations. They expect the museum to use their money efficiently. They also expect acknowledgment and appreciation.

Many fund-raisers use a five-step approach to donations, particularly sizable ones: identification; introduction; cultivation; solicitation; and appreciation.[8] Information gathering about individuals who are or might be donors is the important initial task. If the prospect is already a giver, his pertinent information should be on file. If not, information regarding personal wealth, corporate interests, or charitable donations may be found through numerous sources—museum supporters or other contacts, local newspapers, and philanthropy journals, among others. The person may be able to contribute to a fund-raising effort more significantly because of affiliation with a corporation or foundation.

Once individuals have been identified as potential donors, fund-raisers arrange an introduction. Here is where the social and political network of museum board, staff, and supporters can be critical. Fund-raisers are more warmly received if they are introduced by someone the potential donor knows, rather than merely making a "cold call." Cultivating the donor's interest in the organization is an important step in building support for the museum and increasing the likelihood of a successful solicitation. Asking for a contribution may be most effective if the museum offers a wish list of exciting projects from which donors may choose.

Donors offering substantial gifts may request certain considerations as a consequence of their generosity. Naming of galleries or facilities after a benefactor or as a memorial is commonplace and generally accepted.

Closer scrutiny is given when donors request active involvement in the programming their funding supports. Multi-million-dollar gifts to the Smithsonian's National Museum of American History were accompanied by contracts stipulating donor participation in selection of exhibition contents. Scholars' requests to the Smithsonian's regents (equivalent to the board) asking for review on the basis of "the appearance of impropriety" resulted in two pieces on the opinion/editorial page of the *Washington Post,* one by the secretary of the Smithsonian defending the gifts and corollary contracts, the other by the newspaper reminding museums of their "obligation not to be unduly pushed around by their donors."[9] Clear and consistent communication about donor expectations and museum accommodations and involvement of the director and board in substantial gift negotiations can help ensure that everyone's needs are met and that public perception remains positive. Smithsonian donor Catherine Reynolds ultimately rescinded her gift. The museum, the general public, and even the donor lost out in this case.

In an attempt to assist museums in working effectively with both individual donors and the larger community, the American Association of Museums (AAM) created *Guidelines for Museums on Developing and Managing Individual Donor Support.* Consistent with and expanding on the AAM's *Code of Ethics for Museums,* the guidelines help museums do several important things related to donor support: write their own policies that adhere to an ethical standard that exceeds legal minimums; act in a manner consistent with the museum's mission; maintain control over all museum activities, including content; avoid conflicts of interest; commit to making the museum's actions open, available, and understandable to the public; and maintain responsibility to individual donors. The guidelines are available on the AAM's website, www.aam-us.org.

After the donation has been received, formal acknowledgment and a show of appreciation in an appropriate form are absolutely critical.[10] Small or large donors alike will not repeat gifts that are not received and recognized in a timely fashion.

Remember, not all donations from individuals need be money. Services, expertise, items, or time are valuable resources, even if they don't show directly on the financial ledger. These contributions show support for the museum and may be useful in leveraging other financial gifts.

Corporations

Corporations give for several reasons: good corporate citizenship, enlightened self-interest, individual leadership, location, and *quid pro quo* interests. In this "cause-related" or "strategic" philanthropy, corporations give to help themselves. Corporations are conservative in their giving patterns because they are accountable to stockholders, customers, unions, and executives. They usually do not support projects that are controversial or antibusiness, so as to prevent potential conflicts of interest with their shareholders. Box 6.4 outlines some of the sources corporations tap to make contributions.

The current trend of corporate donations to museums is through corporate sponsorship. Corporation sponsorship to museums rose 41 percent from 1994 to 1997—from $45 million to $65 million.[11] Sponsorship of museums and their programs allows profit-making companies to reach a specific group of consumers and get a bargain for corporate marketing

Box 6.4

Corporate Contributions

Corporations use different channels to contribute funds, including:

Direct corporate giving—Donations are provided directly out of corporate profit. This is the more common method.

Executive discretionary funds—Pools of charitable funds distributed at the discretion of top personnel, usually small grants to community-based organizations, such as museums, for public programs.

Individual plant budget—Each branch in the company makes its own decision on donations. These are usually small contributions given exclusively to the community agencies in cities and towns where the branch is sited.

Marketing budgets—This also is known as corporate sponsorship. The corporation makes a gift to a museum in order to attract its constituency or to join the corporate name with the museum's name.

Corporate foundations—Allow companies to maintain a fairly stable level of giving each year. Corporate foundations tend to view grant proposals in a business-related manner.

Research and development budgets—Funds are usually given to research projects, which a corporation may market in the future.

Source: *Achieving excellence in fund raising* by H. A. Rosso and Associates, 231–232. San Francisco: Jossey-Bass, Inc., 1991.

dollars. In a deal with Subaru of America, for example, the Franklin Institute Science Museum's traveling science show was transported via four Subaru Legacy station wagons donated by the carmaker. In exchange, the museum gave the kids participating a bag of goodies, including an invitation to their parents to test-drive a Subaru. Subaru's marketing director, Timothy Mahoney, estimated sales of one car a week through this type of sponsorship with five museums.

Corporate sponsorship can come in many forms, depending on the needs of the museum and the corporation. The Dallas Museum of Art created a fifty thousand dollar quarterly or semiannual sponsorship that allowed donating corporations to display their logos and use museum facilities during the period. At Henry Ford Museum and Greenfield Village, the sponsorship is year-long. AT&T set aside a half-million-dollar fund to grant to museums for the specific purpose of presenting and acquiring contemporary art.

Increasingly, corporations are exchanging substantial financial support for inclusion of their names on galleries, buildings, or even entire institutions.[12] The Monsanto Insectarium at the St. Louis Zoo, the General Motors Center for African American Art in Detroit, and the Please Touch Museum Presented by McDonald's in Philadelphia exemplify this trend. Corporations appreciate the strengthened image and goodwill that go along with substantial financial underwriting; nonprofits benefit from the big bucks associated with big corporations. But what to some looks like a match made in heaven is causing others grave concern.

Careful consideration must be given to public perception of the supporting corporation and its products and the appearance of potential conflicts of interest. Museums have traditionally been a refuge from commercialism, and some visitors are not happy about having yet another place for their children to be imprinted with corporate logos, or being confronted with the symbols themselves. Other people raise questions about a tobacco company's underwriting of the national tour of the U.S. Constitution. Should profits earned by an industry from sales of harmful products be used, even for a good purpose? Did funding from pest exterminator Orkin compromise the intellectual integrity of a major Smithsonian exhibition on insects?

In addition to public relations issues, corporate sponsorship may subject the museum to tax scrutiny. The Internal Revenue Service has closely examined corporate sponsorships and has called into question the tax deductibility of contributions by corporations and the tax exemption of such income to museums if they appear to be advertising for their sponsors.[13] The 1999 "Sensation" exhibition at the Brooklyn Museum of Art caused controversy, not only because some artwork was decried as obscene, but also because all the pieces were owned by one individual, London advertising executive Charles Saatchi, and the exhibition's principal corporate sponsor, Christie's, stood to gain financially when it auctioned the work after the exhibition closed.

Guarding museums' valuable status as institutions the public can trust, the AAM developed guidelines to help museums develop and implement policies and practices that address their relationships with business. The AAM guidelines concluded

> It is essential that each museum draft its own policies, appropriate to its mission, regarding its interaction with business. Policies provide a consistent position that can be articulated by trustees and staff and understood by the public; they are vital to a museum's public accountability. As new models of business support develop and conventional models evolve at an ever-increasing rate, AAM and the U.S. museum community must remain committed to a continual review of ethical policies and practices and the development of new ones, as needed. Policies addressing business support should be reviewed regularly and updated as necessary. In addition, museums should remain current on all relevant statutory and regulatory developments related to the topic.[14]

Museums that can adapt and work in creative ways to meet the changing concerns of corporations will find an unfailing source of funding for many years. Careful consultation in advance will ensure both parties benefit from the relationship. Numerous resources for information on corporate giving are available; check the bibliography in this book or search online.

Fund-Raising Methods

The most common methods used to solicit funds are membership drives, personal and phone solicitations, direct mailing, and special events.

These methods are primarily aimed at individual contributors but can be used for businesses and community organizations.

Membership Drive

Membership is the most common entry point for donors to become involved in museums. A membership drive is a concentrated effort to generate new members (and contributions) while renewing and upgrading current and past memberships. Paid membership is a vote of support for the ideas and programs a museum represents and serves as a bond between the member and the museum. Paid dues give the museum access to valuable information about the people who really care about the museum's focus, programs, and services. Beyond the dollars they bring, members are a source of potential volunteers, contacts, and donors. Members also can serve an important advocacy function in public policy issues affecting the museum.[15]

Most museums complete a membership drive periodically but promote memberships at the door and through the mail year-round. In selling memberships, museums should consider carefully the benefits offered to members and calculate their cost to ensure that servicing the membership does not cost more than the basic membership brings in. If the benefits of a fifteen-dollar membership (for example, four issues of the museum magazine, twelve monthly newsletters, regular mailings about special events, and free admission) cost the museum twenty dollars to produce, the membership program operates at a loss. Generally the lowest-cost memberships are offered by history museums; art museums and planetariums are usually highest. Typical fees are around thirty dollars for individuals and fifty dollars for families. Additional membership categories that identify special member needs and interests have been used by museums with success; these categories feature benefits supplemental to the free admission and museum store discount that are standard.

Clear, straightforward communication with members about what they are getting for their money, and what it costs the museum to produce those benefits, is important. Not only will members feel a sense of satisfaction about the "good deal" they are getting, they also will start to understand why the museum needs to ask for help with annual, capital, or endowment funds. Member lists are usually the starting point for fund solicitations.

Personal and Phone Solicitations

Many of us would rank asking another person for money as difficult and uncomfortable. This personal touch can be important to the success of the fund-raising effort, but it is easy for fund-raisers to procrastinate in fear of being rejected.

Personal solicitations require the fund-raising member to meet directly with the potential donor. Although the purpose of the meeting is to familiarize the potential donor with the organization, its programs, and successes, it ultimately concludes with a request for support. The most successful face-to-face fund-raisers enthusiastically present an image of a vital and significant organization that they themselves support. They are not so much asking for money as they are extending an invitation to others to become part of something valuable, enduring, and even enjoyable.

Some of us view phone solicitation as slightly easier because the fund-raising member has the protection and the anonymity provided by the telephone. Phone solicitation is most successful and effective when the fund-raising team is relaxed and having fun. Making calls in a group setting over short segments of time (like a telephone marathon) is a frequently used technique. Prizes and food distributed during the allotted time and a social event afterward to thank the fund-raising members make the work more enjoyable for everyone.

Preparation, practice, and presentation are the three key phases of successful solicitation, whether done over the phone or face to face. During the preparation phase, the museum staff will conduct research and prepare material. Compiling potential donor lists and writing a script will comfort volunteers because they will know whom they will be approaching and exactly what to say. The list should include the name, phone number, and address of the potential donor, as well as the amount of the donor's last gift, a suggested increase, and issues of interest. Accuracy of the list is a must; approaches to individuals who have requested not to be contacted or who have experienced a change of circumstances (divorce, death, financial shift) can be embarrassing for both parties and leave a negative impression of the museum. A script for the fund-raising team ensures that all important elements are presented professionally and consistently.[16]

Practice should include a training session, which answers questions and gives the fund-raising team a chance to become familiar with the script. The potential donor should not be approached until the fund-raising member is comfortable with what should be said and how to say it. Training videos, which show taped examples of actual interactions between solicitors and donors, can ease fund-raisers' anxieties. Approaching easiest donors first and visualizing positive responses can also build solicitors' confidence.[17]

During the presentation, whether in person or by phone, the fund-raiser should first establish a comfort level by listening for values and identifying areas of common interest. Some organizations find pairing the volunteer fund-raiser with a staff member creates a more comfortable atmosphere for direct solicitation; the volunteer supplies the enthusiasm and personal connection to the potential donor, and the staff member offers facts and figures. Discussion of an ideal gift range and the variety of giving methods available becomes a three-way, rather than a one-on-one, conversation. The moment of truth is the actual request for the gift. An outright "no" can be countered with a request to approach the individual again at some time in the future. If the potential donor wishes to contemplate the project, set up a return visit or call. Regardless of the answer, it is important to thank potential donors for their time and ensure that any requests for further contacts or removal from consideration be followed up.[18]

Successful solicitations require that the fund-raising member has made his own donation to the project. The amount of support is less critical than the fact a contribution was made. The fund-raiser is contributing a great resource—his or her time—to the museum, but this strong selling point is further strengthened if the solicitor can honestly say, "I put my money where my mouth is." The best advice is to approach and treat potential donors as the fund-raising member expects to be approached.[19]

Direct Mailings

Direct mailing is a method of reaching prospects who cannot be reached personally. Like personal and phone solicitations, direct mailings may be targeted to specific individuals or may be more generally aimed at certain market segments. Direct mailing is not highly popular because of the low returns and relatively high cost. A 1 to 2 percent response is considered successful when mailing to a list of individuals who have never contributed to or been associated with the museum. The goal of the first direct mailing campaign or personal contacts should be the acquisition of new members or potential donors. Subsequent direct mailing campaigns will produce improved financial results as the museum approaches current and past, as well as potential, donors. The goal is to resolicit, renew, and upgrade donations. The response rate usually increases by 6 to 15 percent.[20]

The appearance of the direct-mailing package directly correlates to its effectiveness. Well-designed materials bespeak a professional museum, but overdone or obviously expensive pieces raise questions about appropriate use of financial resources. A cover letter should directly convey the tone of the fund-raising campaign, state the challenge (using specific examples), and make a straightforward request for donor action. Inserts, response forms, and return envelopes may be helpful inclusions. A newsletter or brochure featuring current and future activities might be inserted. Response forms may make record keeping easier for both the museum and the donor. Return envelopes may make giving simpler. Too much paper will annoy potential donors; excess information will distract them from the primary message and goal of the mailing. Careful consideration of the museum's community and constituency will guide staff in creating suitable materials.[21]

Special Events

Special events are an especially effective fund-raising method that help museums reach a broad range of contributors. They also can be expensive and time-consuming undertakings. Before embarking, it is important to analyze the cost/benefit ratio to ensure the event will be profitable. Time and effort of numerous staff and volunteers will be needed to attend to countless details, time necessarily taken away from other museum functions. Careful planning is essential.

The variety of special events a museum can offer is immense; receptions, dinners, exhibit openings, lectures, performances, tours, and auctions are common. Different events attract different participants. Some individuals unlikely to buy memberships or make donations to the museum may be attracted by the nature, location, or subject of the special event. The tax deductibility of the difference between the ticket price and the actual value of the benefit received is icing on the cake, but it is not the principal motivating factor for these participants.

Chocolate was the main attraction at the fund-raiser sponsored by the University of Nebraska State Museum and the Historic Haymarket, in Lincoln, Nebraska. Their "Chocolate Lovers' Fantasy," scheduled prior to Valentine's Day, featured indulgences prepared (and donated) by local celebrity chefs. The four-hour event netted each organization more than ten thousand dollars and introduced nearly seven hundred people to both organizations. Up-front dollar costs were comparatively low (mostly marketing), but hundreds of staff and volunteer hours went into organizing the participation of thirty-plus "chefs" and preparing food for seven hundred people. Other events may require significant cash investments up front (speakers' or performers' fees; rentals; food and beverage service), which will increase pressure on ticket sales to cover costs.

More pressure, too, is being placed on museums to compromise traditional rules in order to accommodate special events. The good news is that more people are viewing museums as great places to hold parties, and they're willing to pay for the privilege of doing so. The bad report is that as revenue sources become tight, it becomes tempting to let the potential of special event income dictate exhibition decisions or alter museum policies. Was it appropriate for the American Craft Museum to pack up half an exhibition so a local politician could host a fund-raiser in one of its galleries? Should the National Civil War Museum have staffers calling bridal boutiques to sell the museum as a wedding location? Is the publicity generated by Rosie O'Donnell's party at the International Center of Photography worth building a special exhibit gallery with giant snapshots of her children?[22]

Special events are a multifaceted tool. Besides raising funds, they have the potential to attract and identify new donors and members, enhance public recognition, promote favorable news coverage, provide a service to the constituency, and recognize community leadership. They also can lose money, take time away from core programs, distract from more difficult (but often more lucrative) personal solicitations, and exclude certain audience segments. Museums need to develop special events policies that take into consideration their mission, ethics, and role in their communities. A realistic appreciation of the resources required, coupled with the creativity and enthusiasm necessary for success, can produce special events that make both friends and money for the museum.

Fund-Raising Maxims

Regardless of the methods used, the nature of the museum being supported, or the fund-raising goal, many fund-raising factors are universal. Here are a few of the basics:

- There are people behind every funding source. Make an effort to become acquainted with donors and to understand their philanthropic approaches and how they fit into a museum's programming activities.
- A blanket approach does not work. Customize the effort based on the donor, giving level, and other factors.
- Board and members should give first. Potential donors, corporations, and public agencies often view support from other sources as an endorsement of the value of a museum's funding effort.
- Incorrectly calculated budget proposals and figures reflect poorly on the planning and execution of a fund-raising effort. Double-check all figures before they are released in any grants, publications, or announcements.
- A good fund-raiser should use positive phrases in all communications.
- Fund-raisers hear "no" more often than "yes." Do not take rejection personally; instead, file the information gained for future use. The project presented may not fit the potential donor's philosophy or timing, but future projects may.
- Use every opportunity to thank donors. Thank them personally in writing, in publicity materials, or through a special event. Major donors should be updated with progress reports. Their sponsorship should be cited in press releases, advertisements, and publications associated with the project. Thanking donors not only shows them your gratitude but also encourages them to contribute to future projects.[23]

Grants

A grant is a gift of money from an established organization designated for a specific purpose. Grants are obtained through an application or proposal process, depending on the organization. Grant seeking is a complex kind of matchmaking; museums need to find organizations that have grant, programming, size, and location requirements that complement the museum's project.

Two basic types of funding organizations, government agencies and private foundations, award grants. Each of these funding entities has its own unique characteristics and objectives, often determined by law. Researching the particular focus and requirements of funding sources is the critical first step in the grant-seeking process. A basic understanding of these types of entities and their general emphases is a good place to start.

Government Agencies

Government grants usually involve long and complex proposals and applications. Grants from government agencies require careful record keeping because the agencies are accountable to taxpayers. The application and review process may take from eight to eighteen months to complete. Government grants are distributed through federal and state agencies.

Federal Agencies

A few federal agencies specifically target museums, while others support the subject matter or audience objective of museum projects. Common sources of federal funding used by museums are the Institute of Museum and Library Services, the National Endowment for the Arts, the National Endowment for the Humanities, and the National Science Foundation.

Institute of Museum and Library Services (IMLS). The mission of the IMLS is to provide distinct support for libraries and museums and to encourage partnerships between them. IMLS is divided into two departments, one to service libraries, the other for museums. IMLS has a number of different programs that provide funding, matching grants, or professional services to improve museums.[24]

Museums for America: The largest IMLS program replaces the former General Operating Support (GOS) category. These grants encourage museums to use their collections, exhibits, and services to sustain our cultural heritage, support lifelong learning, and be centers of community engagement.

Museum Assessment Programs (MAP): The MAP is a noncompetitive grant program designed to help smaller museums identify strengths, weaknesses, and future courses of action. (MAP assessments can help museums develop and put in place the systems and programs necessary for national museum accreditation offered by the AAM.) The museum engages in a rigorous self-study that is complemented by the assessment of one or more museum professionals serving as outside evaluators, who interview the museum staff and board on site. A report is then produced offering observations and recommendations. This assessment process is available for four different areas.

MAP I reviews overall museum operations.

MAP II assesses collections care and management.

MAP III examines public programs and operations

MAP IV focuses on museum governance.

This program is funded by the IMLS but is currently administered by the AAM.

Conservation Project Support (CP): This matching grant program helps museums evaluate and prioritize conservation needs and perform activities to ensure the care and safety of their collections. Grants are awarded for five types of conservation activities—environmental improvements, research, surveys, training, and treatment.

Conservation Assessment Program (CAP): CAP supports a one-time, noncompetitive grant for general assessment of a museum's entire conservation program. CAP funds a two-day assessment by one or two conservation professionals and preparation of a written report. This program is funded by the IMLS but is currently administered by Heritage Preservation.

National Leadership Grants for Museums: These grants help plan and develop relationships and interactions between museums and community-based organizations and the widespread and creative use of new technologies.

National Endowment for the Arts (NEA). The mission of the NEA is to foster the excellence, diversity, and vitality of the arts in the United

States and to broaden public access to the arts. This is accomplished through grants, leadership initiatives, and partnership agreements with a variety of public, private, state, local, and federal organizations. The NEA awards grants to individuals and organizations and funds partnership agreements and leadership initiatives.[25]

National Endowment for the Humanities (NEH). The mission of the NEH is to provide grants to individuals and organizations that will educate, research, and preserve the humanities. Examples of fundable projects are the research and preservation of texts and materials, translation of an important work, and public programming through exhibits, public discussion, television, and radio. NEH projects can be funded through fellowships, grants, and matching grants.[26]

National Science Foundation (NSF). The primary area in which NSF provides grants of interest to museums is informal science education. These are major grants to support science exhibits and other types of public programming in science education. Some NSF programs provide funding to assist in the preservation of systematic and scientific collections and may help underwrite collections storage materials or equipment.[27]

The IMLS is the only government agency set up to address the specific needs of museums. The NEA and NEH are examples of government agencies museums can access. Museums can also access NEA and NEH funding through state and regional sources; these endowments distribute a portion of their funding to state or regional agencies so it can be distributed within a specific geographic area.

State Agencies

State agencies are another funding source for museums. Some state entities are funded by the state's tax dollars, but others receive funds through federal agencies on the premise that the state can better evaluate and set priorities regarding projects and areas of need at the state level.

State-distributed grants are mainly for projects that are strongly supported by the community. Grants from state agencies are easier to access because the state agency is physically closer; this proximity encourages good working relationships and makes assistance in the grant process simpler to obtain. Be aware that grants from state agencies may be more closely scrutinized because they must adhere to both state and federal guidelines.

Each state has a state humanities and state arts agency, but the specific names of these organizations and their configurations vary from state to state. In Nebraska, the agencies are the Nebraska Arts Council and the Nebraska Humanities Council; next door in Colorado, the agencies are combined into the Colorado Council on the Arts & Humanities. The mission of these state agencies is similar to their respective national counterparts, the NEA and the NEH, and part of the state-based programs' funding is appropriated to them by their national equivalents. State-based arts agencies may support annual operation of art-based organizations and projects that educate children and adults about the arts and encourage individual and collaborative projects.[28] Programs state-based humanities agencies sponsor are for preservation, research, and education in areas of the humanities aimed at a state-based audience.[29]

Other Sources

In addition to these traditional sources, museums can tap into other federal and state agencies that may not be obvious matches. A little research and creativity may be needed to find a fit within unorthodox museum partner agencies such as the Department of Energy, Environmental Protection Agency, National Institutes of Health, or Department of Labor. Museums are defined as "educational organizations"; therefore they are eligible to apply under many different federally funded programs. At first glance, neither the Department of Agriculture nor the Department of Education may appear to be an accessible source of funding, yet both have in fact provided funding for museums.

An example of a seemingly incongruous match is a twenty-minute documentary produced by the Wing Luke Asian Museum (WLAM) in Seattle with funding from the USDA Forest Service. The video documents a five-day Chinese Heritage tour of the American West through historical sites in Washington, Oregon, and Idaho. These sites, many of which are on public land, tell the stories of the Chinese pioneers whose labors were instrumental in the development of the West. The video increased public awareness of the national forests and educated about Asian heritages in these national forest lands. In this way it fulfilled both the USDA Forest Service's objective of increasing awareness of the national forest and the WLAM's mission to document and exhibit Asian-American history.

Private Foundations

Foundations are not-for-profit entities that have been established to provide support to charitable organizations through grants. Foundations generally favor giving support to capital funds, demonstration projects, and educational programs. They rarely support requests for operating expenses. Foundations give according to the foundation's charter or mission statement and sometimes according to guidelines set forth by the governing board. Foundations can be categorized according to size, purpose, and the chartering entity.

Family Foundations

Over eighteen thousand family foundations exist in the United States, created to assist organizations that have interests similar to that of the founding family member. Family foundations are generally small, have little structure, and do not maintain a full-time staff.[30] Grant decisions are often made directly by the donor or members of the donor's family.

Community Foundations

Community foundations are created to address the problems and the interests of the community. The community can be a predetermined geographical area such as the city limits or state boundaries. Community foundations incorporate funds from numerous community sources. The Lincoln Community Foundation, for example, operates to provide grants to enrich the quality of life in Lincoln and Lancaster County, Nebraska. Community foundations tend to fund projects that work and can be replicated.

Corporate Foundations

Corporate foundations are extensions of private corporations. Grants are awarded with business objectives in mind; support favors local community projects and educational activities. Corporate foundations such as the AT&T Foundation and the Chevron Corporation Foundation are numerous. Understanding the foundation's philanthropic goals and how its support of your project will further the corporate good name is a key to success with this funding source.

National Foundations

National foundations are large and take a national or international scope. The Ford Foundation, the Johnson Foundation, the W. K. Kellogg Foundation, and the Rockefeller Foundation are well-known examples. Foundations in this classification are prone to support highly visible, pilot, or demonstration programs and programs with national applicability.

Special Purpose Foundations

As with family foundations, special purpose foundations grant awards to areas defined by the foundation's charter.[31] Unlike most family foundations, special purpose foundations may give away millions of dollars. An example is the Robert Wood Johnson Foundation, which focuses on the area of health.

Foundations in each of these categories not only fund different types of proposals; they also look for different characteristics. As a result, it is important to research the foundation to understand its giving pattern before ever considering submission of a grant proposal. Foundation proposal turnaround time is anywhere from three to eighteen months; proposal formats may vary from a one-page letter to more extensive application forms.

The Grant Process

Each government agency and foundation has its own set of guidelines and preferred charitable causes. Yet the steps to finding, applying for, and receiving a grant from these funding sources are essentially similar. Finding a funding organization with guidelines that match a museum's proposed project requires research.

Numerous books, periodicals, and Internet sites provide information about government agencies and foundations. The World Wide Web is a gateway to abundant information on all government agencies and foundations. Two excellent sites to start with are those of the NonProfit Gateway[32] and the Foundation Center. The NonProfit Gateway is the first place to go to find information on government agencies and departments. This site provides links to many federal departments and agencies. There is also a link to an electronic version of *The Catalog of Federal Domestic Assistance.* This site provides a search engine that can be used to find grants that may be applicable to a museum's potential project. The *U. S. Government Manual* describes all federal agencies and provides names of officials.[33] The Foundation Center's *National Directory of Corporate Giving* and *National Data Book of Foundations* offer data in both print and electronic format.[34] The Foundation Center's website provides information and tips on applying for and writing grants as well as updates on grant sources and trends. The site also lists available courses and links to public, private, and community foundations.

Two other useful sources about specific foundations are their individual annual reports and the IRS Form 990PF, which each must file annually. The annual report identifies the focus of the foundation, the types of programs supported, and the amount of funds distributed during the year. The IRS Form 990PF is a valuable source of up-to-date information about the organization (the actual names of trustees, director, and staff), its budget (fiscal details on receipts and expenditures, compensation of officers, and capital gains or losses), and giving patterns (grants paid, grants committed for future payment, and who received them).[35] Many of these reports are becoming available online.

People are a great source of information about government agencies and foundations. A museum's staff interacts daily with board members, other staff members, constituents, and countless public and private organizations. Insights into a government agency or foundation, suggestions on where to search, leads on grant requirements the museum may meet, and introductions to funding sources can come out of these museum relationships.

When pursuing *any* grants from *any* source, it is important to do your homework. Call the funding entity before applying to obtain the most up-to-date information about emphases and application requirements, guidelines, and deadlines. Some funding sources are very hands-on and will guide an applicant from the beginning to the end of the grant process. Other funding sources prefer minimal or no advance contact. Do not hesitate to find out the level of interaction the funding source prefers and utilize the staff's generosity to the fullest. Normally, government agencies and certain foundations prefer the hands-on approach.[36]

Set up an informational meeting with representatives of funding organizations that welcome advance contact. This meeting will: (1) provide the opportunity to initiate and establish a relationship with the funding organization; (2) help determine if the nonprofit organization meets the funding organization's criteria; and (3) offer the museum an opportunity to understand what will be most appealing to the representative in the position to accept or reject the proposal (ideally the same representative with whom the museum staff meets). It is through this rapport that the museum will be able to present its project to the funding organization in the best possible light. If, based on this initial conversation, the museum project is found to be eligible, the funding organization may request a letter of inquiry outlining the proposal or project before it sends out an application or guidelines.

After the grant is submitted, a review board will either reject or accept the grant proposal. Governmental entities involve professional peers in the grants review process, and specialists are likely to examine proposals in more technical categories (e.g., conservation); foundation applications are likely to be reviewed by the same review committee, regardless of the subject matter or emphasis of the grant proposal. There may be circumstances in which the review board will request changes before approving a grant proposal or opt to fund only part of the request. The applying museum must carefully consider the changes proposed and the financial implications of partial funding to determine whether the project can be successfully implemented under new provisions.[37]

Not all grant agencies will provide a form for their application process. Form or not, there are six basic elements a grant proposal should present (see box 6.5).

Who will write the grant? Some museums have a grant writer on staff, but in many cases grant proposal preparation will fall to senior administrative staff with input from the director. If the grant has a particular focus (for example, collections preservation or education programming), then the staff members responsible for those areas may shoulder the major responsibility for the proposal. Broad-based applications such as those for IMLS Learning Opportunities Grants will necessarily involve input from a variety of museum staff. Most proposals will require good communication with and input from the budget accounting office to ensure financial information is accurate and clearly expressed.

Grant proposals are essentially high-stakes marketing tools. The goal is selling the museum's good idea in such a convincing way that the funding entity commits financial resources to make it happen. The museum's

Box 6.5

Elements of Grant Proposals

Introduction/abstract—A brief or condensed summary of the proposed project

Problem/needs statement—A description of the problem or need the museum will be addressing. Documented facts and statistics are commonly used in this section. Devote considerable effort to this statement because it is your initial opportunity to get the interest of the reviewer.

Goals/objectives—The description of project goals should be made in quantitative terms to provide a gauge for measuring the success of the project.

Methods/approaches/program description—How the goals and objectives will be accomplished. It is wise to include a timeline or task schedule.

Evaluation strategy—Identify the methods and benchmarks used to evaluate the success of the project.

Program budget—The budget will justify the amount requested by showing how it will be spent. It is important to show three figures—1) the amount requested for the project; 2) the costs associated with the project such as materials, staff time, use of facilities, and honoraria; 3) additional funding sources, in-kind services, and the amount contributed by the museum. Check and then double check all numbers and calculations. You cannot afford a mistake here.

Source: *Managing a nonprofit organization: In the twenty-first century* by T. Wolf, 262–264. New York: Prentice Hall Press, 1999.

financial need should be made clear, but the appeal should most strongly articulate the vigor of the proposed project and how well it fulfills the museum's mission and goals. Regardless of the source of their funds, all grant-giving entities want to help underwrite successful programs that have significant effects.

Crafting successful grant proposals takes practice. We encourage you to take the time to complete the grant writing and review exercises outlined in boxes 6.6a and 6.6b.

Grants will continue to play a substantial role in creating the museum's financial package. Staff must be constantly alert to the missions, philosophies, and agendas of these funding entities in order to tap their resources effectively for the benefit of the museum and its constituents.

Earned Income

Museums are looking inward as well as outward for ways to generate income. Facilities use, services, and programming are among typical

Box 6.6a

Exercise: Grant Writing

In this exercise, you will prepare a grant application to a state-based humanities council. You will design a project of your own choosing that fits within the funding guidelines of the council, complete a cover sheet, write a one-hundred-word abstract, respond to questions in a project narrative, prepare a budget, and complete scholar participation sheets for humanities resource persons working on the project. We recommend state humanities grant forms for this exercise because these tend to be very general types of proposals and can be used for a wide variety of projects. History museums typically receive funding from these agencies, but natural science and art museums also receive state humanities grants. Your success depends on your ability to write a coherent and convincing grant proposal.

A second part of this exercise is for you to serve as the reviewer for the proposals written by your classmates. This part of the exercise is discussed in Box 6.6b. You may wish to look at that portion of the exercise before beginning to write a proposal because the criteria by which the proposal will be evaluated are listed there. You may find it useful to work on this effort as a group and recruit colleagues, friends, or volunteers to serve as a review panel.

Acquire the current proposal guidelines and forms from the state humanities council in your location. (Many are available on state council websites.) Your state humanities council may also share the materials used by reviewers to evaluate proposals.

Sample Guidelines

Eligibility

Any nonprofit group is eligible to apply for grants. Examples of eligible organizations include libraries, museums, civic groups, service clubs, tribal organizations, professional associations, historical societies, educational institutions, archives, botanical gardens, zoos, and community organizations.

Applications must demonstrate that the humanities are central to the project. The National Endowment for the Humanities has defined the humanities as including, but not limited to, history, literature, languages, jurisprudence, philosophy, comparative religion, archaeology, ethnography, anthropology, ethics, the social sciences when they employ humanistic perspectives, history of science and technology, and the history, theory, and criticism of the arts.

All projects must include humanities resource people. Typically, they are college or university professors in a humanities discipline. If nonacademic humanists are chosen for a project, the applicant must provide sufficient background information on them to demonstrate that they will capably represent the humanities. Examples of such individuals would be people such as tribal elders or longtime members of an ethnic community, whose life experience makes them an expert on a humanistic topic. In place of the résumé or biographical sketch, please complete a scholar participation sheet for each humanities resource person involved in the project.

Any age group may be served. Projects need a creative publicity plan and a means of evaluation by audience participants or an outside reviewer. At least one-half of the total project cost must be provided by the applicant in local cost-share, in either cash or in-kind services. At least 20 percent of this local cost-share must be cash.

Box 6.6b

Exercise: Grant Reviewing

Divide the group into two grant review panels. Exchange grant proposals between the panels so that each member has a full complement of the proposals from the other panel. We do this "blind" so that no one knows whose proposals they are reviewing. Individuals have two weeks to review their group of proposals using the following grant review instructions.

Grant Review Instructions

1. Keep your review of grants strictly confidential. You will discuss them with no one outside of class.
2. Using a separate Grant Evaluation Form for each grant, you will evaluate each aspect of the grant as instructed. At the bottom of the sheet, you will give an overall score for the grant.
3. You will rank the grants from number 1, the most fundable, to the last number, the least fundable.
4. Grant panels will meet for the first forty-five minutes of the class period designated for making funding decisions. Each panel as a group will rank its grants from number 1 through the last.
5. In the last thirty minutes of class, we will come together to decide which grants will receive funding. We will have $12,000 to award. The funded proposals will receive five bonus points.
6. You should remember throughout this entire process that your grading and review will affect the lives and careers of your classmates.

Grant Evaluation Form

Proposal Title ________________________ Proposal No. ________

Scoring should be from 1 to 10, with 1 the lowest and 10 the best.

1. Humanities contents: Are humanities disciplines and methodology central?

Score ________

2. Staff and consultants: Are humanities scholars involved in the planning, implementation, and evaluation of the project? Do the participants have the necessary qualifications?

Score ________

3. Value for the audience: Will the project increase the intended audience's knowledge of the humanities? Is the audience clearly defined?

Score ________

4. Plan of work: Are the project's activities clearly defined and stated? Are the project's goals realistic? Is the timeline reasonable?

Score ________

Box 6.6b (continued)

5. Avoidance of advocacy: Do the project activities avoid bias or advocacy and provide for a balance of viewpoints?

Score ________

6. Budget: Is the budget appropriate in scope and in terms of the anticipated results? Is the budget cost effective?

Score ________

7. Publicity: Are the planned publicity methods appropriate for reaching the intended audience?

Score ________

8. Evaluation: Are adequate provisions made for evaluation of the project?

Score ________

9. Other issues: Does the project reach audiences from across the state or that are underserved by the agency? Is this the first grant to the organization from the agency? Is there a co-sponsor? Is the project innovative?

Score ________

10. Overall impression: How important is it that this project be accomplished? Would it be important to have this project associated with the agency? Reviewer's overall impression of the proposal and project?

Score ________

Total Score ______

Recommendation (circle one)
REJECT RESUBMIT FUND (low priority) FUND (high priority)
Comments & Conditions:

sources of earned income. Museums earn considerably over $1 billion every year through admissions, memberships, gift shops, restaurants, parking, publications, and services to other museums.[38] In the past five years, earned income accounted for one-third of museums' total operating income. These statistics send a signal to museums in need of increased revenue—there are numerous income opportunities within their walls.

Assessing the feasibility, tax implications, and income-generating potential of ventures is a critical first step in developing new earned-income possibilities. Published guides to business development for nonprofit organizations, as well as board members with business planning experience, can assist in this important evaluation.

Admission Fees

Charging admission is a common and sometimes controversial earned-income opportunity. Admission fees provide a source of revenue, but there is concern that they affect the museum's constituents and other museum programming. There are arguments that donations and volunteers will decrease because donors feel they are already contributing to the museum through the admission fees. Others argue that museums are educational institutions. By charging admission fees, museums become elitist organizations because they become inaccessible to low-income individuals.[39]

Admission fees also may discourage visitors from spending on other services offered by a museum, thereby reducing the total amount earned from a group of visitors. However, charging admission may be advantageous in the overall scheme to generate income. Admission fees can be a marketing and membership tool and can provide valuable information on visitor demographics and peak attendance times and days. When a museum charges admission, it also has the power to waive it. Marketing opportunities can be created between businesses and the museum in which businesses can sponsor a free-admission day in exchange for advertisement at the museum. Free admission also can be part of a membership package, encouraging visitors to become members and thus increasing membership revenues.

Charging admission fees is a difficult decision because of the uncertain impact on the museum's viability. Many museums have found a balance by offering a variety of admission options in order to make the museum affordable and accessible. Some museums offer free admission on specific times or days. The admissions policy at the Joslyn Museum in Omaha, Nebraska, is an example: there are different admission fees for adults and children (five to eleven years of age), and admission is free for members, seniors, and children under age five and for everyone on Saturdays from ten A.M. to noon. It is important for each museum to examine what its constituency will support and the impact of admission fees on other museum revenue sources, such as the museum store, dining facility, planetarium, or Imax theater.

Museum Store

Operating a museum store offers many advantages. A store can generate income for a museum, provide additional information about the collection, offer a point of personal contact with the staff, and feature merchandise that reflects the museum's mission and exhibits. Visitors may take home a souvenir of their experience or gain additional educational materials about an exhibit or collection. Ideally the store should be located near an exit or entrance; most people tend to buy goods at the end of their visit. Some newer museums, like the San Francisco Museum of Modern Art, have street-side museum stores accessible through a separate entrance so that the store can serve customers whether or not the museum itself is open.[40] At a small museum, staff can service incoming and outgoing visitors while operating a well-situated gift shop.

Museum merchandise is now offered off the museum premises through print and electronic catalogs and other retail outlets. The Metropolitan Museum of Art, the Boston Museum of Fine Arts, and the Art Institute of Chicago are among museums with stores located off-site. In fact, the Met has fifteen different shops operating around the country and another twenty-two overseas.[41] Museums also are offering their merchandise through both printed and online catalogs and on television in order to reach more consumers.

Several museums—the Boston Museum of Fine Arts, the Metropolitan Museum of Art, the Smithsonian Institution, Winterthur Museum, and Colonial Williamsburg, among others—partnered with the home shopping network QVC. During the "two-hour tour" of each museum QVC broadcast, merchandise related to the museum's collections was marketed. Although these mass marketing campaigns help museums reach more consumers, they have generated controversy about preserving the integrity of both the museums and their collections, particularly in the case of works of art. Do adaptations of artistic motifs in the form of puzzles, mugs, scarves, and prints demean the significance of the art and its creator? Some argue that nontraditional partnerships with entities like QVC draw nonvisitors, make art less threatening and more comfortable, and ultimately attract the nonvisitor to the museum.[42]

A more practical concern is attracting the attention of the Internal Revenue Service and engendering unrelated business income tax (UBIT). Museums maintain their tax-exempt status on the basis of their educational purposes. Increasingly the IRS is questioning the educational value of some museum store merchandise, such as T-shirts or coffee mugs that merely feature the name or logo of the institution. Items that are or that feature reproductions of materials in the museum collections are less subject to scrutiny (and to income tax on the profits from their sales). Museum shop merchandise currently generates nearly $1 billion annually, so it is reasonable to expect increased IRS attention to this substantial revenue generator.[43] Advice on protecting tax-exempt status while offering attractive merchandise to visitors is available from the Museum Store Association.

The proliferation of online shopping is prompting many museums to allow "virtual visitors" to purchase store merchandise via the museum website. Frequent analysis of both print and online catalogs will help determine the benefits and costs of such visitor services. There may be some advantage to an online presence even if sales are not immediately significant since every indicator predicts expansion of this type of commerce.

Dining Facilities

Museums with cafes, restaurants, or refreshment areas can attract and comfort visitors and become community resources. Since the Metropolitan Museum of Art installed a public restaurant in 1954 and others followed suit, visitors have come to anticipate opportunities for refreshment and rest in a pleasant atmosphere. Having a spot to relax and refuel makes visitors more willing to spend several hours at the museum.

A small museum with numerous visitors and limited space may find a "refreshment stand" approach useful. While the primary goal of operating an eating facility is to earn additional income, a well-run food service can help create the ambience that builds a return audience. The number of visitors, their visiting pattern, and the space available will help determine what the museum can offer. A good dining experience can have a strong impact on the visitor's overall museum visit; bad food or service can create negative word-of-mouth publicity.

Some museums, aquariums, and zoos contract with known national or regional brand-name restaurants to provide food service. McDonald's, Taco Bell, Pizza Hut, Wendy's, Burger King, and Starbucks work particularly well in institutions that attract families and children, while "art museums . . . tend to be good partners for well-known local or regional restaurant operators who are interested in lending their names, talent, creativity, and resources to the museum environment," according to Marjorie Schwarzer, chair of the JFK University Museum Studies program.[44] The same visitors who see museums as a refuge from commercialism and therefore criticize promotion of corporate financial partners may complain about museum food service, which encourages brand recognition and purchases.

Museums of any size can maximize their facilities' usage and exposure to the public by offering facilities for after-hour events. Depending on the size and food preparation facilities available, a museum can offer catering service or permit an outside caterer to serve the function. Beware: Each of these catering methods has its downside. An in-house catering service may be convenient to the renter and safer for the museum. The catering staff familiar with the museum will have established procedures on service, setup, and cleanup. The museum's ongoing relationship with catering staff may provide greater security for the museum collection.[45] However, users may find their options limited with an in-house caterer.

Some renters will want to use an outside catering service to provide specific foods and drinks. Allowing outside caterers to serve means a museum does not need to provide cooking facilities, but outside caterers may present security problems. Museum staff or security will need to be present to help facilitate, answer questions, and monitor the event to ensure the collection and facilities are cleaned properly and nothing is damaged or stolen.[46]

Regardless of catering particulars, these details and all other procedures, guidelines, and expectations should be communicated in writing to outside groups using the museum. Acknowledgment of the renters' receipt and acceptance of the requirements should also be received in writing prior to the special event. Effective communication within the museum also is essential to ensure that the special use of the museum facility is a positive experience for all involved and that neither the museum nor its collections are placed at risk.

Planetariums and Theaters

Planetariums and Imax or other large-screen theaters expand a museum's offering to visitors through intense multimedia experiences. These entertaining and educational shows can attract additional dollars because visitors are willing to pay extra for something out of the ordinary. Some visitors may be lured solely by the planetarium or Imax presentation.

These features can provide a comfortable transition to the museum world. The shows can be seen as a form of temporary exhibit. They can be easily changed, making them effective tools for providing new materials to the public and encouraging a return visit. Museums need to be alert to the income stream that large-format theater companies expect to see and ensure that their projected attendance figures are realistic and allow them to meet their contractual obligations. More than one museum has been left with extremely expensive projection equipment when its large-screen film provider canceled its contract.

The Mueller Planetarium of the University of Nebraska State Museum offers "laser shows" (laser light displays set to music shown on the dome) on Friday and Saturday evenings during the academic year. The shows are an excellent source of income for the museum and help hold and expand its audience. High school and college students on weekend dates make up the majority of the audience. This group was difficult to attract to the museum for other events; the laser shows helped bridge the gap between the children's programs and the museum's adult events.

Educational Programming

Museum education departments normally offer tours, lectures, hands-on activities, workshops, and other educational activities for children and adults. These entertaining and educational offerings can be another source of earned income. The Fort Worth Museum of Science and History's "Museum School" for preschool and school-age children includes classes designed for various age levels on subjects related to the museum's collection. The Frye Art Museum in Seattle offers workshops ranging from oil painting to the archeology of pottery for people of different ages, interests, and backgrounds. The Museum of Nebraska History runs hands-on history workshops during week-long breaks at the end of every school quarter.

Programming possibilities are limited only by staff and facilities. Educational activities provide opportunities for the community and museum staff to interact. While the museum's educators are the principal teachers, curators can oversee content or serve as guest experts. Teaching a workshop or facilitating a lecture gives museum staff direct feedback from the community. Well-organized and effective educational programs not only add to the museum's potential for earned income but help humanize the institution in the eyes of its constituents.

Special Exhibits

Changing an exhibit is a common way to offer a new subject for current members to explore and to attract new members who are interested in the subject. Special exhibits may have a brief run or be extended a year or more. In addition to changing exhibits produced for the museum's in-house use, traveling exhibits and blockbuster exhibits are effective at bringing the museum to a larger audience and generating new income.

Traveling Exhibits

Traveling exhibits can maximize a museum's research and design efforts and provide a medium for communicating its message to a wider audience. The potential programming opportunities and audience contact traveling exhibits offer are both exciting and unlimited. Some museums send their exhibits around the nation while others focus on their immediate state. Some traveling exhibits may require professional movers, while others can fit in one minivan. They can comprise two-dimensional or three-dimensional objects or a combination of these two elements. Entities like the Smithsonian Institution Traveling Exhibition Service (SITES) and Exhibits USA provide a broad range of temporary exhibitions to museums nationwide—from the high-cost, high-security variety to the inexpensive, low-security. Michigan State University's traveling exhibits primarily stay in the state and are designed to travel to small venues and fit into one minivan.

The income potential for these exhibits is usually enough to supplement some of the costs to produce the actual exhibit. The museum's primary benefits from traveling exhibits are outreach and exposure. The glimpse of a museum's collection may prompt people to visit the museum to see its other holdings.

Blockbuster Exhibits and Other Partnerships

Blockbusters, temporary exhibits that gather "complete bodies of work or comprehensive period surveys in one location are once-in-a-lifetime, spectacular events."[47] These "really big shows" often feature collections seldom assembled together or toured, so they draw record numbers of visitors. Perhaps the first of the modern blockbuster exhibits was the King Tut exhibit organized by the Metropolitan Museum of Art in 1976.[48] Millions of visitors have attended dozens of blockbusters (primarily art exhibitions) since then. Related revenue generated by tourism-related facilities during these exhibitions was in the hundreds of millions of dollars. Many memberships are sold during blockbuster exhibitions, particularly if membership provides a discount on or preferred time for admission.[49] Retaining those members becomes a subsequent challenge.

Blockbuster exhibits are marketed as projects that are mutually beneficial for corporations, museums, and their communities, but they require huge amounts of time, effort, and money. Governments, foundations, and corporate sponsorships are needed to generate the funds to organize or accommodate these types of exhibits. The Albright-Knox Art Gallery in Buffalo, New York, spearheaded "The Summer of Monet" campaign, a major collaborative effort that capitalized on the influx of tourists to Buffalo for the Gallery's special exhibition, *Monet at Giverny: Masterpieces from the Musée Marmottan.* The Gallery brought together leaders from area businesses, foundations, tourism agencies, and New York State. Through a cultural events brochure and an advertising campaign promoting hotel cultural packages, seventy not-for-profit cultural organizations showcased their activities in Erie and Niagara counties. A survey and analysis of the campaign estimated the economic impact on the City of Buffalo at $11.3 million from visitors outside the area. The effort netted the museum a National Museum Service Award from the IMLS in 2000.[50]

Small- and medium-size museums may not have adequate staff resources or space to hold a blockbuster exhibit, but the overall development concept of blockbuster exhibits is available to all museums. Forming relationships and partnerships with the city, businesses, and other private and public community organizations results in many benefits for museums. Joslyn Art Museum in Omaha, Nebraska, worked with a number of corporate and private sponsors to bring in an exhibition by glass artist Dale Chihuly that drew almost 140,000 visitors, a new museum record.

Partnerships with a related community event can mean joint public relations and marketing efforts. In Nebraska, the Lincoln Children's Museum joined forces with the Star City Holiday Parade to make "kids" the parade theme in conjunction with the opening of the museum's new facility; every piece of parade publicity issued an invitation to the new museum. Partnerships can lead to artifact loans, sponsorship, or donations of services or expertise in addition to directly increasing the museum's earned income.

Conclusion

The effectively administered museum will base its development activities, as it will all of its efforts, on the priorities outlined in the museum's strategic plan. A number of options exist through which museums can diversify and expand their financial resources, but this revenue, whether in the form of contributions, bequests, grants, or earned income, can be generated only through lots of good old-fashioned work. Board commitment to "give, get, or get off" sets the tone for active, committed participation in the effort to ensure the museum has the financial resources to fulfill its mission. Other volunteers and staff with a similar belief in the museum's purpose will be needed to follow the lead set by the board and do the legwork to implement development goals.

Given the amount of staff and board time and resources necessary to successfully pursue any of these development strategies, clear direction is essential. While this course is most specifically laid out in a development plan for the museum, that document should be in harmony with and subservient to the museum's overall strategic plan.

Notes

1. Smith 1985, 8.
2. Lord and Lord 2001, 41.
3. Rosso 1996, 120–25.

4. Rosso and Associates 1991, 52.
5. Rosso 1996, 94.
6. American Association of Fund-Raising Counsel Trust for Philanthropy n.d.
7. Kotler and Kotler 1998, 297.
8. Ibid. , 298.
9. *Washington Post* 2001, A24.
10. Kotler and Kotler 1998, 298.
11. Neuborne 1997, 91.
12. Halpert 2001.
13. Neuborne 1997, 94.
14. American Association of Museums n.d.
15. Trenbeth 1986, 2.
16. Bayley 1988, 102.
17. Ibid., 105.
18. Rosso 1996, 48–54.
19. Ibid., 47.
20. Rosso and Associates 1991, 67.
21. Kotler and Kotler 1998, 248–252.
22. Barnes 2002.
23. Wolf 1999, 270.
24. Institute of Museum and Library Services n.d.
25. National Endowment for the Arts n.d.
26. National Endowment for the Humanities n.d.
27. National Science Foundation n.d.
28. Nebraska Arts Council n.d.
29. Nebraska Humanities Council n.d.
30. Lawe 1980, 19.
31. Ibid.
32. NonProfit Gateway n.d.
33. General Services Administration n.d. U. S. Government Printing Office.
34. Foundation Center n.d.
35. Lawe 1980, 25.
36. Ibid., 34–35.
37. Ibid., 83–84.
38. American Association of Museums 1994, 89.
39. Williams 1991, 113.
40. Schwarzer 1999, 45.
41. Gregg 1997, 121.

42. Ibid., 120.
43. Schwarzer 1999, 45.
44. Ibid., 44–45.
45. Roth 1990, 76–77.
46. Ibid.
47. Csaszar 1997, 27.
48. Ibid., 23.
49. Kotler and Kotler 1998, 277.
50. Institute of Museum and Library Services n.d.

CHAPTER SEVEN
PERSONNEL MANAGEMENT

Personnel Policies

The relationship between the museum administration and its staff has a direct impact on a museum's ability to fulfill its mission. "It is vital that efforts be made to create a working environment that is productive, progressive, and respectful of the needs of the individuals as well as the institution," according to Rebecca Buck and Jean Gilmore.[1] From simple statements to grand, leatherette-bound volumes, policies serve to codify specific procedural elements associated with the museum. Collection management policies, codes of professional conduct, and multicultural policies are among the many policies often found in museums. One area of policy that may be neglected, especially in museums with a small staff, is that of personnel.

Simply defined, a policy is a "declared course of action to be taken in the future." A personnel policy is "a series of such declarations about management objectives in relation to employment within the organization."[2] In short, a personnel policy is designed to provide basic guidelines for all levels of museum staff regarding expectations, obligations, and rights within the museum. Through codification, a personnel policy increases institutional productivity and employee performance and morale.

Why Does a Museum Need a Personnel Policy?

Every museum can and should have a set of written personnel policies. A written policy manual ensures uniformity in response and enhances the employees' faith in that uniformity. Personnel policies guide all levels of staff, establishing consistency in operations and enhancing the integrity and credibility of important operational decisions. This type of organizational consistency serves to protect both the museum and its staff.

In addition, a personnel policy clearly explains existing museum policies and practices, which benefits both new and longtime employees by increasing the clarity of museum policies, reducing dependence on specific individuals, and encouraging more consistent managerial behavior. Policies also allow employees to know their circumstances, and policies act as a response to legal and other external pressures. Development of a personnel policy also aids the museum by forcing it to ask itself basic questions about external laws, delegation of authority, reporting lines, grievance procedures, criteria for disciplinary action or dismissal, and institutional planning.[3]

Policy Development: Where to Begin

Who is responsible for writing the personnel policy? It is recommended that only one person—a member of management with human resources training—be given the task. This person's work should then be reviewed by a committee composed of board, management, and staff representatives who will suggest changes and approve the final draft. This draft should be forwarded to the director and finally to the board for its approval. The comprehensiveness and scope of the personnel policy ought to be determined by the needs and resources of the institution and its employees.

There are a variety of sources and issues a museum should consider when drafting a personnel policy. Other museums, libraries, state and federal agencies, and academic institutions may provide useful models. Suggestions may come from querying legal counsel, insurance personnel, and financial advisors. Professional consultants specializing in personnel matters are usually expensive and necessary only under limited circumstances or in large, complex museums. Because no one knows a museum better than its own staff members, typically it is advisable to generate the policy internally so that it can be tailored to meet specific needs. Additionally, personnel manuals are useful only if they are kept current. The museum director should review the manual at least annually, and the manual should be in a loose-leaf format or available through the museum's website so that it may be easily changed.[4]

An effectively communicated personnel policy is created by identifying the topic, selling the idea, determining the key features, and incorporating the details.[5] Generally, a simple writing style is preferred. Long, complex sentences should be broken up and unneeded words eliminated. Vocabulary should be easily understood or clearly defined, and the policy should be written to communicate ideas. Rules should be stated in a positive manner, and reasons for restrictions should be supplied. Helping the staff understand why rules are necessary makes compliance more palatable and, therefore, more likely to occur.

Policy Development: What to Include

Deciding exactly what information should be included in the personnel policy can be a daunting task. A personnel policy should be comprehensive enough to address typical policy questions without attempting to answer *all* possible policy questions, many of which are more effectively handled on an individual basis. Any potential problem areas should be included in the policy. Existing or desired day-to-day practices, such as work hours, vacation time, and sick leave, should be addressed. Background information on the museum, general advice, and information associated with the workings of the facility itself also may be addressed.

With the exception of the grievance system and other essential elements, policies should provide guidelines or standards for decision making, but not the procedures that specify how action is to be taken. Some elements that might be addressed are initial job probationary period, attendance policies, conduct issues, treatment of patrons, accommodations for the disabled, discounts, discipline, performance reviews, telephone and electronic mail use, and theft.[6] A commitment to employee safety also should be evinced. Following standards set by OSHA (Occupational Safety and Health Administration) will demonstrate the museum's dedication to safety in the workplace. Other potential areas may include museum principles, staffing and development practices, the network for employee relations, conditions of employment, and an equality of opportunity statement. For legal reasons, a museum should include policies governing holidays, jury duty, military leave, maternity-paternity leave, retirement, harassment, and worker's compensation. The policy should be clear on expectations for working hours and workdays, pay differential for night or weekend work, rate of accumulation of sick and vacation days, and scheduling of vacations. Procedures and timing for annual staff evaluations should be described. Clearly defined expectations for each staff member must be established annually as part of the performance evaluation. Finally, an effective personnel policy also will discuss conflict-of-interest policies and termination and grievance procedures.[7]

Volunteers: A Unique Consideration

Because volunteers are such an integral part of a museum's survival and daily operations, it is vital to consider them whenever personnel policy issues are addressed. Volunteers should be treated as formally as paid staff members. If the same level of commitment is expected of them and the same degree of respect is accorded them, outstanding volunteer contributions can result. Because certain personnel policy issues (such as paid holidays and salary benefits) do not apply to volunteers, it is advisable to create a separate volunteer manual that is distributed during volunteer training. This might include a welcoming statement, the museum mission statement, a museum overview, a museum fact sheet, a description of rewards and benefits, a calendar of volunteer activities, job descriptions, grievance procedures, and a code of professional standards.[8] It also is critical to note (with regard to performance and grievance procedures) that volunteers who are dismissed may be subject to the same legal protections as paid staff. Evidence supporting the termination must be presented, and the volunteer must be given the opportunity to appeal the dismissal decision.[9]

Job Descriptions

A good personnel policy will include employee job descriptions. "Each museum should have staff positions and job descriptions appropriate to the needs and financial resources of that institution," according to G. Ellis Burcaw[10] in his *Introduction to Museum Work.* As a museum's mission changes and develops, so should its job descriptions. Staff input should be considered when writing job descriptions. A job description should include a general description of the position, the employee's supervisor, whom the employee will supervise, and a list of the employee's specific responsibilities and functions. More specific details, such as the percentage of time an employee will be expected to devote to each function, should be itemized in individual performance plans.

Implementation

Even the most well-written personnel policy is ineffective if it is not successfully implemented and enforced. Once the final draft is approved, a responsible museum organization will publicize the personnel materials through mass distribution in either written or electronic format, explain the procedures, monitor staff and employee feedback and compliance, and modify the original policy as necessary. In fact, training, distribution, and maintenance are three of the most critical components of policy implementation.[11] Personnel policies will not be effective without a commitment to both the policy itself and the measures required to make it work.

Drafting and implementing a personnel policy is a critical and challenging task. Part of the difficulty lies in the fact that the policy seems to spill into so many different areas—staffing structures, recruitment, and performance evaluation to name only a few. However, personnel policies protect not only the organization but also the staff. An effective personnel policy will be adaptable to meet the changing needs of the museum and staff. The museum will benefit from satisfied employees who will then focus their full attention on fulfilling the museum's mission. Without the hard work and dedication of personnel, after all, a museum is just a building.

Performance Evaluation

Probationary Period

Each new employee of a museum should expect to serve an initial probationary period of three to six months. This period gives both the museum and the employee an opportunity to see if they are well matched. During the probationary period, the employee should be closely supervised. This is a time to introduce the new employee to the museum and build his or her loyalty to the institution and its staff. This also is the time to address any problems that the manager observes before the employee becomes a permanent member of the museum staff.[12]

At the end of the probationary period, the employee may become a permanent member of the museum staff, or the probationary period may be extended. During the initial probationary period, management may terminate an employee at any time without stating reasons or going through a long documentation process. It is advisable for the manager to document the reasons for his or her actions, but these should be kept only to defend his or her action if a later challenge should occur. If the probationary period is extended, the justification and the time period for the extension should be presented to the employee in writing. The desired outcomes should be explicitly stated in the letter and thoroughly discussed with the employee.[13]

Annual Evaluation

One of the more anxiety-producing aspects of a person's employment can be the performance appraisal, a periodic evaluation of job performance. Ask managers which of their duties make them the most uncomfortable and they most probably will mention the formal assessment of employees. Conversely, ask employees which part of their job they like the least, and most probably they will mention the formal examination of their work performance by their supervisor.[14] What exactly is performance appraisal, and why does it have such a negative reputation? How might museums implement an appraisal system so that managers and employees view it in a positive light?

A performance appraisal is broadly defined by Gary Latham and Kenneth Wexley as "any personnel decision that affects the status of employees regarding their retention, termination, promotion, demotion, transfer, salary increase or decrease, or admission into a training program."[15] Periodically evaluating employees' job performance not only serves as an audit of their overall effectiveness for the organization; it also gives employees formal feedback on how well they are doing their job, which can energize and motivate them to increase their level of performance. Periodic reviews also offer opportunities for management to establish or modify goals for individual employees in light of objectives in the strategic plan and to "specify what the employee must start doing, continue doing, or stop doing"[16] to be a success within the organization. After the initial probationary period, these performance evaluations are usually done on an annual basis either at a fixed time during the year, such as the end of the fiscal or calendar year, or on the anniversary of the employee's hiring.

Many intrinsic problems and errors can exist with the typical performance appraisal methodology. These often center on the personal biases of the manager doing the rating and other subjective factors. Regardless of any manager's good-faith efforts to undertake a fair and impartial evaluation of his or her employees, several psychological errors in judgment can enter into the appraisal process.

Perhaps the most common appraisal error is "contrast effect," which is the tendency of the evaluator to rate an employee in comparison to other employees rather than against established job standards and requirements. "Recency effect" is probably the next most common error. This happens when the evaluator's rating is influenced more by recent minor events involving the employee than by major events occurring many months previous. Other appraisal errors include "first impression error" (the persistence of an initial positive or negative judgment), "halo-horns effect" (inappropriate generalization of one incident to all performance), and "similar-to-me effect" (the tendency of managers to give people who resemble themselves a higher rating than they give others).[17]

Many managers tend to rate their employees in the middle of the scale even when actual job performance merits a much higher or lower rating. This error is called "central tendency." The ratings also can suffer from negative or positive skews. In these situations, a manager rates everyone much higher or lower than their actual job performance warrants. Positive skew ("everyone is performing at the highest level possible") and negative skew ("I have very high performance standards and my staff simply does not measure up") offer little constructive feedback and render the evaluation process ineffective.[18]

Other problems include attribution bias and stereotyping. Attribution bias is a manager's tendency to ascribe performance failings to factors under the employee's control, while linking performance successes to causes outside the control of the employee. An evaluator who makes sweeping generalizations about entire groups of employees and ignores differences among individuals is stereotyping.[19]

The appraisal tendency that can have the most damaging effect on an organization's work effectiveness is leniency, positive or negative. A manager who is unfairly tough on his or her employees at appraisal time shows negative leniency. No matter how well the employees perform their assigned tasks, it is never good enough to suit this type of manager. On the other hand, a manager who is unfairly easy on his or her employees in their appraisals displays positive leniency. No matter how poorly the employees perform their assigned tasks, their manager never rebukes or corrects them adequately, leading to unwarranted expectations where raises, new job assignments, and promotions are concerned. Both positive and negative leniency can lead employees to cut back the amount of work they perform and can lower the effectiveness of the entire group. Surveys have shown that employees do not like managers who are unfairly tough, nor do they respect managers who are too lenient.[20]

The quest for a functional and effective process for measuring and assessing employee work performance goes on, due to the extreme importance of proper management and maximization of human resources. Organizations utilize performance appraisal data for determining employee salaries, giving motivational feedback, highlighting individual strengths and weaknesses, and documenting personnel decisions. Performance appraisal data also are used to recognize individual performance, assist in goal setting, make promotion decisions, determine retention or termination of employees, and evaluate goal achievement.[21]

How should such a performance evaluation system be implemented? What steps should a wise museum director take to make sure such a system works to the benefit of the museum? First, the strategic plan and mission must already be established before any assessment of individual employee performance can be made. The institutional strategic plan and mission must be articulated to all employees because the strategic plan will drive the establishment of goals for each individual employee. No appraisal should be performed until the institutional context for it has been established. The ideal performance appraisal-management cycle involves a continuous, five-phase process: planning, execution, assessment, review, and renewal. In the first phase, the manager and employee meet to devise the work plan for the next evaluation period, usually a year. They must come to agreement on two things—the objectives the employee will work to achieve and the ways the employee will go about achieving them. After this "what" and "how" of the plan have been determined, the execution phase of the cycle can proceed. In this phase, the actual work gets done: the employee goes about the job from day to day, and the manager observes, coaches, mentors, guides, and provides feedback as needed.[22]

After the execution period has run its course, a formal assessment is undertaken, during which the employee's work results are compared to the objectives originally set. This management "report card" is reviewed in a meeting between the manager and the subordinate. They discuss the results achieved, overall job performance, and the progress of the employee's development. Any salary or compensation changes can be discussed at this meeting but are probably best deferred to another meeting. The results are passed up to the next level of management for review and approval. Finally, the whole process is renewed: goals are set anew, based on the museum's strategic plans for the next year.

Good management practices will help keep the appraisal system above reproach and minimize the danger from possible legal challenges. Performance appraisals should be based on analysis of job requirements and mutually agreed-upon goals, and performance should be defined and supported by documented, objective evidence. The process should be kept as simple and straightforward as possible, constant monitoring and auditing for discrimination should take place, and evaluators should be trained to assess performance accurately. An open, nonsecretive environment should be encouraged, but the employee's right to privacy should be protected. Upper-level management should review appraisal results before they are discussed with the employee, and employees should be able to present a written response to appraisals they feel are unfair. Many computer software applications are available to help managers gather and administer the wealth of data produced by performance appraisal-management systems.[23]

Termination Procedure

Termination of an employee is often an under-used management tool in nonprofit organizations. It is a difficult process because of the litigious times in which we live. It is critical that the reasons for termination and the termination process be written out in considerable detail. The reasons for termination will vary from museum to museum but will include such things as nonperformance of duties, insubordination, theft, commission of a felony, sexual harassment, conflict of interest, and inappropriate behavior toward visitors. Some of these offenses, such as theft from the collection or commission of a felony, can lead to immediate termination.

Other issues, such as nonperformance of duties and insubordination, require thorough documentation and attempts at corrective measures before termination can be justified.[24]

Documentation of noncompliance with the museum's rules usually begins with verbal reprimands. Although a reprimand should involve only a discussion with the employee, managers should record the event on their personal calendar. Managers must not be obscure about the problem or the appropriate remedy for it. It is very important that the employee leave the meeting with a very clear picture of the manager's expectations. There is no magic number of verbal warnings that should be given before taking stronger measures. It is hoped that a verbal warning or two will correct the problem and no other action will be needed.

If a problem with an employee continues, the next appropriate action is a written warning. Written warnings should follow the same format as verbal warnings—a clear statement of the problem and specific statements of the corrective behavior that is expected. Copies of warnings should be given to the manager's supervisor. As with verbal warnings, no set number of written warnings must be given before a manager moves to the next step toward termination; the severity of the problem and its rate of occurrence will help determine the number.[25]

By the time probation is being considered for the employee, the museum director certainly will want to become involved. The museum's human resources staff and legal counsel (if the museum is large enough to have them) also may be involved. Even at a small museum, the board president should be informed of what is occurring, and the temporary services of a lawyer should be engaged to advise on the further steps. Generally, the employee will be placed on probation for a specific length of time. The amount of time must be sufficient to allow the employee to demonstrate that he or she has solved the difficulty, but the time should not be so long as to allow significant further damage to the museum's programs if the corrective measures are not taken. Generally a period of three to six months is chosen, but the museum should reserve the right to move to termination at any point if the problem worsens. The conditions of the probation should be clearly defined in writing, along with the reasons for the probation, its length, and the expected outcomes if the probation is to be lifted. A third party, such as the museum director or a human resources

Box 7.1

Case Study: Contrary Mary

Mary Jarden has worked as a nursery assistant at the Ajo Public Garden and Arboretum for the past twenty years. She has worked for the current curator, Jack Flowers, for eight years. Mary had a reputation as a hard-working and dependable employee until about three years ago. Since then, her performance has slowly deteriorated, and she has become a very difficult employee. Jack's annual evaluations for Mary have reflected this deterioration, and the evaluations have affected her salary increases. The situation has gotten so bad in the last three months that Jack has given Mary what he considered to be two verbal warnings. Mary missed two days of work last week without giving prior notice or calling in. Jack is seriously considering giving Mary a written warning for absenteeism.

On Saturday morning Jack is reading the local *Ajo Times-Herald* with his wife, Jill. Jack notices a short article on page three of the newspaper about a local man who was arrested on Friday night for spousal abuse. The names catch his eye—Hansel and Mary Jarden. Jack points out the article to Jill, who says "Oh yes, you remember Jack, Mary's second husband. They got married five or six years ago, and I had heard they were having problems." A light comes on in Jack's head, and the last several years' work problems come into focus.

Mary does not come to work until Thursday of the following week and has not called in. When Jack inquires about her whereabouts for the last three days, his overtures are quickly rebuffed in a very gruff manner. In a month, the work situation has only gotten worse, and Mary has missed two more unexcused days. Jack discovers four South African succulents have died because of neglect, and Jack knows the plants were Mary's responsibility. These are prized plants that were received only three months earlier at some considerable expense.

What would your advice to Jack be? Will you discuss Mary's personal problems with her? Outline a course of action for dealing with Mary. What can be done to bring Mary back to being a model employee? Have Jack's actions been consistent? Has he given Mary all of the appropriate supervisory signals? Should Jack bring a third party into this situation?

staff member, should be present at the probationary meeting to be certain that it runs smoothly and that all communications are clear.

If at the end of the probationary period the problem still exists, it is time to move to termination. This should be done immediately, with no additional work time allowed for the employee being terminated. The termination should be presented in writing. The termination letter should briefly state the reasons for termination and little else. Be certain that the meaning of the letter is absolutely clear. A final meeting should be held within a week, if the employee wishes, for reconsideration of the termination action. At this meeting, the employee may present in writing any facts believed relevant to the work and the termination and ask for the termination to be reconsidered. If there do not seem to be any compelling reasons to withdraw the termination, it should stand without further action.

The director of the museum and the supervisor should be fully aware of the impact the termination of an employee will have on other employees of the museum. There will often be a general negative feeling among the staff members. Staff members may wonder if they will be the next to be terminated. Insecurity will run high. The director can help alleviate some of these problems by being as open as possible within the restrictions of confidentiality of personnel actions. The director can be available and can visit various departments, reassuring staff members. Ultimately the museum, and perhaps even the terminated employee, will benefit from having brought the personnel action to the appropriate conclusion.

Notes

1. Buck and Gilmore 1998, 211.
2. Torrington and Hall 1987, 29–34.
3. Miller 1980, 2–3, 58, 87.
4. Lawson 1969.
5. Torrington and Hall 1987.
6. Miller 1980, 3, 40–44, 77–82, 123, 133, 160–162.
7. Berstein 2000, 71, 111, 117, 191; Wolf 1990, 94, 100, 109.
8. Condrey 1998, 508–509.
9. Kuyper et al. 1993, 89.
10. Burcaw 1997, 51.
11. Lawson 1969.
12. Lawson 1969; Miller 1980, 29–30.
13. Lawson 1969.
14. Landy and Farr 1983.
15. Latham and Wexley 1981, 4.
16. Ibid.
17. Condrey 1998, 382; Landy and Farr 1983, 76–77; Latham and Wexley 1981, 100–102.
18. Landy and Farr 1983, 77.

19. Condrey 1998; Landy and Farr 1983.
20. Landy and Farr 1983, 77; Latham and Wexley 1981, 104.
21. Condrey 1998, 368–370; Landy and Farr 1983, 3–4.
22. Wolf 1990.
23. Grote 1996, 352–356.
24. Landy and Farr 1983, 201.
25. Lawson 1969.

CHAPTER EIGHT
COLLECTION MANAGEMENT POLICIES

A museum exists because of its collections. The collections not only give the museum its character but also define the purpose of the museum. It is therefore important for a museum to manage its collections as effectively as possible while preserving the collection for long-term use and staying true to its mission and its public trust. All museums need a well-articulated collection management policy that is understood by the governing board, staff, and volunteers. This policy defines goals for the development and use of the collection and prepares the museum to face controversial or unexpected eventualities such as deaccessioning or a disaster endangering the collection.

Communication is important in drafting a collection management policy. Both staff and board need to agree on all areas of the policy. Although it cannot solve all potential problems, the policy will, according to Marie Malaro, "define areas of responsibility and set forth guidelines for those charged with making certain decisions. . . . completed policy should be approved by the board . . . and once in effect, the policy should serve as formal delegation of responsibilities."[1] Each museum needs to draw from its own history and the needs of its collections to begin drafting its collection policy. The size and scope of a museum's collections will determine the length and complexity of this policy.

There are eight issues that should be covered by all comprehensive collection management policies:

- Collection Mission and Scope
- Acquisitions and Accession
- Cataloging, Inventories, and Records
- Loans

- Care of the Collection
- Collection Access
- Insurance
- Deaccession

Collection Mission and Scope

The collection's mission statement should state the present and future scope of the collection, its uses, and its needs for support.[2] Any statutes or legal documents important to the establishment of the museum and maintenance of the collection can be explained in this section. The roles of the board, committees, and staff involved in collection procedures should be explained, along with the different types of collections and how they are handled.

There are several important points to consider in defining a statement of purpose:

- The focus of the collection: discipline; geography; time period; artists, persons, groups of people, or cultures; types or sizes of objects; research; and interpretation
- The portions of staff time and museum resources devoted to collecting and collection care
- The state and size of the collection and the resources required to support them (record keeping, storage, management, conservation, security, and exhibits)

Acquisition and Accession

Acquisition is the process of legally obtaining objects and their associated data for a museum through gifts, purchases, exchanges, transfers, and field collecting. Acquisition and accessioning are interrelated and should be thoughtful processes that are addressed as such in a museum's acquisition policy. Before accepting objects, the museum needs to study the question of "title," or ownership, and to avoid stolen objects, improperly excavated (illegally removed) materials from archaeological or paleontological sites, and specimens taken in violation of state, national, or international laws.

A museum's collecting scope should define the types of objects to acquire—their sources, time periods, and geographic origins. Museums such as natural history museums may need to add and define other issues, such as geological ages, geographic area, taxonomic groups, and cultural representation.

Criteria

The scope of a museum's collection can be defined by considering its mission statement, which will in turn guide a museum to acquire objects selectively.[3] See box 8.1 for a discussion of ethical problems that might

Box 8.1

Case Review: Inappropriate Acquisitions

Most museum professionals recognize that acquisitions beyond the scope of the missions of their institutions are not appropriate, but some items that fall within the museum's mission also can prove to be inappropriate. The acquisition of Native American ancestral remains and the associated burial goods by museums was at one time considered to be appropriate. By the 1980s, however, public opinion had rallied against the practice, and the resulting legislative changes took place faster than could the ethical and scientific debate within the museum community. Museums now have the Native American Grave Protection and Repatriation Act of 1990 to answer any remaining questions and to guide their conduct in this area.

In another ethical issue of inappropriate holdings in collections, the Smithsonian Institution found that its National Anthropological Archives had nude photographs of students from the Ivy League and Seven Sisters schools, taken as part of an anthropometric study by W. H. Sheldon from the 1940s through the 1960s. Changes in standards for studies involving human subjects, a discredited "scientific" basis for the study, and significant pressures by politically and economically powerful individuals depicted in the so-called posture photographs resulted in the collection being first sealed and then destroyed by the Smithsonian.

It should be clear that no amount of laws or rules of conduct will cover every situation and that an ethical conscience will serve as an excellent guide to members of the museum profession.

Source: "The great Ivy League nude posture photo scandal" by R. Rosenbaum. *The New York Times Magazine*, January 15, 1995 (section 6): 26–31, 40, 46, 55–56.

arise when a museum acquires objects that may be beyond its collecting scope.

Another consideration is whether or not the museum has the resources to care for an object for the long term. The cost to the museum must be weighed against the potential benefit of acquiring the object. Costs that a museum should consider include space, staff time for processing and managing the object, overhead (utilities, storage equipment, housekeeping, and other administrative costs), conservation, and insurance.[4] Even if part of this expense is donated, all costs still need to be considered. Criteria used by the Nebraska State Historical Society to guide its acquisitions are described in box 8.2.

Legal Considerations

An acquisition policy should state that the museum will not violate any local, state, federal, or international laws, treatises, conventions, or regulations.[5] These laws include copyright protection and the Artists Rights Act, Endangered Species Act, Marine Mammal Act, Migratory Bird Treaty Act, American Eagle Protection Act, Lacey Act, Archaeological Resources Protection Act of 1979, Native American Graves Protection and Repatriation Act, Convention on International Trade in

Box 8.2

Acquisition Criteria: Nebraska State Historical Society

- The donor must have clear and legal title.
- If material is for sale, funding must be available.
- The Society must have resources to properly care for the proposed acquisition.
- Materials must have significance to Nebraska history.
- Provenance of the materials should be documented.
- All moral, legal, and ethical implications of the acquisition must have been considered and resolved.
- Acquisition should occur without donor restrictions. Restrictions or conditions may be considered when in the best interest of the Society's fulfillment of its mission. Use and disposition will be at the discretion of the Society unless otherwise specified.
- The acquisition of material must conform to the Society's collections policies.

Endangered Species, 1970 UNESCO Convention, Unidroit Convention, and Hague Convention, among others.[6] The policy also should require the donor to have acquired and possessed the objects legally and ethically. The museum must determine that no archaeological sites, historic sites, natural habitats, or populations were damaged when the object was acquired.

Museums should, under normal circumstances, accept only unencumbered objects—unless their acquisition is in the long-term interest of the museum. The policy needs to have procedures that evaluate encumbrances. Ownership is an important issue to be addressed because if the donor does not have clear title to the object, the museum cannot be positive the object has not been stolen or illegally acquired. If clear title or the right to transfer ownership cannot be established, the museum should not accept the object. Donor restrictions, artist rights, and copyrights must be investigated. The museum must understand what rights it is acquiring and must obtain proper documentation of its rights.

Once a donor's ownership has been verified, a museum obtains clear and complete title by having the donor sign a deed of gift. This document should state that the donor is not putting any restrictions on the object, that he or she legally owns the object, and he or she is transferring ownership to the museum.[7]

Ethical Considerations

Museums also must follow Internal Revenue Service regulations regarding appraisals for tax deductions, which require that third-party appraisals be conducted on acquisitions. It is the responsibility of the donor to have this appraisal performed. Museum employees should not conduct appraisals or refer donors to specific appraisers.

As a general rule, objects outside of the mission of the museum should not be accepted unless they are destined for particular use in the near future, but in some cases an object may be accepted for the sole purpose of exchanging it or putting it up for auction. Art museums do this frequently, and it is not unethical as long as it is done in a forthright manner and the policies of the museum allow such an acquisition.

While museums need to try to acquire objects that fulfill the breadth and depth of their mission and the scope of the collection, they also must be selective. Once an object is accessioned, the museum has a responsibility to properly document, store, conserve, and maintain it. A museum that accepts all objects whether it intends to keep them or not risks losing the trust of the public. Such activities tend to fuel the contention of the U.S. Financial Accounting Standards Board (FASB) that collection materials are assets and should be accounted for as such on financial forms.

Delegation of Authority

The authority to accept objects for the collection lies with the board of trustees or their counterpart, but this authority may be delegated to others. The others may vary from one museum to another, but in most cases the director, curator, or collection committee has the authority.

Accessioning

An acquisition policy needs to include procedures for accessioning. *Accessioning* is the process of entering objects and their proper documentation into the possession of the museum. Not all acquisitions must be accessioned.[8] Accessioning procedures state what records must be completed, where they are stored, and who maintains the records. Each museum has its own record-keeping system, but in most cases a donor file and an accession record are completed. The donor file includes information about the donors and any correspondence with them, whereas an accession file may include a brief description of the object or series of objects obtained from a single source, photographs, collecting permits, and any information available about the objects. The file may contain condition reports and provenance, as well as the donor or collector information.

Objects added to the collections need to be assigned an accession number. The accession record is the museum's legal record of taking possession of and title to an object. All documents pertaining to an object or group of objects need to have the accession number placed on them.[9] Museums develop their own numbering systems, so it is important to provide specific directions on how an object should be numbered. The methods used to label objects should be placed in the collection management policy because the accession record is the museum's legal record of taking possession and title to an object. It is important to have all documents signed and dated.

Cataloging, Inventories, and Records

Cataloging

Cataloging is the creation of a full collection record. The record will contain full descriptive detail about the object, assembly, or lot, cross-referenced to other records and files, such as accession records and donor files. A catalog number is placed on the object associating the record and the object. Catalog data may be recorded on cards, sheets, ledgers, or computerized databases such as FileMaker Pro, Microsoft Access, Microsoft Excel, Quattro Pro, Lotus 1–2–3, PastPerfect, Paradox, Argus, Encoded Archival Description, Re:Discovery, MultiMimsy, or GalleryPro.

Because the catalog file is used when working with and inventorying the collection, it is sometimes called the *working record.* Most museums give each object both a catalog number and an accession number for record-keeping purposes. From the information given on the catalog record, anyone should be able to locate the object, know what it looks like, and find related records or files. Often objects of high monetary value are photographed to document the condition, color, and appearance of the object. Digital images of objects can be incorporated into electronic cataloging systems.

Inventories

Museums need to establish uniform methods to inventory the objects in the collection and their records. Comprehensive and spot-check inventories should be undertaken routinely. A comprehensive inventory locates all objects in the collection and reviews the records to make sure all documents are present and in good order. Because most museums have large collections, there is usually not enough time, staff, or money to take a comprehensive inventory every year, so it is normally done every five to ten years. A spot-check inventory, on the other hand, can be taken more often because it entails finding randomly selected objects in the collection and checking their records. Inventories allow the museum to track the status of objects and their records in the collections. If any objects are missing, they can be located or reported as missing to the proper authorities. The curator, collection manager, or registrar is responsible for completing inventories.

Records

Three other types of records need to be mentioned—photographs, condition reports, and conservation reports. Other records, such as collecting permits and field or collection notes, used mainly in natural history or archaeological collections, need to be stored by individual museums according to the requirements stated in their collection policy. The same

Box 8.3

Inventory: Stan Hywet Hall and Gardens

Stan Hywet Hall and Gardens conducts scheduled inventories of all collections in its care and custody. The curator of collections conducts or directs all inventorying efforts.

Frequency

General inventories of objects on exhibit in museum rooms are made on a yearly basis. Spot inventories are made periodically by museum personnel to ensure control of the inventory of objects within the museum. General inventories of objects housed in storage facilities are scheduled every five to seven years at the discretion of the curator of collections. Spot inventories of these areas are conducted periodically during this span of years.

Method

Manual inventories are taken according to location status. Collections on exhibition are inventoried by museum room, and collections in storage are inventoried by storage room or area, and by bin, rack, and shelf within the storage area. Location inventories will record each object by accession number and object name and will record any remarks or changes in present condition of that object. Verification of inventory findings is conducted after the manual inventory has been completed. When in the course of an inventory an object is discovered to be missing or misplaced, every effort will be made immediately to locate the object through physical inspection of cataloging and processing areas, research, exhibitions, and other appropriate areas.

Source: *Stan Hywet Hall and Gardens* by I. Adams, B. Taxel, and S. Love. Akron, OH: University of Akron Press, 2000.

is true for historical documentation of items, such as archival materials or other paper documents.[10]

Photographs

Photographs can document the condition of an object and give a visual description of it. Most museums take photographs of each object when it is accessioned, and these photographs are placed with the accession file. For condition and conservation reports, photographs show more detail, including all sides of the object and close-ups of specific parts of the object. Because of the expense, photographs are normally taken only of particularly valuable or vulnerable objects, but with the developing digital technology, costs may no longer be a limitation.[11]

Computers allow us to capture a digital image of any printed picture, manipulate pictures, and enhance otherwise poor pictures. Photographs can be taken economically with charge-coupled device (CCD) cameras, and photographs can be downloaded and transferred to a computer to print or store on floppy disks or CD-ROMs. Existing pictures can be captured using standard commercially available scanners and appropriate software such as Abode Illustrator. The chief advantage of digital images is the ease with which they can be moved into databases and stored on such media as CD-ROM. Image formats currently standard on computers (for example, BMP, JPEG, GIF, and TIFF) can facilitate exchange of information via the Internet.[12]

Condition Reports

Condition reports need to be created for any valuable or vulnerable incoming museum objects whether they are new acquisitions, incoming loans, or returning loans. These reports allow the museum to note any damage. Condition reports also protect the museum from liability for damage already present on loaned or borrowed objects. Most condition reports include a name and description of the object, the examiner, the dates it was examined, a description of any physical, chemical, or biological damage, and any potential damage to the object. Photographic documentation should be included in condition reports.

Conservation Reports

Any time an object is altered by the general staff or a conservator, the work should be documented using a conservation report. This report should include the condition of the object, recommended storage, how the object should be and was repaired, information on how cleaning was undertaken, and any other important observations about what was done to the object. This information should be kept in the accession or catalog file.

Loans

Even with the largest collections, a museum may have inadequate objects for an exhibit or for research study and will decide to borrow other objects from a private individual or another institution. Objects may also be received on loan for conservation or research purposes. Whether the loan is incoming or outgoing, a clear loan policy and a loan agreement document stating the rules and procedures for loans will eliminate any potential problems.[13]

Incoming Loans

A museum should never accept a loan without a written contract that clearly states the rights and responsibilities of each party. Each incoming loan should have an agreement that covers specific issues such as insurance, loan conditions, care and use of objects, duration of the loan, the dates and method for returning the loan, and proper packing methods.

In most cases, it is advantageous to have the loan insured because insurance can resolve the lender's claims and protects the museum from possible liability. The borrowing museum may carry the insurance, the lending museum may, or the insurance may be waived. A certificate of insurance should be part of the loan agreement.[14] The lender should provide a value for the object based on fair market value, or in the case of field-collected specimens, the value can be based on the replacement cost.

Borrowing objects is a great responsibility, and therefore only certain persons should be allowed to request a loan. Usually the director or board of trustees must give final approval for a loan request, but in some types of museums, such as natural science museums, the curator has the authority to make requests. Once the loan has been requested, authority needs to be given to a registrar or curator to receive, open, inspect the loan, and keep all records. It is also important to specify who within the lender museum should be notified in case of damage. One person needs to be responsible for notifying the insurance company of damage and negotiating a settlement.

The reasons museums request loans vary. A museum needs to state clearly in its collection policies the purposes for which it will request a loan, whether for exhibition, research, education, or photography. Loans need to comply with international, federal, state, and local regulations concerning wildlife specimens and the Native American Graves Protection and Repatriation Act (NAGPRA), among others.

How the object can be used and any special care it requires should be detailed in the loan agreement, which can cover anything from photography to the wording of the credit line on the exhibit labels. Any intent to photograph or reproduce the object for cataloging, educational, or publicity purposes needs to be stated, along with any fumigation or examination the borrower may wish or be required to do. The requesting museum also should state that it will not repair or restore any object without the written permission of the lender and the employment of a conservator with appropriate expertise. The transportation method and expense responsibility for a loan need to be specified in the agreement. The lender should provide the borrower with instructions on repacking the object for return.[15]

The length of the loan needs to be clearly stated, with the provision that the borrower may terminate the loan at any time. The usual length of a loan is six months; long-term loans vary in length but usually do not exceed three years. Provisions for returning a loan need to be stated clearly, with specific dates for pickup or shipping. If the loaned object is to be returned to the lender by the borrower, written notification of the object's return should be given to the lender. When the object is successfully returned, a return receipt should be signed by the lender and returned.[16]

Outgoing Loans

Outgoing loans are similar to incoming loans, with the roles reversed. Generally, a museum will not lend to an individual, because its collection is for public, not private, use. Most museums will request that the object be maintained in the same environmental conditions as at its home institution, which individuals normally cannot provide. Most museums will make loans only to similar educational or nonprofit organizations. Generally, the authority to approve loans is given to the governing board, but in larger museums, the professional staff or director may be able to approve loans of objects of a certain value or class. It is best to set a definite loan period and state who is responsible for returning the object.[17] It is important for the lending museum to assign a person, usually a registrar in larger museums, to monitor outgoing loans and their termination dates so there is no question about the return of the object.

Objects Left in the Temporary Custody of the Museum

In some cases, such as conservation, identification, or study, objects are left in the temporary care of the museum. When this occurs, a temporary custody receipt should be signed. It is important to outline a way of monitoring these materials and a way for them to be processed expeditiously. Documentation needs to be permanently retained for objects under temporary custody just as for other loaned or accessioned objects.

Many states have passed laws regarding unclaimed loans and undocumented collections. In general, these laws state that after the objects have been abandoned by the owner and left in the care of the museum for a specific period of time (usually five to seven years), the museum may, with proper notification (usually a public notice published in certain newspapers), claim the object as a donation. In Nebraska, for example, under the Museum Property Act, if the object has not been claimed after seven years, the lender must be notified by certified mail or, if an address is not known, a public notice must be placed in a widely circulating newspaper. This notice must be published once a week for three weeks; if the object still is not claimed after a three-year waiting period from the date of notification, the museum legally owns the object. All paperwork must be kept for at least twenty-five years. Most state laws treat undocumented collections in a similar manner.

Long-Term or Permanent Loans

There are no standard definitions for the terms "long-term" and "permanent" loans, but as used here, long-term loans are those made for an extended, but specific, period of time (up to five to ten years), whereas objects on permanent loan are for the use of the holding museum as long as it desires. In permanent loans, the original museum or owner has not relinquished title, so the object must be returned when the holding museum no longer has a use for the object. Although some museums will not accept long-term or permanent loans, others will take them under specific circumstances. Museums avoid these arrangements because they involve the expense of storing and taking responsibility for objects that belong to other organizations or individuals and because of the cumbersome record keeping. Long-term loans may involve the lending of one or a few objects that are needed by an institution for a long-term temporary exhibit. Museums, when they have duplicates of objects, may choose to make such loans to assist another museum's programs. Some examples of permanent loans to museums are those made by the U.S. Fish and Wildlife Service of preserved specimens of endangered species, such as sea otters and whooping cranes. These are given to the museums for their collections and use, but the Service retains title, and the agency's catalog numbers must be maintained on the specimens along with the museum's catalog number. The Service audits the specimens on an irregular schedule.

Care of the Collection

All museums are responsible for providing care for their collections as well as for the health and safety of their staff and visitors. Each museum should tailor its collection management plans to fit its own collections and situation. Issues involving emergency preparedness, integrated pest management, and health and safety will be important parts of any collection management plan; however, because these issues extend beyond collection areas in the museum, they are covered in the next chapter, "Facilities Management." Only a brief discussion of the important issues for preventive conservation are covered here.[18]

Preventive conservation is an emerging field that is concerned with the condition of the overall collection rather than the condition of individual objects. Primary emphasis is placed on environmental and storage conditions. Topics that can be included within preventive conservation are environmental monitoring,[19] climate control, design of storage equipment,[20] use of inert storage materials,[21] building construction, facilities management, security systems, fire protection, emergency preparedness, integrated pest management, fluid preservatives,[22] storage supplies,[23] and health and safety issues.[24] Personnel involved in collections care need to be thoroughly familiar with the latest developments in the rapidly evolving field of preventive conservation.

Temperature and relative humidity are the two most important environmental conditions for museum collections and should be monitored at all times. Because temperature has a direct effect on relative humidity and is more easily controlled, achieving a stable collection storage temperature in the range of 66° to 72° Fahrenheit (19° to 22° Celsius) should be a museum's first priority. Stability in relative humidity (RH) is more difficult to achieve, but it is critical because high RH (greater than sixty percent) can lead to such problems as mildew and mold, which flourish at seventy percent RH on any organic materials, and low RH (less than thirty percent) can lead to the separation of glued materials, the flaking of paint in multimedia objects, and the cracking of wood, bone, and ivory. Summer humidity should be held between forty-five and fifty percent; winter, between thirty-five and forty percent. Stability is most important.[25] The most damage occurs when relative humidity shows repeated changes over the daily cycle or if rapid changes occur over a period of a few days. Storage equipment should be constructed of nonreactive materials that exclude vibrations, light, dust, pests, and pollution. Storage materials should be alkaline buffered. Many collection professionals have found ethafoam to be an ideal storage material with multiple uses, from packing or cushioning material to a cover for reactive surfaces.

Access to the Collection

Access to the collection includes how to provide access to collections, availability of objects and records for study or research, and access for disabled staff and visitors. Legal and ethical considerations are involved in all aspects of making the museum accessible and should be included when planning policies on access to the collections of the museum. Collections are not open to members of the general public; therefore, the hours that the collections are available for use may vary from the museum's public visiting hours. Generally, the collections are available for research and for preparation of exhibits during the hours the collection staff is available.

Availability of Objects and Records

Museums can limit who has access to the collections and their records by establishing criteria for using the collection for research, exhibition, student projects, photography, and loans. It is legitimate to restrict access for the reasons of security and preservation of the collection. Careful documentation and monitoring of users must be done to ensure the safety of the collection and provide data for collection use reports. Authority to determine the use of the collection is usually given to the department chair or curator of a particular collection, but the governing board may choose to have the final say. Part of the criteria for access to the collection should require that the user provide an adequate reason for using the collection and prove competence in handling the objects in the collection. Museums also may establish different levels of access for various users. For example, students may require more supervision, and museum professionals may require less, although theft by professionals can be an issue, as illustrated in box 8.4. Guidelines for the handling of objects should be given to all users, and new users may need an explanation of the collection arrangement.

Besides having access to the collection itself, a user may need to have access to the records of a particular object. Procedures and restrictions for access to records also should be included in the policy. A restriction might, for example, require witholding the specific locality of an endangered species, fossils, or archaeological materials because the user may go to that location for financial gain. Some states, such as Nebraska, have laws pertaining to access to information on sensitive localities and identities and contact information of donors; therefore, state and federal laws need to be examined when determining this specific section of the policy.

Access to the collection should be in accordance with the Americans with Disabilities Act of 1990 and the Rehabilitation Act of 1973. Access involves a multitude of issues and criteria, and procedures need to be stated clearly and documented by the museum in collection policies. Consultation with representatives of disabled populations can create access responsive to the needs of the artifacts and constituents alike.

Box 8.4

Case Review: Security of Collections

Threats to the security of collections can come from a variety of sources, but theft is high among those that the museum must protect itself against. The thief can be a member of the staff, such as the curator for the World War I artifacts at the National Air and Space Museum who sold artifacts to war memorabilia dealers; a researcher, such as the professor from the University of Scranton who stole antique ceramics and glass from a number of museums and donated them to other museums, particularly the Peabody Museum of Salem, Massachusetts, where he became a board member; or unknown outsiders such as the two thieves dressed as policemen who stole thirteen objects worth approximately $200 million from the Isabella Stewart Gardner Museum in Boston in March 1990. Obviously, stealing museum objects is illegal, and the perpetrators can be prosecuted, but museums have an even higher ethical standard to meet, which is to prevent theft of objects by any agent.

Sources:
"The museum insider who became a thief" by W. H. Honan. *The New York Times* (The Living Arts), December 19, 1991, 1–2.
"A professor helps to catch Smithsonian's curator-thief" by D. Johnston. *The New York Times* (National), February 17, 1996, 1, 9.

Insurance

Because most museums' permanent collections are considered irreplaceable and insurance compensates only for the monetary loss, many museums choose not to insure their collections or may insure only parts of them, such as an important piece of art. Insurance should be a last resort for a museum because instead of anticipating reimbursement, a museum should be preventing loss and damage. Risk management becomes very important in this regard. A museum should seek security measures to prevent loss or damage; examples include controlled access, proper storage, exhibit procedures, crowd control, security guard training, inventory, and record procedures.

If insurance is found to be necessary, the museum should identify the type of risks it must cover in order to negotiate intelligently with the insurance company. Some risks that may be covered are hazards like fire, water damage, transportation, and packing. Zoos, arboretums, and other museums with living collections will need to seek special policies and should look at similar institutions to determine how to set up a policy.

Insurance is a difficult decision, but museums need to evaluate carefully the need for insurance and the type of coverage they need for their collection. Unfortunately, there are no standard insurance policies for museums; however, some insurance companies have specialized in coverage designed for museums and related organizations.

Deaccession

Deaccessioning is the process of removing accessioned objects from the museum's collection legally and permanently. Deaccessioning is used to improve the quality and integrity of the collection in respect to the museum's mission. Deaccessioning may be used to reshape the collection by allowing unneeded objects to be removed, freeing needed space and funds. As with accessioning, deaccessioning should be a thoughtful process. If not handled properly, deaccessioning can endanger the museum's reputation and public trust. Stephen E. Weil, who currently serves as the scholar emeritus in the Smithsonian's Center for Education and Museum Studies, states that funds from deaccessioning are never used "for anything other than acquisition or care of collections." Monies from deaccessioning should not be used to generate operating funds, which would be a violation of the current AAM Code of Ethics. With the expanding need to deaccession, many museums have written policies to avoid an appearance of conflict of interest or unethical behavior, according to Steven Miller from the book *A Deaccession Reader.*[26]

Delegation of Authority

As with the accession policy, the deaccession policy needs to specify the persons who can give approval for deaccessioning of an object and who will keep the deaccessioning records. In general, the curator or person in charge of the collection is allowed to make recommendations for deaccessioning, and then the director, or more appropriately the governing board, makes the final decision based on the given criteria. Some museums choose a more layered approach to deaccessioning. For example, if an object is valued at less than $500, the deaccession can be recommended by the curator and approved by the department chairperson; if the object is valued at between $501 and $10,000, the director must approve the deaccession; and anything valued at more than $10,000 must be approved for deaccession by the governing board. This method saves time, especially when small quantities of objects of minimal market or research value are being deaccessioned. How a museum delegates deaccessioning authority should be clearly stated in the policy. All deaccession records must be kept on file permanently by the appropriate person, who in larger museums is usually a registrar.

Criteria

The first step in the deaccession process should be a search of the museum's records to determine if it holds title to the object or if there were any stipulations placed on the object that prohibit deaccessioning. If there are restrictions, it may be necessary to go to court and show that the donor's wishes are impossible to fulfill. Once it is determined that an object can be deaccessioned, this action needs to be justified. A set of criteria must be established to help guide deaccession decisions. The deaccession criteria used by the Sioux City Public Museum, Sioux City, Iowa, are presented in box 8.5.

Methods and Procedures for Disposal

Deaccessioned items may be exchanged with or transferred to another museum or educational institution, donated, used in destructive analysis

Box 8.5

Sioux City Public Museum Deaccession Criteria

1. The object or material is outside the scope of the museum's mission and its acquisition policy;
2. The object's condition has deteriorated beyond usefulness, the item has been damaged beyond repair, or the item's condition endangers human life or other items in the collection;
3. The object or material has failed to retain its identity or authenticity, or has been lost or stolen and remains lost or stolen for longer than two years;
4. The object or material is unnecessarily duplicated in the collection;
5. The object or material has doubtful potential utilization in the foreseeable future;
6. The object has accidentally been accessioned twice.

Box 8.6

Deaccessioning Policy: Sheldon Memorial Art Gallery, University of Nebraska-Lincoln

Deaccessioning is the process used to permanently remove an object from a museum's collection. The decision to deaccession an object from the Sheldon Memorial Art Gallery collection is serious and must be carefully considered. The criteria for deaccessioning are stringent and must support the museum's accessioning policy and standard museum practice as established by the Association of Art Museum Directors. All deaccessions are made to preserve the integrity of the collection and to improve the quality and coherency of the collection.

The director, with the curator, will determine specific justifications for particular proposed deaccessions. However, general reasons for considering deaccessioning an object are

- To maintain the objectives for collecting at the Sheldon Memorial Art Gallery through professional, purposeful refinement and consolidation of the collection
- To reserve costly storage and conservation funds for those objects of relevance to the collection
- To ensure the continued growth of the collection, by judiciously exchanging auxiliary holdings for objects that are in keeping with the priorities of Sheldon Memorial Art Gallery

As an aspect of the acquisition policy, funds received through deaccessioning shall be used only to support and augment acquisitions. These funds shall not be used to provide operating budget, other maintenance funds, exhibition funds, or special events monies. Donors of works sold will be acknowledged on labels and other printed references to art purchased with proceeds from a deaccessioned object.

Recommendations for deaccessions shall be determined by the director, with the curator. Their recommendations will be presented for consideration to the appropriate consulting body. When recommending the deaccessioning of works from the collection of the Nebraska Art Association (NAA), recommendations will be made to the NAA acquisitions committee, with final approval by the NAA board. Recommendations for the deaccessioning of works from the University Collection shall be made to the Sheldon Advisory Board, with final approval by the regents of the University of Nebraska. The respective review groups will support or discourage each proposal to deaccession.

A procedure for disposal of deaccessioned objects should be determined, recommended by the director, and approved by the Sheldon Advisory Board or the NAA board of trustees. Prior to initiating the deaccessioning procedure, the director will attempt to establish clear and unrestricted title to the object under discussion. When title has been verified, or documented to the fullest possible extent, the deaccessioned object will be disposed of appropriately. Typically, the work will be sold through public sale, auction, or trade. No member of the Sheldon Memorial Art Gallery staff, the Nebraska Art Association board of trustees, or the Sheldon Advisory Board will be permitted to directly acquire a work deaccessioned by the Sheldon Memorial Art Gallery. Nor shall any Sheldon staff member, NAA board of trustees member, or member of the Sheldon Advisory Board be permitted to benefit directly from the sale or trade of any deaccessioned object.

for research, sold, destroyed, or discarded. Most museums rank these methods in the deaccession policy.

One of the most controversial methods of disposal is selling deaccessioned objects. This is especially true if the museum chooses to use the proceeds from the sale for general operating expenses. By using the proceeds in this manner, the museum appears to view its collection as a cash reserve to be used anytime it is needed. At the moment, according to the FASB, museums do not have to capitalize their collections (that is, list them as assets) if they use the proceeds from deaccessioning to acquire other objects for their collections.[27] The AAM's Code of Ethics states that the proceeds from a sale are to be used only for the acquisition of material for the collection, or for the conservation or preservation of the collections. For these reasons, many museums outline in detail how their objects should be sold and how the proceeds from the sale should be used. To avoid any appearance of conflict of interest, the policy should prohibit the museum's board, staff, volunteers, and their relatives from purchasing objects for sale. The sale of a deaccessioned object also must be conducted as a public sale, such as an auction.

Whatever method is chosen, the public does need to be notified of the plan to deaccession, and all records (with the possible exception of the donor record) relating to the process should be available to the public. The deaccession policy should state whether or not the donor is to be notified. If there are no restrictions on the object and the donor has no legal interest in it, then the museum has no legal requirement to notify the donor.

Notes

1. Malaro 1998, 47.
2. Hoagland 1994.
3. Buck and Gilmore 1998.
4. Cassar 1995.
5. Buck and Gilmore 1998
6. Malaro 1998; Phelan 1994.
7. Buck and Gilmore 1998.
8. Ibid.
9. Ibid.

10. Zorich 1999.

11. Ibid.

12. Koelling 2002.

13. Professional Practices Committee 1991.

14. Malaro 1998; Reibel 1997.

15. Reibel 1997; Buck and Gilmore 1998.

16. Malaro 1998.

17. Reibel 1997.

18. Blanchegorge 1999; de Guichen 1999; Duckworth et al. 1993; Howie 1992; Krebs 1999.

19. Weintraub and Wolf 1995.

20. Hatchfield 1995; Moore and Williams 1995; von Endt et al. 1995.

21. Baker 1995; Burgess 1995; Hatchfield 1995.

22. Simmons 1995.

23. Baker 1995; Burgess 1995.

24. Grzywacz 1995.

25. Cassar 1995; Weintraub and Wolf 1995.

26. Weil 1997.

27. Malaro 1998.

CHAPTER NINE
FACILITIES MANAGEMENT

Museum Facilities

Proper management of museum facilities includes the orchestration of people working to maintain and secure the day-to-day operations of the institution, its structure, grounds, and areas of special use. A good facilities management plan takes into account the needs of the people who work within the organization, the preservation and exhibition of objects in the museum's collection, and the needs of the people who visit the museum. U. Vincent Wilcox,[1] director of the Smithsonian Institution's Museum Support Center, contends that these needs can be adequately met through the following six basic facility management actions:

1. Provide and maintain "the physical structure necessary to support the functions to be housed in the space"
2. Provide and maintain "the basic utility services necessary to support the functions of the space"
3. Provide housekeeping "services necessary to support the functions of the space"
4. Provide for the "health and safety of all persons using the space"
5. Provide "for the physical security of people and property in the space"
6. Provide "integrated pest management services for the space"

Adherence to this basic outline provides a museum with the framework necessary to develop a facilities management program that should meet the diverse needs of the institution.

Physical Structure

Museum buildings come in a variety of forms, and each has its own requirements for proper upkeep. A museum may be housed in a historic building that requires extreme measures of care in order to retain the structure's historic value. Museums also can be installed within parts of other institutions, such as universities and libraries. Museums may occupy structures that were built entirely for other purposes, such as a fraternal lodge, a library, or a basketball gymnasium. Or, museums may exist in buildings designed to function exclusively as museums. No matter what the type of structure, the administration and facilities staff of the museum should have a detailed knowledge of the infrastructure of the building; an assessment of the maintenance record of the building; a schedule of maintenance work to meet annual maintenance needs; and an appropriate budget that itemizes the expenses of the maintenance schedule.[2]

Those institutions that are able to design a museum must remember several considerations. G. Ellis Burcaw,[3] formerly head of the Museum Studies department at the University of Idaho, declares: "'form must follow function' is the paramount consideration in planning a museum building." It is most important that the building be designed to preserve and maintain the institution's collection. According to Arthur C. Parker,[4] internationally known Native American scholar and historian, "A museum building need not be ornate; but it should be attractive, though it be modest in its outward lines." For this reason, aesthetic concerns, though important, should be relegated to secondary status when designing a museum structure. Museum professionals such as curators, conservators, and facilities managers should be in direct consultation with the architect at all stages of planning and construction to ensure that preservation needs are met.

In addition to the architectural design, a site for a new museum must be selected if one has not been made available already. The site decision may be based on the functions of the museum and its focus. If tourists are to be a principal focus group, a site should be chosen that is close to a main tourist route, such as a major highway. Certainly, accessibility to the site should be taken into consideration. A site in a major metropolitan area should be near public transportation routes or selected on the basis of ample parking. A museum should be easily visible from several directions. Finally, the neighborhood in which a site is situated also must be carefully considered. A museum in the middle of a residential neighborhood may introduce an influx of traffic to the area, which could make residents of the area resentful toward the institution.[5]

The most important area within a museum, whether it is a newly designed building or a 200-year-old Greek Revival mansion, is its collection storage area, which also includes those areas where objects are displayed. The preservation of the collections of a museum becomes a primary concern in any proper facilities management plan. Most museums have many times the number of objects in nonpublic storage as are on exhibit. For this reason, a museum should allocate at least as much space for storage as for exhibits. Proportions of 30 percent to 40 percent are a realistic allocation of space,[6] indicating that of the total space available within a building, 30 percent should be used for collections storage, 30 percent should be used for exhibits, and the remaining 40 percent should be used for everything else (classrooms, offices, auditorium, lobby, bathrooms, libraries, mechanical units, and other areas).

When allocating space in a museum for collection storage, Wilcox's[7] recommendation is to "minimize the number of functions or activities designated for a given area." He advises this because the more activities that are conducted in an area, the greater the chance they will come into conflict with one another. The limitation of activities is especially important in the collection storage areas of a museum for security and conservation reasons. Wilcox[8] continues that a collection storage area should be designed to support three basic functions:

1. maintain the "optimum environmental conditions necessary to ensure the preservation of the collections"
2. provide "physical accessibility to the collections for the placement and retrieval of objects or specimens"
3. allow for the arrangement of "the collections in a manner that will optimize the efficiency of the space"

One of the most important aspects of constructing a storage area is use of proper building materials. Many different woods can be harmful to a collection because these materials "off-gas" (give off gas) over time.[9] Raw concrete, plaster, and brick are common construction materials for walls and ceilings. While off-gassing is a minimal problem for these materials, they present a major conservation problem due to the dust they generate. For this reason, these surfaces should always be sealed and painted. In this context, painting should be viewed not as decoration but rather as a conservation measure. The final structure that is needed for any collection storage area is a vapor barrier. According to May Cassar,[10] "ideal" conditions for the preservation of a museum collection include a relative humidity of about fifty percent and a temperature of 19° C. A vapor barrier consisting of a sheet of heavy-duty polyethylene is recommended on the interior of all exterior walls because it will help to exclude water vapor and outside pollutants.[11]

In addition to its building materials, the actual location of a collection area within a building is extremely important. The ideal storage area will be located away from exterior walls because a controlled environment is easier to achieve within the central part of a building. Additionally, storage areas should be near a hallway that has easy access to the loading dock and exhibit preparation areas. Consideration also should be given to keeping the collection areas away from those parts of a museum that contain activities that may cause harm to a collection; therefore, a storage area should not be located near food, exhibit construction or fabrication, or facility maintenance areas. Passages in and out of collection storage should be kept to a minimum. Many museums have only one access door into a storage area; however, building codes sometimes require two for safety reasons. These entrances should be large enough to accommodate the largest objects in a collection but small enough to be locked easily. Finally, storage areas should be kept out of basements and attics as much as possible. Attics often suffer temperature and humidity fluctuations, and basements may flood.[12]

While the collection areas are vital to the mission of a museum, other space considerations are also important. The entrance to the museum should be easy for a visitor to find. If a building has multiple doors to the outside that are locked, signs should be posted to direct a visitor to the point of admission. Once inside the entrance, the visitor encounters the lobby; this should be a space large enough to handle many people entering the museum at once. If the museum charges for admission, the desk where this is paid should be clearly visible and easily accessible. A cloakroom for hats, coats, and umbrellas should be located just off the lobby, near the entrance. The lobby should be seen as an informational guide to the remainder of the museum. For that reason, adequate signs should be posted to direct visitors to rest rooms, food areas, auditoriums, gift shops, and exhibit areas. If possible, both the food area and the gift shop should be located in places that are visible to visitors when they first enter. A museum also needs to ensure that there are plenty of places throughout the building for the public to sit down and rest.[13] These seats need to be comfortable and should face areas of interest within the institution. Finally, building facilities must be made accessible to people with disabilities. Whenever possible, elevators, gently sloping stairways, and wheelchair ramps should be available.[14] The universal design concept is discussed in chapter 13, under ADA.

Utility Services

One of the challenging tasks for a facilities manager is to maintain an environment that does not harm the objects in the museum's collection but at the same time is pleasant for people. Air ventilation, temperature, and humidity are all factors that must be controlled in the modern museum.[15] These conditions are often controlled by systems known as heating, ventilating, and air-conditioning systems (HVAC).[16] The mechanical systems that work together to provide HVAC control over a building's environment are often complicated and sophisticated. For this reason, computers often control HVACs, monitoring the systems for problems and providing a record of past performance. These systems require regular maintenance and should be located in areas that are easily accessible for such maintenance.

One of the most important functions of an HVAC system is movement of air throughout the building at a controlled temperature and humidity level. The input vent in the collection area should be located at one end of the room and the air return at the opposite end. This layout helps to ensure that clean, conditioned air is constantly being circulated throughout collection areas. The same manner of air circulation also is important in maintaining a healthy environment for the people in the museum, both workers and visitors. To ensure that the air circulating within the building is clean, intake ducts should be placed as far as possible from loading docks, laboratory exhaust hoods, and waste storage areas. The use of high-efficiency, particulate-air (HEPA) filters also helps to reduce the amount of pollutants within an HVAC system by as much as 99.9 percent. HEPA filters are much more expensive than lesser-quality filters and require more energy to circulate air. However, the HEPA filter greatly reduces the presence of dust particles within a building and will cut down on custodial work.[17]

The other major utility that must be closely monitored is the lighting of a museum. According to museum planners Barry and Gail Lord,[18] lighting "is perhaps the most important single factor in establishing an atmosphere and highlighting the presentation of individual objects." Lighting levels, however, must be monitored closely because of their potentially damaging effects on objects. Even though fluorescent lights emit ultraviolet (UV) rays that are as damaging to objects as natural light is, fluorescent lighting is the most popular choice. The reasons for its popularity are its low maintenance, low power usage, and low heat generation. The problem of damaging light can be partly offset by using UV filters on the fluorescent tubes.[19]

When choosing a light fixture, a facilities manager should consult with the curator or a conservator about the level of light that is safe for objects. Light levels can be measured using a light meter.[20] Proper light levels and limits on the amount of time that objects are illuminated can greatly reduce the harmful effects of lighting on objects. The facilities management staff can ensure proper lighting by following a regular maintenance schedule for the replacement of bulbs.

Facility Operations

Housekeeping

Creation of a comprehensive cleaning program should be a top priority in the development of any facilities management plan for a museum. The maintenance of a clean workplace is, according to Wilcox,[21] "part of the overall environmental requirements for the preservation of the collections as well as for the general health and safety of the people using the space." Many times custodial work is contracted to outside companies or done by another part of a parent organization. While this arrangement is fine for the typical office setting, museums have unique custodial concerns that require a conservator to work closely with those who train the custodial staff—whether in-house or out. The conservator should train any member of the cleaning staff in proper techniques for cleaning *around* collection objects and exhibit cases. Of course, artifacts and specimens in the collections should be cleaned only by a professional conservator or someone working directly under the supervision of a conservator.[22]

A formal cleaning plan for the general museum environment should be developed. According to Franklin Becker,[23] cleaning performance specifications for contract staff must state in writing the standards that must be achieved in every cleaning action. Because chemicals can often be harmful to objects in a collection, care must be taken to outline how and when products are to be used. This manual will also indicate how often various areas of a museum need to be cleaned. For example, carpeted floors retain dust and dirt at a high level; these surfaces should be cleaned at least every other day.

Emergency Preparedness

An emergency preparedness plan can be used to prevent or greatly reduce damage that occurs during a disaster and to help prepare a museum in advance for the aftermath of a disaster. The emergency preparedness planning committee should include representatives from each major function in the museum, a conservator, and board members. The plan should identify possible emergencies the museum may face, what procedures should be followed, and who will be in charge during an emergency.[24]

After a list of possible emergencies has been established, the museum can prepare for or prevent them. Potential hazards like faulty plumbing, mold, overloaded electrical circuits, and storage of reactive chemicals and other materials in inappropriate areas can all be easily monitored and remedied before they become a disaster. Maintenance staff and the local fire marshal should inspect the facility to ensure the safety of the building. Listing the location of fire extinguishers, first aid supplies, rolls of plastic, basic hand tools, and other resources will save valuable time because the staff will be able to find the resources easily. Emergency numbers, phone numbers of key staff members, and plans or diagrams of the facility should also be accessible.[25]

In deciding who is in charge, one method that can be used is the *Incident Command System,* a method developed for the California fire service in the 1970s. The organizational chart for emergencies is set forth by areas of responsibility, not by individuals, so it does not matter which key personnel are present at the time. For each essential emergency assignment, a line of succession by title, as deep as the museum can support, is established. This system allows for the adjustment of the plan depending on the magnitude of the emergency. A checklist giving step-by-step instructions for tasks such as shutting off natural gas, water, or electrical supply is a useful guideline.[26] After developing an emergency preparedness plan, all personnel, paid and volunteer, must be trained to use the plan, and drills should be held to test the plan. The drill also allows the committee and staff to improve the plan before it is actually needed.

The most common factor to be dealt with after a disaster is water, whether it is caused by fire, earthquake, hurricane, tornado, or a broken pipe. Objects must be dried and cleaned as soon as possible. Some museums make arrangements in advance with meat plants and factories to use their freezers in case of emergencies. This allows for objects, especially papers, to be frozen in order to provide time for treatment. No matter what kind of damage a museum has endured, a conservator needs to be brought in as soon as possible to evaluate damage and determine methods of treatment.[27]

The understanding of the meaning of emergency preparedness was changed forever with the events of September 11, 2001, likely to be referred to for a long time to come simply as 9/11. Among the many things affected by the destruction of the World Trade Center and a portion of the Pentagon were cultural and historic resources. The Heritage Emergency National Task Force and Heritage Preservation studied and prepared a report on the impact of 9/11 and prepared recommendations for collecting institutions to mitigate future terrorist acts or major disasters.[28] Here is a summary of the major recommendations:

- First, protect human life.
- "Collecting institutions should integrate emergency management into all parts of their planning, budget, and operations."
- "Emergency management plans should address both protection of collections and continuity of operations."

- "Emergency management training should be provided to all staff of collecting institutions, not just those charged with specific responsibilities such as security or engineering."
- "Priority should be given to maintaining complete and updated collection inventories and to placing such records in off-site storage. These efforts should be incorporated into emergency plans and should be considered essential to disaster mitigation."
- "Emergency management agencies and collecting institutions should maintain an ongoing dialogue aimed at strengthening affiliations between the two communities."

Health and Safety

Health and safety planning can include aspects of the emergency preparedness plan, but it also incorporates procedures for protection of staff and visitors through the prevention of fire, the use of Material Safety Data Sheets (MSDS), the proper storage of hazardous materials, and the disposal of biological waste materials. Specific procedures and documentation that meet federal, state, and local regulations should be established for each of these issues. The director must help establish a strong commitment to health and safety through financial and programmatic support. A safety officer should be appointed who has authority to require compliance with the health and safety procedures of the museum. The safety officer should carry out semiannual inspections, investigate complaints, and evaluate accidents, illnesses, and other incidents. The goal of all health and safety plans should be to improve working conditions and to eliminate as many dangers as possible to staff, visitors, and the collections.[29]

Fire Prevention

The most important health and safety component of a facilities management plan involves the installation of a high-quality fire protection system.[30] Fire protection should include preventing, detecting, controlling, and extinguishing fires. In order to protect staff, visitors, and collections, a fire detection and suppression system must be installed throughout the facility. Once a fire detection system is in place, the staff needs to be trained in fire prevention, which should include the use of a fire extinguisher. Safety features such as emergency exits should be clearly marked and accessible throughout the museum. Regular inspections by the local fire department and maintenance of fire protection equipment and systems should be included in the fire safety policy. Smoking should be banned throughout the museum, and all important records, such as accession and catalog records, should be kept in fireproof cabinets, with copies kept off site. Drills and evaluations of evacuation procedures should be conducted on a regular basis to ensure the protection of visitors and staff. Specific measures to protect the collection should be established, such as keeping storage and work areas clean and not storing objects or materials too close to furnaces or water heaters.[31]

The most common fire suppressant used by museums is a water-based sprinkler system. The sprinkler heads are governed by heat sensors that release water when enough heat is generated in a given area.[32] These heads can be set to go off individually, rather than in concert, when the designated temperature is reached. For maintenance purposes, the pump, pipes, and valves of a fire protection system, according to D. W. Brown,[33] "should be painted red or black with red valves and connections" for easy identification. Although wet-pipe sprinkler systems are the cheapest and statistically most efficient fire suppressant systems, water also can cause significant damage to collections and libraries. For this reason, museums that can afford the more expensive CO_2 fire suppressant systems should invest in them for their collection storage areas. These systems suffocate fire by quickly removing available oxygen in an area without the damaging effects of water. Be aware that these systems can also suffocate any staff members caught within the area and that oxygen masks must therefore be provided in all areas where a CO_2 system is installed.[34]

A facilities manager, in conjunction with the collections staff, should form a disaster preparedness plan that distinguishes which objects in storage or on exhibit should receive the highest rescue priority. This plan should be implemented only if objects can be removed safely from a building without risk to staff members. All those developing such a plan must keep in mind that the most important resource of any institution is its human resources. A life should never be sacrificed to save any object, no matter its cultural or monetary value.

Material Safety Data Sheet

A Material Safety Data Sheet (MSDS) is provided by the manufacturer and contains information about the composition of any materials that may be hazardous. These sheets include the product's name; its components; its volatility, flammability, and toxicity levels; and precautions for its safe handling.[35] The museum should have an MSDS for each hazardous material or chemical used in the museum. The sheet must be available to all who use the chemical or material or work in the area where the chemicals or materials are used. There must be a designated place for these sheets in the work area, and a master file should be kept of all MSDSs and other important information. This information can help the museum staff learn how to store, handle, dispose of, and prevent accidents when using hazardous products. All people who will use the product must be required to read its MSDS and initial it when they finish reading it.

Hazardous Materials

A museum should establish an Emergency Response Team and a chain of command for emergencies involving hazardous materials.[36] A file regarding all federal, state, and local regulations for the handling and disposal of hazardous chemical, biological, and radioactive waste on site should be assembled. An inventory of all chemicals, infectious agents, and other potential hazards at the museum should be included in the file.

Careful documentation of all purchases and disposals of hazardous materials should be kept on file, along with information about contaminated objects in the collection. Specific procedures for handling hazardous materials should be established and practiced by all staff members. Some common hazardous materials in museum collections are alcohol and formaldehyde (in wet-preserved specimens); lead (in paints); arsenic and mercury (in taxidermy specimens and other specimens and artifacts); gunpowder, ammunition, bombs, hand grenades, and artillery shells; most laboratory chemicals; copy machine toner; janitorial cleaning supplies; and fumigants and pesticides.[37] All of these hazardous materials should be clearly labeled and documented, and procedures for handling and using hazardous materials should be stated in the health and safety policy.

Special cabinets must be used for storing these materials and should be specifically labeled as such. The Occupational Safety and Health

Administration (OSHA) has specific regulations governing the type of cabinet to be used and which materials can be stored together. The cabinets need to be kept closed at all times.

Safe disposal of hazardous materials and anything that has come into contact with them is important. Any containers, gloves, instruments, or other materials used in connection with the hazardous material need to be disposed of in a specific sealed container or bag. These items, like the hazardous materials themselves, must be picked up by an authorized company or government agency that will dispose of them properly. None of these materials should be thrown away in normal receptacles or poured down the drain. State and federal regulations for both the storage and the disposal of hazardous materials need to be studied and included in the policy. When handling hazardous materials, people must wear appropriate dress, such as rubber or latex gloves, rubber aprons, respirators, or goggles, and/or use a fume hood.[38]

Biological Waste Materials

Biological waste includes dead animals, animal parts, absorbents containing body fluids, animal waste, food service organic wastes, and material coming in contact with any of them (for example, rubber gloves and scalpel blades). Each museum will need to develop its own disposal system for these materials in accordance with federal, state, and local regulations. The University of Nebraska State Museum has a specific method for the disposal of biological waste materials from its collection areas, which involves sealing the waste in a plastic bag that is then placed in a plastic-lined receptacle and held in a freezer. Once a week the bags are picked up by a special crew and taken for incineration. Any sharp materials must be placed in a crush-proof container that has a one-way opening. This container, when full, is then placed in a plastic bag and placed in normal housekeeping receptacles.

Integrated Pest Management

Pest damage can be one of the worst natural disasters to befall a museum; no geographical area or climatic region of the country is exempt from this possibility. Integrated Pest Management (IPM) was originally developed for commercial agriculture for both environmental and economic benefit, and the concept can be transferred to museums.[39] IPM can lower the costs of chemical treatments, and it can also reduce the long-term exposure of staff and objects to such chemicals while reducing the opportunity for insects to proliferate. Basically, IPM is an ecosystem approach to pest control.[40]

Pests are a concern for collection preservation and a health risk, and both issues must be addressed by a facilities management plan. Pest management starts with good housekeeping, so the museum's overall custodial staff must be considered part of the pest management team. A program should be established that looks for likely invasion routes of pests into a museum facility and takes steps to prevent use of these routes. Museums may be viewed as a series of nested boxes, with the objects in the collection at the center. The outer box is the museum building itself. Efforts should be made to prevent pests from entering the building at points such as visitor entrances, service entrances, air intake points, food services, windows, and cracks and breaks in the building. Housekeeping should be concentrated at these points of entry. Outside the building, certain types of flowers and other plantings that can attract insect pests should be avoided.

The next box is the room in which the collections are stored or exhibited. Efforts must be made to keep these spaces as airtight and dust free as possible, especially at floor level, where creeping insects travel. Food should be excluded from these areas, and trash should be removed on a daily basis. No shipping boxes or packing materials should enter the collection areas without fumigation or freezing, and they should not be stored in collection areas. Housekeeping must focus on removing all dust and other materials that accumulate on floors, in cracks in the floors and walls, on light fixtures, in corners, and between and under storage cases because this material makes excellent food for insects.[41] Some museums have started elevating cases so that the dust and other particles can be accessed easily and removed.

The final box is the storage case or exhibit case that contains the objects. These must be acid free and airtight to exclude insects, dust, and other pollutants and to help maintain constant temperature and relative humidity.

Organic materials such as bone, horn, fur, textiles, wood, paper, and leather are the most vulnerable to pest infestation. Damage from pests can range from surface soiling and spotting to complete destruction of the object owing to some of the more common museum pests' feeding directly on it. Pests can be placed in three categories: microorganisms (molds and fungi); insects; and vertebrates (birds and mammals). Unfortunately, all three can support one another, and each can contribute to the damage caused by the others. Cloth moths, wood borers (beetles), dermestid beetles (carpet beetles), silverfish, firebrats, cockroaches, rodents, and birds, such as pigeons and starlings, are commonly found affecting museum collections.[42]

Monitoring for pests by direct observation and sampling is critical. Direct observation includes looking through the collection for signs of insect infestation, such as frass, insect carcasses or remains, or damage to artifacts. Sampling can be done by setting and carefully monitoring insect traps throughout the facility. All pests found in and around the traps should be identified and documented so the museum can identify any present or potential problems. By knowing the types of pests that are invading the museum, those responsible can determine the best method of dealing with the infestation.

Museums also need to establish methods of stopping infestation once it has occurred. A special quarantine room needs to be created for infested objects and objects entering the museum.[43] All incoming objects should be placed in quarantine for approximately seven days and inspected in order to determine if they are infested. If they are infested, various methods can be used to rid the object of pests. As an alternative to using chemical controls, many museums now are using freezing. The object should first be isolated from the remainder of the collection and then sealed in clear polyethylene. The bag should be sealed with heat sealing or polyester tape. If the bag is completely sealed, organic objects can control the environment inside the bag. The object should then be placed in the freezer for a minimum of one week at a temperature below -20° C. The bag should then be removed and a twenty-four-hour period allowed for the object to come to room temperature. If the bag was sealed correctly, condensation will occur only on the outside of the bag, and so the risk of mold will be eliminated. The object should again be quarantined for several days to check for surviving insects.[44] Once the object is free of pests, it should be carefully cleaned to remove all pest remains. This step not only removes material that might attract other pests; removing the signs of the old infestation also prevents false alarms of a new infestation. There are other methods of stopping infestations. The Canadian Conservation Institute in Ottawa is especially helpful in advising museums on proper methods for dealing with an infestation.

Pest management procedures need to be developed with the safety of both collections and people in mind. It is important that all staff members be educated on pest management because the key to any pest management program is constant vigilance.

Security

Museums are repositories for items held in the public trust; therefore, collections must be secured. As Timothy Ambrose, director of the Scottish Museums Council, and Crispin Paine,[45] secretary to the Committee of Area Museum Councils in Britain, contend, "Museums have a special responsibility to ensure that their buildings are secure, and that effective security systems and procedures, physical defenses and appropriate levels of staffing are in place day and night."

Museum security can be developed by following a checklist that includes assessment of security risks (such as neighborhood crime rates and traffic patterns); reviewing roofs, walls, windows, and doors for strength and stability; checking locks for function and appropriateness; and reviewing staff and visitor ingress and egress routes. Museum staff should survey the building from the perspective of a thief or vandal; this type of observation may lead to a more acute assessment of museum security and a better identification of weaknesses.[46]

The human factor is also important to consider in evaluating the security of museum structures. Wilcox[47] asserts that museum personnel "can be physically controlled by limiting their access to keys or devices that unlock the physical barriers that control storage spaces." All visitors should be monitored and their parcels inspected. Moreover, Steven Keller, formerly of the Art Institute of Chicago, and Darrell Wilson,[48] deputy administrator of the National Gallery of Art, emphasize that internal security is essential: "Hiring honest people and impeding dishonest behavior" are keys to successful museum security. Although such actions are theoretically useful, these values are often difficult to assess because even the most thorough of background checks and strictest of policies may not prevent human error.

Security Guard Staff

In most museums, the security staff will not be armed and will provide many services, such as visitor information, in addition to security. It is, therefore, essential to clearly define the duties of the security force and the priority for security of the collections, staff, and visitors. It also is essential that security staff be properly trained in all security issues, such as prevention of theft, fire, and accidents. A member of the security staff or another full-time staff member should have certification in CPR. In small museums, staff and volunteers with other duties also will perform security responsibilities; the museum is obliged to properly train these personnel in security issues.

Alarm Systems

Museums should have alarm systems that monitor indications of fire, theft, and flood. The monitor for fire should always be connected to the local fire department. Security staff should work with the local fire department before any problems occur so that the emergency personnel are familiar with the museum's facilities and the needs of exhibits and collections.[49] Motion and infrared detectors are commonly used to secure areas from intrusion during both open and closed hours. If the security staff is not on the premises twenty-four hours a day, then the security alarms should be connected to the local police department. Panic alarms connected directly to security firms and local police should be installed in areas where significant amounts of cash are handled. Flood alarms should be connected off the premises to appropriate staff members during those hours when the security staff is not on duty.

Video Monitors

Museums with large facilities commonly use closed-circuit television to enhance security. Surveillance of the museum building and grounds can be achieved with cameras that can pan and tilt. The security staff manipulates the cameras from a central station where they can monitor activities in many areas of the museum building at one time. The closed-circuit television is not an alarm in itself but an aide to the museum's security staff.[50]

Visitor Services

Museums provide a learning experience for their visitors, and this learning can be enhanced or undermined by the quality of other services provided. Some visitor services are mandated by law; others are not mandated but are still essential to customer satisfaction, while still others are "icing on the cake." A visitor service is anything that adds value to the visitor's experience at the museum. Visitor service is inseparable and undistinguishable from the museum's programs and is therefore indispensable. "We can blow thirty years of research in 30 seconds" with poor visitor service that causes someone to turn away. And since it takes five times the effort to find and attract a new visitor than it does to keep a current one, and ten times the effort to erase a tale told of bad visitor service, a strong commitment on the part of *all* staff to visitor service is critical to the museum's success.[51]

Previsit Information

Most museums solicit the patronage of "potential visitors" through the use of brochures, posters, and other promotional literature. Museums should take care that all information, such as telephone numbers, addresses, hours, and directions to parking, is current and correct.

Museums also should be certain that their telephone numbers and addresses are listed in the yellow pages of the local telephone book under "Museums," and they should be certain that the information remains correct over the years. The listed telephone number should be answered by either a person or a message machine with information about the museum. It is always preferable to have a person answering visitors' calls, but many times there are not enough staff members available. If a machine is used, the museum should be careful that two things are done: keep the message short and updated, and be certain that early in the message a telephone number is given to reach a person.

Usually, only the larger museums can consider using paid advertising, but there are ways for smaller institutions to participate in advertising as well. Smaller institutions should consider joining in cooperative advertising campaigns with other local or regional nonprofit organizations, local convention and visitors' bureaus, or state departments of tourism. Local radio and television stations will air public service announcements (PSAs) free of charge for nonprofit organizations. Paid advertising can take the form of radio, television, and newspaper advertisements, billboards, and bus signs, among others.

Many museums have worked to get on- and off-right-of-way highway signs. Many cities are more than willing to work with museums that are significant tourist attractions in acquiring directional signs that help visitors in the last short distance to the facility. Museums should work to make their buildings, and especially the front entrance, highly visible and welcoming.

Parking

A museum ideally should have a dedicated parking lot within easy walking distance of the front door. Unfortunately, many museums are presented with challenges in providing appropriate parking for their visitors. In cities, availability of a mass transit system will help resolve this issue. In other places, a shuttle bus or other dedicated transportation between parking areas and the museum will be helpful. Museums should make every effort to mark the routes from remote parking to their front doors and include information on the availability of parking in their advertising brochures and press releases.

Accessibility for the Disabled

The Americans with Disabilities Act has mandated that all public facilities be made accessible to the disabled, although exceptions are made for certain structures, such as historic buildings, in existence prior to the act's passage.[52] Once patrons are in the museum, there are a variety of issues of accessibility, including rest rooms, drinking fountains, and, of course, the exhibits and programs offered by the museum. Making the exhibits accessible will involve placing the exhibit labels, lighting, and cases and objects at an appropriate level. Braille labels or oversized letters can be helpful for visually disabled visitors. Those museums capable of doing so should make touchable objects available to all visitors. Because presentations in museums are primarily visual in nature, visually disabled visitors will continue to present museums with the greatest challenges. Those museum professionals who work to improve the museum experience for visually impaired constituents deserve the recognition of the entire museum profession. Museums may need to provide sign language interpretation for hearing-disabled visitors, especially for some educational programs and special exhibits. Chapter 13 gives a longer discussion of the requirements of ADA.

Staff on Duty

The patron of a museum is offered a sense of security by knowing that someone is present who can answer questions, provide general information, or respond in case of an emergency. Museums, of course, want to have persons on duty during museum hours not only to provide these services as a courtesy to patrons but also to provide security. Front-door staff should be trained in greeting visitors, so that the visitors realize they have been seen, and in making visitors feel welcome to the institution. Maps showing cloak rooms, rest rooms, and exhibits should be readily available.

Museum Stores

Museums are always searching for additional sources of revenue, and museum stores offer such an opportunity. Museum stores also meet visitor needs by providing gifts, publications for further learning, and mementos of the visit. In addition, many visitors derive some satisfaction from knowing that proceeds from sales help to fund the museum. In recent years, museums wanting to maximize the receipts from their stores have turned over store management to volunteers from their support groups or have hired concessionaires that operate regional or national chains of museum stores.

Rest Rooms

Although not always a major topic of conversation, rest rooms are probably the one place that visitors will remember if they have a bad experience. Ideally rest rooms are located in "obvious" places such as adjacent to lobbies, are well marked, and are accessible to persons with disabilities. The rest rooms should be kept clean and well supplied with towels and toilet paper at all times, which should be a responsibility of *all* staff members. A nice service to have available is changing stations for babies in both women's *and men's* rest rooms. This does not seem like a critical issue for members of the museum profession, but rest room quality is high on the visitors' list of significant parts of their visit.

Food Service

Food service can be one of the most challenging services to offer to visitors. Because most museum staff members lack food service experience, providing it means evaluating and hiring staff with this expertise. Food service brings the museum under the purview of a variety of public health inspections and laws. Many museums have found it extremely difficult to generate profits from food services, because to do so requires specialized marketing and management knowledge. For these reasons, many museums have contracted or franchised this service. Food service also means more materials entering the museum and more garbage to be removed. If not properly monitored, these functions can add to the museum's pest management problems; consequently, extra effort in pest control and additional rules, such as no food or drink outside the food service area, are required. Despite all these considerations, however, many museums have found it profitable and good public relations to provide food service for their visitors.

Many small museums will not be able to consider providing food service because of a low number of visitors or a lack of space to provide the service. These institutions should consider cooperative agreements with one or more local food service businesses. The museum can provide display space with directions to these businesses, and they, in turn, can prominently display posters and brochures from the museum. Such an arrangement can build good relations with the local business community while providing more exposure for the museum.

Educational Services

The primary function of a museum is to educate the public in the field of the museum's mission. The number of educational programs a museum can offer depends upon such factors as museum size, resources, and demand for programs. The National Park Service[53] recommends surveying visitor flow patterns through the museum and removing any obstacles that may be encountered. Obviously, a museum will want to prevent injuries to visitors concentrating on viewing the exhibits, and having to

Box 9.1

Exercise: Visitor Services Survey

To gain a better understanding of the importance of visitor services, conduct a survey of these services at a local museum. Obtain permission from the director of the museum before doing a survey. Use the chart below for your survey. It will be best if you make your visit unannounced so that you can come close to the real visitor experience. Try not to disrupt the museum experience of other persons visiting the museum during your survey.

In the chart below, use the rating of 1 for services that are as good as any you have seen in a museum, 3 for average service, and 5 for services as poor as any you have seen in a museum. Use NA if the service is not available or if the statement is not applicable.

Visitor Survey Chart

Previsit Information						
Quality of listing in the local telephone book						
White pages	NA	1	2	3	4	5
Yellow pages	NA	1	2	3	4	5
Brochures in local hotels and restaurants	NA	1	2	3	4	5
Quality of museum contact						
Answering machine information at museum's contact number	NA	1	2	3	4	5
Ability to reach by telephone a person at the museum	NA	1	2	3	4	5
Quality of directions received from person at the museum for finding the museum and its parking facilities	NA	1	2	3	4	5
Travel to Museum						
Quality of directional signs to museum	NA	1	2	3	4	5
Quality of directional signs to public parking	NA	1	2	3	4	5
Adequacy of parking area	NA	1	2	3	4	5
Marked parking for disabled visitors	NA	1	2	3	4	5
Quality of directional signs to guide visitors from parking to museum's entrance	NA	1	2	3	4	5
Compliance of entrance with ADA standards	NA	1	2	3	4	5
First impression of the museum's exterior and its grounds		1	2	3	4	5
The Greeting						
Greeting by a staff member	NA	1	2	3	4	5
Amount of admission fee posted clearly	NA	1	2	3	4	5
Museum maps (floor plan)	NA	1	2	3	4	5

Box 9.1 (continued)

Museum's mission obvious at this point	NA	1	2	3	4	5
Quality of the front-line staff's knowledge and understanding of the museum's mission	NA	1	2	3	4	5
Responses of front-line staff to questions about programs available on the day of your visit	NA	1	2	3	4	5
Responses of front-line staff to questions about future educational and exhibit programs	NA	1	2	3	4	5
Quality of other museum information available at front entrance	NA	1	2	3	4	5
Quality of directional signs to rest rooms	NA	1	2	3	4	5
Quality of directional signs to exhibits	NA	1	2	3	4	5
Rest Rooms						
Your first impression of the rest room		1	2	3	4	5
Compliance of rest room with ADA standards		1	2	3	4	5
Cleanliness of rest room		1	2	3	4	5
Availability of toilet paper		1	2	3	4	5
Privacy within rest room		1	2	3	4	5
Availability of baby changing station (in both men's and women's rest rooms)	NA	1	2	3	4	5
Exhibitions						
Overall impression of quality of exhibits		1	2	3	4	5
Impression of conservation measures for exhibits	NA	1	2	3	4	5
Adequacy of lighting in exhibits	NA	1	2	3	4	5
Accessibility of exhibit labels	NA	1	2	3	4	5
Wheelchair accessibility of exhibits	NA	1	2	3	4	5
Accessibility of exhibits for the visually disabled	NA	1	2	3	4	5
Special accommodations for hearing disabled	NA	1	2	3	4	5
Multicultural interpretation within exhibits apparent	NA	1	2	3	4	5
Educational Programs						
Quality of educational presentation	NA	1	2	3	4	5
Appearance and demeanor of the staff or volunteer presenter	NA	1	2	3	4	5
Accessibility of presentation space	NA	1	2	3	4	5
Accommodations made for hearing or visually disabled	NA	1	2	3	4	5
Quality of multicultural materials in presentation	NA	1	2	3	4	5
Museum Store						
General appearance of museum store	NA	1	2	3	4	5
Greeting and appearance of store staff	NA	1	2	3	4	5

Box 9.1 (continued)

Accessibility					
Wheelchair	NA	1	2	3	4	5
Visually disabled	NA	1	2	3	4	5
Appropriateness of items for sale (any UBIT problems)	NA	1	2	3	4	5
Food Service						
General appearance of food service area	NA	1	2	3	4	5
Greeting and appearance of food service staff	NA	1	2	3	4	5
Accessibility						
Wheelchair	NA	1	2	3	4	5
Visually disabled	NA	1	2	3	4	5
Hearing disabled	NA	1	2	3	4	5
General quality of menu and food	NA	1	2	3	4	5
General						
Overall impression of facilities		1	2	3	4	5
Overall impression of staff		1	2	3	4	5
Overall impression of commitment to accessibility		1	2	3	4	5
Overall impression of commitment to multiculturalism		1	2	3	4	5
Overall impression of museum experience		1	2	3	4	5

Following your museum visit, write a two-page evaluation of the museum's visitor services. Share the report with the museum director who gave you permission to visit the museum. Remember that this evaluation could contain sensitive material, so be certain to keep it confidential.

When we have used this exercise in the classroom, we have invited representatives of the museums being surveyed to come and hear oral reports from the students. Even large museums may be surprised at what is missing. In some cases, you will get a demonstration of how sensitive the issues raised by this visitor services survey can be. Try to avoid confrontation, which is best done by being professional and constructive in the evaluation. It is important to give as much coverage to services that are being provided well as to areas needing improvement, rather than just dwelling on the latter.

avoid obstacles detracts from the experience.[54] Another reason for establishing foot traffic routes is preservation, especially in a historic structure. If a historic house is open to the public, the museum personnel should be concerned with the effects of foot traffic on surfaces such as steps and flooring.

People visit museums for varied reasons—to have a learning experience, to satisfy a curiosity, or simply for enjoyment. It is incumbent on museums through their services to provide visitors an educational, safe, and enjoyable experience.

Notes

1. Wilcox 1995, 31.
2. Brown 1996; Wilcox 1995.
3. Burcaw 1997.
4. Parker 1966, 41.
5. Lord and Lord 1983.
6. Hillberry 1995.
7. Wilcox 1995, 30.
8. Ibid.
9. Hatchfield 1995.
10. Cassar 1995.
11. Hatchfield 1995; Sebor 1995.
12. Cassar 1995; Hatchfield 1995; Hillberry 1995; Sebor 1995; Wilcox 1995.
13. Ambrose and Paine 1993.
14. Hillberry 1995; Wilcox 1995.
15. Ambrose and Paine 1993; Cassar 1995.
16. Sebor 1995; Wilcox 1995.
17. Wilcox 1995.
18. Lord and Lord 1983, 119.
19. Wilcox 1995.
20. Ambrose and Paine 1993.
21. Wilcox 1995, 35.
22. Sandwith and Stainton 1993.
23. Becker 1990.
24. CCI 1995; Candee and Casagrande 1993; Faulk 1993; Haskins 1996; Kahn 1995; Nelson 1991; Roberts 1995; Vaughan 1999.
25. Faulk 1993.

26. Ibid.
27. CCI 1995.
28. Hargraves 2002.
29. Liston 1993.
30. Wilson 1995, 1999.
31. Wilson 1995.
32. Ibid.
33. Brown 1996, 29.
34. Wilcox 1995.
35. NPS 1990.
36. Makos and Dietrich 1995.
37. NPS 1990.
38. Makos and Dietrich 1995.
39. Olkowski et al. 1988.
40. Edwards et al. 1981; Florian 1997; Jacobs 1995; Jessup 1995; Linnie 1996; NPS 1990; Ryan 1995; Zycherman and Schrock 1988.
41. NPS 1990.
42. Ibid.
43. Linnie 1996.
44. Strang 1997.
45. Ambrose and Paine 1993, 212.
46. Ambrose and Paine 1993; Liston 1993.
47. Wilcox 1995, 40.
48. Keller and Wilson 1995, 55.
49. Wilson 1995.
50. Liston 1993.
51. Born 2001.
52. Phelan 1994.
53. Lewis 1976.
54. McLean 1993.

CHAPTER TEN
ETHICS AND PROFESSIONAL CONDUCT

Ethical principles are one of the cornerstones of the museum profession. There is almost universal agreement that standards should be articulated as a way to guide the thoughts and actions of museum professionals and to provide some basis for judging the performance of institutions and individuals. But what those standards should entail, how they should be expressed and promulgated, and what methods should exist for their enforcement have been a source of considerable conflict. The American Association of Museums (AAM) brought together professionals from all types of museums and charged them with creating a new code of ethics for the field. The resulting 1991 *Code of Ethics for Museums* sparked a firestorm of controversy, which led to some revisions and a reissue of the code in 1994. Although many issues were debated, the most hotly contested were the use of funds from the sale of collections (see box 10.2), adherence to the code as a requirement of institutional membership in the AAM, and the threatened withdrawal of membership from institutions found to be in violation of the code.[1]

Since the time of Aristotle, ethics has been considered one of humankind's highest pursuits because it results in the elucidation of human good. These discussions concerning museum ethics, then, were to be expected, but the tone and content of the dialogue were unanticipated. How could leaders in the museum profession, who espouse the highest professional ethical standards, disagree so strongly over what should be included in this code of ethics?

Part of the difficulty is semantic; there is great variation in the use and understanding of terms such as "ethics," "morals," "codes," and "regulations." Part of the problem is philosophical; there are widely disparate interpretations of what ethics should address and of whether and how they can be enforced. The need for using correct, appropriate, and standardized terminology is well recognized within the museum profession, and we would urge a similar attention to detail in this all-important area of discussion.[2] We believe more effective communication can result from precisely used language and the creation of a distinction between statements of ethics and codes of conduct.

Ethics

What Is Ethics?

"Ethics" is derived from the Greek word *ethos,* meaning character, custom, a person's natural state. Aristotle, author of the first major systematic treatise on ethics in Western philosophy, conceived of ethics as the search for the highest good, for how one ought to act in the world. Ethics relies on rational thought as the means by which one chooses the highest good through open discourse about such universal values as virtue and justice. Ethical thought prompts us to ask questions about how to achieve excellence in both our private and public lives, thus promoting dialogue. This dialogue, coupled with practice and habit, enables individuals to make good choices, to do their work well. Rational thought enables us to make appropriate choices between right and wrong, or more often, "difficult choices between competing goods."[3]

An example of these difficult choices in museums is the conflict between preservation and exhibition: "The curator's dilemma is the reconciliation of these disparate functions."[4] The true conundrum is this: "The museum—in its most fundamental role—is that place where objects are preserved for the public to see."[5] Ideally, with adequate resources, objects can be placed on display in a way that does not endanger them. In a world of limited resources, actions that benefit one side of the equation do so to the detriment of the other. When we raise exhibit light levels in galleries so that seniors and visually impaired visitors can see artifacts and read labels, we raise the potential for damage to the artifacts. We are compelled to make tough choices between these "competing goods." Perhaps through the consideration of ethics (based on rational thought) we may have the capacity to make appropriate decisions in each unique situation.

The Ethics Task Force of the AAM, attempting to write the 1991 code, gave as its number one conclusion, "Ethics is not a list of commandments dictated from above but the traditional values drawn from experience on which standards and practices are based" and explained that the code was an attempt to reflect the traditional values of American museums.[6] Ethicist Robin Lovin, dean of the Southern Methodist University Perkins School of Theology, echoed this idea in stating, "ethics will not begin with a list of 'dos' and 'don'ts,' commands and prohibitions." What is required first is "some preliminary thinking about how museums and what they do relate to the human good that ethics seek. What does a museum contribute to the good lives of the people who visit it? How can the people who work for the museums enhance that contribution, and what are the characteristic ways that they might diminish it?"[7]

Robert Macdonald, director emeritus of the Museum of the City of New York, and Lovin both make a distinction in their writings between "values" and "rules," and we suggest that this is the difference that should separate statements of ethics from codes of conduct. According to Mary Anne Andrei and Hugh Genoways, "The difference between a value and a rule is that it makes sense to maximize a value—to increase it as much as possible—whereas you can only comply with a rule"[8] Values (for example, honesty) may spawn rules (tell the truth), but it's quite possible to behave in ways contrary to the value (telling only part of the story) without actually breaking the rule (lying). Adherence to values is difficult to measure or enforce; adherence to rules is more easily gauged, with compliance "encouraged" via the negative consequences for rule breaking. In an ideal world, belief in and acceptance of values would be universal; these values would guide conduct so effectively that rules simply would not be necessary.

But museums exist in the real world and are institutions composed of people; these individuals make ethical decisions that affect the museum community and our whole society. Through the development of museum ethics, we may look beyond our human frailties to consider how museums contribute to the endeavor of human excellence and ultimately the highest good. A statement or code of ethics should inspire ethical thought by raising the awareness of museum professionals, ultimately creating an atmosphere that encourages honesty, fairness, respect, excellence, and accountability.

Museums are entrusted with the very objects—scientific, historic, cultural, and artistic—that represent our humanity. These objects embody the entire spectrum of human behavior and the products of such behavior. "What makes museum work morally risky is that those objects are often fragile and sometimes irreplaceable, so that it is possible to deprive future generations of an experience by exhibiting objects improperly or disposing of them in ways that make them unavailable to the public."[9] We must then strive to develop ethical standards based on universal values that are then translated into practice in all matters. The root value must be a commitment to serve society as a whole, to serve the highest good.

Museum Ethics

A good statement of museum ethics will articulate the traditional values or morals and communal standards of the museum profession. These statements are essentially unenforceable since no structure exists for the discovery or censure of violators, and the attempt to create such a system via the 1991 AAM code turned out to be both philosophically untenable and logistically impractical. It should be our shared professional expectation, however, that there will be observance of these ethical standards. Moral suasion more than legislation will govern our professional attitudes and behavior. These traditional museum values are what define the museum profession. Acceptance of these values and embodiment of them in our work marks the difference between simply being an employee of a museum and being a museum professional.[10]

Members of the museum profession will personify these values no matter where their institutions lie within the diversity of disciplines among museums or no matter what their range of duties may be. In a highly mobile work force, employees of one type of museum may be expected to move to a different type during their careers. Although their specific duties may change, we would not expect a change in museum professionals' traditional values any more than we would expect the ethical behavior of a family practice doctor in a small rural clinic to change once she sought further training and became a surgeon in an urban hospital.

The compilation of museum ethics that follows is based on traditional museum values. Some of these are ideas expressed in earlier codes (see box 10.1). Each of these statements is a work in progress because members of the museum profession can only *attempt* to embody these aims; if individuals or institutions attained these ends, they would exist in a utopia. These

Box 10.1

Sources for Museum Codes of Ethics

American Association of Museums (AAM)

Code of ethics for museum workers. Washington, D.C.: American Association of Museums, 1925.

Museum ethics. *Museum News* 56(4) (1978):21–30.

Code of ethics for museums. Washington, D.C.: American Association of Museums, 1994.

International Council of Museums (ICOM)

Code of professional ethics. Paris, France: International Council of Museums, 1987.

Museum Association (MA)

"Code of conduct for museum professionals." In *Museum provision and professionalism,* ed. G. Kavanagh, 293–304. London and New York: Routledge, 1994.

values will not change with place or time, but the mechanisms through which they are realized may evolve with new technologies, new pedagogical methods, and new understanding of social responsibilities. Museum professionals will be able to judge their ethical behavior by measuring the progress of their institution in terms of these values during their tenure. It should be kept in mind that a focus on progress toward one value that has a negative impact on progress toward other values may not be judged as ethical behavior. Balance in reflecting each of these values will always be the key goal.

Another semantic note: the word "museums" is used in the broadest possible meaning and includes institutions and their staff, trustees, volunteers, contract employees, and anyone else associated with the institution.

Museum Ethics

Museums will strive to maintain as their highest goal serving the public through the enhancement of the search for human knowledge, beauty, and understanding.

Museums will strive to maintain their public trust responsibilities.

Museums will strive to be guided by their missions in all activities, including collection acquisition and development of public programs.

Museums will strive to conduct their business and programs in a legal and moral fashion and will strive to avoid even the appearance of impropriety.

Museums will strive to identify actions that reveal all discriminatory behavior and will strive to overcome these behaviors by education and active diversification of their work forces.

Museums will strive to maintain their not-for-profit status.

Museums will strive to ensure the expenses for their operations and programs do not exceed their revenues.

Museums will strive to manage objects and artifacts placed in their care in such a manner as to ensure the long-term preservation and conservation of the objects and artifacts.

Museums will strive to maintain their collections and the associated records in an accurate and ordered manner.

Museums will strive to work cooperatively with native groups to provide patrimonial collections care that includes respect for the traditions of the cultural groups that produced them.

Museums will strive to maintain the educational value of their pedagogical objects, but recognize that these objects will receive different use and treatment from those in the permanent collections.

Museums will strive to create and disseminate new knowledge based on research with collections, informal education, preservation and conservation, and new technologies in exhibition and collection care.

Museums will strive to make their public programs available for the education of a broad and diverse audience that is truly representative of the communities they serve.

Museums will strive to involve the most knowledgeable experts available, including representatives of cultural groups when depicted, when planning and implementing exhibits and other public programs.[11]

Codes of Professional Museum Conduct

Professional ethics are the standards of conduct for any given occupation. These standards usually mandate more exacting expectations for behavior by members of the profession than that demanded of the general population. An individual citizen who collects, buys, and sells objects, for example, would be considered to be acting ethically so long as she was giving and asking fair value and was not dealing in stolen or otherwise illegal materials; a museum professional's behavior would be considerably more constrained. Some codes of conduct would prohibit the latter from accumulating or maintaining a personal collection; others would prohibit engaging in any trades or sales; others would limit the nature of materials collected; others would require disclosure of personal property. Similarly, corporations are regarded as ethically selling property they own as long as the transaction reflects a fair value and laws regulating commerce are observed. Museums, however, which are nonprofit corporations, are held to a higher standard when contemplating the sale of property in the form of museum collections.

Future AAM and International Council of Museums (ICOM) Codes of Professional Museum Conduct

We agree with Hugh Genoways and Mary Anne Andrei that the AAM and ICOM have written codes of professional conduct rather than codes of ethics.[12] The Museum Alliance in England has aptly identified its work as a code of conduct. Much of the material included in the current "codes of ethics" of the AAM and ICOM can be used, with some reformatting and modification of emphasis, as standards for writing codes of professional museum conduct. As such, it could be included in any future behavior code for these groups.

The AAM will have a fairly extensive set of rules to include in a Code of Professional Museum Conduct if it bases its work on the listing of museum ethics presented here and on federal laws and regulations. Some of the rules will be based primarily on ethical issues—for example, all museums' obligation to serve the public, to care for objects in their collections, and to avoid conflicts of interest—whereas others will be included because of legal requirements. Recent concerns about issues grouped under the term "multiculturalism," for example, are primarily of an ethical nature; desired staff behavior in response should be set out in a code of conduct. The Native American Graves Protection and Repatriation Act (NAGPRA), provisions of the Americans with Disabilities Act (ADA),

Box 10.2

Case Review: Conflict of Interest and Use of Funds from Deaccessioned Items

Concerns in the early 1970s over conflict of interest by staff and board members at the Brooklyn Museum, the Metropolitan Museum of Art, and the Museum of the American Indian in New York State and the subsequent intervention by the New York attorney general led the museum profession, through the American Association of Museums (AAM), to issue *Museum Ethics* in 1978. These cases involved staff and board members who interacted with private dealers in obtaining and dealing in deaccessioned objects from their institutions' collections. The AAM's stand was clearly articulated: Staff and those responsible for governance of museums should avoid conflict of interest or even the appearance of impropriety. The Association of Art Museum Directors has taken a similar position. These strong statements concerning the conduct of members of the museum profession have decreased problematic activities, and no government legislation has been imposed on museums.

When the AAM sought to expand its statement into a code of ethics in the late 1980s, the most controversial portion dealt with the use of funds resulting from the sale of deaccessioned collection items. Although the 1991 code, amended and finally accepted in 1994, allowed the use of these funds for new collection acquisitions and for care of collections, selling collections as a general fund-raising technique continues to be a point of ethical debate within the profession and a growing public concern. A number of cases have arisen in which the conduct of museum boards or staff has appeared to be in conflict with museum values.

One of the most public of these controversies in recent years involved the 1995 sale of portions of the collection of the "notoriously mismanaged" New-York Historical Society. The *Wall Street Journal* called the sale "a low point in cultural stewardship." In a case in the 1980s, the Pennsylvania attorney general, acting on behalf of the people of the Commonwealth, initially blocked and finally substantially altered the sale of the coin and stamp collections of the Carnegie Museum of Natural History. A few years later, the board of the Barnes Foundation petitioned the courts in Pennsylvania to amend the trust under which it operated to allow sale of some of the "lesser" Impressionist artworks in its collection. Proceeds from the sale were to fund repair of the deteriorating structure in which the collection was housed. Legal issues aside, the board used circular logic to create its questionable ethical argument by seeking to sell part of the collection to repair the house that existed solely to preserve the collection. The 1991 AAM code's extremely strict language on the use of proceeds from deaccession was written, in part, as a response to this highly questionable board action.

In addition to generating negative public opinion, decisions to sell portions of the collection also caused internal dissension, such as at the Shelburne Museum in Vermont. The sale in 1996 of five pieces from the collection netted $31 million, before commissions; it also precipitated the resignation of the chairman of the board, who was the son of the museum's founder. The remaining board and staff were deeply divided over the action. The AAM and the Association of Art Museum Directors disapproved of the sale, despite reassurances from board member John Wilmerding, the

Box 10.2 (continued)

founder's nephew, that funds would go into an endowment for "new acquisition, conservation, preservation and enhanced security." Critics rightly point out that creating an endowment is no guarantee of how funds will be used; the Barnes Foundation in 2000 spent the last of the $10 million endowment left to it by its founder and continues to teeter on the brink of financial disaster.

Museums exist to collect and preserve materials. Should they be allowed to sell part of their collections in order to stay in business? Museums have vehemently resisted attempts by the Financial Accounting Standards Board to categorize collections materials as assets; museums argue that collections are not disposable resources but are to be maintained in perpetuity. Yet if collections are sold and the cash proceeds used to finance general operating costs, how are the museum's objects any different from its monetary resources? Museums' tax-exempt status is granted in exchange for their operating as public trusts; does selling collections objects violate that trust function? Without restrictions on the use of proceeds from the sale of collections materials, what is the distinction between museums and art, antique, and natural history specimen dealers?

As the ethical debate continues within the profession, there is always the potential that growing public concern over this issue will lead to legislative action. Far better for the museum profession to be self-regulatory and address the practice through a code of professional museum conduct than to have its actions in this area regulated by law.

Sources:
Museum Ethics by the American Association of Museums. *Museum News* 56(4) (1978):21–30.
"Sketching Out a Plan for Survival" by D. E. Blum. *Chronicle of Philanthropy*, March 8, 2001: 57–59.
"Codes of Professional Museum Conduct" by H. H. Genoways and M. A. Andrei. *Curator, The Museum Journal* 40 (1997): 87–88.
"New-York Historical Society Sells New York Heritage" by L. Rosenbaum. *Wall Street Journal*, January 19, 1995.
"A Museum's Fortunes Rise by $31 Million at an Auction" by C. Vogel. *New York Times*, November 14, 1996: B1, B4.

and the Internal Revenue Service criteria for exempt status and unrelated business income tax (UBIT) are among the laws covering a broad range of museums. Compliance with laws may be expressly addressed through codes of professional conduct.

Controversy is often the impetus for reexamination and reworking of codes of conduct, and just as the repatriation issue flavored the AAM code dialogues of the 1990s, so, too, may concerns about objects of cultural patrimony instigate ethical debate among ICOM members in the early twenty-first century (see box 10.3).

Box 10.3

Case Study: Repatriation Redux

DATELINE—*The Near Future*

"In what can only be described as a stunning victory for the Egyptian culture, the United Nations has enacted the UN Egyptian Antiquities Protection and Repatriation Act (UNEAPRA). This act, in part, will repatriate 'culturally significant artifacts' to Egypt from national museums around the world. Cultural significance will be determined by the Egyptian government and supervised by a specially commissioned, multinational task force installed by the United Nations. Leading this special task force is a team of Egyptologists from the United States, Great Britain, France, and Russia.

"It is expected that compliance with this act will be voluntary, but heavy UN sanctions (in the form of travel restrictions and export tariffs on certain commodities) will be placed upon nations refusing to comply. Implementation will begin within 180 days of the enactment of UNEAPRA, with total returns to be made or scheduled no more than five years from the date of enactment.

"No details are yet forthcoming that outline fiscal responsibility of the returning nations. There are presently several bunkered warehouse locations in Egypt that will serve as the temporary repository of these artifacts, pending final approval of a $13 billion loan from the World Bank, which will be paid out in increments of $1.3 billion a year for the next ten years."

DATELINE—*The Present*

This parody news account may at first glance seem like something out of science fiction. But with the relative success of the Native American Graves Protection and Repatriation Act (NAGPRA) in the United States, and the Greek government's demand that friezes from the Parthenon, long held by the British Museum, be repatriated, it may be possible that we will soon be entering a new era. Could there come a time when all the plundering from wars will have to be accounted for, and perhaps on a grand scale? We have in recent years seen numerous accounts of Holocaust survivors' art collections being returned to them and their family fortunes being given back to their heirs. The spirit of righting past wrongs may be upon us, as shown by Papal apologies for the lack of moral courage to stand up for what was right.

But how can we settle accounts with cultural groups and nations? Legal, ethical, and moral standards vary from country to country, region to region; even within a single town, there is often no consensus about "the greater good."

Museums are public institutions; their holdings are intended to be exposed for all the world to see, and with this exposure come claims to pieces within a museum's collection. These claims may be individual or family-based, and increasingly they are being made in the name of a culture as a whole.

It has been said that the sins of the father migrate through his offspring, even to the fourth or fifth generation, but we now have a moral standard in which children disclaim responsibility for the wrongs committed by their ancestors. This attitude is strongly evidenced in a statement by directors of leading European and U.S. museums opposing the wholesale repatriation of cultural artifacts seized during imperial

Box 10.3 (continued)

rule or by means now considered unethical (see declaration below). They say the universal role played by objects in promoting culture outweighs the desire by individual countries or racial groups for their return. At issue are not only such "booty" as the Elgin Marbles, which the Greek government desperately wants back, the Benin bronzes in the British Museum, and thousands of Egyptian works in the Louvre, but Australian Aboriginal requests for the return of artifacts and human remains from Europe.

Is repatriation "a disservice to all visitors," as the directors declare? Although they are opposed to illegal trafficking in objects, they draw a distinction for material seized "decades or even centuries ago" and now held in museums. "We should recognise that objects acquired in earlier times must be viewed in the light of different sensitivities and values, reflective of that era."

Still, if subsequent generations are capable of righting what they perceive as wrongs, should they do so? Several European institutions have returned artifacts to countries of origin or traditional owners. Italy has agreed to repatriate an obelisk Mussolini seized from Ethiopia in 1937, and a Scottish museum returned a spiritually significant ghost-dance shirt, worn at the battle of Wounded Knee in 1890, to the Sioux.

"We hold these truths to be self-evident, that all men are created equal," begins the Declaration of Independence, but these words, which are the cornerstone of the United States' system of government, were written at a time when only some men (and no women) were considered equal, and human beings who were owned—slaves—didn't count at all. Times have changed, and we now consider slavery repugnant and indefensible, but the psychological damage to our country continues into the twenty-first century. As a society we have attempted to acknowledge the great wrong, create compensatory programs that try to offer equal opportunity, and teach our children that all people are truly created equal. We have other moral and legal precedents (reparations for WW II-interned Japanese Americans, for example) for trying to make right the wrongs of the past.

But will returning artifacts to their place of origin in fact right a past wrong? Opponents of object repatriation say that collections are universal, whether they consist of material culture or human remains.

In many cultures, the remains of deceased individuals are expected to stay within the care of the family or society, and their protection is a moral obligation. This is one reason the repatriation mandated under NAGPRA has been such an emotional issue. Claimants feel the bones of their ancestors have been desecrated and used in a manner less than honorable. Orthodox Jews have similar feelings about Jewish remains that have been disturbed by archaeological excavations. Almost two-thirds of European and British museums are believed to hold thousands of Aboriginal bones, hair, and soft tissues, removed from Australia usually against the wishes of local people or without their knowledge. The Tasmanian Aboriginal Centre and the Foundation for Aboriginal and Island Research Action have campaigned for more than twenty years for the return of remains.

And what about unclaimed human remains? Is it any less wrong to possess human remains that have no one to speak up for them? Can we claim, for example, Egyptian mummies may appropriately reside in museums because their ancient culture is no

Box 10.3 (continued)

longer vital? Have we the right to claim their ceremonial goods, in the name of science, because there are no longer any practitioners of the ancient faith?

Do museums have the right to own the bodily remains or possessions of any individual, whether their culture is living or extinct? Should this fact influence museum practice? Do we retain or repatriate materials based on moral and ethical standards or political expediency? If it is ethically and morally right to return aboriginal remains and materials in North America and Australia, shouldn't non-Egyptian museums give Egyptian materials back?

Museums are not likely to give away their collections and close their doors. But how do they find the right balance in these complex issues of who has the legal, moral, and ethical right to what? How will you help your museum make its choices and develop its policies?

Declaration on the importance and value of universal museums

The international museum community shares the conviction that illegal traffic in archaeological, artistic, and ethnic objects must be firmly discouraged. We should, however, recognize that objects acquired in earlier times must be viewed in the light of different sensitivities and values, reflective of that earlier era. The objects and monumental works that were installed decades and even centuries ago in museums throughout Europe and America were acquired under conditions that are not comparable with current ones.

Over time, objects so acquired—whether by purchase, gift, or bequest—have become part of the museums that have cared for them, and by extension part of the heritage of the nations which house them. Today we are especially sensitive to the subject of a work's original context, but we should not lose sight of the fact that museums too provide a valid and valuable context for objects that were long ago displaced from their original source.

The universal admiration for ancient civilizations would not be so deeply established today were it not for the influence exercised by the artifacts of these cultures, widely available to an international public in major museums. Indeed, the sculpture of classical Greece, to take but one example, is an excellent illustration of this point and of the importance of public collecting. The centuries-long history of appreciation of Greek art began in antiquity, was renewed in Renaissance Italy, and subsequently spread through the rest of Europe and to the Americas. Its accession into the collections of public museums throughout the world marked the significance of Greek sculpture for mankind as a whole and its enduring value for the contemporary world. Moreover, the distinctly Greek aesthetic of these works appears all the more strongly as the result of their being seen and studied in direct proximity to products of other great civilizations. Calls to repatriate objects that have belonged to museum collections for many years have become an important issue for museums. Although each case has to be judged individually, we should acknowledge that museums serve not just the citizens of one nation but the people of every nation. Museums are agents in the development of culture, whose mission is to foster knowledge by a continuous process of reinterpretation. Each object contributes to that process. To narrow the focus of museums whose collections are diverse and multifaceted would therefore be a disservice to all visitors.

Box 10.3 (continued)

Signed by the directors of:

The Art Institute of Chicago
Bavarian State Museum, Munich
State Museums, Berlin
Cleveland Museum of Art
J. Paul Getty Museum, Los Angeles
Solomon R. Guggenheim Museum, New York
Los Angeles County Museum of Art
Louvre Museum, Paris
The Metropolitan Museum of Art, New York
The Museum of Fine Arts, Boston
The Museum of Modern Art, New York
Opificio delle Pietre Dure, Florence
Philadelphia Museum of Art
Prado Museum, Madrid
Rijksmuseum, Amsterdam
State Hermitage Museum, St. Petersburg
Thyssen-Bornemisza Museum, Madrid
Whitney Museum of American Art, New York
The British Museum, London

Sources:
British Museum. *Newsroom.* Retrieved December 15, 2002, World Wide Web: http://www.thebritish museum.ac.uk/newsroom/current/universalmuseums.html.
Fray, P. Museums get tough on "trophy" returns. *The Age.* Retrieved December 16, 2002, World Wide Web: http://www.theage.com.au/articles/2002/12/10/1039379835169.html.

Institutional Codes of Professional Museum Conduct

Individual museums should construct their codes of professional museum conduct through an inclusive and public process that allows input from the larger profession and members of the museum staff and board. The 1994 AAM code concluded with a call to institutions "to regulate the ethical behavior of members of their governing authority, employees and volunteers," noting that "formal adoption of an institutional code promotes higher and more consistent ethical standards."[13]

All museums should use the AAM *Code of Ethics for Museums* or its future replacement as their starting point and include all of its contents in their codes of professional conduct. Institutions will also have several other sources to consider when developing a code of conduct. Certainly there will be institution-specific components to add, which will include federal and state laws and regulations that apply in their specific circumstances. Among the laws and regulations that may require rules of conduct are those that deal with employee relations, such as the Equal Pay Act, Age Discrimination in Employment Act, and Civil Rights Act of 1964; those that deal with copyright and intellectual property in relation to works made for hire, fair use, and licensing of copyrighted materials; and those that deal with legal liability, workers' compensation, and contracts. Institutions also will have unique issues to include in their codes, based upon their internal policies for hiring and dismissal, acquisition, collection management, health and safety, and emergency preparedness, among others.[14]

Institutions preparing their own codes of conduct will want to include appropriate materials from current profession-specific "codes of ethics" (actually primarily codes of conduct) that are applicable to their activities (see box 10.4).

There may come a time when various groups of discipline-specific museums (art, history, natural science, children's, technology) through their umbrella organizations, such as the Association of Art Museum

Box 10.4

Profession-Specific "Codes of Ethics"

Art history—"A code of ethics for art historians and guidelines for the professional practice of art history," by the Committee on Professional Practices for Art Historians. *Art Journal* 23:129–32 (1974).

Conservation—"A code of ethics for conservators," by the American Institute for Conservation. *Museum News* 58(4):27–34 (1980).

Curation—"A code of ethics for curators," by J. Lester. *Museum News* 61(3):36–40 (1983).

Education—"On the ethics of museum education," by D. Rice. *Museum News* 65(5):13–19 (1987).

History—"Statement of professional ethics," by the American Association for State and Local History. 1992. http://www.aaslh.org/ethics.htm.

Museum stores—"A code of ethics for museum stores," by B. Barsook. *Museum News* 60(3):50–52 (1982).

Public relations—"Museums and the public interest," by A. Searle. *Museum News* 63(1):53–58 (1984).

Registration—"A Code of ethics for registrars," by C. Rose. *Museum News* 63(3):42–46 (1985).

Directors, Association of Systematics Collections, Association of Youth Museums, and Association of Science-Technology Centers, may wish to promulgate a code of professional conduct that would apply to all of their affiliated institutions. There are already discipline-specific issues museums will need to consider. For example, the federal laws covering the collection and holding of plants, animals, and cultural objects (Lacy Act, Endangered Species Act, Marine Mammal Protection Act, American Eagle Protection Act, Migratory Bird Treaty Act, and Antiquities Act) will be primarily of interest to museums of natural science. The Visual Artists Rights Act of 1990 will be most applicable to museums of fine art.

This process will result in a complex and unique code of professional museum conduct for each institution, yet each code would also share many common elements. Because these codes are inevitably complex, each museum should employ the widest possible diversity of staff in creating this document. If this process is conducted openly and fairly, it should result in all members of the staff, board, and support organizations becoming stakeholders in the document, which will make internal implementation far simpler.[15] In the final analysis, though, implementation will be a question of individual commitment. The most inspired and well-articulated code in the world will have meaning only if individuals use it as their personal guide in making choices and then acting on them (see box 10.5).

Enforcement

The lack of an enforcement mechanism has been cited as one of the major failures of the 1994 AAM Code of Ethics.[16] Yet a proposed system for enforcement in the 1991 version raised even more concerns. The 1991 code stated: "Beginning January 1, 1992, each nonprofit museum shall, upon joining AAM or renewing its membership, subscribe to the code as a condition of membership. No later than January 1, 1997 . . . each nonprofit museum member of the AAM shall also affirm, as a condition of membership that it has adopted and promulgated its separate code of ethics, applying the Code of Ethics for Museums to its own institutional setting." An Ethics Commission, to be nominated by the president of the AAM and confirmed by the board of directors, was to be appointed and charged with "reviewing alleged violations of the Code of Ethics for

Box 10.5

The Scarf Dance

Constance Rader sighed as she inched her way to the back of the cluttered antique store. All the usual suspects were there—depression glass, crocks and stoneware bowls, bits and braces and crescent wrenches, tintypes and cabinet card portraits of people long dead, commemorative plates, horse collars, embroidered day-of-the-week tea towels—all stacked precariously in the dank cave. She breathed in the familiar smell of slow decay and was turning to go when she saw it. There, draped over the back of a chair at the edge of a stack of feed sacks—a bright bit of silk. She carefully extricated the sheer square from the pile of muslin and burlap (she was a curator, after all, so she knew yanking on old fabric could shred it). Yes, it was a scarf, and yes, it was a souvenir scarf with pictures and words all over it, and as she moved into better light, she saw that yes, unbelievably, it was a souvenir scarf of Nebraska!

Now Connie had quite an extensive collection of souvenir headscarves from states and locations across the United States. She enjoyed wearing the scarves; their funky depictions of the French Quarter and Yosemite and Mount Rushmore were an interesting contrast to her solid colored "curator suits." The scarves seemed like a safe thing to collect because her museum wasn't interested in materials from California or Maine. In all her perusing of antique stores and junk shops and museum collections, she'd never seen a souvenir scarf of Nebraska. But here it was—goldenrod (the state flower), field corn, meadow larks, the towering State Capitol, herds of cattle, and Boys Town—all depicted in yellow and green and black and fuchsia! She scanned the silk and saw something strange in the midst of all the familiar symbols—a little Victorian house. "Home of General Lew Wallace, author of *Ben Hur,*" the black letters said. Now she'd studied history for almost two decades, but she'd never heard that General Wallace lived in Nebraska. Still, it was a souvenir scarf of Nebraska, and the price was right. She put down her money and left the store in a glow. What a find!

Once Connie got home, she spread out the scarf on the dining room table and then looked up Wallace in the encyclopedia. She was right; he'd never lived in Nebraska. The house depicted on the scarf was in Indiana. A double find! Not only a Nebraska souvenir scarf, but one with a mistake! She imagined some overworked scarf designer in a faraway country, sorting through piles of building sketches that all looked the same, and a post-World War II factory with no proofreaders to catch the error. She scooped up the scarf and draped it around her neck, admiring "Nebraska" spelled out in green block letters. But as she caught her reflection in the curved glass front of her china cabinet, her smile faded.

"What am I thinking?" she said out loud. She was Constance Q. Rader, in charge of museum collections at the Nebraska Museum. She had signed a copy of the museum's code of conduct, agreeing to abide by its provisions, including offering the museum the right of first refusal on an item she might acquire that was within the museum's collecting scope. She *knew* the acquisitions committee would want the scarf the minute it was offered, even with the mistake printed on it, because there were no other such souvenir Nebraska scarves in the collection.

Still, she thought, the mistake made it a flawed piece. And since she'd never seen

Box 10.5 (continued)

anything like it, what was the likelihood that her colleagues on the acquisition committee knew such an item even existed? And if she never wore it around work, who would know she had it? The museum often declined items without provenance, and the owner of the antique store, she was sure, would know nothing about who had owned or used the scarf or even where he had come across it.

It was only a twelve dollar scarf . . . it would probably just go into storage . . . she could always donate it later. If only she hadn't suggested, just yesterday, to her intern that a good guide to behavior was "the mom test"—if you couldn't tell your mother what you were going to do, you probably shouldn't do it.

What are Connie's obligations (legal, moral, ethical) in this case?

What would you do?

What should Connie's intern do if she sees Connie at a local restaurant wearing the scarf?

Museums under procedures approved by the Board . . . and recommending that membership of the institutions in violation be withdrawn."

Many museum professionals objected to these provisions, not only because of the lack of clearly stated due process, but because they believe, as we do, that it is far better for the AAM to be an inclusive rather than exclusive organization. We believe the only requirement for membership should be embracing the statement of museum ethics presented in the previous section of this chapter and the payment of membership dues. As many institutions as possible should be encouraged to be involved in the AAM, to ensure a broad and diverse membership and to try to elevate the professionalism of as many institutions as possible.

To the AAM's credit, the revised 1994 language indicates museum members *should* subscribe to the AAM code and set about framing their own institutional code, in conformance with the AAM's.

Enforcement of the code of professional museum conduct by the AAM could occur during the accreditation process. Only those museums that adhere to the AAM code and have their own code written and implemented would be accredited. This means that enforcement will be guided by the Accreditation Commission with a thorough review of documentation presented by the institution and input from members of the profession, who through an on-site visit become knowledgeable about the museum under review.

Accreditation reviews take place initially at the request of a museum; once granted, accreditation is reconsidered after five years, and if regranted, at ten-year intervals thereafter. Is this schedule sufficient for an enforcement tool? Should there be a swifter response to situations in which museums appear to be behaving badly? Consider the case in box 10.6.

Museum Accreditation

Museums in the United States that meet the highest professional standards while fulfilling their stated missions may be accredited by the AAM. Of the nearly 16,000 museums believed to exist in the country, about 750 are accredited at any one time. A museum will be accredited for five years initially; after undergoing a subsequent accreditation review, it can be accredited for ten years. The accreditation process is supervised for the AAM by the Accreditation Commission, composed of a chair and six members appointed by the AAM president.

The process begins when a museum voluntarily applies for accreditation or is notified by the Accreditation Commission that it is time for a subsequent accreditation review. The accreditation staff will send the museum a self-study questionnaire that must be completed and returned within one year. The self-study is an exhaustive, and sometimes exhausting, review and documentation of the museum's programs and operations. Museum administrators should remember that the Institute of Museum and Library Services (IMLS) supports programs that can help museums prepare to undergo the initial accreditation process (see IMLS grant descriptions in chapter 6). The Museum Assessment Program (MAP I-IV) and the Conservation Assessment Program (CAP) were designed with accreditation as the ultimate goal. These noncompetitive grant programs feature self-studies and on-site peer review of administrative operations, policies and procedures, collection care procedures, collection condition, public programs, and governance. During the visit, reviewing professionals will meet with the staff and the governing board and subsequently write a report citing both strengths and deficiencies of the institution. These reports help identify issues to be addressed before moving ahead for accreditation.[17]

Box 10.6

Case Review: Creating a Sensation

The Brooklyn Museum of Art's display of "Sensation: Young British Artists from the Saatchi Collection" caused an uproar because of content some perceived as obscene and sacrilegious, and because of then New York Mayor Rudolph Giuliani's attempt to pull city funding from the museum. Of greater concern to the museum community, however, was the extent to which fundraising and exhibition content intertwined to create the perception that space in the museum was for hire, and that exhibition sponsors dictated curatorial decisions. The facts that all the artworks in the exhibition belonged to a sole collector and that the principal corporate sponsor, Christie's, stood to gain substantially from subsequent auctioning of the works seemed particularly egregious. Defenders of the BMA suggested "Sensation" presented cutting-edge contemporary art and drew thousands of new museum goers to the facility. Detractors countered that some museums will do anything for a buck (or in this case, several million).

Traveling exhibitions have become an important source of earned income for many museums, but do those institutions have an ethical responsibility to ensure that loaned exhibits meet their missions? The Colorado Historical Society hosted "Vatican Treasures: 2,000 Years of Art and Culture in the Vatican and Italy" in 1993 and set a new attendance record. The Western Heritage Museum in Omaha booked animatronics dinosaur exhibits a number of times over the past decade. A regional historical society is contemplating borrowing an exhibition on the life of holocaust victim Anne Frank. The connections between the content of these exhibits and the missions of the sponsoring museums are remote. But is scheduling a surefire crowd pleaser unethical?

Financial conflicts of interest, irrelevance to mission, and intellectual control concerns prompted a response from the museum community. Consider these excerpts from the American Association of Museums's "Guidelines on Exhibiting Borrowed Objects," an outgrowth of the "Sensation" sensation. (The full text is available online at www.aam-us.org.) Do you agree with these findings? What would your museum's written policy include?

Guidelines on Exhibiting Borrowed Objects (excerpted)

As society has come to rely more on museums for education about, as well as preservation of, its cultural heritage, it has also come to expect more of its museums—more accountability, more transparency of action, and more leadership in the community. Recognizing that concerns, both inside and outside the museum community, had arisen over time about what constituted ethical activity in exhibiting borrowed objects, the AAM Board of Directors created a task force on this topic . . . [to] provide the museum community with more detailed guidance on the development of institutional policies and standards for exhibiting borrowed objects, consistent with and following from the AAM *Code of Ethics for Museums.*

On July 13, 2000, the AAM Board adopted the following guidelines:

Before considering exhibiting borrowed objects, a museum should have in place a written policy, approved by its governing authority and publicly accessible on request, that addresses the following issues:

Box 10.6 (continued)

I. Borrowing Objects. The policy will contain provisions:

A. Ensuring that the museum determines that there is a clear connection between the exhibition of the object(s) and the museum's mission, and that the inclusion of the object(s) is consistent with the intellectual integrity of the exhibition.

B. Requiring the museum to examine the lender's relationship to the institution to determine if there are potential conflicts of interest, or an appearance of a conflict, such as in cases where the lender has a formal or informal connection to museum decision making (for example, as a board member, staff member or donor).

C. Including guidelines and procedures to address such conflicts or the appearance of conflicts or influence. Such guidelines and procedures may require withdrawal from the decision-making process of those with a real or perceived conflict, extra vigilance by decision-makers, disclosure of the conflict or declining the loan.

D. Prohibiting the museum from accepting any commission or fee from the sale of objects borrowed for exhibition. This prohibition does not apply to displays of objects explicitly organized for the sale of those objects, for example craft shows.

II. Lender Involvement. The policy should assure that the museum will maintain intellectual integrity and institutional control over the exhibition. In following its policy, the museum:

A. Should retain full decision making authority over the content and presentation of the exhibition.

B. May, while retaining the full decision making authority, consult with a potential lender on objects to be selected from the lender's collection and the significance to be given to those objects in the exhibition.

C. Should make public the source of funding where the lender is also a funder of the exhibition. If a museum receives a request for anonymity, the museum should avoid such anonymity where it would conceal a conflict of interest (real or perceived) or raise other ethical issues.

Sources:

American Association of Museums. *Guidelines on Exhibiting Borrowed Objects.* July 2000. World Wide Web: www.aam-us.org.

"Vatican art draws record crowd" by J. McCord. *Omaha World Herald,* August 25, 1993, 37–38.

The self-study questionnaire causes museums to examine the following components:

Stated charter purpose
Governance and governing body
Staff
Volunteers
Membership and affiliated organizations

Finances
Physical facilities
Health, safety, and security
Collections
Research
Preservation and conservation
Public relations and marketing
Exhibitions
Programs and Education
Publications
Changes since last accreditation (if applicable)

We submit that the museum's code of professional conduct should be added to the list of required documentation. Rejection of the accreditation application or reaccreditation request because a museum lacks a code or has failed to live up to it could be a powerful enforcement tool to ensure ethical museum conduct.

The museum must supply photographic as well as written documentation. Photographs must depict the museum's interior and exterior, collections, exhibitions, storage facilities, environmental systems, and other appropriate locations and activities. Several sizable binders may be required to house the completed self-study questionnaire with all of its accompanying documents, even for a medium-size museum.

The self-study documents go to the Accreditation Commission for initial consideration, with three possible outcomes: (1) The application may be moved forward; (2) it may be tabled for six to twelve months for gathering of additional information or correction of deficiencies; or (3) the museum may be advised to withdraw its application because it will not be approved.[18]

Those museums moving forward toward accreditation will next prepare for the visiting committee, composed of two or three museum professionals from comparable museums. The committee will tour all facilities and collections, review documentation from the self-study, and have discussions with the director, staff, and representatives of the governing authority. Following the visit, the committee will complete a narrative report analyzing all aspects of the museum's operation, including both the self-study and the on-site materials, and recommending whether accreditation for the museum should be granted, tabled, or withheld.

The Accreditation Commission will review the visiting committee's narrative report, recommendation, and on-site evaluation questionnaire and the museum's self-study questionnaire and supporting documents. After careful deliberation, the commission will grant accreditation, table the museum's application for more information or correction of specific deficiencies, or withhold accreditation. The museum director, chair of the governing board, and members of the visiting committee are informed of the Accreditation Commission's decision. Museums for which accreditation has been withheld may appeal with information to correct the record or evidence to show that deficiencies have been corrected. A museum for which accreditation has been withheld may reapply for accreditation after one year.[19]

Conclusion

A statement of museum ethics outlining museum values and the principles for which the institution stands is an important moral compass that can guide board and staff in their fulfillment of the museum's mission. Just as the strategic plan outlines specific courses of action, a code of professional conduct should delineate specific expected behaviors. The strategic plan will explicate what will be accomplished; the code of professional conduct will reveal how staff will go about doing that work in ways that are consistent with articulated museum values and protective of the public trust.

Active self-regulation by the museum profession will minimize the likelihood of outside regulation, but that should not be our principal motivation in writing statements and creating codes. We in the museum community will continue to explore both the philosophical and pragmatic issues of ethical thought and behavior because it is the right thing to do.

Notes

1. Macdonald 1992.
2. Andrei and Genoways 1997, 6.
3. Lovin 1994.

4. Wilson 1982, 65.
5. Weil 1983, 31.
6. Macdonald 1992.
7. Lovin 1994.
8. Andrei and Genoways 1997, 7.
9. Lovin 1994.
10. Andrei and Genoways 1997, 9.
11. Ibid., 10–11.
12. Genoways and Andrei 1997.
13. American Association of Museums 1994.
14. Genoways and Andrei, 1997, 88.
15. Ibid., 89–90.
16. Ibid., 90–91.
17. American Association of Museums n.d.
18. Taylor 1990, 13.
19. Ibid., 71–79.

CHAPTER ELEVEN
MARKETING AND PUBLIC RELATIONS

Many large museums have separate marketing and public relations departments, but the majority of museums will be fortunate to have a single staff member who is responsible for both marketing and public relations. Because these two functions are frequently intertwined, they are presented together in this chapter.

Marketing

Marketing has sometimes been viewed as an amoral, commercialistic practice—a "sales job." But museum professionals are becoming more sophisticated in their understanding of marketing and its value to their museums and audiences. Fundamentally, marketing is a process that helps people exchange something of value for something they need or want. Both museums and audiences are the beneficiaries of the marketing process "in which individuals and groups obtain what they need and want through creating, offering, and exchanging products, services, experiences and ultimately values with others," concludes marketing professor Philip Kotler.[1]

Most museum managers have little or no training in business or marketing, so in circumstances where they work with marketing professionals, mutual understanding must be built up carefully over time. In cases where the museum manager has to serve as the marketing "professional," that person must acquire skills in the area in order to apply marketing strategies in a meaningful way. Remembering that all marketing activities, no matter what type of organization conducts them, are about linking consumers (audience) and the product (museum) may help museum staff view marketing in an appropriately positive light. "Marketing is so basic that it cannot be considered a separate function. It is the whole business seen from the point of view of its final result, that is, from the customer's point of view," states management maestro Peter Drucker.[2]

Motivations for Marketing

Why do organizations market themselves? Most people would say they do so in order to increase awareness of the organization and the goods it produces. The Amherst H. Wilder Foundation recognizes, "Marketing is necessary to help nonprofits promote their values, accomplish their missions, and develop increased resources to address a range of compelling concerns."[3] But marketing isn't just about what the museum wants. Good marketing puts the museum constituents at the center of the process.

Many museums consider marketing in order to improve public perceptions and eliminate stereotypes or misconceptions. The old notion that "most museums display and explain in the archaic and restrained fashion that encourages fast walking through static rooms with suspicious or indifferent guards and no place to sit" is fading, but slowly, even though there are fewer and fewer museums where this is the case.[4]

Financial pressures, a changing social and technological environment, or the need for publicity for publicly funded programs may also inspire organizations to "do some marketing." Museums realize there is a limit to the amount of revenue that can be generated from increasing admission fees, so they promote themselves within the community and surrounding area in order to increase interest in their "products," thereby increasing their "volume" (or attendance).

The changing social and technological environment may be a motivation for museum marketing. A museum might tout itself as full of state-of-the-art interactive computers so as to portray itself as being in line with the current interests of the community. The challenge is that the "change" will necessitate an unfamiliar behavior on the part of the audience, and this proposed action could be difficult for the audience to imagine. For example, children may be attracted to the state-of-the-art interactives, but the grandparents who take the children might not be able to envision using a computer in a museum, or they may hope the museum is a place to get the kids away from the computer screen and see something real. In addition, the public may find it difficult to separate its perception of a museum and its past performance from a current project. An example might be a community art museum, which is seen as an elitist organization that typically showcases the dominant culture, deciding to exhibit work by minority artists. Members of the minority community might not attend the exhibition, simply because the organization was not perceived as a welcoming environment.[5]

Museums frequently market themselves in order to maximize the effectiveness of publicly funded programs, the theory being that if "the public" is paying for it, the public should know about it. Some granting agencies such as state humanities councils require public notice of programs that they fund. If "the public" does not attend a publicly funded program, in the next budget year the museum may not get the money for such programs. If the program has been well positioned and well publicized but is not well attended, marketing research will try to ascertain whether content, scheduling, pricing, or other factors resulted in the poor response.[6]

Marketing in reaction to particular needs or circumstances can be useful in addressing those specific cases, but the well-managed museum is one that has a comprehensive marketing plan. Ongoing, strategically designed marketing efforts will produce more effective and lasting results than case-by-case marketing. What is needed is a strategic marketing plan.

History of Marketing Activities

An understanding of the institution's marketing history is vital to development of plans for the future. Former marketing efforts can reveal the commitment the museum has to certain programs or activities, the ways in which the museum has shown its appreciation to its audience, and how it has implemented changes in order to better serve this audience. Former activities give clues to what the organization sees as acceptable marketing practices. Some governmental museums, for example, such as state museums, may be prohibited from certain types or forms of marketing.

Many marketing histories will show limited and inconsistent efforts, with emphasis on special events and a hodgepodge of unrelated advertisements and mailings and other communications. Some museums' marketing histories will reveal significant activity and decline, dependent on economic conditions or changes in leadership. Knowing why past marketing campaigns have been conducted, who pushed for them, how they were implemented, and their degree of success can be most important clues in developing a new marketing plan.[7]

The Four Ps of Marketing

Traditionally, there are four main elements in preparing a marketing strategy. These are often called "The Four Ps of Marketing": Product, Place, Price, and Promotion. Current customer-oriented approaches suggest that the "Four Ps" reflect the seller's, not the buyer's (or customer's or visitor's) point of view. A customer-centered concept features "the four Cs" (see box 11.1).

Marketers may see themselves as selling a product, while customers see themselves buying value. Customers also want the product or service to be conveniently available. More than simply knowing the price, customers want to know their total costs in obtaining and using a product. Furthermore, they don't want promotion; they want two-way communication. Museum marketing planners may do well to first think through the customer's "four Cs" and then build their own "four Ps" on that platform.

Product/Customer Value

A product is generally defined as a tangible good; however, products can be intangible, as is often the case with museums. And even if a prod-

Box 11.1

Marketing Ps & Cs

The Four Ps	The Four Cs
Product	Customer value
Place	Convenience
Price	Customer Cost
Promotion	Communication

uct is tangible, it has intangible elements as well, called quality perception. Many marketers find it is more difficult to communicate and sell intangible services or concepts than it is to market physical products, although they are intrinsically linked. Service-related companies, museums included, find quality to be a "particularly elusive concept."[8] Tangible goods are easily evaluated for quality by assessing size, shape, texture, fit, and color. Intangible goods like "the museum visit" are often judged on the basis of tangible cues such as physical facilities, equipment, and personnel. If a museum has dirty bathrooms, broken interactives, and curt staff, visitor perception of quality will be low, despite excellent programs, labels, and exhibits. Differences between service quality and goods quality are presented in box 11.2.

Quality is a key word. A quality exhibit, interpretation, or collection can be maintained no matter what the size of the museum. One of the best ways to ensure that the audience is aware of the quality is to concentrate on one thing, do that thing well, and tell people effectively what it is that you do so well.[9] Effectively communicating that strength will help refine visitor expectations and will likely result in a positive assessment of that particular museum service.

Place/Convenience

Place is defined generally as proximity of customers to product. Museums in many communities are often in the business district or the

Box 11.2

Differences Between Goods and Service Quality

Service quality is more difficult for consumers to evaluate than goods quality
Service quality perceptions result from a comparison of consumer *expectations* with actual service *performance*
Quality evaluations are not made solely on the *outcome* of a service; they also involve evaluations of the *process* of service delivery
Service quality is a measure of how well the actual service level matches customer expectations; delivering quality service means conforming to customer expectations on a consistent basis

Source: *Handbook of cross-cultural marketing* by P. A. Herbig. New York and London: The International Business Press, 261, 1998.

inner city, away from many residential centers. Marketing has prompted some museums to eliminate place as a restriction on reaching their audience. "Branch" museums in local shopping malls are one example. Traveling exhibitions are another way to address place. Rural dwellers unable to attend museums in a large urban center may visit a traveling exhibition in a town closer to them. Museums often reach national audiences though traveling exhibits.

Virtual exhibits and other online offerings are bringing the museum home, so "the place" becomes as close as your personal computer. Special "Met Net" memberships developed by the Metropolitan Museum of Art provide a number of computer-based benefits (free downloads of screen savers, views of collections, and chat room access).[10] Museums like the Austin Children's Museum are finding e-mail an effective and inexpensive way to communicate with members; "viral marketing" occurs when members forward e-mails of interest on to their friends.[11] Mail-order or online catalogs are opening up museum collections all over the world. Many museums gain income and goodwill from the sale of replicas of pieces from their collections. Statuary, postcards, tote bags, tee shirts, and computer mouse pads featuring the museum's collections and name can now be delivered for a price all over the world.[12]

Price/Customer Cost

Price is the cost to the individual for services or goods. As with many leisure activities, prices do factor into museum attendance. When determining price, businesses, including museums, must evaluate the cost in dollars relative to the objectives of the organization as well as to the museum's ability to earn funds. That means if the mission of a children's museum is to serve all children within a community, yet the admission fee is too high for many residents, the mission of the museum is not being fulfilled because of price. Problems often occur when admissions or fees are imposed on previously free services or activities and the audience does not understand why. Psychological costs can also discourage or restrict use of museums or museum programs. Visitors who perceive a museum as being in a "bad" neighborhood may hesitate to attend. Museum hours may be perceived as inconvenient. People may not go to a history museum because "boring old stuff" is a waste of time. The price people pay in time and effort may be a far greater determinant of participation than monetary cost.[13]

Promotion/Communication

Promotion is what nonmarketers consider "marketing." Promotion or promotional strategy is defined as communicating effectively with and persuading potential customers. Several misconceptions about promotion exist, especially in nonprofit enterprises. Many museums see promotion as commercialistic and unnecessary. Many administrators and staff see promotional campaigns, which spend money on radio and newspaper ads, as unjustifiable to donors, particularly where financial resources are slim.[14]

As museums become more subject to competitive pressures in attracting visitors and raising support, promotion and communication become increasingly important aspects of the marketing plan. The Internet is frequently used as an inexpensive way to communicate with members and potential visitors and to let them talk back. A mix of media and messages can reach varied audiences with an image of the museum that is consistent and effective.[15]

The Marketing Plan

Museums need to create marketing plans that spell out marketing projects, activities, and costs. A written plan in this critical area is as important as written plans and policies for any other aspect of the museum. Committing the plan to paper makes it easier to identify inconsistencies, unknowns, gaps, and implausibilities. More important, the plan helps management and staff focus on new market conditions or key marketing issues. The written plan establishes performance goals and sets out a timetable for achieving them.[16]

Plans may include sections addressing the following issues:

The *current marketing situation,* which includes relevant background on the market, product offerings, competition, and environmental scan results.

Opportunities and issue analysis, which considers threats, opportunities, strengths, weaknesses, and issues the museum will face in the plan's time frame.

Market research, the process of collecting information on audience preferences to help identify the needs, desires, and capabilities of the audiences. Market research may show that 42 percent of a community's population is elderly and visually impaired and does not go to the museum because low light levels in the galleries make it difficult for them to see the items exhibited. Once a need has been identified, the museum can take steps to address it and then communicate the changes to that particular segment of the population.[17]

Market research can also identify desires of the visitors as well. Perhaps families do not visit a museum because there is no concession stand or cafe, and perhaps it is not feasible to have one. Collaboration with a nearby restaurant to offer museum visitors discounts on meals could be beneficial to the museum, the restaurant, and the visitors.

The capabilities of the audience should not be taken for granted. Not all people can reach the museum and enjoy it easily. Lack of bus routes or reliable and convenient parking may be an impediment. With an increase in foreign visitors and English language learners in a community, language barriers may block the museum's message.

Goals, which include marketing goals (regaining lapsed members, building underserved audiences, and creating a new image) and financial goals (maximizing revenues and full-cost recovery based on admissions). Many marketing campaigns fail because they lack clear goals. A museum marketing campaign designed to increase visitation to the museum will be more effective if measurable objectives are set, such as a 10 percent increase in attendance or an increase of fifty visits per week. This measurement is important in order to determine the success of the campaign; otherwise, an increase of one visit per week could be considered a success.[18]

Abstract goals, such as having people know the name of the museum and what the museum does, can be made measurable. Perhaps a museum wants to increase its recognition within the community by 15 percent. This increased recognition can be measured through interviews and opinion polls.

Most marketing campaigns, no matter how effective in the beginning, lose impact after six months. Museums must keep evaluating and updating their marketing campaign in order to keep the public's attention and to stay consistent with their goals.

Marketing strategy, including general positioning and initiatives the museum will pursue related to its product portfolio (offerings, products, and services currently available) and its plans for product and market expansion (deeper penetration into existing market segments, broader geographic base, new market segments, and modifications to attract the existing market). One of the greatest temptations the novice marketer must resist is directing major marketing efforts toward people who are different from current consumers. The principle articulated nearly two decades ago still holds: "Marketing efforts should be concentrated on people who have characteristics similar to those who already are supporting the activity or buying the product."[19]

The potential to attract new audiences is seductive, but unfortunately, efforts to lure them will be largely wasted. The experienced marketer knows that the greatest success will come from those people who are already loyal supporters and others who are like them. There is no question that an arts organization will be more successful in increasing an individual's patronage from three times a month to four or five times a month than it will be in getting somebody who has never come to a performance to attend once a month. Politicians have learned this lesson well. The greatest efforts in a well-managed political campaign will be directed at those elements of the constituency that are already providing the candidate a large base of support. It's time for the museum world to learn this lesson, too.

This is not to say that museums and other institutions should not try to attract new audiences. Their responsibility to serve their communities demands such efforts. But major marketing campaigns will have the greatest success if they focus on people who already attend museums.[20]

Market segmentation, the process of dividing the total market (audience) into relatively homogeneous groups. These groups are based on affluence, age, location, education, gender, and/or a multitude of other characteristics.

Women have long been a major segment of the museum community, but the changing roles of women in society are changing their involvement in museums. Women's increased levels of personal affluence are making them a larger force in the area of institutional development, but their full-time employment is decreasing their contributions of time.

Seekers of social benefits are another museum market segment. Some individuals may be drawn to the status and prestige that go along with supporting museums. Networking may be another reason for involvement. Upwardly mobile people may be interested in supporting museums in order to meet others who would be interested in them or their companies and to enter new social circles.[21]

Action programs, which spell out specific programs and steps to be taken by specific staff in specific time periods. What will be done? When will it be done? Who will do it? How much will it cost? What kind of benefit will it generate?

Budget figures, which identify the amount of money needed to carry out the plan.

Controls, to ensure that progress is made in achieving the goals. Controls may include collection and evaluation of data on a regular basis. Each quarter, for example, the museum may want to evaluate the information it's been gathering about the number and nature of people affected by a particular marketing strategy. The plan should identify who will take corrective action if elements of the plan prove unsuccessful; it may also include contingency plans.[22]

Incorporating these features into a marketing plan for the museum will give staff and board a blueprint for improving the museum's exchange of something of value with its audiences.

Multicultural Marketing

One of the "hottest" new markets is that of multicultural and ethnic groups. According to the United States Census Bureau, 34.7 million African Americans (12.3 percent of the population) and 35.3 million Hispanic Americans (12.5 percent of the population) lived in this country in 2000. Projections suggest that by 2005 there will be more than 36 million members of each group. Adding to this figure the number of Asian Americans brings the total to more than 25 percent of the United States population. Some estimate that by 2010, more than one-third of the population will consist of African Americans, Hispanic Americans, and Asian Americans; by 2050, the number will make up more than 50 percent of the population. Estimates of 2002 buying power for both African Americans and Hispanic Americans are around $580 billion. These numbers vividly depict the necessity of marketing museums to these groups of consumers.[23] Product image is not created or changed overnight—it takes many years to change perceptions, especially about cultural institutions. Museums that are not already doing so should begin marketing to these groups, not only in order to better serve and increase audiences, but to cultivate future financial support.

Many marketers are not sure where to start when it comes to marketing to various cultural, ethnic, and religious groups. As is the case with the dominant culture, only certain portions of these groups will be receptive to museum marketing. One approach taken by many museums is to establish advisory boards composed of members of the ethnic or religious communities they are trying to reach. Culturally specific print media and television outlets are rapidly expanding and may offer other options.

Cross-Cultural Implications for Marketers

Most marketing miscommunication from organizations stems from a lack of knowledge and research about the culture to which the museum is marketing. Box 11.3 presents guidelines to help museums avoid the mis-

Box 11.3

Suggestions to Minimize Cross-Cultural Marketing Mistakes

Be sensitive to do's and taboos. Develop cultural empathy.
Recognize, understand, accept, and respect another's culture and differences.
Be culturally neutral . . . different is not necessarily better or worse.
Never assume transferability of a concept from one culture to another.
Use the following steps to avoid problems when moving products to a new cultural market.

Examine those cultural and environmental attributes of the product you wish to market that make it a success in your home market.
Compare these attributes to those found in the target market.
Note those particular attributes where substantial differences exist.
Changes in the product or promotion must be made to account for the differences noted; in some cases, differences are too great, and the best option is not to enter the market.

Source: *Handbook of cross-cultural marketing* by P. A. Herbig. New York and London: The International Business Press, 302–303, 1998.

communication that has plagued many large corporations; many more resources are available in print and on the World Wide Web.

The Marketing Mandate

Marketing has been on the periphery of many museums' activities, but the combination of increased competition for leisure time activities and diminished individual, corporate, and governmental support is creating a marketing mandate. Just as care of the collections and prudent financial management are critical to the survival of the museum, so too is marketing. As for-profit corporations expand their positioning as purveyors of exhibitions, cultural programming, and "edutainment" (see box 11.4), museums must find effective and efficient ways of presenting themselves as "the real thing"—the places where meaningful objects and trustworthy information are offered in ways that people can use to meet their needs.

Not merely a "sales job," strategic museum marketing can help museums enlarge and diversify their audiences, identify key audience segments and appropriate mechanisms for serving them effectively, retain members, reach program goals, achieve higher quality and broader support, and thrive in a quickly changing world.[24] Many museums lack the resources to create a marketing staff or hire an expert, but they can train their managers and staff members in marketing principles and methods and take on the point of view of visitors and members. Many tools are available—including printed resources like the model marketing practices of specific museums outlined by Kotler and Kotler in *Museum Strategy and Marketing* and human resources like the reviewers in the Museum Assessment Program Public Dimension Assessment (MAP III) process—to help museums assess public perception and create more effective marketing strategies to better serve their audiences.

Public Relations

From ancient to modern times, museums have served many varied purposes and audiences. John Cotton Dana, a museum master, championed the idea that museums should be accessible and relevant to people's lives. He believed public programming and community activities were an

Box 11.4

Case Review: Coming Soon from a Corporation Near You

The end of the twentieth century and the beginning of the twenty-first have been a time of significant transformation in American museums. From the Metropolitan Museum to the National Museum of Roller Skating, institutions are finding their way in the marketplace. As they expand their efforts to position their products and services in compelling ways to attract broad and diverse audiences, they're facing stiff competition from marketing masters: for-profit corporations that are creating and touring exhibitions and media programming.

Clear Channel Communications Inc. owns more than a thousand radio stations across the United States as well as its own touring company, Clear Channel Exhibitions. The firm has some nineteen touring exhibitions, ranging from "Titanic" and "Brain" to its latest venture, "St. Peter and the Vatican: The Legacy of the Popes." A Vatican curator worked with the company and created a show that includes original sketches by Michelangelo and other rare materials.

Museums' attractive facilities and wholesome atmosphere appeal to corporate partners, but not everyone on the museum side of the equation is enthused. "Museums are one of the few things left that people trust, and we're trying to keep that," Don Otto, president of the Fort Worth Museum of Science and History, notes. Some museums are concerned that if they appear too close to commercial entertainment providers, they likely will lose credibility with visitors and, just as important, donors. "We don't want to blur the line on whether we're an educational venue or an entertainment venue," said Christian Greer, theater-programs manager at the Denver Museum of Nature and Science, which had been approached about showing Hollywood releases on its Imax screen.

Stacy King, chief executive of Clear Channel Exhibitions, thinks the company offers positive opportunities for museums. The company absorbs and recoups the significant costs of big exhibits from ticket sales and takes a share of the revenue after that, but "It's a financial model that's appealing to a risk-averse segment" (museums) because the company bears the development costs.

The Houston Museum of Natural Science, the Fort Lauderdale Museum of Art, the Cincinnati Museum Center, and the San Diego Museum of Art agree with this perspective and are venues for the Vatican exhibit. The expert curators Clear Channel uses lend academic legitimacy to the displays.

Smaller companies, including theme park exhibitors and animatronics makers, are creating exhibits based on children's books, such as BRC Imagination Arts' science exhibit featuring the Berenstain Bears or science-based ventures like Advanced Animations' "Grossology" and "Booger Shoot." Children's museums and science centers offer a ready market for these corporations' products.

If you were on the staff of a museum approached by such a corporation about an exhibition that fit within your mission and public program policies, would you support hosting such an exhibition? Why or why not?

Source: "Entertainment companies aim to thrill museum throngs" by Anna Wilde Mathews. *The Wall Street Journal,* November 25, 2002, B1, B5.

important part of the work of any museum. In the early twentieth century, museums were among the few sources of information and education outside schools. With limited opportunities for leisure activities, the public viewed museums as places to spend free time.

Television, mass media, and electronic media have changed the public's recreational activities. For many people, museums no longer hold an attraction. Museums need to increase the public's awareness of their presence and reassert their place in community life. Museums, like most businesses, also need to bring in customers to pay their bills. These customers can be paying attendees, or they can be donors. For museums to thrive in an ever-changing and increasingly fragmented society, they need to market and promote themselves. One way museums can regain visibility in the community is through public relations.

Definition of Public Relations

Public relations is "the process of planning, executing, and evaluating programs that encourage purchase and consumer satisfaction through credible communication of information and impressions that identify organizations and their products with the needs, wants, concerns, and interests of their publics," contends *The Marketer's Guide to Public Relations*.[25] Public relations includes "non-advertising media activities which increase your [organization's] profitability."[26] Museum ethics demand that museums operate in the public trust and exist for the public good; therefore, "profitability" is not the most important outcome of a public relations program for a museum. Still, the museum's "profits" from donations of money, objects, and volunteer time are all directly affected by the public's goodwill. A public relations program that ties the work of the museum to the interests of the community and increases the community's understanding of what the museum does can increase attendance and membership.

Public relations differs from marketing or advertising. Marketing develops and sells the product using advertising, which persuades the public to buy the product. Public relations seeks to increase awareness of the product and influence the public's perceptions of and attitudes toward the product. The museum is the product. The image it presents can attract or detract from public support. A museum's image is based on its significance in the community, its values, policies, personnel, and programs. The community includes people who are museum enthusiasts, people who are interested in museums, and people who don't attend. The objective of the public relations program is to find ways to reach each of these groups in order to gain their support in some form.[27]

Public relations programs also increase the staff's stake in the museum's mission and increase employee performance and morale. An internal public relations program can increase dialogue between the staff and administrators. Staff will develop a sense of ownership of the museum if they feel managers take their thoughts and ideas seriously.

Public relations programs can be either active or reactive.[28] An active public relations program allows the museum to control its image and influence how others see it. The reactive public relations program is always putting out fires and coping with complaints and problems and serves only a limited range of the interests of the museum. In a reactive scenario, the environment rather than the museum sets the public relations agenda, crisis defines the museum's image, and the public relations program has little to do with the museum's strategic goals. The active public relations program provides control over public perception of the museum. The museum can establish its image and develop a full strategy of publicity and promotional programs to enhance that image. By providing a positive image to the media and public, the active public relations program is also better able to manage a crisis.[29]

Incorporating Public Relations

The board of trustees and the museum administrator are responsible for the proper stewardship of the museum, including its public relations. Budget, board member or volunteer expertise, levels of activity and programs, and staffing availability will determine the public relations program at each museum. The stage in a museum's life cycle and its reputation in the community will influence public relations budgeting, as well as community size and the level of existing audience interest. Special events and activities may influence public relations budgeting and decisions as well. The particulars of the program are not as critical as the fact that an active program exists.

The position of the public relations professional within the museum is based on the board's or executive director's commitment to the importance of public relations. The public relations slot can be an executive-level position or a staff position. The placement of the position within the organization will sometimes influence the duties assigned to it. At the executive level, the public relations professional may be involved in setting direction and policy for the museum. At the staff level, this person provides more technical service. In cases where museums do not have the budget to hire a full-time public relations professional, a volunteer may provide similar service. In any case, the public relations professional should be an active member of the museum team.[30]

The public relations director will have many ways to serve the museum beyond writing news releases and arranging openings. This professional can be a valuable part of the planning process. Through research and study of the museum's audience and the community in general, the public relations professional can offer insight into whether goals and objectives of any plan will meet public needs and acceptance. These employees should be involved in all aspects of the museum's operation; through involvement, they can identify opportunities for publicity, which will get the museum's message out and increase awareness and visibility.

Public relations officers also have a role in training staff to increase their visibility within the community through public presentations or media contacts. Public relations officers do not have to be the mouthpieces of their museums; in many instances the media and public will grow tired of the same person representing the organization. By training staff to handle interviews, the museum develops a more personal image with its constituents and the public. Staff can be trained in what makes a good interview and what type of information the various media prefer, making the media feel more comfortable with the prospect of working with the museum on a regular basis. They will know that they can depend on staff of the museum to do a good job with little editing on their part. Public relations professionals can also train staff in crisis management so that staff will not be caught off guard in a crisis and will be better able to present the museum in a favorable light when a crisis occurs.[31] Part of the museum's emergency preparedness planning should be a designation of who will speak for the museum; a clearly communicated protocol for staff interaction with the media should apply to day-to-day operations as well to ensure that no staff members are surprised by what they read in the papers.

When it is not possible for the museum to hire a public relations professional, and there is no expertise within the board or volunteer staff, the museum must seek outside assistance. While it might be tempting to have staff from other areas of the museum fill in on publicity tasks, their expertise might not coincide with the task to be done. An excellent exhibit designer may have no knowledge of brochure design, or the curator of education may not have the expertise to write news releases; looking outside the museum may be best in some instances. Some advertising and public relations firms will provide *pro bono* work, but this donated support is often tied to major campaigns or publicity projects. It may be possible to hire a freelance professional or local agency on a retainer for much less than the salary of a full-time staff person. In these instances, the professional must be used more selectively.[32]

Public Relations Activities

Public relations activities fall into four separate categories offering various opportunities to provide information about the museum and its services:

Creation of an image of the museum that is attractive to government, businesses, and community leaders is an important activity of public relations. Museums need the goodwill of the community to survive; with that goodwill comes support. An AAM communications kit, *America's Museums: Building Community*, offers a variety of suggestions, data, and strategies for helping these policy and decision makers better appreciate the significant role of museums in the life of our communities.

Product publicity that reaches the general public and establishes the museum's audience is in many ways the most important aspect of public relations for museums. What does the museum have to offer? What is its area of expertise? What can a visitor expect upon entering the museum? Providing information to the public enables decisions about participation in museum programs. A public relations officer should always be on the lookout for media outlets through which to publicize the museum.

Financial public relations efforts provide information about the museum to potential donors, the board of directors, the membership, and the public. The financial information includes annual and quarterly reports.

Internal marketing helps the museum promote itself to its staff and employees. Internal public relations builds a sense of family and enhances overall museum performance.[33]

All public relations activities and promotional efforts begin with planning. All museum public relations programs must involve strategies to accomplish objectives that will serve the museum. If the public relations program is not based on clearly defined goals, it will fail. Several steps make up the public relations strategic planning process[34]:

Identify the museum's relevant public. In the first step, the museum focuses on discovering its audience and audience segments.

Measure image and attitudes. Once the museum has identified the various segments of its audience, it needs to conduct formal research into each group's perception of the museum. One way to accomplish this is through focus groups; another is through surveys. MAP III provides some funds to conduct these activities.

Establish image and attitude goals for key publics. As the museum becomes familiar with its audience and the audience's perception, it can compare its goals with the audience's perception and prepare a plan and indicate the amount of effort needed to reach each audience type.

Identify cost-effective strategies. What methods for changing audience attitudes will require the least amount of money and staff time? The museum will need to evaluate the potential benefits of the change in attitude versus the amount of time and money available for the project.

Prepare for public relations crisis. Once the plan for achieving increased public awareness has been determined, the next step is to evaluate crisis management. The museum must consider the possibility that a crisis will occur and that it will have to deal with negative publicity. The public relations professional or designated staff member must work to establish relationships with the media that will enable the museum to address and overcome negative publicity without being on the defensive. Crisis management is an important part of the public relations program, but one the museum hopes never to use. (See box 11.5.)

Choose specific public relations tools. Once the cost-effective strategies for the public relations program have been identified, the museum must evaluate the various tools available. For a publicity tool to be effective, it must be presented to the target audience in a manner that maximizes its impact. This may mean different tools for different audiences—print pieces may be more effective for seniors than broadcast or electronic messages, for example.

Implement actions and evaluate results. Measuring the success of the public relations activity is the final step in the process. Changes in attitudes and public awareness of the museum may be measured by an increase in attendance or memberships. If getting the message out is the goal, the number of times an interview ran, or the number of times a public service announcement was heard would be effective measures of success. Ultimately, the best measure of success of a public relations program is positive change in public perception of the museum. To identify the public's perception, the museum needs to go back to step one, identify its audience, and begin the process all over again with focus groups and survey respondents to see if audience views have changed.[35]

The public relations strategic planning process is key to the development and maintenance of a museum's image and so must be tied into the museum's overall strategic plan. The museum and its goals drive the public relations program, not vice versa. The museum must clearly identify its goals and use them as a foundation for the public relations program. Museum staff need to participate in the public relations process so that all will feel ownership in the publicity activities and understand their roles as representatives of the museum.

Public Relations Tools

The variety of public relations tools and the possibilities for their use are as diverse as the museums that can benefit from them. Museums have many different levels of commitment to and expectations from public relations activities. The tools the museum chooses to use will depend on the museum's expectations and staffing abilities.

Box 11.5

Case Study: the Case of the Corlis City Rumor Mill

Cindy James recently accepted a job as a public relations officer for the Corlis City Museum of American Art. The museum boasts a 100-acre campus and over 500,000 objects in its collection. It has been a strong asset to the Corlis City community for 130 years. Currently the CCMAA has twenty employees and seventy-five volunteers.

Ms. James will replace the newly retired Ed Fogey, who worked for the museum for thirty years and was well known and respected in the community. The museum director and board want Ms. James to foster public relations with Corlis City's twenty- and thirty-something audience, a public that was largely ignored by Mr. Fogey, who favored constituents closer to his age. The city is well known for being home to some of the country's top Internet moguls and software gurus, most of whom are below the age of forty. This generation has a potential for high dollar donations to the museum. They also have young children. In one year, the museum will begin a campaign to raise funds for a new educational component to the museum. The new wing will house a variety of classes and art-related, hands-on activities geared toward kindergartners through twelfth graders. For adults, the museum will hold a monthly art history lecture and wine reception to highlight artists in the collection. The museum plans to solicit this younger public for most of the funds.

Two weeks before Ms. James was scheduled to begin work, the museum director, Garrison Grundy, complained to a friend at the local field club that the new software the museum had just purchased was "full of bugs." A local computer guru made the software. One of the guru's competitors overheard the disgruntled Grundy gripe and shared the news with his girlfriend, Ms. Verbatim, who just happens to be a business reporter at the *Corlis Daily News.* The next day a story reporting "serious defects" in the locally produced software cited the museum director's comments. The software maker's mother, Mrs. Chatterly, just happens to be on the museum's board of trustees, and she was not particularly pleased to see her son's new product bashed. Insulted by the director's comments, she decided it was time to share the news that she had walked in on the director and the museum curator in a compromising position in the board room. Soon the community grapevine was buzzing with news of the extramarital affair. In a follow-up newspaper story on the software bugs, the software guru suggested that the director's comments were a smokescreen to take attention away from his inappropriate personal behavior and mismanagement of the museum.

When Ms. James arrived at the museum two weeks later to begin her job as public relations officer, she found the museum staff and board in a state of chaos and finger-pointing. Morale was at an all-time low. The museum curator resigned from her job, and the director took a sudden three-week vacation without any further comments to the press. Animosity among the board members was growing; some were threatening to resign, while others were torn between their friendships with Mr. Grundy and Mrs. Chatterly, who was loudly demanding they choose sides and fire the director. Board members on both sides of the conflict had made statements to the media regarding the director's behavior.

Older members of the community who were Mrs. Chatterly's friends are consid-

Box 11.5 (continued)

ering withdrawing support from the museum. Younger members of the public are writing angry letters to the editors of the local and regional newspapers, with comments ranging from disgust at the unprofessional behavior to distress at the lack of postmodern art in the galleries.

Ms. James has her hands full. What was supposed to be an easy walk to a promising job has turned out to be a public relations nightmare, and it is too late for her to withdraw from her contract. The museum's public image has been tainted and intramuseum relations are in turmoil.

Using the public relations strategic planning process outline, decide what steps Ms. James should take to rectify this situation.

How will Ms. James control intramuseum conflicts?

What should she say to the director or the board member who spread the news about the affair?

How should she handle media relations?

What should she do to regain support from the museum's older constituency?

How could she clear up the image of the museum and establish a relationship with the younger members of the community?

No museum can implement a public relations program without people; when evaluating the possible participants in the museum's public relations program, the museum needs to look at all its human resources, including the board of directors, employees, members, interns, clients, customers, family and friends, contributors, volunteers, retirees, neighbors, vendors, and civic groups. Next the museum needs to look at all the possible communications tools available, including the annual report, newsletters, brochures, the museum website, public service announcements, print advertising, news releases, feature articles, letters to the editor, documentary and public education programming, film and slide shows, speaker's bureaus, bulletin boards, posters and flyers, specialty advertising (T-shirts, balloons, pens, and calendars), classified advertising, chamber of commerce promotions, public address systems, billboards, corporate-sponsored advertising, personal contact, bus cards, staff meetings, service clubs, and photography.[36]

Perhaps the most cost-effective public relations tool is word of mouth. It does not cost a thing and its value is beyond measure. Museums should encourage their staff and volunteers to provide the best possible experience to the visiting public. Visitors who have a positive museum experience are more likely to tell their friends and neighbors about their visit and encourage them to attend. Visitors who have a positive experience are more likely to return to the museum. Electronic word of mouth is proving to be another effective and low-cost way to create positive public relations.[37]

The news release is another low-cost but effective public relations tool. News media are always looking for stories that are of interest to their readers and viewers.[38] One news article about a museum is as powerful as three or four advertisements. Editorial copy is a very strong third-party endorsement of your museum. Making contact with news reporters and news editors is an investment that will generate great dividends. When museum representatives make contact with the media, they should remember that they are in a partnership that benefits not only their museum, but the news outlet as well. Asking questions about media interests in the museum and reporters' goals will guide the content and approach of news releases. Whenever possible, include a photograph with the news release. If the newspaper does not have room for the full article, it will often print the photograph and a caption. Many readers will look at a photograph even if they skip over an article.

Museums and Community

Museums continue to grow as important participants in the lives of their communities, and these relationships carry positive public relations benefits. The AAM-sponsored Museums and Community Initiative created opportunities for dialogue between museum and community leaders as well as outside experts on community life in the year 2000. The report *Mastering Civic Engagement* offers lessons learned and strategies for enhancing this critical interaction.

National efforts aside, the process of enhancing a museum's image within the community can be as simple as inviting community leaders to exhibit openings and including them in the program. The presence of the mayor, the governor, or a prominent business leader at a museum event will generate publicity and enhance the stature of the museum. Likewise, the inclusion of a local high school band or theater groups in a museum program will bring a new audience—parents and school leaders—to the museum and generate goodwill within the community. Providing staff the opportunity to participate in a speaker's bureau will open new opportunities for the museum to get its message out and demonstrate support for staff.

Increasing the goodwill of those who already volunteer and donate to the museum will increase their feelings of satisfaction with the museum and may encourage them to volunteer and donate more. Thank-you notes and special correspondence are good public relations practices that will promote feelings of connection. Holding special recognition ceremonies for board members and volunteers will increase their sense of importance to the organization and will identify them to the community. When the public sees an individual it respects connected to a museum, the museum gains from the positive association.

Joint promotions with other museums in the community are effective ways to publicize the presence of the museums and their services.[39] For example, in Lincoln, Nebraska, the museums formed the Lincoln Attractions and Museums Association for joint promotion and programming. The group was successful in getting financial and personnel support for promotion from the local convention and visitors' bureau and the state division of travel and tourism. Brochures, advertising, and World Wide Web listings were produced with this support that would not have come to any one of the individual institutions. In Chicago, the nine museums located on Park District land throughout the city collaborate on advocacy to legislators and business leaders, public information materials in various media, programs, and temporary exhibitions.[40]

The museum should also reach outside the museum community and look for opportunities to work with service groups and others on special projects. If a local business sponsors an after-school program or summer camp for disadvantaged children, the museum could volunteer its staff to provide a program, or the museum could open its doors to the group for special activities. The museum benefits from being associated with the other group's public service. A museum might consider sponsoring a kids' sports team and encourage interested staff to volunteer as coaches. These types of activities also help to make the museum relevant in the community's daily life. When museum employees volunteer in activities, they should identify themselves with the museum in some way, with a name tag or a museum T-shirt. Increased visibility is the goal of public relations, and the museum should be prepared to take advantage of community involvement.[41]

It is particularly important for the museum director to be seen as being actively involved in the community. The director should consider being a member of the chamber of commerce and one of the local service clubs, such as Rotary, Kiwanis, Elks, Lions, Optimists, or Women's Club. If the director has children, it will be important to be involved with school academic and athletic programs. The director may want to be a member of a local faith-based group. Directors of museums must remember that no matter where they are and what they are doing, they will be seen as the representative of the museum. This is especially true in smaller communities, where the number of people available to participate in community activities is limited. If the museum director wants the support and involvement of the community, he must be seen to support and be involved in the community.

Conclusion

Effective marketing and public relations are vital elements in a museum's success. As with all the aspects of museum operation, the mission and values of the organization and its strategic plan are critical guides for marketing and public relations efforts.

Recent shifts in both marketing strategy and museums' understanding of their roles in our communities have placed the visitor at the center. Visitor desires, needs, and capacities must be considered and married to the museum's programs and services in order for museums to compete successfully against the myriad of leisure-time choices now available.

Technology is expanding the ways in which museums can communicate with audiences, and global outreach is truly possible through the World Wide Web. Museums will want to match their use of technology and the messages they send to the diversity of their audiences.

Diversity will continue to be a watchword, influencing marketing and public relations efforts as it does nearly every other aspect of museum operations. Museum professionals are presented with an exciting opportunity to expand their understanding of all the people and cultures that make up their communities and to use that new learning to match the museum's offerings with new kinds of visitors.

Envisioning marketing and public relations programs as vehicles through which the museum can have meaningful exchanges with its audiences will enable museum professionals to engage in something more than a "sales job." Appropriately conceived, managed, and communicated, museum marketing and public relations programs can help museums and audiences share something of real value.

Notes

1. Kotler 1997, 6.
2. Drucker 1974.
3. Stern 1990.
4. Levy 1980, 14.
5. Lovelock and Weinberg 1978, 30.
6. Ibid.
7. Ibid.
8. Herbig 1998.
9. Ibid.
10. Kotler and Kotler 1998, 210.
11. London 2001.
12. Stern 1990, 43.
13. Stern 1990, 48.
14. Stern 1990, 52.
15. Kotler and Kotler 1998.
16. Ibid., B24.
17. Strang and Gutman 1980, 227.
18. Ibid., 226.
19. Searles 1980, 67.
20. Ibid., 68.
21. Levy 1980, 36–37.
22. Kotler and Kotler 1998, 324–5.
23. Ketchum Vanguard Cultural Marketing. Home page. Retrieved November 26, 2002, World Wide Web: http://www/ketchum.com/DisplayWebPage/0,1003,214,C00.html.
24. Kotler and Kotler 1998.
25. Harris 1991, 12.
26. Bangs 1992, 147.
27. Kotler and Andreasen 1991, 572.

28. Ibid., 91–92.
29. Kotler and Andreasen 1991.
30. Ibid., 569.
31. Ibid.
32. Strang and Gutman 1980, 233.
33. Luther 1992, 112–114.
34. Kotler and Andreasen 1991, 591.
35. Kotler and Andreasen 1991.
36. Ibid.
37. London 2001.
38. Boone and Kurtz 1993, 631.
39. Ibid., 632.
40. Atkins 2001.
41. Boone and Kurtz 1993, 630, 639.

CHAPTER TWELVE
PUBLIC PROGRAMS

In 1984, the American Association of Museums issued *Museums for a New Century,* which identified education as the "primary" purpose of museums. This report was followed in 1992 by *Excellence and Equity: Education and the Public Dimension of Museums,* which urged museums to place education at the center of their public service roles. Museums were to develop, expand, and use objects and the unique learning opportunities they present to serve their audiences. The report states that museums are "institutions of public service and education, a term that includes exploration, study, observation, critical thinking, contemplation, and dialogue."[1]

Of the ten recommendations[2] made in the report, at least three are entirely relevant to the public programs of museums:

> "Assert that museums place education—in the broadest sense of the word—at the center of their public service role. Assure that the commitment to serve the public is clearly stated in every museum's mission and central to every museum's activities."
>
> "Understand, develop, expand, and use the learning opportunities that museums offer their audiences."
>
> "Enrich our knowledge, understanding, and appreciation of our collections and of the variety of cultures and ideas they represent and evoke."

If these recommendations are fully implemented, museums will become a more important part of their communities as they educate and enlighten their audiences.

The learning that occurs in museums and similar places is termed "informal learning."[3] According to Judy Diamond, informal learning differs from formal learning, which occurs primarily in schools, because it is "voluntary . . . has no established sequence or curriculum . . . can occur in a variety of settings . . . [and] is ubiquitous."[4] The National Science Foundation describes it as "voluntary and self-directed, life-long, and motivated mainly by intrinsic interests, curiosity, exploration, manipulation, fantasy, task completion, and social interaction."[5] Informal learning often involves social interaction, especially with family or peers, that involves a large element of play.[6] Within museums, informal learning occurs primarily through planned educational programs and tours of exhibits, either as part of a regular program or as part of a group, family, or personal excursion.

Education Programs

Although it is suggested that collections are the core around which most museums are built, education generally is regarded as the primary purpose of all museums. The education function is what gives the collection meaning. It is the responsibility of the education department to make the museum's "collections accessible—physically, emotionally and intellectually—to the widest possible audience," according to P. B. Williams.[7] This responsibility includes presenting a diversity of perspectives through a wide range of media in order to increase the modes of understanding for as many people as possible. It also requires consideration of physical, language, and other barriers that may affect visitors' understanding of the collections. Museums offer many types of programs that serve the public: exhibitions, gallery guides, hands-on displays, demonstrations, classes, guided tours, self-guided tours, films, lectures, special events, workshops, volunteer training, outreach programs, teacher training, educational resources, resource kits, museum stores, libraries, and publications.[8]

As Americans have become more and more dissatisfied with public schools, a wide variety of educational experiments are being tried. Some of these experiments have been conducted using museum facilities as the school venues. The New York City Museum School, which is one of sixteen "New Visions" schools developed in Manhattan, meets the educational needs of students in the critical adolescent years of sixth and seventh grades. This consortium uses four New York museums three days per week to host the students, while the students spend the other two days in their public school facility.[9] In Lincoln, Nebraska, the Lincoln Public

Schools and the Folsom Children's Zoo and Botanical Gardens have formed the "Zoo School." This school serves a select group of high school students with a curriculum emphasis in the sciences, but one that integrates all other subjects, such as English, mathematics, and history, in the science studies.

With the average age of the population of the United States steadily rising, museums cannot afford to ignore nonschool audiences.[10] In many institutions, it is the responsibility of the education program to find and develop new audiences, such as working adults, the retired traveling public, or audiences with special needs. One of the newest, most innovative developments in educational programming in the museum field today is use of the Internet. This recent technological wonder, developing at unprecedented speed, provides a medium to serve a community in the largest sense—a global community. According to David Bearman and Jennifer Trant,[11] "a museum website can shape interactions between people and virtual objects, people and others visiting virtual spaces, and connect a new type of museum 'visitor' to museum personnel." Just as programming within the museum aims to create a venue for people with many perspectives to enjoy, learn, and interact with the physical museum, so must the museum aim for the same with its online programming.

When embarking on the creation of a website, it is vital, as it is in all educational programming development, to focus on fulfilling the mission of the education department and the museum. The guidance and support of educators, curators, and the director are mandatory. Will the website focus on content and access to collections or on marketing and visitor services? The creator of the website must have a clear understanding of the needs of the desired audience, knowledge of how to design and present instructional and educational materials, the skills to support the site technologically, and the resources to keep the content up to date.[12] Because Internet technology continues to change with increasing speed, museums often find contracting for website services to be the preferred route. Although very exciting, website development and subsequent maintenance can be quite expensive. Museums with smaller budgets must give attention to their budgets and develop websites that they are financially able to maintain.

With such a broad scope of possible activities filling such crucial roles in the community, the importance of creating museum policies regarding education programs seems clear. The museum acts as a public trust, caring for objects and providing programs to the community. The museum is supported by the community through donations from individuals, groups, and corporations, and occasionally by government funding. David Carr,[13] professor in the School of Information and Library Science at the University of North Carolina, states, "Every cultural institution is challenged to live up to the trust placed in it by the mere presence of the user, a trust or contract or alliance devoted to creating a situation that offers the optimal experience of art and attention." The museum is, therefore, responsible to the community ethically and financially. Establishing program policies and guidelines is one way to ensure that the museum fulfills this responsibility in an appropriate manner.

Guidelines and Policies

In most museums, the educational function is delegated to a public program or education staff member or department. Through its programs and through the voices of individual staff and volunteers, this department speaks to the public for the museum as a whole. If the institution is unable to set clear guidelines for the education department, its position within the community may be at risk. A well-defined education program with clear goals and policies provides a positive atmosphere and builds long-term relationships with the community.[14]

The purpose of guidelines is to clarify the goals of public programs and describe the steps to meet those goals. Specifically, the scope of the particular programs and the role of individuals within the programs should be defined. The policies and guidelines will help focus the efforts of the staff to meet the specific needs of the community and institution. Program policies and guidelines should include relevant job descriptions for paid and volunteer staff, the expectations regarding the conduct of the staff, and the training provided for the staff and volunteers. Policies should address the overall goals of the program as well as the specific issues of accessibility, diversity, and outreach. A means of evaluating the program should also be provided. Ideally this evaluation will provide opportunities for feedback from both the staff and the community.[15]

Many education programs have a mission statement that builds on the general mission of the institution but addresses the specific goals of the education program. Defining the goal of the education program will provide focus for paid and volunteer staff members. Education in a museum setting is about the exploration of concepts, the shaping of opinions, and the stimulation of ideas. Carr[16] states that "Flexibility, openness, diversity of interpretations are essential for the creation of a situation where multiple kinds of becoming are possible. . . . The museum that embodies mindfulness naturally attracts minds." The mission of the education program should be used as a tool to nurture an attitude of mindfulness in the educational staff. For them, the most important characteristic is an attitude that nurtures learning. Carr's[17] statement "Learners learn from learners" should be the motto of any museum education department. This is equally important whether that staff is composed of a part-time coordinator with a few loyal volunteers or a department with many paid professionals.

Guidelines for professional conduct are also critical. As basic as such issues may seem, if there is no policy, there can be no enforcement. The AAM provides guidelines for professional conduct for museum staff. The best time to create codes of conduct and job descriptions is before a problem arises.

Certain expectations are possible regarding the experience and abilities of paid staff members. If they have been properly trained for the position of educator, they will have familiarity with educational method and theory, an understanding of the practices of education in an informal setting, and some education experience as well as an appropriate background in the relevant subject matter of the museum. For volunteers, however, expectations of previous experience or background are not appropriate. A thorough training program should be implemented for all volunteers, especially those who will be interacting with the public.

Evaluation

Museums, like all publicly funded institutions, are under increasing pressure to show outcomes, not merely output. Stephen Weil and John Falk, in separate articles published in the summer 1999 issue of *Dædalus*, emphasize the importance of museums being able to document that learning is occurring in their programs. Weil[18] states, "The demand is that the American museum provide some verifiable added value to the lives of those it serves in exchange for their continued support." In Weil's view, the museum's portion of this social contract is to provide educational experiences. Museums must be able to provide evidence from outcome-based evaluations that they are fulfilling this social contract. Falk[19] believes that museums have provided learning experiences all along, but have failed in the documentation of this learning through erroneous assumptions and approaches to learning assessment. He[20] points out that immediate assessments may miss the most important part of the museum learning process: "It may take days, weeks, or months for the experience to be sufficiently integrated with prior knowledge for learning to be noticeable even to the learner himself, let alone measurable."

Providing for the evaluation of programs most often falls into the responsibilities of the education department. The evaluation of museum programs should provide opportunities for feedback from both the staff and the community. Judy Diamond, in her 1999 *Practical Evaluation Guide,* outlines instructions on how to design, implement, and present an evaluation study.[21] She discusses three main types of evaluations that any department should incorporate into its evaluation process: "Front-end evaluation provides background information for future program planning . . . formative evaluation provides information about how a program or exhibit can be improved . . . [and] summative evaluation tells about the impact of a project after it is completed." The purpose of such evaluation is not just to build a pile of paperwork; it should provide meaningful suggestions that can be implemented in current and future programming.[22]

Exhibits

"Visitors" is not just another word to museum exhibit staff members. Michael Belcher[23] calls visitors the "lifeblood of museum exhibitions," and they must be considered throughout the design, building, and evaluation process. Visitors are the people for whom exhibitions are, and should be, designed in the first place, and they should be the focus of the overall aims and objectives of the exhibit. It takes the imaginative ideas of the exhibit staff to create a plan that serves the needs of visitors, employees, the museum's mission, and the objects displayed. John Falk and Lynn Dierking[24] say that museum visitors come for the same reasons that they use other media—for information, personal identity, reinforcement of personal values, social interaction, and entertainment and relaxation. These reasons are not mutually exclusive, and information may not necessarily be the most important reason for visiting a museum.

Eugene Bergmann[25] argues that an exhibit policy is essential to ensure that dreams do not overtake reality, and conversely, that reality does not squash dreams. Every museum should have a strategic plan for exhibits, and that plan "should be put on paper for all to see."[26] "With written guidelines, all participants in the exhibit-making process will know exactly why, how, and toward what end the exhibit is being made and how it fits into the overall museum exhibit program. The guidelines should be firm in overall direction, yet flexible enough to adapt to specific circumstances."[27]

Plans for individual museums will vary, depending on their mission, resources, location, and a myriad of other concerns, but a lack of planning will lead to the same conclusion for all museums. David Dean[28] expresses the concern that museums would become "driven by the demand to fill space, rather than by ethical purpose and educational design." When creating a plan, it quickly becomes obvious that the exhibit staff does not create exhibitions alone. There are six key areas that must work in tandem to implement an exhibit policy. They are collections; locations and facilities; museum marketing and visitors; sponsorships, grants, and gifts; finance and staff; and the museum communicators.[29]

Collections

Concerns about preserving the collection should be as much of an issue for the exhibits staff as it is for the collections staff. There are important questions to be answered: What are the best items to tell the story of the exhibit? What is the condition of the object? Can it withstand permanent exhibition, or any exhibition time at all? Will this item be secure in the exhibit?

According to Belcher,[30] security is an important aspect in the development of every exhibit, and it must be considered before, not after, an exhibit is assembled. Security measures involve locking cases, adding weight or fastening cases to the floor to prevent tipping, keeping a record of what objects are on exhibit and where they are, installing a security system, and having a strolling guard or other staff member in the exhibit space.[31] The proper security procedures for a museum will vary depending on the size of the museum, the locale, and the collection objects used. "The safety of objects must be an overriding consideration, and conservation and security requirements must be satisfied."[32]

Conservation is a major concern when objects leave the storage environment for the unknown of the exhibit floor. Threats appear from materials used in case construction, light and humidity levels, improper mounts, pests, and human negligence. The safest route is to create micro-environments in which the objects can spend time in the so-called limelight without suffering any adverse effects. Exhibition policy should outline ways to neutralize as many threats as possible, but it must also allow the visitor access to the object and exhibit. Each area should have a listing of acceptable values, such as five foot-candles for dyed textiles, UV filters placed on lighting, relative humidity of 40 to 50 percent, and buffering to prevent off-gassing of materials. Maintenance schedules, including case inspection, should be part of the policy. All measures to preserve the collection must be taken seriously and incorporated into the exhibit policy in order to preserve the objects and the public trust given to museums.[33]

"Public trust cannot be undervalued," says David Dean;[34] "Properly presented exhibitions confirm public trust in the museum as a place for conservation and careful presentation. Potential donors of objects or collections will be much more inclined to place their treasures in institutions that will care for the objects properly, and will present those objects for public good in a thoughtful and informative manner."

Locations and Facilities

"Don't squish me." "I feel like a sardine." "I'm getting claustrophobic." "I can't breathe." These are not the words museum staff members want to hear in an exhibit area. It is essential that adequate space be allocated for exhibits. There must be space for the artifacts and space for visitors to view them comfortably, whether they are many in a large school group or an individual using a wheelchair.

Museums commonly exhibit objects in two ways—permanent exhibits and temporary or special exhibits. Permanent exhibits must contain enough material and experiences to attract repeat visitors and provide them with opportunities for new discoveries as well as old memories. Permanent exhibits are expected to last for ten years or more before renovation, so durability is a virtue.[35] They can set the character of an institution, becoming in some cases an icon or signature image for a museum (as "Archie" the mammoth has become for the University of Nebraska State Museum in Lincoln or the dinosaur *Diplodicus* for the Carnegie Museum of Natural History in Pittsburgh, Pennsylvania).

Museums cannot live by permanent exhibits alone. Temporary or special exhibits can maximize use of space. They provide a chance for change and for sustaining visitor interest and attracting new visitors. The time frame for temporary exhibits is generally six months to five years.

"Blockbuster" shows have become part of the temporary exhibit world. "Blockbuster" refers to shows that attract significant attention, such as the Van Gogh exhibition at the National Gallery of Art in Washington, D.C., which sold out its advance tickets, or the "King Tut" exhibit, which started the modern "blockbuster" craze. "Blockbusters" often involve sponsors from the for-profit business world.[36]

An issue that museum administrators have had to take more seriously since 1990 is ensuring that exhibition spaces are available to people of all abilities. The Americans with Disabilities Act requires museums to provide visitors with disabilities equal access to public programs and spaces, including exhibits. By focusing on details such as audio descriptions, items for tactile examination, adequate lighting, height of display cases, and readability of text, exhibit staff members can broaden audiences.[37] The Smithsonian Guidelines for Accessible Exhibition Design outline specifics for these components, as well as proper language for symbols and nonoffensive terminology. Museums are finding that the guidelines do not create design problems but instead create a better visitor experience for all.[38]

Museum Marketing and Visitors

"Only as they [visitors] trickle through and fill the various passageways and spaces to interact with the exhibits do these otherwise passive, dead areas come to life."[39] Who exactly are these visitors and what does it take to satisfy them? Each museum will find different answers to this question, and that is why it is vital for each museum to connect with its own audience. For example, if a college science museum thinks that its main visitors are the academic faculty, the labels would most likely be technical on the assumption that visitors have prior knowledge of basic concepts. However, if the majority of its visitors are young children with parents, the label text will be too difficult—for children and parents alike. Museum fatigue will set in quickly and drive out those visitors.[40]

Labels truly are an important aspect of the exhibit experience and should be treated as such, not as the last item on a checklist.[41] Label content will vary depending on the type of exhibition as well as the emphasis of the museum. Art museums most often use descriptive labels, which provide the most basic information for identification of the object (title of work, artist, medium, date). Interpretive labels, more often used in science and history museums, are lengthier and explain not only what an object is but also why it is significant.

Decisions about exhibition content are all too often based on staff assumptions about community needs rather than information actually gathered from the community itself. Research involves determining the interests and understanding of visitors.[42] The MAP (Museum Assessment Program) III of the Institute of Museum and Library Services provides funds for assessing public programs, including the undertaking of visitor research. This often takes the form of front-end evaluation as a way to test an exhibition idea.

If an exhibit idea makes it through the formative evaluation stage, it is created and placed in the museum. At that point, a summative evaluation will determine how visitors react to the finished product. In the exhibit world, finished is never finished. By using the summative evaluation results, an exhibit can be refined and used as an example when creating other exhibits.

Does this emphasis on visitors mean all exhibit decisions are left to their desires? Definitely not! Before visitors are involved in an idea, the museum staff must follow its exhibit policy and evaluate whether the exhibit is true to the museum's mission and its standards. Will it serve the community's needs and the museum's needs equally well? Management also must be thinking about approving and scheduling the exhibit and assessing available or potential resources.[43]

Spending money wisely should result in attracting visitors. It is becoming increasingly important for museums to attract a culturally and ethnically diverse audience. All visitors, even seemingly look-alike Caucasians, have their own cultural identities and experiences; no two visitors are alike. However, museums have tended to consider the European American viewpoint first, or at least to look at the world from that perspective. Exhibits that draw on the experiences and viewpoints of other ethnic groups in the community and the world are changing those thoughts. Cross-cultural exhibitions often present such stark contrasts between what the majority knows and what the majority needs to know that the challenge of reorganizing one's knowledge becomes an aspect of the exhibition experience. The challenge to exhibition makers is to provide within exhibits the contexts and resources that enable audiences to reorganize their knowledge.

Cross-cultural exhibitions present the challenge of who has the authority to speak for different cultural groups. Museums have approached this idea in different ways. Some institutions, like the Birmingham Museum in Alabama, have used the traditional curatorial authoring voice but broadened it with the involvement of specialist advisers for an updated exhibit of its ethnographic collection of art and material culture from North America, Africa, and Oceania.

An active approach for any museum would be to draft a multicultural policy statement and incorporate it into the exhibit policy. The statement should be created by a diverse group of people involved in the museum's activities, including board members, staff, and constituents (including cultural representatives). Not only will the museum become better informed about its collections, but cultural representatives will know that objects essential to their particular culture's life are being preserved and presented in an appropriate manner.

One group of visitors museums are attempting to reach is made up of people who want to be active, to become involved in the exhibition. Michael Spock, former director of the Boston Children's Museum, was one of the early proponents of hands-on exhibits, but even he had concerns about introducing them to the public. The concern was that "the exhibit was going to be vulnerable and would be vandalized."[44] Happily, children were respectful and did not try to steal the objects, which was a significant revelation. Hands-on exhibits do experience significant usage, however, and a repair or replacement cycle and resultant budget costs should be planned for any such component.[45]

Box 12.1

Exercise: Evaluation of Exhibits

At a local museum with which you are familiar and where you have received permission, evaluate visitors' use of one of the important exhibit galleries. You should make your observations over a period of at least four hours. Try to be inconspicuous while observing so that you do not change visitor behavior.

Sketch the floor plan of the exhibit gallery and trace the routes individual visitors or groups of visitors take through the gallery. Record how long visitors spend at each of the exhibits in the gallery. Record any intragroup or intergroup interactions you observe, especially as these interactions relate to the exhibits.

Write a two-page summary of your observations to be given to the museum. What part of the gallery seemed to be of most interest to visitors? Why do you think this is true? What part of the gallery seemed to be least interesting to visitors? Can you give reasons why this area seemed to be of the least interest? What could the museum do to enhance visitors' experience in this gallery? What recommendations can you make to guide the museum as it plans future exhibits?

Sponsorships, Grants, and Gifts

Exhibits are among the most expensive public programs the museum produces, and, as the most visible of programs, exhibits can attract monetary support. This support can take the form of corporate sponsorship of exhibits, whether they are "blockbusters" or small displays. How the money for exhibits is spent and the results of those expenses will be the business of the trustees, the community, and regional and national funding bodies. Editorial control must not be exchanged for monetary or other forms of support because to do so would undercut the ethical structure of the museum and erode public trust. Museums must be proactive and outline partnership rules for sponsors. These rules should be included in the exhibit policy.[46]

More money means more advertising, more prestige, and more visitors, but it also has drawbacks. Corporations may say they are not involved in the exhibition, but the public still sees the connections. Sometimes the connections are blatant—Mattel Inc.'s funding of a 1994 touring exhibition on "Barbie" included editorial control that the public perceived as censorship. The Smithsonian's exhibition on the building of the Alaska Pipeline, funded in part by the Alyeska Pipeline Service Company; the

Metropolitan Museum of Art's retrospective of works of Louis Comfort Tiffany, supported by Tiffany & Company; and the Carnegie Museum of Art's "Aluminum by Design: Jewelry to Jets," funded by the ALCOA Foundation, are examples of corporate sponsorships that raise questions as well as eyebrows. Less obvious connections—ad executive Charles Saatchi's underwriting of the "Sensation" art exhibit that featured his collection, and Giorgio Armani's $15 million contribution to the Guggenheim capital campaign in 1999, followed in the same year by the show "Giorgio Armani" at the museum—undermine museum credibility when they are revealed. The AAM has established a task force to examine the ethics of sponsorship, but in the interim, the principles at the core of museum ethics should serve as a guide—honesty, transparency of all dealings, independence, and "preventing at all costs both the perception and the reality of conflict of interest."[47] The museum must remember that as the corporation benefits from the museum's reputation, so the reputation of the corporation, for good or bad, will reflect on the museum.

Another source of revenue comes from the private sector. When museums approach individual givers, they must learn what a potential donor's interests are and match them to the appropriate exhibition or program. A careful consideration of the museum's mission and its commitment to intellectual integrity will ensure an appropriate mesh of donor wishes and museum needs. Museums that offer donors significant input into program content will find themselves subject to constituent criticism at the least, if not editorial castigation in the media.[48] Similar considerations should be made when approaching foundations. Generally, local foundations will be more interested in the programs of a local museum than foundations in other regions of the country. The exception to this rule is large foundations, such as the Ford Foundation or the Pew Charitable Trust, that provide grants nationwide.

Although exhibits are expensive, they also help to support the institution financially by giving people a reason to visit the museum; therefore, exhibits should be treated with respect and an eye to the future. Exhibitions provide a highly visible justification for a museum's existence and its expectation for continued support. Donors, both public and private, are more likely to give to a museum with an active and popular exhibition schedule.[49]

Finance and Staff

How grants, sponsorships, gifts, and general museum dollars are spent on exhibits will ultimately become the responsibility of the museum director and the museum's board. They must spend money wisely in the creation of good exhibits. Exhibits are a critical investment. Limited finances and ensuing restrictions on exhibitions could result in a decrease in visitor interest and museum attendance.[50] Museums must remember that their competition is amusement parks, movies, video games, computers, television, and similar activities. It behooves the museum administration to find the financial resources necessary to support a healthy exhibits program.

The tasks that relate directly to exhibit planning and production include scheduling and contracting for exhibitions, contracting for services, production and resource management, documentation and registration, and publicity and marketing. It is essential that every person involved in planning, managing, producing, and maintaining exhibitions be aware of the project's progress.[51] This means that the exhibits staff should be involved in the budget process. The operating costs of maintaining an exhibit must be considered along with the costs of planning and installing it.

One way to keep the exhibit development process moving smoothly for all parties involved is to employ a checklist. It must include a method of determining a project's status, a budgeting section both for obtaining funds and for dispersing them, a timeline of required tasks, and task assignments. It acts as a tracking document and provides a quick reference that shows the exhibit's current stage of development.[52]

Museum Communicators

In some museums, the curator will act alone as the museum communicator, but more often in recent years, exhibits have been created by a team of museum communicators—educators, curators, collection managers, exhibit designers, and others.[53] This group will select objects for the proposed exhibit and determine how they will be displayed. It will use exhibit policy guidelines to determine if the topic is a good fit for the museum and its mission. It will appoint a project expediter to make sure everything rolls along as it should. One of the most common features of successful team projects is, according to Alan Friedman,[54] "a single individual on the team who is charged with responsibility for each element of presentation, from conception through final installation." A successful team also needs the full backing and support of the museum director.

Putting It All Together

All of these aspects of exhibit policy and procedure—collections; location and facilities; museum marketing and visitors; sponsorships, grants, and gifts; finances and staff; and museum communicators—have one thing in common. They all focus on visitors, who are the key to success. Visitors should be the first and last thought, no matter what kind of challenges arise. A good exhibit policy will reflect the importance of keeping visitors in mind during every step of the planning process. With an exhibits policy in hand and visitors foremost in mind, museums have the best chance of ensuring that all of these components will work together and produce the best possible product.

Conclusion

Regardless of its mission, size, or emphasis, a museum will be known to its audiences through its public programs. According to Neil Kotler of the Smithsonian Institution and Philip Kotler of Northwestern University, "Museums offer the public rich, multidimensional sensory experiences with rare authentic objects, along with the research, knowledge, and interpretation behind them."[55] We in museums also have the potential to offer a valuable alternative to people who feel oversaturated with mass media and the products of entertainment conglomerates. Through creative and effective public programs, museums can give visitors "safe public spaces for recreation, learning, and sociability" as well as "enchanting, celebrative, and transforming experiences."[56]

Notes

1. AAM 1992, 6.
2. Ibid., 7.
3. Diamond 1999.

CHAPTER 12

4. Ibid., 25.
5. NSF 1998, 7.
6. Diamond 1999.
7. Williams 1992, 62.
8. Alexander 1996.
9. O'Donnell 1995.
10. Falk and Dierking 1992.
11. Bearman and Trant 1999, 9.
12. Bearman and Trant 1999.
13. Carr 1999, 32.
14. Belcher 1991.
15. Dean 1994.
16. Carr 1999, 34.
17. Ibid., 35.
18. Weil 1999, 244.
19. Falk 1999.
20. Ibid., 260.
21. Diamond 1999, 16–17.
22. Diamond 1999.
23. Belcher 1991, 171.
24. Falk and Dierking 1992.
25. Bergmann 1992.
26. Ibid., 81.
27. Ibid.
28. Dean 1994, 13.
29. Belcher 1991.
30. Ibid.
31. Dean 1994.
32. Belcher 1991, 73.
33. Dean 1994; Miles 1988.
34. Dean 1994, 2.
35. Belcher 1991.
36. Ibid.
37. Miles 1988.
38. Smithsonian n.d.
39. Belcher 1991, 171.
40. Belcher 1991; Miles 1988.
41. Dean 1994.
42. Belcher 1991.

43. Belcher 1991; Miles 1988.
44. Garfield 1993, 58.
45. Garfield 1993.
46. Belcher 1991.
47. Lord 2000, 79.
48. Balzar 2001.
49. Belcher 1991.
50. Ibid.
51. Ibid.
52. Dean 1994.
53. Blackmon et al. 1988.
54. Friedman 1991, 80.
55. Kotler and Kotler 1998, 361.
56. Ibid.

CHAPTER THIRTEEN
LEGAL ISSUES

Nothing in this chapter should be considered legal advice. This material is presented solely to raise awareness concerning six legal issues that commonly confront museum administrators and managers. The museum profession indeed is fortunate to have three excellent texts available concerning legal issues for museums—*Museum Law: A Guide for Officers, Director and Counsel,* by Marilyn E. Phelan, Professor of Law and Museum Science, Texas Tech University; the 1998 update of *A Legal Primer on Managing Museum Collections,* by Marie C. Malero, formerly director of the Museum Studies Program at George Washington University and legal counsel for the Smithsonian Institution; and *Art and Museum Law: Cases and Materials,* by Robert C. Lind, Professor of Law, Southwestern University School of Law, Robert M. Jarvis, Professor of Law, Nova Southeastern University Law Center, and Professor Phelan. We urge all museum professionals to purchase these primary books on museum law.

Americans with Disabilities Act (ADA)

Museums must work to enhance the experiences of their visitors with disabilities. Providing experiences for disabled visitors always has been the ethical thing to do, and with the passage of the Americans with Disabilities Act,[1] it is also the legal thing to do. (A good starting point for museums in understanding accessibility issues is the Association of Science-Technology Centers website.[2])

What Is ADA?

President George Bush signed Public Law §101–336, the Americans with Disabilities Act (ADA), on July 26, 1990.[3] ADA is a Federal law that gives individuals with disabilities civil rights protection similar to that provided against discrimination on the basis of race, color, sex, national origin, age, and religion. This law prohibits discrimination based on disability and guarantees individuals with disabilities equal opportunities in employment, state and local government services, places of public accommodation, transportation, and telecommunications.[4] ADA extended the protections of the Civil Rights Act of 1964 to the 53 million Americans with some form of disability. ADA is modeled after the Civil Rights Act and Section 504 of the Rehabilitation Act of 1973. The Rehabilitation Act of 1973[5] is regarded as the most important "program accessibility" legislation before ADA.

Contents of ADA

Title I—Employment

Title I of ADA provides protection for qualified individuals with a disability against discrimination in employment and includes specific features related to reasonable accommodation, qualification standards, and other management issues. Employers, including museums, must reasonably accommodate the disabilities of qualified applicants or employees, including modifying workstations and equipment, unless undue hardship would result.[6]

Title II—Public Services

The Public Services section of ADA consists of two subtitles, but only Subtitle a—Prohibition Against Discrimination and other Generally Applicable Provisions—has application for museums. This portion of Title II prohibits any public entity, defined as any part of state or local government, from discriminating against individuals based upon their disabilities in the provision of "services, programs, or activities." If a museum is a part of any branch of a state or local government, it will be covered by provisions of Title II.

Title III—Public Accommodations and Services Operated by Private Entities

If a museum is not covered by Title II, it will follow provisions of Title III, which prohibits discrimination on the basis of disability by private entities in places of public accommodation. This rule requires that all new places of public accommodation and commercial facilities be designed and constructed to be readily accessible to and usable by persons with disabilities. Those alterations must be to the maximum extent feasible.

Title IV—Telecommunications

Title IV of ADA sets forth two major requirements to expand telecommunication services for individuals with hearing impairments—telecommunications relay services and closed captioning of all federally funded television public service announcements. Both of these requirements may affect museums. Museums are expected to provide TDD "telephone" service, and any video used in exhibits or programs should be captioned.

Definitions of Terms

The definitions of the following terms for ADA must be understood in order to properly implement the law.

Disability

There are several general categories of disability that comprise most of the disabled population—mobility, visual, hearing, and cognitive. According to the Americans with Disabilities Act, a person with a disability is defined as: "a person with a physical or mental impairment that substantially limits one or more major life activities; or a person with a record of such a physical or mental impairment; or a person who is regarded as having such an impairment." Under ADA, the term "qualified individual with a disability" means an individual with a disability who is, with or without reasonable modifications to rules, policies, or practices, qualified for the removal of architectural, communication, or transportation barriers, or the participation in programs or activities provided by a public entity.

Accessibility

Under ADA, accessibility means compliance with the requirements of the Americans with Disabilities Act Standards for Accessible Design for new construction or alterations. To museums, accessibility means making the site's exhibits and programs available to all visitors. Standards for new construction differ from standards for alterations. ADA Accessibility Guidelines set standards that are applied during the design, construction, and alteration of buildings and facilities covered by Titles II and III.[7]

Universal Design

Universal design is the design of spaces, elements, and systems to make them as usable as possible by as wide a range of people as possible. One basic characteristic of universal design is the redesign of existing elements to broaden their functionality instead of the introduction of new elements into the environment. Universal design creates a safer, more functional, and more convenient environment for everyone, not just those with disabilities. Universal design has replaced the older term "barrier-free design."[8]

Public Accommodation

Places of public accommodation are classified into twelve categories: places of lodging, establishments serving food or drink, places of exhibition or entertainment, places of public gathering, sales or rental establishments, service establishments, stations used for specified public transportation, places of public display or collection, places of recreation, places of education, social service center establishments, and places of exercise or recreation.

Accessibility for Museums

Accessibility is one of the most important factors for public places. Janice Majewski,[9] accessibility coordinator for the Smithsonian Institution, stated, "Accessibility is for the majority, not just for the largest minority in the country, and accessibility is for people who have different learning styles and communication problems as well as for people who use wheelchairs." According to P. B. Williams,[10] "Each museum should strive to make itself and its collections accessible—physically, emotionally, and intellectually—to the widest possible audience." The American Association of Museums[11] stated in *Everyone's Welcome,* "From museum guards to tour guides, curators to administrators, all of the public must be treated with dignity, courtesy, and human understanding. And accessibility for people with disabilities will make everyone's daily life easier." The AAM[12] also sets forth "Nine Building Blocks to Accessibility," encouraging museums to take the following steps:

- include a statement of commitment to accessibility in the museum's general policy or mission statement
- designate an accessibility coordinator
- obtain input from people with disabilities [and] organize an Accessibility Advisory Council of people with disabilities
- train staff on accessibility, the ADA, and strategies for serving all visitors
- conduct a review of facilities and programs to identify existing barriers and discriminatory policies or practices
- implement short- and long-term institution-wide accessibility
- promote and advertise accessibility in the museum
- establish a grievance process
- conduct an ongoing review of accessibility efforts

Barrier Removal

Barrier removal is the key to an accessible design and a universal design; it is an essential factor in Title III of ADA. ADA requires the removal of architectural barriers that are structural in nature from existing public accommodations where such removal is readily achievable.[13] "Readily achievable" means easily accomplished and carried out without much difficulty or expense.[14] ADA regulations offer twenty-one examples of readily achievable steps to remove barriers, but the following list is not all-inclusive or limiting: (1) installing ramps; (2) making curb cuts in sidewalks and entrances; (3) lowering shelves; (4) rearranging tables, chairs, vending machines, display racks, and other features; (5) lowering telephones; (6) adding raised-letter markings on elevator control buttons; (7) installing flashing alarm lights; (8) widening doors; (9) installing hinges to widen doorways; (10) eliminating a turnstile or providing an alternative accessible path; (11) installing accessible door hardware; (12) installing grab bars in toilet stalls; (13) rearranging toilet partitions to increase maneuvering space; (14) installing lavatory pipes; (15) installing a raised toilet seat; (16) installing full-length mirrors; (17) lowering the paper towel dispenser in a bathroom; (18) creating a designated accessible parking space; (19) installing an accessible paper cup dispenser at an existing inaccessible water fountain; (20) removing high-pile, low-density carpeting; and (21) installing vehicle hand controls.

Because it is difficult to achieve all alterations at once, the ADA regulations suggest this order of priorities:

- Priority 1: Items that must be navigated to get into the building (parking spaces, curb cuts, access ramps, wider entrances, thresholds, easy-open doors)
- Priority 2: Basic items that must be used for interior circulation, use of the facilities, or acquiring products or services offered (door hardware, furniture arrangement, visual alarms, Braille and raised-character signs, ramps)
- Priority 3: Items that provide access to facilities, with rest rooms a chief concern (doors, ramps, signs, internal maneuvering room, fixture design and installation, grab bars)
- Priority 4: Any other items that do not comply but constitute a bar to access to the goods, services, privileges, or accommodations offered (such as telephones and water fountains)

Concluding Thoughts

Museum workers must study ADA prudently. Alan Quick[15] emphasizes that "an error can be, and probably will be, expensive in both human and financial terms." For example, the civil penalties for violating Title III may be as high as $50,000 for a first violation and $100,000 for any subsequent violation. However, it is hoped that rather than being driven by fear

Box 13.1

Exercise: ADA Inspection

With someone knowledgeable about the Americans with Disabilities Act, such as an affirmative action officer, an architect, a volunteer from a local social services agency, a representative from an organization serving senior citizens, or a volunteer from a local agency for the disabled, visit your museum or another local museum. Make a list of physical barriers that detract from the museum experience of visitors.

Which of these physical barriers should be removed under ADA?

Which physical barriers would be good to remove even though their removal would not be required under ADA?

Make a list of barriers to be removed and indicate which should be addressed immediately and which could be delayed until later.

If you were planning a new museum or renovating an existing building for use as a museum facility, what would be the most important physical barriers to avoid or eliminate from the future museum building?

of legal actions, museums will be motivated by a higher calling to provide accessibility and will do it because it is the right thing to do.

Native American Graves Protection and Repatriation Act (NAGPRA)

Throughout the past century, Native Americans have fought for control of their cultural heritage as they have seen their traditional ways of life disappear.[16] Raymond Thompson,[17] director of Arizona State Museum at the University of Arizona, states, "The last half of the 20th century has not been a good time for the continuity and preservation of American Indian traditions, languages and religions." Yet Native Americans began searching for ways to revive their culture, and the search eventually led them to museums where the physical remains of Native American culture often are kept. Over time, museums had acquired a wide range of Native American artifacts, including sacred materials that are an essential part of revitalizing Native American religions and traditions. "Historically, Native Americans had found themselves disconnected from museums in this country; they were studied and interpreted from a distance, with little opportunity to speak for themselves. In addition, Native American artifacts and human remains that were part of museum collections seemed beyond their reach," according to Malaro.[18]

President George Bush signed the Native American Graves Protection and Repatriation Act[19] into law on November 16, 1990. T. H. Boyd and Jonathan Haas[20] have observed: "This law may mark the 'beginning, not the end, of a dialogue between museums and native groups about the treatment, care and repose of ethnographic and archeological collections.'" According to Geoffrey Platt,[21] "A guiding principal in crafting the final legislation was a desire to balance the need for respect of the human rights of Native Americans, with the value of scientific study and public education—all within a complex legal framework." In trying to strike a balance between competing interests, NAGPRA only sets standards, conditions, and definitions under which certain Native American objects and remains can be repatriated; it encourages cooperation and consultation in its implementation.[22]

NAGPRA required all agencies and museums that receive federal funds (including state, local, and private institutions) to inventory all Native American ancestral remains and associated funerary objects and to develop written summaries of all sacred objects, objects of cultural patrimony, and unassociated funerary objects within their collections. During this process, these institutions were to consult with Native American tribes, Native Alaskans, and Native Hawaiian organizations to reach agreements on repatriation or other disposition of these remains and objects. NAGPRA not only affirms the right of individuals with lineal or culturally affiliated descent to decide on the disposition of or take possession of these items; it also increases protection for unmarked Native American graves located on federal and tribal lands.[23] In addition, NAGPRA prohibits trafficking in Native American human remains and cultural items.

Inventories

By November 16, 1993, museums and federal agencies were required to have a written summary for all sacred objects, objects of cultural patrimony, and unassociated funerary goods in their collection. During this process, museums and agencies were required to consult with tribal, Native Alaskan, and Native Hawaiian organizations and traditional religious leaders identified as having a likely cultural affiliation with the items. The written summaries were to include information on the scope of these collections, kinds of objects included, information on the geographical location of origin, means and period of acquisition, and cultural affiliation. As of July 22, 1998, 1,032 museums and federally funded institutions had submitted written summaries of these objects in their collections.

By November 16, 1995, museums were required to complete inventories of human remains and associated funerary objects and to prepare two documents based upon the inventories. One was a list of remains and objects that had been identified as affiliated with one or more Native American groups; the other was a list of remains and objects for which such affiliation could not be determined.[24] As of April 13, 1998, 733 museums and federally funded institutions had submitted a NAGPRA inventory.

Federal agencies and museums were to notify the appropriate tribes of inventory completion within six months of the date of compilation. This notification was to describe each set of human remains and associated funerary objects, including information on the acquisition of the objects. A copy of each notification was to have been sent to the Secretary of the Interior for eventual publication in the *Federal Register*. Under NAGPRA, all information discovered during the inventory process was to be made available to Native American tribes, Native Alaskans, or Hawaiian organizations.

Repatriation

NAGPRA provides a mechanism through which materials may be repatriated to lineal descendants, tribes that demonstrate ownership, or tribes with a cultural affiliation. NAGPRA defines cultural affiliation as follows: "a relationship of shared group identity which can be reasonably traced historically or prehistorically between a present day tribe, Native Alaskan, or Native Hawaiian organization and an identifiable earlier group." Several different types of evidence can be used to show cultural affiliation, including geographical, kinship, biological, archaeological, anthropological, historical, or linguistic evidence; oral tradition; or other relevant information. Because it may be impossible for claimants to prove an absolute continuity of lineage from present-day tribes to older tribes, the evaluation of cultural affiliation is to be based on a preponderance of information pertaining to the relationship between the claimant and the claimed material. When cultural affiliation cannot be ascertained, NAGPRA provides criteria for placing the affiliated tribes in priority order.

The repatriation of cultural items involves a four-part process. First, native peoples must show that the requested items fall under the definition of objects of cultural patrimony, associated funerary objects, sacred objects, or unassociated funerary objects. Second, native people must be able to prove a cultural affiliation with the object or show prior ownership. If these requirements are met, then native people must prove that the federal agency or museum does not have right of possession to the object. The criterion for the right of possession is defined in NAGPRA: "possession obtained with the voluntary consent of an individual or group that had authority of alienation."

Disputes concerning ownership can be resolved with the help of a review committee established by the secretary of the interior. If the review committee cannot come to a solution, disputes can be resolved in the federal courts. All objects meeting the four-part process requirements will be returned following publication in the *Federal Register* by the museum or federal agency of a "notice of intent to repatriate" to the lineal descendant or tribe. NAGPRA states that lineal descendants or culturally affiliated Indian tribes, Native Alaskans, and Native Hawaiian organizations have the right to make final judgments on the treatment of their ancestral remains and cultural items.

Implementation

The implementation of NAGPRA was assigned to the secretary of the interior, who is responsible for promulgating regulations to carry out the law. Under the direction of the secretary of the interior, a seven-member review committee was established to help monitor and review all inventories, identifications, and repatriation activities; to make recommendations for future care of repatriated cultural items; and to submit an annual report to Congress. NAGPRA provides the secretary of the interior with the right to assess civil penalties against museums and federal agencies that do not comply with the law. If a museum repatriates an item in good faith, however, it is not liable for claims against it predicated upon a claim of wrongful repatriation, breach of fiduciary duty, public trust, or violations of state law.

Concluding Thoughts

Many Native Americans describe a love-hate relationship with museums. They appreciate that museums have preserved material necessary to preserve their religious and cultural heritage. On the other hand, they dislike the fact that these museums are so far away from their homes and that access to objects vital to the restoration of their dwindling culture is extremely limited.[25] Museums are benefiting from NAGPRA because it has increased their communication with native groups and has helped establish new partnerships with them. Native American people have begun to play a role in the planning of museum exhibits and public programs. Creating these new partnerships allows museums to work together with Native Americans to increase the understanding of American Indian culture and history.[26]

Unrelated Business Taxable Income

Nonprofit organizations are subject to taxation on specific activities if these activities are unrelated to their exempt purposes. The source of the income, rather than how the proceeds are ultimately used, determines whether it is taxable or not. Those museums with more than one thousand dollars in income from unrelated business activities must file an IRS form 990T. Phelan[27] states, "'Unrelated business taxable income is defined as gross income derived from any unrelated trade or business, regularly carried on." "Regularly carried on" is open to interpretation but is generally determined by comparing the "sequence and continuity" of the activity carried on by the nonprofit organization with similar commercial activities of a taxable business. If they are similar, then the activity will most likely be judged to be "regularly carried on" and will be taxable. The purpose of this tax is to prevent nonprofit organizations from enjoying an unfair advantage in certain business activities compared with taxable organizations.[28]

Activities Excluded from Taxation

Three activities conducted by museums are specifically exempt from unrelated business income taxation. Activities conducted for a museum by volunteers are not subject to taxation. The receipts from the sale of donated merchandise are not subject to taxation. Any activity conducted primarily for the benefit of staff, volunteers, members, students, and visitors will not be taxed.

Potentially Taxable Activities

Museum administrators should evaluate a variety of the museum's activities for the possibility of incurring unrelated business income tax (UBIT) on their receipts. Among those activities that should be examined are museum stores, eating facilities, parking, travel tours, sales of collection objects, fundraising, advertising, income from investments, rentals, royalties, and certain programming.

Generally, eating facilities and parking lots that operate for the convenience of the staff, volunteers, members, and visitors will not be taxed. If used for other unrelated activities, the income from these facilities will be taxable. Fundraising activities are usually not regarded as unrelated business taxable income because they are not "regularly carried on" and they use a considerable number of volunteers. Income from investments should not be taxable, thus protecting the income from endowments that is vital to the operation of many museums. Royalties from licensing in most cases will not be taxed as unrelated business taxable income.

Receipts from the sale of items from the collection are usually taxed. This is an important issue for art museums and zoos that regularly sell items from their collections at moderate to extremely high prices. The theory is that if the item is being removed from the museum's or zoo's collections, the item can no longer support the mission of the organization. Generally, receipts from the sale of advertising in an organization's publication also are subject to taxes.

Rent from real property is not taxed as unrelated business income, whereas rent from personal property is generally taxed. Again, this can be seen as the museum being allowed to use its real property to the benefit of the museum and its programs. Some parts of a museum's programming also may need to be assessed for potential unrelated business taxable income. For example, a planetarium could use its theater for educational programs for school groups during weekdays but use it for public entertainment programs on weekends. Receipts from the former would not be taxable, but receipts from the latter would be. Income from tours for which a staff member is the leader of the tour and income from educational programs offered as part of the tour should not be taxed, but if the museum works with a travel agency that pays the museum a fee per person, this income is taxable.

The museum store will be the most difficult part of a museum's operation to assess for potential taxation of unrelated business income. The taxable status of merchandise to be sold in the gift shop must be determined on an item-by-item basis. Those items relating to the museum's exempt status will not be taxed, whereas those items not contributing to the museum's exempt status will be taxed. Although this sounds like a fairly straightforward issue, it has proved to be anything but, because the Internal Revenue Service (IRS) continues to make new determinations. For example, items of apparel carrying the museum's logo were at one time exempt from taxation, but at the time of this writing this determination is under review by the IRS.[29]

Concluding Thoughts

Unrelated business taxable income is an important issue for museum administrators, especially directors, because an assessment of unrelated business income taxes could have a significant impact on the museum and its programs. Museums certainly can engage in unrelated business activities, but the resulting taxes must be taken into account as the financial benefit of the activity is calculated. The real challenge of unrelated business income tax is the constantly shifting determinations by the IRS of what will be taxed and what will be exempt. This means that the museum's director and business manager must monitor these changes at all times.

Legal Liability

We live in an increasingly litigious society. Sometimes it seems as if just about everyone is being sued or is busily suing someone else. As the tendency to settle matters in the courtroom has grown, there has been a corresponding decline in the traditional protection from legal peril afforded nonprofit organizations. The immunity once enjoyed by public service organizations has evaporated, and even museums are no longer safe from attack in courts as a result of their official activities.

Liability

Ultimate accountability and responsibility for ensuring the museum follows the law fall to the museum's board of trustees. The board is legally responsible to the state attorney general for all the museum does, and it is the entity against which any legal action will be directed. In some instances, individual trustees can also be sued and held liable for failing to carry out their duties, although this action is relatively infrequent. More commonly, trustees become involved in threatened lawsuits that are settled before they get to court. These legal maneuverings require the diversion of valuable resources from the museum's primary mission and may be just as damaging in the long run as a suit that runs its legal course. The museum also is indirectly liable for the acts of its officials, employees, docents, volunteers, and even outside contractors. This means the museum's board of trustees and director must be aware of the museum's legal obligations in a plethora of situations.

Tort and Contract Law

The museum may limit its liability by knowing which activities to undertake and which to avoid. Liability can stem from one of two branches of the law—either tort law or contract law. A tort is defined as any wrongful act, or failure to act, that does not involve a breach of contract; all other wrongs fall under contract law and are considered breaches of contract.

Loan agreements and work performed by outside contractors are examples of activities covered by contract law. The defining issue in tort law is the concept of "negligence," which Phelan[30] defines as "conduct that falls below a standard established by law for the protection of others." In defining negligence, the legal system assumes that the museum director and the trustees are "prudent" people. That is, their standard of conduct will be measured against the conduct of a reasonable person under like circumstances. A museum director would thus be held to the care or skill that an ordinarily prudent museum director would exercise under similar circumstances. If his or her conduct does not meet this standard, the director would be negligent, and the museum is thus liable under tort law.

The Illinois Heritage Association (IHA) suggests a less threatening way of looking at museum liability. In an article by executive director Patricia Miller,[31] the IHA advises museum directors to develop written rules for legal protection covering six main areas of potential liability: governance, personnel, collections management, risk management, copyright, and earned income. If rules and standards are in place covering these six areas, a museum should be able to minimize the extent of its liability. Copyright and earned income are discussed elsewhere in this chapter; the remaining four areas are covered below.[32]

Governance

The documents, policies, papers, and contracts a museum uses in the operation of its business are called its governing documents. These may include the documents issued by a museum relating to the roles and responsibilities of trustees, the museum's bylaws, and its codes of conduct, including its position on conflict of interest and personal collecting. The governing documents may also include warranties, contracts, sales policies, and licensing agreements—in other words, virtually everything a museum may publish relating to its methods of governance. From a legal standpoint, the position taken in each of these documents defines the museum's stated duties and responsibilities to the public; they form the basis of the museum's standards for meeting its obligations. For obvious reasons, most of the governance liability will relate to contract law and breaches of contract. A museum director should carefully examine and be familiar with all governing documents because they form the foundation of any legal claim the museum may wish, or be forced, to make in the future.

Personnel

Another area of potential liability relates to the policies that outline the responsibilities and privileges of the museum staff. If these policies are written in an employee handbook, they form a contract between the employees and the museum and thus are covered under contract law. The museum's lawyer or legal advisor should view all employee handbooks for their legal implications, just as he or she also should see all other contracts. The key here is equitable treatment in recruiting, hiring, evaluating, and terminating employees. Museums are not immune from legal actions brought by disgruntled employees or volunteers. Personnel problems, and the liability that may be incurred, would be subject to a breach of contract judgment. Tort law would apply in noncontractual issues involving negligence. For example, if a docent allows a group of children to play on a sculpture, and one child is subsequently injured in a fall, the museum is liable for negligence because the volunteer would legally be considered the museum's representative.

Collections Management

One of the most likely areas of liability for a museum comes from failure to properly conserve its collections. As Alan Ullberg and Robert Lind[33] note, "All of this attention to collections becomes important when considering a museum's potential liability for failing to conserve its collection." Besides the negligence problems associated with allowing a collection to deteriorate, museums are also legally liable over questions of object ownership and indefinite loans.[34] Malaro[35] reports that insurance claims are highest in collections management because many claims result from accidents occurring while objects are being handled or transported.

Risk Management

Risk management is a process whereby potential loss is evaluated and a program to decrease the possibility of loss is initiated and monitored on a regular basis. Most museum personnel think of risk management as fire safety, tornado drills, or shoveling snow off the museum's steps, but risk management extends much farther than keeping the fire exits unlocked during business hours. There are also issues relating to the Occupational Safety and Health Act of 1970 (OSHA), the Americans with Disabilities Act (ADA) (see above), the use of Material Safety Data Sheets (MSDS) (chapter 9), and a host of others. Good risk management should reduce insurance costs by lessening the likelihood of litigation.

Concluding Thoughts

A museum director or board of trustees can employ a variety of strategies to minimize the museum's liability:

- Avoid problems by being proactive instead of reactive.
- Include a lawyer or other qualified legal counsel on the board of trustees or at least have legal counsel available to the board.
- Carry insurance, including liability, comprehensive, and workers' compensation.
- Develop written policies to cover as many contingencies as possible. This includes having written employee manuals (see chapter 7); bylaws (see chapter 2); collections care policies (see chapter 8); and a code professional conduct (see chapter 10).
- When, despite the board's precautions, a situation does evolve into a legal issue, there are still a few options to pursue in the courtroom. Phelan[36] outlines some legal defenses a museum may wish to investigate should it be sued for negligence.

Artists' Rights

The Berne Convention Implementation Act of 1988 and the Visual Artists Rights Act of 1990 have expanded legal protection to recognize an artist's moral rights as well as his property rights to work he creates.[37]

Moral Rights

Phelan[38] has stated, "The personal right or moral right . . . is a recognition that literary or artistic works are extensions of the personalities of the creators, giving them special protection or an inherent right in their works." Moral rights have two elements—the right of paternity and the right of integrity. The right of paternity ensures that the public knows the creator of a work and prevents a work from being attributed to the wrong artist. The right of integrity prevents any contortions of the work through distortion, mutilation, modification, or derogatory action. The right of integrity and right of paternity remain with the artist for life and are not transferred to subsequent copyright holders.

Freedom of Expression

Artists are guaranteed the right of free expression by the First Amendment, but this right does have limits. The interests of others must be considered in this expression. Obscene materials as defined by community standards are not protected.

Property Rights

In the United States, the property of artists and writers is protected primarily by copyright laws. Property right affirms that the creator of a work has a temporary monopoly on its use.

Copyright

Copyright issues seem to change constantly as the subject becomes more complex due to new ways of displaying and reproducing images (by electronic digitization, for example).[39] Copyright is defined as the exclusive right to publish and sell the substance and form of a literary, musical, or artistic work.[40] Museums and other institutions need to have a clear understanding of who owns the copyright for materials in their collections. Museums must honor and be aware of these copyrights not only to respect the artist or creator but also to protect themselves from illegal uses and subsequent litigation.[41]

Legal Basis

Congress passed two major copyright laws during the twentieth century. The first was the "1909 Act." This was Title 17 of the U.S. Code, and it was amended on several occasions starting in 1947.[42] Copyright law was modified significantly by the Copyright Act of 1976, which became effective on January 1, 1978.[43] This modification provided a single, national system of protection for works that can be copyrighted, instead of allowing regulation by the states.

Items Covered

Copyright covers tangible works of intellectual creation in the areas of literature, music, art, and science. Ideas, procedures, processes, systems, methods of operation, concepts, principles, or discoveries do not fall under the governance of copyright law, but they may be patented. The following items can be copyrighted:

- Works of art
- Photographs
- Literary works
- Musical works (including any accompanying words)
- Dramatic works (including any accompanying music)
- Pantomimes and choreographic works
- Pictorial, graphic, and sculptural works
- Motion pictures and other audiovisual works
- Sound recordings
- Architectural works

The copyright owner has five rights in copyright material, including the right to reproduce the work, the right to make derivative works, the right to sell the work, the right of performance, and the right to publicly display the work. The copyright owner can transfer these rights singly or together. However, if no transfer occurs, the creator or copyright owner reserves all rights. The right to sell is terminated for the owner of copyright once the copyright holder sells the work. For this reason, a copyright owner cannot determine the subsequent sales of the work. Significantly for museums, the creator also loses the right to exhibit or display the sold work; however, the copyright owner can still reproduce the sold work. Museums need to exercise extreme care when accepting donations where copyrights may or may not be conveyed with the donation; a determination as to exactly who owns the copyright should be made upon acceptance of each new gift.

Work Made for Hire

In creating a new publication, work of art, or similar commodity, the museum will hold the copyright only if the individual creating the work does so under a contract that specifies it is a "work made for hire." This contract should be written and the terms clearly stated. A work created by an employee of a museum will be considered a "work made for hire" if it is created by the employee within his or her scope of employment.

Protecting a Work

For a museum to protect the copyright of a work, the work should be marked, when possible, with © or "Copyright," the year of creation of the work, and the name of the museum. Two copies of a work bearing a copyright notice must be deposited with the Library of Congress within three months of publication. To assert the copyright protection, the museum must register the work with the Copyright Office sometime during the term of the copyright.

Fair Use

"Fair use" of an item under copyright is not illegal. According to Phelan,[44] it is the use "by reproduction of copyrighted works for criticism, comment, news reporting, teaching (including multiple copies for classroom use), scholarship, or research." To ensure that an item under copyright is utilized for "fair use" purposes only, four factors should be considered by the user: (1) whether the use of the work is for commercial gain or nonprofit educational purposes; (2) the nature of the copyrighted work; (3) the amount and substance of the portion used in relation to the complete work; and (4) the effect of the use of the copyrighted material upon the public and the market.

Concluding Thoughts

Visual artist and copyright laws present museum administrators with a dual set of challenges. The museum must be careful to protect its interests when it has works created, either by regular staff or by contract. An explanation of "works for hire" should be included in the staff handbook to cover works created by the regular staff. The museum should be certain as it writes a contract for creation of a work that all copyrights are transferred to the museum.

The other challenge for museum administrators is researching the copyright status of created works donated to the museum for its collections and exhibition. Even more challenging can be determining the status of works that have been in the collection for a number of years. Does the museum own the work, the right to exhibit the work, the right to reproduce the work, or the right to create derivative works? Before making use of works in the collection, the museum must know which of these rights it owns. Also, the museum must know the creators of the works so that they can be acknowledged. The museum also has the responsibility of protecting the work from damage or alteration. Because these issues carry the force of law, museum administrators must avoid violations.

Notes

1. Americans with Disabilities Act 1990, Equal opportunities for individuals with disabilities, 2001.
2. Association of Science-Technology Centers n.d.
3. Homepage: http://www.usdoj.gov/crt/ada/statute.html.
4. Abercrombie 1993; Committee on Education and Labor 1990; Disability Rights Education and Defense Fund 1994; Quick n.d.; U.S. Department of Justice 1996, 1997; U.S. Equal Opportunity Commission 1992.
5. Rehabilitation Act of 1973. *U.S. Code.* Title 29, chapter 16, sections 701–797, Vocational rehabilitation and other rehabilitation services, 2001.
6. President's Committee on Employment of People with Disabilities 1993.
7. Evan Terry Associates 1993.
8. Wilkoff and Abed 1994.
9. Majewski 1993.
10. Williams 1989.
11. Salmen 1998.
12. Ibid., 35.
13. Briggs 1993; Evan Terry Associates 1993; Majewski 1993; Quick n.d.; Wilkoff and Abed 1994.
14. Malaro 1998, 446.
15. Quick n.d.
16. Hill 1979.
17. Thompson 1991, 38.
18. Malaro 1998, 112.
19. Native American Graves Protection and Repatriation Act (NAGPRA).

U.S. Code. Title 25, chapter 32, section 3001–3013, Native American graves protection and repatriation, 2001.

20. Boyd and Haas 1992, 253.

21. Platt 1991, 91.

22. Dongoske 1996; Echo-Hawk 1992; Ferguson et al. 1993; Ferguson et al. 1996; McManamon and Nordby 1991.

23. Green et al. 1996; Killheffer 1995; Tabah 1993.

24. U.S. Public Law 101–601 n.d.

25. Dongoske 1996; Ferguson et al. 1993; Ferguson et al. 1996; Horse Capture 1991; Monroe and Echo-Hawk 1991; Platt 1991.

26. Sackler 1992; Thompson 1991; Zimmerman 1996.

27. Phelan 1994, 170.

28. Phelan 1994.

29. Ibid.

30. Phelan 1994, 204.

31. Miller 1989.

32. Ibid.

33. Ullberg and Lind 1989, 32.

34. Teichman et al. 1989.

35. Malaro 1998, 42.

36. Phelan 1994.

37. Ibid.

38. Phelan 1994, 240.

39. Shapiro and Miller 2000.

40. Hutter 2000.

41. Phelan 1994.

42. Kent and Lancour 1972.

43. UNESCO; and Library of Congress, Copyright Office http://www.loc.gov/copyright.

44. Phelan 1994, 258.

CHAPTER FOURTEEN
THE "ISMS": CHALLENGES FOR MODERN MUSEUMS

Multiculturalism, colonialism, racism, commercialism, and sexism are five important issues challenging the modern-day museum and its administrators. Knowledge of all five issues is necessary in order for the museum to successfully navigate the hazards and pitfalls they can create. Multiculturalism is the effort of organizations, including museums, to represent the cultural diversity of their communities and nation through their staff and the contents of their exhibits and programs. Colonialism creates many pitfalls, including an "us versus them" mentality and institutionalized dogma. It also calls into question the provenience of collections "collected" from other cultures. Racism raises issues of audience, diversity, exhibit and program content, exhibition and program voice, institutionalized racism, and the place and importance of ethnic museums. Commercialism can create an unfavorable image for the museum. On the one hand, a museum needs money to survive; on the other hand, what makes money may fail to educate the public. Where does a museum draw the line? Sexism is behavior, conditions, and attitudes that foster stereotypes of social roles based on gender. Museums must work to prevent their exhibits and public programs from reinforcing cultural stereotypes, while simultaneously presenting the factual reality of other cultural systems, which may have different values about gender.

Multiculturalism

In the 1950s and 1960s, non-European peoples within the United States began an intensive quest for recognition and enforcement of social rights. These movements led to an ever-growing awareness throughout Europe and the United States of the inadequate and often insensitive representation indigenous groups have received. Mainstream museums often reflected the prevailing Eurocentric notions prior to the 1960s and understandably later became a target of these groups. Since that time, museum professionals have sought to incorporate methods of exhibit and program development that would ensure a sensitive and accurate representation of the ethnographic "Other."

Ethnocentrism arises out of the concept of "otherness," the idea that there are limits to who belongs to a particular society. Susan Pearce, professor of museum studies at the University of Leicester, explains that "otherness" reflects the common human characteristic that "each of us, lonely and fearful individuals, needs to feel that there is an 'us,' a broader grouping of like souls with shared culture, which can, of course, be defined only in relation to something which is seen as 'different.'"[1]

The cultural diversity of the United States is steadily increasing. It is estimated that by the year 2050, no more than fifty percent of the population will be of western European ancestry.[2] In addition, advances in technologies have increased each person's ability and likelihood of interacting with people of cultural backgrounds quite different from his or her own. In discussing multiculturalism, there are three major areas that museums should consider: multiculturalism within the composition of the museum staff; multiculturalism within the community served by the museum; and the multicultural aspect of collections and exhibitions. The museum has direct control over the diversity within its staff. If the museum successfully assembles a diverse staff, that staff will directly influence its success in dealing with its exhibits and community.

Internal Multiculturalism

Many employers are beginning to write directly into policy statements the need for a multicultural composition to their staff. The National Parks Conservation Association has worked as a partner in opening communication between the National Park Service of the U. S. Department of the Interior and underserved minority communities. The objective of this effort is to diversify both the public visiting the national parks and the staff of the National Park Service. They have created a Community Partners Program bringing together community and staff of the National Park Service. The Association is promoting the hiring of minority staff by the

Service by preparing tips (available online) for applying for positions in the National Park Service, offering instructions for supervisors to follow in hiring interviews, and promoting special hiring programs.[3] Those museums that have not made similar efforts need to review their multicultural and hiring policies and try to get all members of the staff involved in the ethnic, cultural, and social events produced by the museum. A goal of the museum should be to promote a better understanding and a broader base of knowledge of cultural diversity among its staff as well as its audience.

External Multiculturalism

Community relations are more effective when a museum reaches out to create a genuine dialogue with diverse groups of people who will be impacted by the museum's programs. Trust and credibility are two essential ingredients in establishing effective communication with cultural groups. Genuine dialogue with the multicultural public and an effort to find common ground on issues are key to achieving a common understanding. Often the best way to establish trust and credibility with a cultural group is to have that group represented on the museum staff. Here we begin to see the relationship between internal and external multiculturalism come into play.[4] Box 14.1 presents a case in which internal and external multicultural needs were not in accord. However, when the ideal of broad cultural representation among staff members is not possible, involving representatives of cultural groups in the museum's programming can offer its own level of success.

Multiculturalism in Collections and Exhibitions

Museum professionals should keep in mind that the very act of placing another culture on display reinforces the idea of "different." There is no way around this. There are no easy solutions, nor is there a catchall formula for avoiding conflict in portraying the "Other." "Until the lions have their historians, tales of hunting will always glorify the hunter." This African proverb, as used by Helen Coxall[5] in her essay *Speaking Other Voices,* appropriately denotes the problematic task of museum staff members in making exhibitions about cultures that are not their own. The movement toward multiculturalism in staffing practices in museums will

Box 14.1

Case Review: The Art of Provocation

In 1969, New York City's Metropolitan Museum of Art exhibition *Harlem on My Mind* was intended to be a mildly provocative presentation of the rise and decline of the African American community of Harlem in upper Manhattan. A white male curated the exhibition, which featured the photographs of a nearly forgotten black photographer, James Van der Zee, as well as slides and videos. The exhibition catalog featured an essay by a young black woman on the difficulties of life in the ghettos of Harlem. The contents of the essay angered members of the Jewish community, whom it cited as antagonists in the economic and social decay of Harlem.

The African American community resented the control over the presentation and interpretation of their community by a privileged "white" curator in an elitist "white" institution. The lack of contemporary black artist and community input into the content and text resulted in protests before the exhibition opened. Graffiti and vandalism of artworks targeted the director of the museum, Thomas Hoving, who refused to acknowledge the concerns of the Harlem community. Hoving did recognize the concerns of the Jewish community and was eventually forced to pull the exhibition catalog after receiving political and financial threats from Jewish supporters and politicians.

Although the exhibition was successful, the damage to the artworks and the reputations of the museum and staff was a heavy price to pay. The controversy led other museums in New York City to develop exhibitions relative to the African American community and other growing minority communities of the city. Throughout the 1970s, museums throughout the world evaluated the issues of cultural colonialism and cultural diversity, and consciousness of the multicultural identity of America grew.

Source: *Making the mummies dance* by T. Hoving. New York: Simon and Schuster, 1993.

help to give a more appropriate voice to museums. However, because no museum staff can reflect the range of cultural diversity of our nation, or probably even its own community, alternative methods have been sought to inform cultural exhibits and public programs.

The most successful procedure museums have attempted has been to include cultural representatives in the planning process for exhibits and other public programs whenever feasible. Some museums have used cultural representatives in only an advisory capacity, whereas others have made them fully integrated members of the planning and implementation teams. When this method is honestly and fully employed, the results are

Box 14.2

Case Study: Dr. Climber's Dilemma

Dr. Aster Climber is the assistant director for public programs at the medium-size Midwest Museum of Cultural Understanding located in a midwestern city of 400,000 people. The Museum has 40,000 square feet of permanent exhibit galleries, 5,000 square feet of short-term changing exhibit space, and about 10,000 square feet of exhibit space devoted to long-term (up to five years) temporary exhibits. Dr. Climber has worked with her staff for more than a year to plan a long-term temporary exhibit that uses the museum's excellent collections of Middle Eastern objects. Last month the board reviewed the design and approved the funds to create the exhibit. It is scheduled to open in six months, on Founders' Day, which is the museum's largest annual event. The museum's Middle Eastern collection contains about 500 religious and secular objects from Syria, Iran, Saudi Arabia, Yemen, Jordan, and Iraq. The main themes of the exhibit are everyday living activities, religious customs, and marriage and the family.

On Monday morning, Dr. Climber arrives in her office to find a copy of the *Daily Planet* in the middle of her desk. The banner headline is about a local story concerning an Iraqi family who fled their home country as political refugees about two years earlier. The newspaper article reports that the father and mother had been arrested for child endangerment for having arranged marriages for their fifteen- and thirteen-year-old daughters. The two husbands, both Iraqi refugees in their early thirties, were arrested for child abuse. The defense presented by all four at their preliminary hearings was that they were simply following the customs of their country, where marriages are arranged and young girls of these ages are regularly given in marriage.

The story has remained in the newspaper on almost a daily basis and has stirred a major debate throughout the city over respecting traditional customs versus respecting the laws of the United States. The date of the trial for the parents has been set for about a month before the museum's exhibit is scheduled to open; the husbands' trial will begin about four months later.

Members of the board of directors have become very nervous about the exhibit they approved. Some want to delay it, some want to cancel it, and some want to remove the section on marriage and the family. Staff members have become very upset that their work has been questioned and wish to use the exhibit to educate the community. At the same time, the staff is split over whether to promote one side of the debate or the other or to simply present information and to allow the public to draw its own conclusions.

As director of the museum, you must deal with the issue. In a meeting with Dr. Climber, you must respond to the following questions:

1. Will you proceed with the exhibit? Why?
2. Will you delay the opening of the exhibit? Why?
3. Will you change the contents of the exhibit? How? Why?
4. If you are proceeding with the exhibit, how will you handle public relations?

Box 14.2 (continued)

5. Will you involve experts in Middle Eastern customs in your exhibit opening and public relations? How?
6. What unique problems should you and the staff be expecting at the opening and during the run of this exhibit?
7. What advice will you give Dr. Climber about dealing with the feelings of her staff?

positive and can provide a certain amount of satisfaction for the interested parties.[6]

Consulting cultural representatives when designing exhibits is an excellent method of arriving at a more accurate and sensitive portrayal of non-European societies. It allows the "other" voices to be heard within the museum. Despite open-minded efforts, it is nearly impossible for the curator and exhibit staff to portray another culture accurately because culture entails so much more than "the facts." Intangibles (attitudes, beliefs, perspectives) are critical to the appropriate interpretation of tangible artifacts. The museum's staff needs the help of experts in these intangible aspects of a group's culture. Consulting with cultural representatives is not always possible, but it is desirable as long as its limitations are considered. In many cases, curators may not wish to relinquish their control but will want to maintain a mediating position. A part of their expertise is to make decisions as to the development of the final product.[7]

For the really brave museums and museum professionals, there is an even larger risk and potential reward: to give full control to the cultural representatives in selecting and interpreting objects and presenting their cultural meaning and context. The museum would supply the objects, space, expertise in the construction of exhibits and presentation of objects, and financial control. As with all exhibit production, there would need to be give and take when the limitations of space, time, and budget come into play. Those museums willing to accept this risk and loss of control will be amply rewarded by a new relationship with a new community and an exhibit with a more authentic voice.

The successes possible from consulting with cultural representatives are not always achieved without problems. Limitations should be considered carefully in the planning stages of joint-participation undertakings. However, because the issue of providing the "Other" a voice in museum exhibits is of great importance to the profession, it will be worth the extra effort. It can lead to greater accuracy and will work to correct the insensitive portrayals of the past. Museum professionals should recognize this importance and consult with cultural representatives whenever possible.

Colonialism

Colonialism may be thought of as an appropriate subject for a museum exhibit, but it usually is not considered to have much of an impact on the operation of modern museums. This type of thinking can be dangerous for museum administrators and staff. Colonialism is more than just a pre-twentieth-century phenomenon; it is a process that has shaped the way in which Western nations and the remainder of the world interact. It also is seen by much of the world as a continuing phenomenon because the United States still focuses a large amount of its resources on maintaining its global economic dominance. Along with this "dominance" come a dogma and an attitude, borrowed from older colonial powers such as the British, French, Germans, Spanish, and Portuguese, among others, that are entrenched in the minds of some U.S. citizens.[8]

Box 14.3

Exercise: Write a Multicultural Policy

Individually or in a group, prepare a one-paragraph multicultural policy for a museum of your choosing. Try to avoid generalizations and words with indefinite meanings, such as "appropriate" and "professional." What areas and programs of the museum will your statement cover? What is the multicultural mission of your museum? Who is responsible for the implementation and "enforcement" of your policy?

Share your or your group's policy with other members of the class. What weaknesses and strengths do you see in the other policy statements? How would you revise your policy after seeing the other statements?

If you are working on this policy statement on your own, share your policy with other staff members. Ask for their feedback on your statement. After receiving this feedback, how would you revise your multicultural policy?

It is important to understand that colonialism has a major impact on museums and the way they are operated today. Museums in Western nations have inherited artifacts and traditions of collecting that are a direct result of colonialism. Many of the attitudes in Western societies, particularly those about peoples and cultures, have been shaped by colonialism. It is sometimes difficult to identify when these attitudes are affecting one's decisions. The problem stems in part from the way in which nineteenth-century scholars began acquiring their knowledge about other cultures. Many such researchers operated from a "mind set" of superiority. Many cultures being studied were seen as inferior, less cultivated, and less significant because the people from those cultures had attitudes, values, and beliefs that did not adhere to Western beliefs.[9]

According to Carol Tator and others, this dogma includes several frequently observed characteristics: (1) the idea of Western superiority; (2) an "us versus them" mentality; (3) a view of non-Westerners as outsiders; (4) a view of non-Westerners as primitives, often referred to as "natives"; (5) a view of non-Western culture, values, and traditions as inferior; (6) a view of non-Westerners as irrational; and (7) a view of non-Westerners as less than human.[10] An example of how colonial-influenced thinking can become a problem for museums even today is presented in box 14.4.

Racism

Without a doubt race is a complex issue. The issues of racism are similar to those of colonialism in many ways because colonial powers used doctrines of racial superiority, such as Social Darwinism, to make their conquest more acceptable in the minds of their populaces. As noted in the preceding section on colonialism, racism is an infused dogma that is often hard for the dominant culture to identify. Museum officials trying to present a multicultural view may be unwittingly constrained by beliefs taught to them by their own society. Years of colonialism and improperly applied scientific theory have ingrained in the Western subconscious a dogma of racism. Museum administrators need to watch for this dogma so they do not fall into the same trap as countless others. By being aware of the existence of such dogma, officials are better able to avoid its appearance in exhibits and programs. There are numerous examples of racism in Ameri-

Box 14.4

Case Review: Into the Heart of Africa

In 1989, the Royal Ontario Museum in Toronto created an exhibition titled *Into the Heart of Africa* in which African artifacts collected by colonial soldiers and missionaries were displayed. The exhibit was presented from the perspective of the conquering British and Canadian troops. The central narrative voice was Dr. David Livingstone's. Livingstone is viewed by Westerners as an adventurer who pulled back the mysterious African veil. To people of African descent, he is seen as another invader who assisted in the conquest of several African tribes and their subsequent subjugation.

In addition, words like "Dark Continent" and "savages" were used in exhibit text and placed inside quotation marks. The quotation marks were intended to distance the museum from the words in an effort to show that, while it would use them, it didn't necessarily agree with them. This subtlety was lost on the majority of the public. People of western European as well as African descent took the words literally.

The exhibit was designed to portray only the perspective of the British and Canadian troops. It failed to present the perspective of the African people who were subjugated by the colonialists. Members of the African Canadian community were outraged by this exhibit and staged a protest. True to form, the media marginalized them, and the museum that controlled access to the resources claimed the right to interpret them. A few changes were made, most notably in the brochure, but the museum seemed to take the stance that it was correct in its display and interpretation. The Royal Ontario Museum called police to control protesters, and a riot ensued. The exhibit was canceled after nine months.

Source: *Challenging racism in the arts: Case studies of controversy and conflict* by C. Tator, F. Henry, and W. Mattis. Toronto, Canada: University of Toronto Press, 1998.

can museums; an example of how racial attitudes contributed to the passage of the Native American Graves Protection and Repatriation Act in 1990 is discussed in box 14.5.

Commercialism

Museums are places of education and preservation, but financial realities are causing many institutions to turn their attention toward commercial activities. Most museums are, in some part, dependent on admissions and merchandise sales for income. This means that administrators need to be aware of what the public wants, but they cannot always give the public everything it desires. Museums have a higher ideal to uphold and cannot accomplish their missions if they become theme park–like fun houses. On

Box 14.5

Case Review: Mounds of Trouble

The Dickson Mounds Museum, near Lewiston, Illinois, spent $2.5 million on a new museum in the early 1970s. The focus of the museum was 237 excavated Paleo-Indian graves discovered and preserved by amateur archaeologist Dr. Donald Dickson. The site, which contains several thousand graves, was sold to the state of Illinois in 1945.

The skeletal remains, pottery, tools, and burial objects were popular with tourists and researchers. The financial benefit of the tourism was a significant factor in the local economy, but the museum closed its primary exhibition in 1990 because of the protests initiated by Native Americans. They continued to apply public pressure on political candidates. Native Americans believed the excavation and exhibition of their ancestral remains was insensitive.

The passage of the Native American Graves Protection and Repatriation Act (NAGPRA) one month after the closing indicated the national concern over the exhibition of burial remains. The closure of the site was a result of action by the American Indian Movement and other Native American groups concerned with respect for their cultural heritage and history. The reluctance by the community to close the museum stemmed from its commercial success and the economic needs of the community. The site has now reopened under the administration of the Illinois State Museum. It houses permanent exhibits, including audiovisual programs, a discovery center, and a resource center, but not human remains.

Source: *Making representations: Museums in the post-colonial era* by M. G. Simpson. New York: Routledge, 1996.

the other hand, they cannot fulfill their missions if they are closed because of a shortage of funds. It is a tightrope that must be successfully navigated by the modern director if the museum is to survive.

Museums are competing for tourist and entertainment dollars. This forces museums to make their exhibits entertaining as well as informative. Computers and interactive exhibits are becoming staples of the American museum. No longer do visitors look but not touch; now they can touch and interact while still being informed. It is important that exhibit designers not go overboard with these devices, as their purpose is to enhance the artifacts, not replace them.

At the Museum 2000 conference, Ian Spero spoke for the betterment of museums through reaction to market forces, stating, "If by reacting to market forces you get better restaurants and a better museum there's nothing wrong with that." On the other side was Patrick Boylan,[11] with a strong warning against blindly acquiescing to market pressures. In response to a statement by Victor Middleton, Boylan said,

> Who is to be the spokesperson for future generations of users and scholars and visitors that are not going to be born for some hundreds of years, but to whom we as curators believe we have a clear responsibility? We are extremely rude about the Ashmolean Museum which at the end of the eighteenth century burned almost all of its natural history collections, including the only stuffed specimen of the extinct dodo. Nowadays we think this was a pretty disgraceful thing to do, but nobody at that time cared about the dodo. There wasn't a local market force. . . . Who is going to play God in relation to those future generations?

In late 2002, the sons of Audrey Hepburn decided to remove all of their mother's memorabilia from a museum dedicated to her in Tolochenaz, Switzerland, where Hepburn lived for thirty years. They cited as their reason the "crass commercialization" of their mother's name. Among the things that the family found upsetting were the posting of signs in the village directing visitors to Hepburn's grave and the selling of souvenirs such as "Audrey Hepburn jam."[12]

There are a few general rules that the museum may follow to keep the appearance of commercialism at bay. There should be no on-site sale of objects and artifacts from the museum's collections. Items that have been deaccessioned should never be sold in the museum store but rather at public auction or some other off-site location. Keeping items for sale in the museum store that are within the education mission of the museum will help avoid the appearance of commercialism as well as avoid problems with unrelated business taxable income. Other actions that appear to be openly commercial are presenting exhibits, especially those that offer high financial return, that clearly fall outside of the museum's mission, such as dinosaur exhibits in history or art museums. The justification that it adds to the museum's bottom line is not enough. Controversial exhibits, such as the "Sensation" exhibit at the Brooklyn Museum of Art, may raise the question of whether education or commercialism associated with huge visitation is the principal intent of such exhibits.

Sexism

Sexism is defined as prejudice or discrimination based on sex. Alternatively, it is defined as behavior, conditions, and attitudes that foster stereotypes of social roles based on sex. Sexism can manifest itself in many ways. Historically, women have been confined to traditional gender roles and were faced with many barriers when entering the workforce. Sexism in the modern workplace takes the form of sexual harassment, the "glass ceiling," unequal pay for women and men, and stereotyping. Although most of the available information about sexism refers to academia and the corporate world rather than to museums, sexism is part of the larger societal fabric and can be a problem in museums as well.

Gender Perspectives: Essays on Women in Museums, edited by Jane Glaser and Artermis A. Zenetou, contains numerous essays by museum professionals from many disciplines. They are useful for gauging the status of women in museums and for learning about the ways in which sexism affects personnel and visitors. The essay by Margery Gordon,[13] for example, suggests, "Institutions should listen to women because women have a long history as nurturers and caretakers. As such, women can affect the decision-making process and design programs and spaces that make a museum special to a visitor." Some might conclude that even though she is attempting to promote inclusion and equality in museums, her thinking reinforces traditional gender roles. This is a good illustration of the complex issues of sexism that challenge the modern museum. If museums are to be inclusive, they need to be certain to include feminine as well as masculine attributes and attitudes.

Exhibits and Interpretation

Increasing interest in women's roles has led to greater visibility of women's history in many museums. It is important when including women's history in exhibits to move beyond token programming to a way of making stories more inclusive of experiences of men and women. A 1997 issue of *Cultural Resource Management* titled "Placing Women in the Past" illustrates tangible ways to retrieve women's history and shows how researchers, preservationists, and interpreters can utilize women's history to enhance their own learning, as well as in teaching. Heather Huyck states that three principles inform this effort: First, women were present both physically and through influence; second, the diverse experiences of women can be uncovered using historic structures, sites, and objects; and third, historic sites provide tangible resources for researchers and visitors to understand more about our collective past.[14]

Sexism in exhibits can be subtle. Robert Sullivan[15] pointed out that museums are ritual places that make visible the objects we value and decide what and how objects will be remembered. In 1976, the museum where he worked evaluated its permanent exhibits for gender bias. It found six forms: (1) invisibility and underrepresentation—omission of women and minority groups; (2) stereotyping—assigning rigid, traditional gender roles to a subject; (3) imbalance or selectivity—presenting only one narrow interpretation of an issue; (4) fragmentation or isolation—separating issues relating to women from the main body of the text; and (5) linguistic bias—using only masculine nouns and pronouns.

Sexism in the Workplace

Now more than 60 percent of women work outside the home, and over one-half of the workforce is composed of women. Issues that concern working women include maternity-paternity leave and day-care subsidies. Women want to be able to have children without being left behind and passed over for promotions. Women hope that "parent track" work patterns will become more acceptable in time.

No studies about museums mention that children and family would interfere with hiring.[16] However, women just entering the field may need to relocate geographically in order to find work. This could pose a strain within a two-career relationship if there are expectations based on traditional gender roles. It also can lead to a woman abandoning her career plans temporarily or permanently if she is unable to relocate or make other career choices. These situations reflect stereotypical gender roles and are not specific to museums but reflect the larger society.

A 1998–1999 study conducted by GuideStar shows that unequal pay for women and men is still a reality even in the nonprofit sector. The study revealed that male executives in the largest nonprofit organizations make about 35 percent more than women in similar-size organizations, and a similar gap in salaries was found in smaller organizations. Women were found to earn less than men in top positions in all job categories of the nonprofit sector, including "development, administration, education programs, marketing, business operations, public relations, technology, finance, and law."[17]

Many options have opened for women in the past three decades. As more women enter the workplace, they will have a greater voice in programming as well as in the workplace more broadly. In the interim, it is the responsibility of directors and administrators to be aware of gender issues and sexism and to deal with complaints with sensitivity.

Conclusion

Museums are "precious institutions" uniquely capable of defining, recording, and sustaining human civilization. "Without museums humankind would hardly understand its past, cope with its present, advance in its future and enjoy and learn from transcendent experiences of beauty, history, nature, and universe."[18] By directly confronting and addressing the various "isms" that limit our thinking as well as our programming, museum professionals can create institutions where the full range of human culture and experience may be explored.

Notes

1. Hooper-Greenhill 1997, 15.
2. National Parks Conservation Association n.d.
3. Ibid.
4. Hooper-Greenhill 1997.
5. Coxall 1997, 99.
6. Coxall 1997.
7. Simpson 1996.
8. Bal 1996.
9. Ibid.; Messenger 1989.
10. Tator et al. 1998.
11. Boylan 1992.
12. Langley 2002.
13. Gordon 1994, 110.
14. Huyck 1997.
15. Sullivan 1994.
16. Etzowitz et al. 1994.
17. Lewin 2001.
18. Kotler and Kotler 1998, 348.

CHAPTER FIFTEEN
INTO THE THIRD MILLENNIUM

In the late 1990s, the American Association of Museums gathered the following facts about museums in the United States:

- There are approximately 15,000 museums in the United States (one museum for every 16,500 Americans).
- 75 percent are small museums.
- 43 percent are located in rural areas.
- $4.3 billion was to be spent on museum infrastructure between 1998 and 2000, and 150 museums were to be built or expanded during the same period.
- American museums average approximately 865 million visits per year, which is more than the yearly attendance at all professional sporting events in the United States.
- 36 percent of all travelers will visit a museum, resulting in part from the fact that museums rank in the top three family vacation destinations.
- A 1999 study showed that Americans from all income and education ranges visit and value museums.
- Museums care for over 750 million objects and living specimens.
- After their families, Americans ranked authentic artifacts in history museums and historic sites most significant in creating a strong connection to the past.

- Tourists who visit museums spend nearly twice as much on their travel as those who do not.
- In 1994 alone, Utah museums generated an additional $5.97 million in household earnings and nearly $500,000 in state tax revenue.
- Of Americans aged eighteen and older, one in 480 is a museum volunteer.[1]

David Carr has written that society "needs" museums because of the educative conversations they generate. Museums hold and exhibit the icons of our countries and cultures, which help us define who we are. These objects include a record of our earth's history and of mankind's accomplishments. In Carr's words, "I believe that people go to museums for profound reasons of hope, identity, and self-construction."[2]

This is a very bright outlook for museums in the dawning days of the third millennium. However, there also are challenges on the horizon because financial pressures have increased, and many museums have been forced to implement strategies for reductions in operating costs—reductions that have been realized, at least partially, through decreases in staffing.

Challenges for Third-Millennium Museums

What will be the challenges for museums in the third millennium? At first they will be the same challenges faced by museums at the end of the twentieth century. Museums in the new millennium will be faced with increasing expectations and demands, but they will be equipped with decreasing, or at best static, resources. A group of twelve senior managers from museum organizations in the United Kingdom listed these as current issues facing museums and galleries: declining public funding; constant change; demand for accountability; National Lottery; increasing expectations; market forces; costs; productivity; politics.[3]

The list for museums in the United States would look much the same. There has been decreased or static funding from such public sources as the National Endowment for the Arts, the National Endowment for the Humanities, and the Institute of Museum and Library Services. Private foundation funding levels have increased in recent years, but so has the competition for these funds, especially from social service organizations that also have lost public funding. Museums with endowment funds did well in the late 1990s, but what went up has come down in the early days of the third millennium. State and local museums have not faired particularly well with the falling economy and will remain dependent upon fluctuations in national and local economies. Predictions for the next several years suggest nearly level funding for museum-related organizations. These economic fluctuations can be expected to repeat innumerable times in the third millennium.

At the same time that funding is expected to remain static, costs can be expected to grow. Museums are labor-intensive organizations. Creation of one-of-a-kind exhibits and complex public programs requires highly skilled people and considerable time. Care of collections requires highly trained staff and unique storage equipment and supplies. All of this is expensive. When museums look for ways to cut expenses, they find that most of their budget (70 to 95 percent) is in salaries. Cutting the budget inevitably means cutting staff, producing another problem museums face—understaffing.

In the United States as in the United Kingdom, museums face increasing expectations from outside the museum. An expanding and increasingly sophisticated audience will expect higher quality in museum programs. At the same time, museums will face increasing expectations from inside the institution—from board members and the staff itself. Members of the museum profession are aware of improvements in the field, and they will expect their museums to keep up.

One issue facing museums in the United States that was not discussed by the United Kingdom group is the changing demographics of the museum audience. In the United States, the median age of the audience will keep rising. Furthermore, the 2000 census reports a decline in marriage rates at a time when many museums have focused their programs on school-age children. As the size of this audience continues to decline, a good strategy may be to bring more programs for adults online.

In the first half of the twenty-first century, groups that are currently considered to be minorities will constitute more than half of the U.S. population. Museums must continue to improve their programs for this multicultural audience. The audience for U.S. museums will become more urban as well. Dozens of museums are under construction or on the drawing board in cities across the country.

Although we do not have a National Lottery in the United States, we have experienced a great expansion in gambling in all forms. In the 1990s, gambling has expanded from Nevada and Atlantic City to nearly every part of the country. Museums in the United States, as in the United Kingdom, face new market competition from other parts of the education-entertainment industry. Among these competitors are theme parks, television, movies, the Internet and the World Wide Web, and sporting events. This "Disney effect" (glitzy, high-tech, feel-good programming) will continue to challenge museums for audiences and the dollars they bring.

Meeting the Challenges

It will require many resources, both fiscal and human, to meet these ongoing challenges. The focus here, however, is on four key responses—leadership, museums and community, technology, and increasing professionalism. These responses rest for the most part within the realm of museum administration and thus seem most appropriate for the conclusion of this book.

Leadership

Leadership in museums is an important daily function that is complicated but indispensable. The issues faced by museum leaders must be dealt with efficiently, carefully, and in a timely manner in order to ensure the survival of the museum as an institution. At the beginning of this book, we suggested that museum administrative issues are really the concern of all museum staff members. Although it can be said that all museum staff members must exercise leadership, the reality is that museum leadership is first and foremost the responsibility of the museum director. It is true that division heads and curators are responsible for the leadership of their units within the museum, but the burden of leadership rests primarily with the director.

What is leadership? This elusive concept is at the base of a growth industry because leadership has new importance within both for-profit businesses and nonprofit organizations. It can be said that "I can't define leadership, but I know it when I see it."[4] There is considerable discussion within the literature as to whether leaders are born or, with proper education and experience, can be made. Anne Ackerson[5] offered this insight: "Leadership is as much an *art* as it is an *act*." Many leadership skills can be learned and honed with experience, but leadership is more than technical competence. Leadership is a combination of acquired *skills* and intangible *talents*.

The model for a museum director has changed significantly since the late 1960s and early 1970s. In those times (and previously), the museum director was seen as the intellectual and social leader of the museum. The route to the directorship was curatorship of one of the museum's disciplinary divisions or public program areas. After a successful career in one of these positions, those people with an interest in the social (and political) activities surrounding the director's position could expect to have the opportunity to ascend to a directorship.

The position of a museum director is now, however, a multifaceted position with responsibilities in such broad areas as fund-raising, public relations, marketing, strategic planning, public programming, legal issues, budget management, collection policies, conflict management, interpersonal relations, and staff evaluation. Successful museum directors are unique individuals with many skills and talents. Museums have begun to look outside the museum for these individuals and hire directors from successful careers in business and other nonprofit organizations. Museums also have recognized the benefits of hiring social and political leaders in their communities, especially when fundraising and garnering resources are the primary emphases of the position. In recent years, larger museums have split the responsibilities of the museum director among two or three people; one person serves primarily as a fund-raiser and social leader of the museum and another leads the day-to-day operations and serves as the intellectual and public programming leader within the museum.

John Durel offers an interesting discussion of the leadership problems that new museum directors may face. A survey of new directors found that nearly two-thirds reported significant surprises in the first year of their tenure that hampered their progress or led to their early departure from the position. Learning that the museum had significant financial problems or learning that the museum did not know its financial position was likely at the top of the list of surprises. Many times boards could not or would not actively participate in fund-raising. Inaction on the part of the board on this or other issues may lead to tension and misunderstandings between the board and the new director, a situation that cannot last for long. New directors also found staff problems they were expected to solve almost immediately, but in many instances their actions were not supported. Problems with the heart of the museum, its collections, were found by many new directors to be significant, resulting from board or staff ignorance or limited resources. Finally, new directors found there was a gap between the rhetoric of the board and staff and their actual willingness to participate in transformational change. These major issues can challenge the leadership abilities of even a seasoned museum director and can be devastating to new, inexperienced directors.[6]

Many authorities have provided lists and discussions of the characteristics by which leadership can be defined. Some of these are summarized in box 15.1. Characteristics of leadership with special reference to museum directors are discussed below. Obviously no one person is going to have all of these talents and skills, but it is important that those aspiring to museum leadership have strengths in many of these areas. The traditional view that museum directors or those aspiring to the position should work on improving their areas of weakness has been challenged by Donald O. Clifton, chair and CEO of Gallup International. "Focus on strengths and manage the weaknesses" is the new mantra.[7] Strengths are more than things you do well, and include patterns of behavior, thoughts, and feelings that indicate "measurable progress toward excellence."[8] Weaknesses, in this view, are more than what you do not do well; they also include anything that intrudes "on your areas of productivity or lessens your self-esteem."[9] The conclusion: "There is no alchemy for weaknesses. They can be removed but they cannot be transformed into strengths. The goal, therefore, is to manage weaknesses so the strengths can be freed to develop and become so powerful they make the weaknesses irrelevant."[10] These assessments of one's strengths and weaknesses should be accomplished well before ascending to leadership positions within museums, or any organization, and the patterns of behavior that emphasize strengths and manage weaknesses should be well established.

From other authors' ideas about what constitutes leadership (box 15.1), we developed the following list of criteria we believe are most important for leaders in the museum field.

Box 15.1

Leadership Characteristics and Responsibilities

"Visionary Leadership and Missionary Zeal" by S. W. Davies

Roles
An individual
Visionary
Advocate and ambassador
Professional
Mentor
Empowerer
Communicator
Manager of learning
Strategic manager
Executive

"Leadership" by D. Fleming

Desire to achieve things
Genuine passion
Self-belief
Compelling vision
Recognition that nothing can be achieved alone
Ability to communicate
Honesty or trust building
Courage
Loyalty
Enthusiasm
Charisma
Determination and confidence
Ruthlessness
Teambuilder
Teacher
Nurturer and developer of people's skills
Standard setter

***New Director! New Directions?* by A. W. Ackerson**

Roles
Facilitator
Steward-standard-bearer
Catalyst-crusader

Box 15.1 (continued)

Key Characteristics
Possesses passion for the work
Shows signs of strength and momentum
Is open to new ways of doing things
Encourages everyone to seek innovative opportunities
Is willing to risk making mistakes; learns from them
Uses consultants and other voices to broaden the museum's vision
Forges new partnerships
Communicates well with staff and stakeholders
Makes change and success shared responsibilities
Plans constantly
Cultivates and educates the governing board
Takes dramatic action only after thorough study
Reports results and continuing needs
Celebrates success

"What It Takes to Lead into the Next Millennium" by W. Phillips

Reality—brings reality to the museum
Vision—presents inspiring vision of the future
Courage—has courage to pursue reality and vision
Charisma—possesses ability to coalesce stakeholders

"Not Enough Generals Were Killed" by P. F. Drucker

Things Leaders Know
A leader is someone who has followers.
Popularity is not leadership, but results are.
Leaders are highly visible and set examples.
Leadership is a responsibility.

Ways Leaders Behave
They start out asking: What needs to be done?
They next ask: What can and should I do to make a difference?
They ask: What are the organization's mission and goals?
They are extremely tolerant of diversity in people, but intolerant when it comes to a person's performance, standards, and values.
They are not afraid of strength in their associates.
They make certain that they are the kind of person they want to be.

"The New Language of Organizing and Its Implications for Leaders" by C. Handy

A belief in oneself
A decent doubt
A passion for the job

Box 15.1 (continued)

An awareness of other worlds
A love of people
A capacity for aloneness
An ability to be out front

"Seven Lessons for Leading the Voyage to the Future" by J. M. Kouzes and B. Z. Posner

Lessons
Leaders don't wait.
Character counts.
Leaders have their heads in the clouds and their feet on the ground.
Shared values make a difference.
You can't do it alone.
The legacy you leave is the life you lead.
Leadership is everyone's business.

"An 'Outsider's' View of Leadership" by S. E. Meléndez

Vision
Diversity
Passion
Clarity of goals
Perseverance
Kindness
Honesty and integrity
Ongoing renewal
Teacher
Sense of humor
Self-knowledge

"Leadership and Organizational Culture" by E. H. Schein

Roles
Animator
Creator of culture
Sustainer of culture
Agent of change

Characteristics
Extraordinary levels of perception and insight
Extraordinary levels of motivation
Emotional strength
New skills in analyzing cultural assumptions
Willingness and ability to involve others and elicit their participation
Willingness and ability to share power and control

Box 15.1 (continued)

The Handbook for Museums by G. Edson and D. Dean

Director Responsibilities
Policy-making and funding in concert with board
Planning
Organizing
Staffing
Supervising and coordinating activities of staff
Professional practices
Financial management
Legal aspects of museum operations

"Seven Critical Issues for Museum Leaders" by R. G. Simerly

Leadership Issues
Ethics
Collections
Multiculturalism and diversity
Censorship
The community
Budgeting
Strategic planning

***Leadership for the Future* by B. F. Tolles, Jr.**

Intellectual leader and educator
Leader for social responsibilities
Initiator of professional standards and training
Leader in collection development, management, and conservation
Leader in exhibition and educational interpretation
Leader in research functions
Legal guardian
Organizer and energizer for planning
Fund-raiser, marketing agent, and cultivator of institutional support
Internal communicator
Fiscal, facilities, and security manager
Public policy manager

***Why Leaders Can't Lead: The Unconscious Conspiracy Continues* by W. Bennis**

Vision in the sense of outcome, goal, or direction
Communication of their vision
Management of trust or reliability or constancy
Management of self, knowing one's skills
Pace and energy to do the work and empower the work force

Possesses Passion for the Work

"A passion for the job provides the energy and focus that drive the organization and act as an example to others."[11] "When we love our work, we need not be managed by hopes of reward or fears of punishment . . . as Robert Frost says, 'Love and need are one.'"[12] Successful museum directors must have a passion for their work, their museum, and the museum profession. They have extremely demanding jobs, and the financial compensation certainly is not commensurate with the expectations placed on the position or with that of comparable positions in the for-profit world. The motivation must be largely internal.

A distinction should be made between a passion for the work and the job and the love of the position. "Leaders must be driven by a desire to achieve things."[13] Museum directors must possess a desire to have their museums accomplish things—build new exhibits, create new public programs, renovate existing facilities, construct new facilities, or strengthen collections. Individuals who are motivated to pursue the position of museum director because of the real or perceived prestige of the position are not true leaders, and their museums will reflect this deficiency.

As passionate and dedicated as museum directors must be, they must find a balance between their work and their private lives. Being a museum director is not an 8 A.M. to 5 P.M. Monday through Friday type of position. However, time away from the pressures and stresses of the position must be found on a regular basis; otherwise, professional "burn-out" will occur, and the profession will have lost a valuable member.

Planned Vision

All leaders have a vision of the future. Sara Meléndez goes so far as to state, "Vision is the first important characteristic of leadership."[14] Museums need direction and leaders who have the vision to see that direction. A leader's vision must be rooted in reality. It usually finds expression in mission statements and strategic plans. "A true mission statement expresses the company's raison d'être, the purpose for its existence, and often becomes the invisible life force that drives and unifies."[15] This statement is equally true, if not more so, for museums. A well-designed strategic planning process will give a museum the direction it needs and a group of active stakeholders that will help implement the vision. Will Phillips notes this interrelationship between reality, vision, and success: "If the leader provides a process for stakeholders to agree on the current reality and to become energized about the vision for the future, it can be achieved."[16]

The mission statement and strategic plan for a museum should be committed to writing. The museum director should be certain that the shaping of the mission and construction of the strategic plan are an inclusive process including board, staff, audience, and nonaudience members. An inclusive process will help ensure that these statements are rooted in reality and that a maximum number of stakeholders result from the process.

A strategic plan puts a museum on a path for growth; the museum director holds the pivotal position in the implementation of any mission or strategic plan. The director works with the board to gather the resources necessary for accomplishing the plan, and the director works with the staff to see that the work is actually accomplished. Because museum directors hold this critical position, they must make the mission and strategic plan their very own. Directors should not need to refer to the mission or the plan but should have it so well ingrained in their minds that it simply infuses their every thought.

Charisma

Charisma is probably the most controversial leadership characteristic listed here. This is well illustrated by the statements of two experts in the study of leadership skills: Peter Drucker states that the only characteristic leaders he studied had in common was that "they had little or no 'charisma' and little use either for the term or for what it signifies,"[17] whereas Will Phillips wrote, "Charisma is the word I use to describe the leader's ability to coalesce stakeholders to acknowledge the current reality and pursue a future vision."[18] This controversy has arisen at least in part because in the popular mind, the word "charisma" has become associated with political leaders who have few other leadership skills and may not use their talent for the general good, whereas the dictionary definition of charisma is basically the special virtue of a person that confers an unusual ability for leadership. This denotative meaning of charisma, then, would seem to belong in a list of leadership characteristics. Charisma is the intangible talent possessed by some people that induces other people to follow them. If charisma is exhibited in conjunction with other leadership skills and is used for the general good, it should not be feared in museum leaders. In fact, most museum directors would be happy to have a little charisma to move the programs of their institutions forward.

Courage

Leaders must have the courage to pursue their vision and "not become immobilized by the potential risks, or be caught on the horns of indecision."[19] Clifton and Nelson found that outstanding leaders' success did not occur because they made quick decisions, but because they showed a tolerance for ambiguity and could delay making decisions until all the facts were in.[20] Museum directors are fortunate to have many good advisors at hand—staff, board members, volunteers, and other stakeholders—but when the data are in, it is time for the director to make the decisions. Decisions that are delayed will often result in institutional paralysis. It is important that museum directors have enough courage to make the decision and move forward even if it proves to be wrong. Leaders learn from their mistakes and grow with the experience.[21]

Many times the courage to make difficult decisions results from a person's belief in self; it is "the only thing that gives an individual the self-confidence to step into the unknown and to persuade others to go where no one has gone before, but this has to be combined with a decent self-doubt." A leader must also have "a capacity for aloneness, because leaders have to be out front. Leaders have to walk alone from time to time."[22] On the other hand, leaders are never afraid to surround themselves with strong people who may not always agree with them. This again is clearly an attribute that is rooted in a belief in one's own abilities, but it is a critical one if a leader is to have access to all of the necessary facts and input for decision making.[23]

Interestingly, David Fleming[24] included ruthlessness—a win-at-all-cost attitude—among the characteristics of leaders. This seems to be an incongruous characteristic unless it is thought of in terms of the unflinching willingness to do the unpleasant jobs, such as terminating staff members and making unpopular decisions opposed by the staff. Here again, however, decisions delayed are never in the best interest of the museum;

therefore, placing the interests of the institution above any one individual or group may be seen as ruthless, but others will see it only as doing what is expected of a leader.

Embraces Change

Changing times and changing environments mean that organizations, including museums, must be prepared to change so they can adapt and survive in the third millennium. In museums, the directors must be the agents of change. Edgar Schein makes the excellent point that change is not easy "because the problem is not only how to acquire new concepts and skills, but also how to *unlearn* things that are no longer serving the organization."[25] Museum directors cannot arbitrarily force change, but they can evolve change by building on the museums' strengths while leaving their outdated programs to atrophy. Even staff and board members who say they want change will resist if areas of interest to them are slated for elimination or change. Leading museums while changing them at the same time is a difficult task and certainly accounts for a share of the turnover in museum directorships.

Embraces Diversity

Our country is a wonderful mix of cultures and races, each with unique characteristics, and this diversity will certainly increase in the third millennium. The challenge for museums and their leaders will be twofold. First, as Sara Meléndez has written, "leaders must be able to see talent and skills in the diverse individuals and groups that comprise the current work force."[26] It will be important for museum staffs to reflect the diversity of the community that they serve. The person in the position to enforce, promote, and glory in this staff diversity is the director. It must be clear to the staff, board, and audience that the director embraces this diversity without reservation.

Second, museums will need to design culturally and linguistically appropriate programs and strategies for the particular needs of their heterogeneous audiences. Museums must be prepared and willing to serve their diverse audiences if they wish to continue to have the support of the community. A critical step in meeting the diverse needs of the community is a diverse staff that has an understanding of the unique characteristics of this mix of cultures and races.

Museum directors should be certain their institutions have a multicultural policy so that multiculturalism is not pushed into the background. It is the responsibility of museum leaders to determine the proper ways to represent cultures in their institution. Museums can be culturally informed by having a diverse staff, but some museums, especially when planning new exhibits, have benefited from representatives of the cultural or ethnic groups represented in the exhibits. Whatever methods are employed, museums must position themselves as agents of diversity, and it is the responsibility of the museum director to be certain that this occurs in an appropriate manner throughout the institution.

Team

Very little is accomplished in museums by individuals acting alone. Probably the principal mode for accomplishing tasks in museums is teams forming for one project and then dissolving to form new teams. The museum director will be responsible for assembling the team, but the director must keep in mind that the team will not be successful without the skills and dedication of the staff members who compose it. One of the primary responsibilities of museum directors is to make certain that they are hiring the right people to do the work. Furthermore, the museum director must foster a work climate in which people feel comfortable with leaving their traditional roles and forming teams to do the work the museum needs.

It should be clear that the museum director must be willing to delegate authority, when appropriate, in order to get the necessary work done. In this way current museum directors can prepare the leaders of the future for the roles they will eventually assume. A museum needs a good staff in order to run well, but it is the museum leader who can ensure that the museum's good staff forms good teams and nurtures leaders from within.

Takes Responsibility and Promotes Results

Leaders, including museum directors, are doers, and many will act with a sense of urgency. Peter Drucker hit it right on the head: "Leadership is not rank, privileges, titles, or money. It is *responsibility*," and "Popularity is not leadership. *Results* are." He further observed that leaders "were extremely tolerant of diversity in people and did not look for carbon copies of themselves. But they were totally—fiendishly—intolerant when it came to a person's performance, standards, and values."[27] Even with a good staff in place, the museum director will be the one who sets the mood and tempo of work and drives the organization to get results. It is the leader's responsibility to get staff "to think and act like owners rather than employees."[28] This should be relatively easy to accomplish in museums with talented and dedicated staff members who derive considerable satisfaction from the results of their work.

Celebrates and Shares Success

"Leaders have to live vicariously, deriving their satisfaction from the successes of others and giving those others the recognition that they themselves are often denied."[29] This is particularly true for museum directors and others who head nonprofit organizations, because the financial rewards that their staff receives are not large. For most professionals in the nonprofit sector, motivating factors near the top of the list are a feeling of working for the greater good and pride in their work. Recognition for their work is on occasion more satisfying than money. Museum directors must appreciate the work of their staff and be certain their work is given public notice. It costs the museum essentially nothing to publicly acknowledge the work of staff at opening events and to place their names in exhibits or on printed materials.

Budget

Budgeting is a necessity for every person, group, museum, and organization. A managed budget shows that a museum is well organized and fiscally sound. To move their organizations forward, leaders must be able to utilize resources within the organization and community and be able to deal with uncertain and limited resources. This is accomplished through budget management. All museum directors must be able to manage the finances of their museum. A balanced budget is a must if nonprofit organizations, such as museums, are to operate efficiently and smoothly.

Robert Simerly sets out four rules for having successful financial management: "1. Learn your budget. 2. Learn your budget. 3. Learn your budget. 4. Learn how to *manage* your budget."[30] Leaders must learn their budgets inside and out and then learn how to manage them. This is a skill that can be practiced and learned, so no leader should be without the knowledge of budget management.

Management of the budget should not be confused with accounting (chapter 5). Accounting helps museum directors understand and manage their budgets, but the accounting certainly does not need to be done by the director. Small organizations (one staff member and volunteers) should make an effort to have someone, such as the treasurer of the board, do the accounting to prevent a conflict of interest and give the director another viewpoint in the management of the financial resources.

Resources

Simerly[31] discusses the scarcity of resources for museums and the ferocity of the competition for those limited resources. Museum directors take note. A leader's ability to fight for resources, both financial and human, will be the key to success. Museum directors must work hard on fund-raising for the institution. The community surrounding a museum is important for many reasons; it is an important source of visitors, funding, volunteers, and general support. A museum director must work to build a good relationship between the museum and the community in order for the museum to survive. For good or ill, how a museum leader deals with the community will always be an issue.

Good Communicator

The director of a museum must speak for the institution at all times. The director will meet with the media when requested or arrange for the most appropriate member of the staff to do so. However, the director's role as spokesperson for the museum is even more complicated. David Fleming explains the situation this way: "The essence of leadership is the relationships which a leader must develop and maintain, not just with subordinates, but also with superiors, and with others outside one's own organization or sphere of activity. Such relationships are built upon the personal qualities that the leader has, and especially on the leader's ability to communicate."[32]

Promotes Professional Standards and Actions

"The first milestone on the journey to leadership credibility is *clarity of personal values.*"[33] Simerly further advises leaders to "identify and analyze the major types of value systems underlying your museum." Once they are determined, the leader must establish a value system conducive to the museum and "adopt the highest standards of ethical conduct." Ethics and ethical behavior are always difficult for individuals and organizations because the choices to be made are usually between two competing goods rather than between right and wrong.[34]

The decision to exhibit an object, for example, is always a difficult one. Displaying any object is to place it at risk from fluctuating environmental conditions, light exposure, and mechanical damage. The object is always safer in storage under controlled conditions. The choice, then, is whether to place the object on display for the enjoyment and education of the audience or to keep it safe in storage. Which serves the greater good? This is the ethical question. It is the responsibility of the director to see that the staff is aware of museum ethics and that a code of professional conduct is in place. The director must set the standard by careful adherence to these codes.

Skills to Understand and Balance Public, Collection, and Research Functions

Directors must understand the natural tension that exists in museums among the staff members with responsibility for public programs, research, and collections care. Directors will understand that it is a waste of everyone's time to try to eliminate this conflict; rather, the conflict must be managed. It is the job of the director to focus and direct this energy for the benefit of the museum. The director must balance the needs and available resources so that all of the museum parts are able to function and succeed.

Cultivates and Educates Board

The museum director serves at the pleasure of the board, so it should be axiomatic that the director must establish and maintain a good working relationship with it. However, there is more to the director-board relationship than employee-employer; the director must see the board as a source of funds and fund-raising support. The board is really both the director's and the museum's most direct contact with the community.

The board must see the director as its primary source of information concerning the museum and its needs; therefore, the director has a primary educational function and responsibility to the board. By building this educational relationship, the director can also help shape the board and its policies. It is critical that the board reflect the diversity of the staff and community, and it may be the director who will need to educate them about this need. This and other difficult changes may fall to the director as the "outside" member of the board.

On many occasions, despite efforts to nurture and maintain the relationship between the director and the board, it will deteriorate over time after many changes and decisions. It is the director who should gauge the status of this relationship and be prepared to move to a new position. It should be clear that the museum is the real loser if the director and the board become estranged. If you are interested in pursuing a career in museum administration or any other sector of the nonprofit world, you must understand that your skills and talents will match the needs of institutions at certain points in their evolution. These needs change over a director's tenure, and if the institution is to continue to progress, a renewal of leadership may well be necessary.

Museums and Community

As we have discussed above, the museum's relationship with its community is inseparable from the success of the museum. The community offers the museum visitors, money, volunteers—including board members—and general support. In 1999 the American Association of Museums (AAM) developed an initiative titled "America's Museums: Building Community" in an effort to strengthen and improve this vital relationship. The initial objective of the effort was to educate people who influence or make public policy. The public has "voted with its feet" to show its appreciation and desire for museums, but a major criticism from media and public opinion leaders is the sense that "museums primarily serve a limited segment of the population."[35] Despite perceptions that museums serve the intellectual elite, 865 million visits per year to museums in the United States clearly demonstrate that museums are serving a broad range

Box 15.2

Case Review: Directors' Defense of Questionable Acquisition Practices

In 1997, the *Boston Globe* launched an investigative series titled "Lost Art," which focused on the questionable acquisition practices of many prominent Boston museums, including the Arthur M. Sackler Museum at Harvard University and the Boston Museum of Fine Arts (MFA). The series revealed that both of these institutions have, in recent years, obtained for their collections unprovenanced archaeological materials that were likely illegally excavated and sold on the antiquities black market.

On December 4, 1997, the *Globe* reported that a number of objects in the MFA's new exhibit of African, Oceanic, and Pre-Columbian treasures were looted and illegally exported from Guatemala and Mali. Museum trustee Landon T. Clay donated the Mayan materials to the museum in 1988, and scholars believe the pieces may have been stolen from Guatemala's Mirador River basin. Museum officials stated they were certain the pieces entered the country prior to the 1982 Convention on Cultural Property Implementation Act, which bound the United States to the 1970 UNESCO convention aimed at stopping the international trafficking of looted artifacts. Guatemala, however, has prohibited the export of such artifacts without a permit since 1947, and the museum's attorney acknowledged in the article that the museum disregarded this law as the Guatemalan government had not objected to the items' presence in the United States. The Mali pieces were loaned to the museum by William E. Teel, a member of the museum's board of overseers, and are believed by archaeologists to have been looted from Mali, which has prohibited the export of antiquities since at least 1969. Despite the fact that Teel refused to reveal—even to the museum—how and when he obtained the items, the museum's director, Malcolm Rogers, stated that he had "no qualms" about exhibiting the pieces.

Another article, dated January 16, 1998, reported that scholars believe many items recently acquired by the Arthur M. Sackler Museum to be of questionable origin. Furthermore, the article detailed a number of transactions that have taken place between the museum and dealer Robert E. Hecht, who has been expelled from both Italy and Turkey for his alleged involvement in the illicit trade of antiquities. In 1997, Hecht sold the museum a rare silver cup for $400,000. When asked where the artifact originated, Hecht reportedly replied, "What does it matter?"

James Cuno, director of Harvard's art museums, defended an acquisition of 182 Greek vases believed to have been looted from Italian tombs: "The decision I took was, I thought, a very ethical one and I would stand by it and do it again. If we hadn't acquired them, they might be in some private collection lord knows where." Cuno also is reported to have stated that an "innocent until proven guilty" policy is sufficient, and that if the museum cannot prove that an item was looted, then it can continue to buy undocumented specimens.

Although it is not certain that any American laws have been broken in either of these cases, it is certain that these institutions and their directors have failed to adhere to the prevailing ethical standards of the museum and archaeological professions. The ICOM (International Council of Museums) Code of Professional Ethics, for example, states that a museum should not acquire any object unless the governing body and

Box 15.2 (continued)

responsible officer are satisfied that "it has not been acquired in, or exported from, its country of origin and/or any intermediate country in which it may have been owned legally (including the museum's own country), in violation of that country's laws." In an article dated January 13, 1998, Elizabeth des Portes, president of the ICOM, condemned the MFA for its reluctance to return the Mayan artifacts to Guatemala. The Illicit Antiquities Research Center argues that "unprovenanced artifacts which cannot be shown to have been known and published prior to 1970 should be regarded as illicit and should not be acquired by public collections whether by purchase, gift, or bequest nor exhibited by them on long or short-term loan."

Because as much as 80 percent of antiquities on the market today are looted in recent decades, the prevailing ethical standard is "guilty until proven innocent," a reversal of Cuno's personal standard. Cuno's assertion that the museum is somehow ethically bound to obtain artifacts that might otherwise end up in a private collection is also an argument that has long been rejected by the archaeological profession. The Society for American Archeology's "Principles of Archeological Ethics" discourages any activity that increases the commercial value of archaeological materials. The active participation by these directors in the purchase of unprovenanced materials from suspect dealers clearly violated this principle. It is also quite apparent that these museums are operating under the assumption that laws and ethics are one and the same. A 1986 statement by former MFA director Alan Shestack clarifies this point: "I cried out for stringent laws that would give museum directors a reason for not doing the evil thing."

As noted in chapter 10, many of the ethical codes promulgated by museums are really codes of conduct because ethics cannot be a matter of external origin. A museum director cannot enforce ethical standards. The museum director must, however, through his or her own behavior, set the standard for professional conduct as well as ethical behavior. Issues surrounding cultural patrimony will continue to dominate our professional discourse as we enter the third millennium, and museum leaders must be sensitive to these concerns. Hiding behind the law, or adopting a thinly veiled paternalism, such as that expressed by Cuno, are not tactics that will move museums forward in the centuries to come.

of the American public.[36] In 2000–2001, AAM sponsored a series of community dialogues in six locations across the United States. More than seven hundred people, 65 percent representing the community perspective, participated. Among their observations: museums are civic enterprises with substantial but unrealized potential.[37]

One way for museums to show their commitment to the community is through strategic partnerships. Local schools are one logical partner. Partnerships with schools help museums emphasize their commitment to their primary mission of education. Museums should look for a relationship that goes beyond being simply a field trip destination. Museums should find ways to make their programs an integral part of the schools' curriculum and look for special opportunities, such as forming magnet schools, charter schools, or latch-key programs. The Folsom Children's Zoo and Botanical Gardens in Lincoln, Nebraska, worked with the local school district to form a science-focus "Zoo School"; a secondary school with an arts and humanities focus makes regular use of the city's varied museums.

A significant number of museums are located on university and college campuses. Even here, museums must continually demonstrate their contributions to the academic programs of the institution. These museums also have a special opportunity to serve the museum community through their access to individuals who will be the next generation of policy makers and news media. These museums should make a special effort to reach out to students and start educating them about the value and role of museums in society.

Another ideal partnership for museums is with other local museums and related nonprofit organizations. Forming local consortia and associations demonstrates that the museums care about the community in general and, under the theory that a rising tide raises all ships, they can realize significant additional benefits. Ten museums and other attractions in Lincoln, Nebraska, formed the Lincoln Attractions and Museums Association (LAMA) to do joint marketing and promotion. By representing a group of attractions, LAMA was able to get support, including funding, from the Lincoln Convention and Visitors Bureau and the Nebraska Tourism Department for such things as brochure production and distribution statewide, production of posters, local promotion for National Museum Day and National Tourism Week, and improved highway signing from the state department of roads. These organizations acting alone would not have been able to accomplish any of these promotions.

It is important that museums inform opinion leaders in the community concerning their economic impact, which results from attracting and "delaying" tourists at the museum's facilities. The longer tourists stay in a community, the more likely they are to buy a meal, stay overnight, or purchase gas. This is economic impact! The other economic factor to which museums contribute is the quality of life of the community. When the ratings for America's most livable cities appear, one can be certain that the presence of museums, parks, and recreational facilities significantly aids those at the top of the list.

Museums must work with their local media. The director and the museum's staff should get to know the reporters on the museum beat and be available to the reporters at all times. News releases, press kits, and media openings can help make the media's job easier. The strongest messages come from museums with ties in the community and those that address broader community concerns such as after-school or similar types of programs. The electronic media must provide a certain number of public service announcements, so even smaller museums can acquire professional spots and have them readily available.

The World Wide Web has opened a new audience for museums and a whole new mechanism for serving audiences far and wide. Exploration of the possibilities continues as museum websites, virtual museums, and digitized collections materials come online. Internet marketing is becoming an increasingly important tool for many museums, which are also using electronic mail to manage membership acquisition and retention and to regularly and cheaply communicate with visitors.[38] This developing technology and its convergence with digital television offer myriad possibilities.

All of these potential partnerships reinforce the finding of the AAM's museum-community dialogue: true civic enterprises succeed through comprehensive, flexible organization-to-organization relationships, not episodic partnerships. Museums can build relationships that overcome the perceptions that limit community involvement: that museums control knowledge, expertise, and learning, and are led and staffed by a homogeneous group that floats above or passes through the community.[39]

Museum directors need to always keep in mind that museums must continually prove their value to the community if they wish to retain and enhance the community's support. The leader of the museum must remember that if the museum wants community support, it (and its staff) must be part of the community. This cycle all begins with the example set by the director.

Technology

With mention of technology, most people's thoughts will turn to computers; the rapidly evolving field of computer technology will be both a boon and a challenge to museums. Computers are already performing such tasks in museums as word processing and accounting, as well as enhancing exhibit and educational programs and managing collection data. These and many other tasks will become ever more dependent on computer technology. The challenge for museums will be in trying to keep their computer technology current while covering the costs of rapid changes.

Computer technology in museums had its origins in the 1960s with mainframe computers that were used for automatic processing of collection data. Museum catalog and similar data could be entered in the computer and then queried to answer a variety of questions that were difficult or impossible to answer without the computer technology. Although these databases could be queried, they could not be shared and were not portable. The 1980s brought desktop computers into database management, and ever improving software, networking, and increasing data storage capacity made them into powerful tools for data management.[40] The technology has now progressed to the point that the databases can be published on the World Wide Web and shared and queried electronically.[41]

Recalling the state of computer technology in the early 1980s makes clear the difficulty of foreseeing what this technology will bring by 2020. Computers will enhance the amount of work done by individual staff members and will allow museums to combat, at least in part, their reductions in staff. Convergence of television and Internet systems with the broad bandwidth that fiber-optic technology allows will create the possibility of a mind-boggling variety of programming for consumers to select. How museums will provide high-quality content and identity in this sea of data remains to be seen. Undoubtedly more museums will be using this technology, and those museums currently involved in computer technology will be making larger databases electronically available. These databases will continue to contain the text of collection data and archival records and certainly will be combined with digital images of collection objects, photographs, and entire exhibits. Digital moving images will allow access to historic films and videos and offer Internet users virtual tours of facilities.

Digital imaging technology for collection objects, photographs, and text documents is only beginning to realize its potential at the opening of the third millennium.[42] These images may be shared via networking on the World Wide Web, produced in CD-ROM and other formats, and used in multimedia presentations[43] both within and outside the museum. This technology also will present challenges to museums as they try to control use of the images of materials in their collections. Howard Besser[44] discusses how imaging technology and its availability through networking may change the basic nature of museums: "Museums are likely to act less like traditional repositories that offer visitors a passive experience primarily through exhibitions and publications, and more like institutions that encourage visitors to take an interactive role. The general public may view culture less as something to consume and more as something to interact with. When the patron no longer has to visit the gallery or museum in order to see a particular image, the authority of the institution will likely begin to erode."

Technology is already being used to create virtual museums and virtual exhibits.[45] Certainly museums will want to lead this effort because it will make their resources available to a far broader audience, but anyone with access to digital images will be able to compete in cyberspace. Here is another technology that will offer museums great opportunities and great challenges that will only be fully understood and appreciated in the decades ahead. Kristine Morrissey and Douglas Worts[46] caution that the real challenge for museums in using technology "lies in considering not just the technology or the tools, but the individual, the group, our cultures, and our institutions. The real challenge is in better understanding how technology can illuminate and enhance the complex relationships between people and objects."

With all of the technological advances, museums must remember that their most powerful educational tools are the real objects. Ann Mintz notes, "Information technology is a means, not an end. It can enhance the experience of the real thing in wonderful, meaningful ways. It cannot replace it."[47] Therefore, it will be important for museums to search for other new technology, which will both improve presentation and provide better preservation of objects. Technological developments and technology transfer from industry are almost certain to revolutionize exhibit presentation and collections care. These changes may be in the form of new materials for the construction of exhibits and storage of collections, control of environmental conditions, new forms of lighting, and improvements in conservation techniques and materials. These technological improvements should help museums to better fulfill their missions of long-term preservation of collection objects and their presentation to the public.[48]

Increasing Professionalism

There will be a need and a demand for people entering the museum profession to have more academic education. Museums with reduced budgets and reduced staff will no longer find acceptable the extended apprenticeship period that was the traditional method of training museum personnel. It will simply be too expensive, in both time and dollars. This is especially true if museums can access a workforce of people who have paid for their own education and introductory experience within museums. Demand for a highly trained workforce for museums will place increased pressure on the existing museum studies, public history, and archive management programs and will provide opportunities for the creation of new educational programs. Prospective students will find excellent resources available in publications of the American Association of Museums, which list over 200 programs providing some type of museum, public history, or archival academic education[49] and supply information students need when choosing an appropriate academic program.[50]

The need for an educated workforce also will create a need for mid-career training programs. This need will far outstrip the capacity of the current programs and will undoubtedly result in a number of additional on-site programs. This area of educational need will be ideally suited to new methods of delivery through distance learning. These methods could include Internet or satellite technology or other methods that have not yet been explored.

The entire museum profession must become far more scholarly. The profession must move from the current word-of-mouth approach to a more academic orientation, in which ideas are published, reviewed, criticized, contemplated, revised and restructured, and published again. This process will result in further progress within the museum profession. Far more scholarly journals will be needed than the four or five available today.

In summary, it will be the professional societies and associations, including the American Association of Museums, the American Associa-

Box 15.3

Case Study: On the First Day

You are reporting for your first day of work as director of a museum. It is July 1, the first day of a new fiscal year. Your interviewing and negotiating process took nearly a year, but you feel good about the position of the museum and your opportunity to work there. Having twenty-five staff members will certainly make life easier compared with the three people you had at your previous museum. You did notice during the interview process that staff morale was low, and they seemed to lack direction, but this was not surprising, since the museum has lacked a permanent director for four years.

You walk into the office, and your lovely young secretary, Ms. Bright, says cheerfully, "Good morning sir! We are certainly happy to have you here. You have a busy schedule this morning. Just about everyone wants to talk with you!" You reply, "Good morning," and you think to yourself, "She looks a little different than I remember, but, oh well, it sounds great that everyone wants to see me." You go into your office and begin unloading your briefcase. "Dr. Doe, this is Mr. Boyle, our chief of maintenance; he is your very first appointment." "Well it certainly is good to see you again. What can I do for you today?" Mr. Boyle begins, "Well sir, I hate to bring this news to you on your first day, but they didn't want me to say anything when you were interviewing, but I thought that you should know that the HVAC system is going on eighteen years old, and I can't be responsible for keeping it running anymore."

As your meeting with Mr. Boyle is ending, your secretary enters your office saying Ms. Moneybags, chair of the museum trustees, is on the telephone and Will Paint, head of exhibits, is waiting to see you. You pick up the telephone and hear the firm, reassuring voice of Ms. Moneybags. "How are you this morning, John? I wanted to call and welcome you on your first day of work. How are things at the museum?" You respond. Moneybags proceeds, "I was talking with Mr. Debit (treasurer of the trustees) yesterday, and he was telling me that he believes the folks down there at the museum may have overspent their budget as much as $20,000 last year. You will need to give this some thought, and we will need to figure out how we will handle this. Sorry to tell you this on your first day, but I thought you should know."

Later in the conversation, Ms. Moneybags inquires, "Has anyone brought you up to date on our $5 million fund-raising campaign?" "No," you reply; this was the one commitment that had been discussed with the trustees at length during your interviews; they had committed to having the campaign completed or nearly so upon your arrival. "Well, we have had some unexpected problems. You know how that happens on such big projects. We have collected about 25 percent of the money, but then the fund-raising company we hired wasn't doing a good job, so we fired it, and Mrs. Civic Duty, who was heading the campaign for the trustees, had a granddaughter born in California, so she was gone for two months. Now that you are here, we will be looking for your advice and leadership to get this campaign finished quickly. This is something we (referring to herself, Mr. Debit, and Mrs. Duty) can discuss at lunch tomorrow. I look forward to seeing you then."

Almost before the telephone hits the hook, Will Paint bursts into the room. "Good morning, sir! We have a big problem! Sorry to bring this to you today, but we

Box 15.3 (continued)

have a major temporary exhibit opening in two months, and we are having problems with the financial donors." "Good morning, Will! Why don't you explain the problem to me?" you reply. "We have two financial backers for this major traveling exhibit. We haven't heard from one in nine months, and the other called last month and was surprised when I asked about the money. They have given $25,000 to the fund-raising campaign, and they assumed that this would cover the temporary exhibit."

As Will departs, your secretary enters. "Sorry, Dr. Doe, I just couldn't restrain him anymore. Here is a note left by Dr. Farrah Field, our chief curator, and, of course, the interim director for the last eighteen months." You knew these facts, but it was nice to be reminded. The note, dated June 28, reads, "I leave in about five minutes for central Mexico. I haven't left an address because it will be impossible to reach me for the next six weeks while I am in the field, and then I will be on vacation for two weeks. I should be back around the first of September. There may be a problem with last year's budget, but if there is, it is those people in education who have been on a spending spree. Sorry to tell you this on your first day, but I thought that you should be warned. See you in a few weeks."

It is about 11 A.M., and Harry Broom, head of custodial services, is waiting to see you. Harry is a distinguished-looking man in his late forties. "Good morning Harry!" "Good morning, sir. I hate to tell you this on your first day, but you have a problem. We have three other custodians workin' here at the museum, and there's goin' to be a strike because this rich museum run by rich people is not paying them anything." He presents you with a photocopy of one page of the budget, which seems to indicate that the custodians are making $5.00 per hour. You ask a few questions and promise to look into the matter.

Ms. Bright comes into your office all smiles. "Can I have a few minutes of your time." "Certainly," you reply. "Well, I don't know if anyone has told you yet or not, but I am five months pregnant. I am just so excited! Aren't you excited?!" She continues, "I suppose Dr. Field has already told you she has approved three months of maternity leave for me starting in about three months. Oh, I am just so excited!" As she starts to leave your office, she turns and says, "Now don't forget the all-staff meeting at 1:30 P.M. Everyone is looking forward to hearing your vision and direction for the museum for the next year! We have been looking forward to having your new leadership. I will see you after lunch!"

It is about 12:15 P.M., and you are starting to think about getting some lunch and gathering your thoughts for the all-staff meeting. You hear running footsteps approaching your office. A wide-eyed young woman bursts into the office. "The boys have plugged the commode on the second floor and the water is running into the exhibit gallery!!!! What should we do????" Suddenly, she sees your surprised face and realizes that no one she knows is in the office. Without waiting for your stuttered response, she is off at a faster pace than she arrived.

Outline the four major points you will make in your 1:30 P.M. talk to demonstrate your new leadership for the museum. What will be your priorities for leading the museum in the next year? What three issues will you raise with your major museum supporters tomorrow at lunch? Defend your decisions in relationship to your leadership style.

tion for State and Local History, the Society of American Archivists, the National Council on Public History, the American Zoo and Aquarium Association, and the American Association of Botanical Gardens and Arboreta that must provide leadership in increasing the professionalism of America's museums and related organizations. We believe that three new or continued actions by these organizations can provide this leadership: first, an accreditation program for member organizations, which already is in place for several of these professional groups; second, an increase in scholarly communication—the number of scholarly journals and open sessions at annual meetings in which scholars present their ideas and findings should be expanded, as should the use of modern communications for live distance education and workshop presentations for mid-career professionals; and third, accreditation of museum professional education programs. Guidelines have been presented for beginning many of these programs, which had their origins in the 1970s and 1980s. It is now time to see how these programs measure up to these standards. Universities depend on professional organizations to accredit many of their programs to be certain that students are receiving an appropriate academic education, and they should do so in the areas of museum studies, public history, and archives management. These actions will ensure a relevant standard for museums and museum professionals.

Notes

1. AAM 1999.
2. Carr 1999, 32.
3. Davies 1999, 115–116.
4. Leigh and Maynard 1996.
5. Ackerson 1998.
6. Durel 1998, 19.
7. Clifton and Nelson 1992, 19.
8. Ibid., 42.
9. Ibid., 72.
10. Ibid.
11. Handy 1996, 8.
12. Bennis 1989, 24.
13. Fleming 1999, 94.

14. Meléndez 1996, 297.
15. Clifton and Nelson 1992, 113–114.
16. Phillips 1998, 29.
17. Drucker 1996, xii.
18. Phillips 1998, 29.
19. Ibid.
20. Clifton and Nelson 1992.
21. Ibid., 27.
22. Handy 1996, 8–9.
23. Drucker 1996, xi-xv.
24. Fleming 1999.
25. Schein 1996, 63.
26. Meléndez 1996, 297.
27. Drucker 1996, xii–xiii.
28. Belasco and Stead 1999, 24.
29. Handy 1996, 9.
30. Simerly 1991, 23.
31. Simerly, 1991.
32. Fleming 1999, 95.
33. Kouzes and Posner 1996, 103.
34. Simerly 1991, 23.
35. AAM 1999.
36. Ibid.
37. AAM 2001.
38. London 2001.
39. AAM 2001.
40. Jones-Garmil 1997.
41. Speck 2001; Ioanid and Bowman 2001.
42. Koelling 2000, 2002; Jones-Garmil 1997; Johnston 1997; Levenson 1998.
43. Sayre, 1998.
44. Besser 1997.
45. Perlin 1998.
46. Morrissey and Worts 1998.
47. Mintz 1998.
48. Duckworth et al. 1993.
49. Adams and Ritzenthaler 1999.
50. Schwarzer 2001.

REFERENCES AND ADDITIONAL READINGS

Chapter 1

Adams, R., and T. J. Ritzenthaler. 1999. *Guide to museum studies and training in the United States, 1999–2000.* Washington, DC: Professional Practice Series, Technical Information Service, American Association of Museums.

Alexander, E. P. 1979. *Museums in motion: An introduction to the history and functions of museums.* Nashville, TN: American Association for State and Local History.

———. 1997. *The museum in America: Innovators and pioneers.* Walnut Creek, CA: AltaMira Press.

AAM (American Association of Museums). 2000. *The official museum directory.* New Providence, NJ: National Register Publishing.

Anderson, G., and C. Matelic. 1988. Museum studies programs: Ethics and professionalism. *Museum News* 67(2):36–41.

Andrei, M. A., and H. H. Genoways. 1997. Museum ethics. *Curator, The Museum Journal* 40:6–12.

Brinati, T. M., ed. 2002. Home page. The Society of American Archivists. World Wide Web: http://www.archivists.org/. Retrieved August 27, 2002.

Burcaw, G. E. 1997. *Introduction to museum work.* 3rd ed. Walnut Creek, CA: AltaMira Press.

Cato, P. S., R. R. Waller, L. Sharp, J. Simmons, and S. L. Williams. 1996. Developing staff resources for managing collections. *Special Publication, Virginia Museum of Natural History* 4:1–71.

Coleman, L. V. 1939. *The museum in America,* vol. 2. Washington, DC: American Association of Museums.

Danilov, V. J. 1994. *Museum careers and training: A professional guide.* Westport, CT: Greenwood Press.

Dolan, D. C. 1986. The historian in the local historical museum. In *Public history: An introduction,* eds. B. J. Howe and E.L. Kemp, 241–250. Malabar, FL: Robert E. Kriegar Publishing Company.

Dubberly, S. 2001. *Organizing your museum: The essentials.* Washington, DC:

Professional Practice Series, Technical Information Service, American Association of Museums.

Fishel, L. H. 1986. Public history and the academy. In *Public history: An introduction,* eds. B. J. Howe and E. L. Kemp, 8–19. Malabar, FL: Robert E. Kriegar Publishing Company.

Fleming, D. 1999. Leadership. In *Management in museums,* ed. K. Moore, 93–132. New Brunswick, NJ: Athlone Press.

Foundation Center. World Wide Web: http://fdncenter.org. Retrieved November 11, 2002.

Francell, M. 1988. Ethics codes: Past, present, and future. *Museum News* 67(2):35.

General Services Administration. *The catalog of domestic assistance*, World Wide Web: http://www.cfda.gov. Retrieved November 11, 2002.

Genoways, H. H., and M. A. Andrei. 1997. Codes of professional museum conduct. *Curator, The Museum Journal* 40:86–92.

Glaser, J. R., and A. A. Zenetou. 1996. *Museums: A place to work—planning museum careers.* London: Routledge.

Hein, H. 2000. *The museum in transition—A philosophical perspective.* Washington, DC: Smithsonian Institution Press.

Howe, B. J., and E. L. Kemp, eds. 1986. *Public history: An introduction.* Malabar, FL: Robert E. Kriegar Publishing Company.

Institute of Museum and Library Services. World Wide Web: http://www.imls.gov. Retrieved November 11, 2002.

Janes, R. R. 1999. Embracing organizational change in museums: A work in progress. In *Management in museums,* ed. K. Moore, 7–27. New Brunswick, NJ: Athlone Press.

Knell, S. J., ed. 1994. *A bibliography of museum studies.* Hants, UK: Scolar Press.

Matelic, C. T., and E. M. Brick, eds. 1990. *Cooperstown conference on professional training: Needs, issues, and opportunities for the future.* Nashville, TN: American Association for State and Local History.

Mock, D. B. 1986. History in the public arena. In *Public history: An introduction,* eds. B. J. Howe and E.L. Kemp, 401–413. Malabar, FL: Robert E. Kriegar Publishing Company.

National Endowment for the Arts. World Wide Web: http://www.arts.gov. Retrieved November 11, 2002.

National Endowment for the Humanities. World Wide Web: http://www.neh.gov. Retrieved November 11, 2002.

National Science Foundation. World Wide Web: http://www.nsf.gov. Retrieved November 11, 2002.

Nebraska Arts Council. World Wide Web: http://www.nebraskaartscouncil.org. Retrieved November 11, 2002.

Nebraska Humanities Council. World Wide Web: http://www.lincolnne.com/nonprofit/nhc/. Retrieved November 11, 2002.

Nichols, S. K. 1989. *Organizing your museum: The essentials.* Washington, DC: Professional Practice Series, Technical Information Service, American Association of Museums.

NonProfit Gateway. World Wide Web: http://www.nonprofit.gov/. Retrieved November 11, 2002.

Parr, A. E. 1960. Is there a museum profession? *Curator, The Museum Journal* 3:101–106.

———. 1964. A plurality of professions. *Curator, The Museum Journal* 7:287–295.

Professional Practices Committee. 1983. Criteria for examining professional museum studies programs. *Museum News* 61(5):70–71, 99–108.

Ruthven, A. G. 1931. *A naturalist in a university museum.* Ann Arbor, MI: Privately published.

Taylor, R. L. 1990. *Museum accreditation: A handbook for the institution.* Washington, DC: American Association of Museums.

U.S. Government Printing Office. *U.S. Government Manual.* World Wide Web: http://www.access.gpo.gov/nara/nara001.html. Retrieved November 11, 2002.

Ward, D., ed. 2001. The National Council on Public History. World Wide Web: http://www.ncph.org/. Retrieved February 16, 2001.

Webster's II New Riverside University Dictionary. 1984. Boston, MA: The Riverside Publishing Company.

Weil, S. E. 1988. The ongoing pursuit of professional status: The progress of museum work in America. *Museum News* 67(2):30–34.

Chapter 2

Able, E. H. 1993. Corporate sponsors and the IRS. *Museum News* 72(5):71.

Ambrose, T., and C. Paine. 1993. *Museum basics.* New York: Routledge.

Anderson, G. 1998. *Museum mission statements: Building a distinct identity.* Washington, DC: American Association of Museums.

Garfield, D. 1992. Frances Hesselbein: Managing for the mission. *Museum News* 71(2):66–67.

Hendricks, W. 1990. Museum director's journal: To build the support you need, hold fast to your mission. *Museum News* 69(1):73–74.

Hoagland, K. E., ed. 1994. *Guidelines for institutional policies and planning in natural history collections.* Washington, DC: Association of Systematics Collections.

IRS (Internal Revenue Service). 2001. Tax exempt status for your organization. Internal Revenue Service, Department of the Treasury, Publication 557:1–60.

Kavanagh, G., ed. 1994. *Museum provision and professionalism.* London: Routledge.

Kearnes, K. P. 2000. *Private sector strategies for social sector success: The guide to strategy and planning for public and nonprofit organizations.* San Francisco: Jossey-Bass, Inc.

Lord, G. D., and B. Lord. 1997. *The manual of museum management.* Walnut Creek, CA: AltaMira Press.

Malaro, M. C. 1994. *Museum governance: Mission, ethics, policy.* Washington and London: Smithsonian Institution Press.

———. 1998. *A legal primer on managing museum collections.* Washington and London: Smithsonian Institution Press.

Moore, K., ed. 1999. *Management in museums.* London and New Brunswick, NJ: The Athlone Press.

Nebraska Continuing Legal Education. 2000. *Nonprofit law: Keeping the public trust.* Lincoln, NE: Nebraska Continuing Legal Education.

Nebraska Department of Economic Development. n.d. "Information on Nonprofit Incorporation in Nebraska." World Wide Web: http://63.239.54.223/npincorp.html.

Nichols, S. K., ed. 1989. *Organizing your museum: The essentials.* Washington, DC: American Association of Museums.

Pepperl, J. M. 1997. *Revised statutes of Nebraska: Reissue of volume 1A.* Published by Joanne M. Pepperl, Revisor of Statutes, pp. 830–915.

Phelan, M. E. 1994. *Museum law.* Evanston, IL: Kalos Kapp Press.

Robert, H. M., III, and W. J. Evans, eds. 1990. *Robert's rules of order newly revised.* 9th ed. Cambridge, MA: Perseus Books.

Schwarzer, M. 1999. Schizophrenic agora: Mission, market and the multi-tasking museum. *Museum News* 78(6):40–47.

Simpson, S. D. 2000. *Tax-exempt organizations: Organizational and operational requirements.* Washington, DC: Tax Management Inc.

Wolf, T. 1990. *Managing a nonprofit organization.* New York: Prentice Hall Press.

Zeitlin, K. A., and S. E. Dorn. 1996. *The nonprofit board's guide to bylaws: Creating a framework for effective governance.* Washington, DC: National Center for Nonprofit Boards.

Chapter 3

Allen, D. 2001. *Getting things done: The art of stress free productivity.* Cambridge, MA: Viking Press.

Axelrod, N. R. 1994. Board leadership and board development. In *The Jossey-Bass handbook of nonprofit leadership and management,* ed. R. D. Herman, 119–136. San Francisco: Jossey-Bass, Inc.

Bailey, M. 1996. *The troublesome board member.* Washington, DC: National Center for Nonprofit Boards.

Bales, R. F., S. P. Cohen, and S. A. Williamson. 1970. *Personality and interpersonal behavior.* New York: Holt, Rinehart & Winston.

Benedetto, R. R. 1985. *Matrix management: Theory in practice.* Dubuque, IA: Kendall/Hunt.

Benjamin, J., J. Bessant, and R. Watts. 1997. *Making groups work: Rethinking practice.* St. Leonards, Australia: Allen & Unwin.

Benne, K. D., and P. Sheats. 1970. Functional roles of group members. In *Small group communication: A reader,* eds. R. S. Cathcart and L. A. Samovar, 133–142. Dubuque, IA: Wm. C. Brown Company.

Bergmann, T. J., and R. J. Volkema. 1981. *An empirical investigation of problem formulation and problem-purpose expansion.* Madison, WI: University of Wisconsin.

Bienkowski, P. 1995. Soft systems in museums. *Museum Management and Curatorship* 13:233–250.

Binsted, D. 1986. *Developments in interpersonal skills training.* Aldershot, England: Gower Publishing Co.

Blackman, C. P. 1988. *Open conversations: Strategies for professional development in museums.* Chicago: Field Museum of Natural History.

Bradford, D., and A. Cohen. 1984. *Managing for excellence: The guide to developing high performance in contemporary organizations.* New York: John Wiley & Sons.

Case, M., and W. Phillips. 1993. A cooperative decision process. *Management briefings.* World Wide Web: http://www.qm2.org/mbrief/12.html. Retrieved December 8, 2002.

Chait, R. P. 1993. *How to help your board govern more and manage less.* Washington, DC: National Center for Nonprofit Boards.

Chell, E. 1987. *The psychology of behavior in organizations.* London: Macmillan Press.

Cloyd, J. S. 1964. Patterns of role behavior in informal interaction. *Sociometry* 27:161–173.

REFERENCES

Cohen, A. R., and D. Bradford. 1990. *Influence without authority.* New York: John Wiley and Sons.

Conger, J., R. Egherman, and G. Mallard. 1979. The museum as employer. *Museum News* 57(6):22–28.

Deep, S., and L. Sussman. 2000. *Act on it! Solving 101 of the toughest management challenges.* New York: Perseus Print.

Des, G., M. Abraham, and J. Crawford. 1999. Effective management of museums in the 1990s. *Curator, The Museum Journal* 42:37–53.

Deutsch, M. 1973. *The resolution of conflict, constructive and destructive processes.* New Haven, CT: Yale University Press.

Dickenson, V. 1994. An inquiry into the relationship between museum boards and management. In *Museum management,* ed. Kevin Moore, 95–103. London: Routledge.

Drucker, P. F. 1990. *Managing the nonprofit organization.* New York: Harper Collins.

Dubrin, A. J. 1997. *Fundamentals of organizational behavior.* Cincinnati, OH: South-Western.

Duca, D. J. 1996. *Nonprofit boards: Roles, responsibilities, and performance.* New York: John Wiley and Sons.

Emery, A. R. 1990. The management of change: The case of the Canadian Museum of Nature. *MUSE* 8(3):76–79.

Fletcher, K. 2000. *Policy sampler: A resource for non profit boards.* Washington, DC: National Center for Nonprofit Boards.

Folger, J. P., M. S. Poole, and R. K. Stutman. 1997. *Working through conflict: Strategies for relationships, groups, and organizations.* 3rd ed. New York: Longman.

Frantzreb, A. C. 1989. Recruiting and working with your governing board. In *Organizing your museum: The essentials.* 1st ed. Washington, DC: American Association of Museums, Technical Information Service.

Friedman, A. J. 1991. Mix and match. *Museum News* 70(4):28–42.

Gastil, J. W. 1993. *Democracy in small groups: Participation, decision making and communications.* Philadelphia, PA: New Society.

Gurian, E. H. 1995. *Institutional trauma.* Washington, DC: American Association of Museums.

Hackman, J. R., and C. G. Morris. 1983. Group tasks, group interaction process, and group performance effectiveness. In *Small groups and social interaction,* ed. H. H. Blumberg, 331–345. New York: John Wiley & Sons.

Handy, C. B. 1989. *The age of unreason.* London: Century Hutchinson Books.

———. 1994. *The age of paradox.* Boston, MA: Harvard Business School Press.

———. 2000. *21 Ideas for managers: Practical wisdom for managing your company and yourself.* San Francisco: Jossey-Bass, Inc.

Hare, A. P. 1982. Roles. In *Creativity in small groups,* ed. A. P. Hare, 122–140. Beverly Hills, CA: Sage Publications.

Hay, R. D. 1990. *Strategic management in non-profit organizations: An administrator's handbook.* New York: Quorum Books.

Heimovics, D., and R. D. Herman. 1994. Executive leadership. In *The Jossey-Bass handbook of nonprofit leadership and management,* ed. R. D. Herman, 137–153. San Francisco: Jossey-Bass, Inc.

Hirzy, E. C. 1998. *The chair's role in leading the nonprofit board.* Washington, DC: National Center for Nonprofit Boards.

Howe, F. 1995. *Welcome to the board: Your guide to effective participation.* San Francisco: Jossey-Bass, Inc.

Hughes, S. R., B. M. Lakey, and M. J. Bobowick. 2000. *The board building cycle: Nine steps to finding, recruiting, and engaging nonprofit board members.* Washington, DC: National Center for Nonprofit Boards.

Ingram, R. T. 1996. *Ten basic responsibilities of nonprofit boards.* Washington, DC: National Center for Nonprofit Boards.

Janes, R. R. 1997. *Museums and the paradox of change: A case study in urgent adaptation.* 2nd ed. Calgary, Alberta, Canada: Glenbow Museum.

Johnson, D. W., and R. T. Johnson. 1998. Cooperative learning and social interdependence theory. In *Theory and research on small groups,* eds. R. S. Tindale et al., 9–35. New York: Plenum Press.

Kahn, H., and S. Garden. 1993. Job attitudes and occupational stress in the United Kingdom museum sector. *Museum Management and Curatorship* 12:285–302.

Kane, K. 1991. Bridging the gap. *Museum News* 70(6):46–48

Katz, N. H., and J. W. Lawyer. 1985. *Communication and conflict resolution skill.* Dubuque, IA: Kendall/Hunt.

Kotler, N. G., and P. Kotler. 1998. *Museum strategy and marketing.* San Francisco: Jossey-Bass, Inc.

Lord, B., and G. D. Lord. 1997. *The manual of museum management.* Walnut Creek, CA: AltaMira Press.

Lundin, W., and K. Lundin. 1995. *Working with difficult people.* New York: Amacom.

Malaro, M. C. 1994. *Museum governance: Mission, ethics, policy.* Washington, DC: Smithsonian Institution Press.

McLean, K. 1993. *Planning for people in museum exhibitions.* Washington, DC: Association of Science-Technology Centers.

National Center for Nonprofit Boards. 1992. *Good governance: Answers to seven common questions.* Washington, DC: The Board Information Center.

Naumer, H. 1977. *Of mutual respect and other things: An essay on museum trusteeship.* Washington, DC: American Association of Museums.

Nemiroff, P. M., and D. C. King. 1975. Group decision-making performance as influenced by consensus and self-orientation. *Human Relations* 28(1):1–21.

Petty, R. E., J. T. Cacioppo, and S. G. Harkins. 1983. Group size effects on cognitive effort and attitude change. In *Small groups and social interaction,* ed. H. H. Blumberg, 177–178. Chichester, NY: John Wiley & Sons.

Rahim, M. A. 2000. *Managing conflict in organizations.* 3rd ed. Westport, CT: Quorum Books.

Reina, D. S., and M. L. Reina. 1999. *Trust and betrayal in the workplace: Building effective relationships in your organization.* Williston, VT: Barrett-Koeler Publishers, Inc.

Robinson, M. K. 1998. *The chief executive's role in developing the nonprofit board.* Washington, DC: National Center for Nonprofit Boards.

Rothwell, J. D. 1992. *Mixed company: Small group communication.* Fort Worth, TX: Harcourt Brace Jovanovich College Publishers.

Sessa, V. I. 1996. Using perspective taking to manage conflict and affect in teams. *Journal of Applied Behavioral Science* 32(1):101–115.

Simmons, K., and G. J. Stern. 1999. *Creating strong board-staff partnerships.* Washington, DC: National Center for Nonprofit Boards.

Smiley, M. 1992. *Strategic planning for nonprofit organizations.* Washington, DC: Information Series, National Trust for Historic Preservation.

Szanton, P. 1998. *Evaluation and the nonprofit board.* Washington, DC: National Center for Nonprofit Boards.

Tolles, B.F., Jr. 1991. Looking for leaders. *Museum News* 70(4):43–44.

Weil, S. E. 1999. Transformed from a century of bric-a-brac. In *Perspectives on outcome based evaluation for libraries and museum,* 4–15. Washington, DC: Institute of Museum and Library Services.

Wilson, M. 1981. *Survival skills for managers.* Boulder, CO: Volunteer Management Associates.

Wolf, T. 1990. *Managing a nonprofit organization.* New York: Simon & Schuster.

Chapter 4

American Productivity and Quality Center. 1999. *Strategic planning: What works and what doesn't: Presentations from APQC's third knowledge symposium.* Houston, TX: American Productivity and Quality Center.

Bryson J. M. 1988. *Strategic planning for public and nonprofit organizations: A guide to strengthening and sustaining organizational achievement.* San Francisco: Jossey-Bass Publishers.

Bryson, J. M., and F. K. Alston. 1996. *Creating and implementing your strategic plan: A workbook for public and nonprofit organizations.* San Francisco: Jossey-Bass Publishers.

Burkhart, P., and S. Reuss. 1993. *Successful strategic planning: A guide for nonprofit agencies and organizations.* Newbury Park, CA: Sage Publishers.

Curtis, K. 1994. *From management goal setting to organizational results.* Westport, CT: Quorum Books.

Forester, J. 1989. *Planning in the face of power.* Berkeley and Los Angeles, CA: University of California Press.

Gardner, J. R., R. Rochlin, and H. W. A. Sweeny, eds. 1986. *Handbook of strategic planning.* New York: John Wiley & Sons Publishers.

Gottschalk, P. 1999. *Strategic information systems planning: The implementation challenge.* Henley-on-Thames, England: Henley Management College.

Grace, K. S. 1996. *The board's role in strategic planning.* Washington, DC: National Center for Nonprofit Boards.

Katsioloudes, M. I. 2002. *Global strategic planning: Cultural perspectives for profit and non-profit organizations.* Oxford, UK: Butterworth-Heinemann.

Phillips, W. 1995. *Why plans fail.* San Diego, CA: Qm2.

McHugh, A. 1980. Strategic planning for museums. *Museum News* 58(6):23–29.

Simerly, R. 1985. *Strategic long range planning: A practical guide for museum leaders.* Champaign, IL: Museum Management Institute.

Smiley, M. 1992. Strategic planning for nonprofit organizations. *National Trust for Historic Preservation Information Series* 66:1–24.

Chapter 5

Anthony, R., and R. Herzlinger. 1980. *Management control in nonprofit organizations.* Homewood, IL: Richard D. Irwin, Inc.

Bergman, J. I., W. G. Bowen, and T. I. Nygren. 1996. *Managing change in the nonprofit sector: Lessons from the evolution of five independent research libraries.* San Francisco: Jossey-Bass, Inc.

Chabotar, K. 1991. *Financial management and retrenchment.* Lecture. Museum Management Institute, Berkeley, CA.

Chapo, J. 2000. *Building a budget.* Lecture. Graduate Program in Museum Studies, University of Nebraska-Lincoln.

REFERENCES

Dalsimer, J. P. 1996. *Understanding nonprofit financial statements.* Washington, DC: National Center for Nonprofit Boards.

Dropkin, M., and B. LaTouche. 1998. *The budget-building book for nonprofits: A step-by-step guide for managers and boards.* San Francisco: Jossey-Bass, Inc.

Dropkin, M., and A. Hayden. 2001. *The cash flow management book for nonprofits: A step-by-step guide for managers and boards.* San Francisco: Jossey-Bass, Inc.

Gambino, A. J., and T. J. Reardon. 1981. *Financial planning and evaluation for the nonprofit organization.* New York: National Association of Accountants.

Garner, C. W. 1991. *Accounting and budgeting in public and nonprofit organizations: A manager's guide.* San Francisco: Jossey-Bass, Inc.

Harrison, W. T., C. T. Horngren, and W. M. Lemon. 1997. *Financial accounting.* Toronto, Ontario: Prentice-Hall.

Hotchner, H. 1995. Life on a fiscal precipice. In *Institutional trauma: Major change in museums and its effects on staff,* ed. E.H. Gurian, 135–155. Washington, DC: American Association of Museums.

Lang, A. S. 1998. *Financial responsibilities of the nonprofit board.* Washington, DC: National Center for Nonprofit Boards.

Lord, B., and G. D. Lord. 1997. *The manual of museum management.* Walnut Creek, CA: AltaMira Press.

Maddox, D. C. 1999. *Budgeting for not-for-profit organizations.* New York: John Wiley and Sons, Inc.

Maitland, I. 2000. *Budgeting for non-financial managers: How to master and maintain effective budgets.* San Francisco: Jossey-Bass, Inc.

Meigs, R. F., J. R. Williams, S. F. Haka, and S. K. Bettner. 1999. *Accounting.* Boston: Irwin McGraw-Hill.

Miller, P. 2001. Putting your house in order: More accountability equals less liability. In *Organizing your museum: The essentials,* ed. S. Dubberly, 110–111. Washington, DC: American Association of Museums.

Phelan, M. E. 1994. *Museum law.* Evanston, IL: Kalos Kapp Press.

Pizer, L. R. 2001. Practically speaking: How to prepare (and live with) a budget. In *Organizing your museum: The essentials,* ed. S. Dubberly, 106–109. Washington, DC: American Association of Museums.

Powell, R. M. 1980. *Budgetary control procedures for institutions.* South Bend, IN: University of Notre Dame Press.

Rosso, H. A. 1996. *Rosso on fund raising: Lessons from a master's lifetime experience.* San Francisco: Jossey-Bass, Inc.

Sheeran, T. E. 1992. Budgeting on the cutting edge: Using PCs to improve budget management. *School Business Affairs* (58)10:14–20.

Ullberg, A. D., and P. Ullberg. 1981. *Museum trusteeship.* Washington, DC: American Association of Museums.
Vinter, R. D., and R. K. Kish. 1984. *Budgeting for not-for-profit organizations.* New York: Collier Macmillan Publishers.
Wolf, T. 1999. *Managing a nonprofit organization in the twenty-first century.* New York: Simon and Schuster.

Chapter 6

Ambrose, T., and C. Paine. 1993. *Museum basics.* New York: Routledge.
American Association of Fund-Raising Counsel Trust for Philanthropy. *Giving USA 2001.* World Wide Web: http://www.aafrc.org/. Retrieved December 16, 2002.
American Association of Museums. *Guidelines for developing and managing business support.* World Wide Web: http://www.aam-us.org/resources/ethics_guidelines/business_support.cfm. Retrieved December 16, 2002.
American Association of Museums. 1994. *Museums count.* Washington, DC: American Association of Museums.
Barnes, B. 2002. Museums' new mantra: Party on! *The Wall Street Journal* July 19, W4.
Bauer, D. G. 1995. *The "how to" grants manual.* 3rd ed. Phoenix, AZ: American Council on Education and The Oryx Press.
Bayley, T. D. 1988. *The fund raiser's guide to successful campaigns.* New York: McGraw-Hill, Inc.
Brentinger, M. 1987. *The ultimate benefit book.* Cleveland, OH: Octavia Press.
Cilella, S. 1988. Fund raising, remembering the human aspect. *Museum News* 66(3):28–29.
Csaszar, T. 1997. The spectacular record-breaking sold-out smash-hit blockbuster supershow! phenomenon of museum culture. *New Art Examiner* December/January, 22–27.
Dove, K. E., V. L. Martin, K. L. Wilson, M. M. Bonk, and S. C. Beggs. 2002. *Conducting a successful development services program: A comprehensive guide and resource.* San Francisco: Jossey-Bass, Inc.
Flanagan, J. 1991. *Successful fundraising: A complete handbook for volunteers and professionals.* Chicago: Contemporary Books, Inc.
Gregg, G. 1997. From bathers to beach towels. *ARTnews* April, 120–123.
Halpert, J. E. 2001. Dr. Pepper hospital? Perhaps, for a price. *New York Times* February 18, 3:1.

REFERENCES

Howe, F. 1991. *The board member's guide to fund raising.* San Francisco: Jossey-Bass, Inc.

Johnson, P., and B. Thomas. 1991. Museums: An economic perspective. In *Museum economics and the community,* ed. Susan Pearce, 5–40. Atlantic Highlands, NJ: The Athlone Press Ltd.

Kotler, N. G., and P. Kotler. 1998. *Museum strategy and marketing: Designing missions, building audiences, generating revenue and resources.* San Francisco: Jossey-Bass, Inc.

Landy, L. 1989. *Something ventured, something gained: A business development guide for nonprofit organizations.* New York: American Council for the Arts.

Lawe, T. M. 1980. *How to secure and manage foundation and federal funds in the 1980's.* Dallas, TX: MRDC Educational Institute.

Lord, B., and G. D. Lord. 2001. The museum planning process. In *Organizing your museum: The essentials,* ed. S. Dubberly, 37–41. Washington DC: American Association of Museums.

Malaro, M. C. 1998. *A legal primer on managing museum collections.* Washington, DC: Smithsonian Institution Press.

Manask Report, The. 1999. Burbank: *Food Service News and Views for Museums, Aquariums and Zoos,* Spring.

Neuborne, E. 1997. This exhibit is brought to you by . . . *Business Week,* November 10, 91.

Reger, L. L. 1995. Collections care: Catalyst for funding. In *Storage of natural history collections: A preventive conservation approach,* eds. C. L. Rose, C. A. Hawks, and H. H. Genoways, 411–422. York, PA: Society for the Preservation of Natural History Collections.

Reiss, A. H. 1988. Anniversaries pay off, a chronicle of successes. *Museum News* 66(2):50.

Rosenbaum, L. 1996. Met shops run deficit (or do they?). *Art In America* February, 112.

Rosso, H. A. 1996. *Rosso on fund raising: Lessons from a master's lifetime experience.* San Francisco: Jossey-Bass, Inc.

Rosso, H. A., and Associates. 1991. *Achieving excellence in fund raising.* San Francisco: Jossey-Bass, Inc.

Roth, E. 1990. Add meals to the menu of options you offer visitors. *Museum News* 69(6):76–77.

Schwarzer, M. 1999. Schizophrenic agora: Mission, market and the multi-tasking museum. *Museum News* 78(6):40–47.

Smith, W. J. 1985. *The art of raising money.* New York: American Management Association.

Trenbeth, R. P. 1986. The membership mystique: How to create income and influence with membership programs. Rockville, MD: The Fund Raising Institute.

Washington Post. 2001. Museums and money. May 31, A24.

Williams, R. 1991. Museums: Education or commerce? *Museum* 43(2):113–114.

Wireman, P. 1997. *Partnerships for prosperity: Museums and economic development.* Washington, DC: American Association of Museums.

Wolf, T. 1999. *Managing a nonprofit organization: In the twenty-first century.* New York: Prentice Hall Press.

Wolfe, M., and R. Ferguson. 2001. New money, new demands: The arrival of the venture philanthropist. *Museum News* 80(1):56–9.

Chapter 7

Ambrose, T., and C. Paine. 1993. *Museum basics.* London and New York: Routledge.

Bernardin, H. J., C. M. Hagan, J. S. Kane, and P. Villanova. 1998. Effective performance management: A focus on precision, customers, and situational constraints. In *Performance appraisal: State of the art in practice,* ed. J. W. Smither, 3–48. San Francisco: Jossey-Bass Publishers.

Berstein, L. 2000. *Creating your employee handbook: A do-it-yourself kit for nonprofits.* San Francisco: Jossey-Bass Publishers.

Buck, R. A., and J. A. Gilmore, eds. 1998. *The new museum registration methods.* Washington, DC: American Association of Museums.

Burcaw, G. E. 1997. *Introduction to museum work.* 3rd ed. Walnut Creek, CA: AltaMira Press.

Condrey, S. 1998. *Handbook of human resource management in government.* San Francisco: Jossey-Bass Publishers.

Grote, D. 1996. *The complete guide to performance appraisal.* New York: American Management Association.

Henderson, R. 1980. *Performance appraisal: Theory to practice.* Reston, VA: Reston Publishing Company.

Komisarjevsky, C., and R. Komisarjevsky. 2000. *Peanut butter and jelly management: Tales from parenthood, lessons for managers.* New York: AMACOM.

Kuyper, J., E. C. Hirzy, and K. Huftalen. 1993. *Volunteer program administration: A handbook for museums and other cultural institutions.* New York: American Association for Museum Volunteers.

Landy, F. J., and J. L. Farr. 1983. *The measurement of work performance: Methods, theory, and applications.* New York: Academic Press.

Latham, G. P., and K. N. Wexley. 1981. *Increasing productivity through performance appraisal.* Reading, MA: Addison-Wesley Publishing Company.

Lawson, J. W., II. 1969. *How to develop a company personnel policy manual.* Chicago: Dartnell Press, Inc.

Lecky-Thompson, R. 1999. *Constructive appraisals.* New York: AMACOM.

Levesque, J. D. 1993. *Manual of personnel policies, procedures, and operations.* 2nd ed. Englewood Cliffs, NJ: Prentice-Hall, Inc.

Levine, M. J. 1982. *Public personnel management: Structure, process, and practice.* Sun Lakes, AZ: Thomas Horton and Daughters.

Malaro, M. C. 1998. *A legal primer on managing museum collections.* Washington, DC: Smithsonian Institution Press.

Miller, R. L. 1980. *Personnel policies for museums: A handbook for management.* Washington DC: American Association of Museums.

Murphy, K. R., and J. N. Cleveland. 1995. *Understanding performance appraisal: Social, organizational, and goal-based perspectives.* Thousand Oaks, CA: Sage Publications, Inc.

Reaves, M. 1992. *Developing a company policy manual that both you and your employees can live with.* Chicago: Probus Publishing Company.

Robinson, F. W. 1999. Why I believe in affirmative action. *Museum News* 78(6):35–36, 38.

Rossett, A. 1999. *First things fast: A handbook for performance analysis.* San Francisco: Jossey-Bass Publishers.

Simmons, A. 1998. *Territorial games: Understanding and ending turf wars at work.* New York: AMACOM.

Thompson, F. 1979. *Classics of personnel policy.* Oak Park, IL: Moore Publishing Co.

Torrington, D., and L. Hall. 1987. *Personnel management: A new approach.* London: Prentice-Hall International.

Wolf, T. 1990. *Managing a nonprofit organization.* New York: Prentice-Hall Press.

Chapter 8

Adams, I., B. Taxel, and S. Love. 2000. *Stan Hywet Hall and Garden.* Akron, OH: University of Akron Press.

Appelbaum, B. 1991. *Guide to environmental protection of collections.* Madison, CT: Sound View Press.

Bachmann, K., ed. 1992. *Conservation concerns: A guide for collectors and curators.* Washington, DC: Smithsonian Institution Press.

Baker, M. T. 1995. Synthetic polymers. In *Storage of natural history collections: A preventive conservation approach,* eds. C. L. Rose, C. A. Hawks, and H. H. Genoways, 305–323. York, PA: Society for the Preservation of Natural History Collections.

Blackaby, J. R., and P. Greeno. 1995. *The revised nomenclature for museum cataloging.* Walnut Creek, CA: AltaMira Press.

Blanchegorge, E. 1999. Preventive conservation on a day-to-day basis: The Antoine Vivenel Museum in Compiègne. *Museum International* 51(1):16–21.

Buck, R. A., and J. A. Gilmore, eds. 1998. *The new museum registration methods.* Washington, DC: American Association of Museums.

Burgess, H. D. 1995. Other cellulosic materials. In *Storage of natural history collections: A preventive conservation approach,* eds. C. L. Rose, C. A. Hawks, and H. H. Genoways, 291–303. York, PA: Society for the Preservation of Natural History Collections.

Butcher-Younghans, S. 1993. *Historic house museums: A practical handbook for their care, preservation, and management.* New York: Oxford University.

Calmes, A. 1995. Video tapes. In *Storage of natural history collections: A preventive conservation approach,* eds. C. L. Rose, C. A. Hawks, and H. H. Genoways, 395–400. York, PA: Society for the Preservation of Natural History Collections.

Case, M., ed. 1995. *Registrars on record: Essays on museum collections management.* Washington, DC: American Association of Museums.

Cassar, M. 1995. *Environmental management: Guideline for museums and galleries.* New York: Routledge.

de Guichen, G. 1999. Preventive conservation: A mere fad or far-reaching change? *Museum International* 51(1):4–6.

Dietrich, B., R. Etherington, and T. Laurenson. 1997. Policy writing: A blueprint for the future. *Museum International* 49(1):46–48.

Duckworth, W. D., H. H. Genoways, and C. L. Rose. 1993. *Preserving natural science collections: Chronicle of our environmental heritage.* Washington, DC: National Institute for the Conservation of Cultural Property.

Dudley, D. H., and I. B. Wilkinson. 1979. *Museum registration methods.* 3rd ed. Washington, DC: American Association of Museums.

Edson, G., and D. Dean. 1994. *The handbook for museums.* New York: Routledge.

Fahy, A., ed. 1995. *Collections management.* New York: Routledge.

Genoways, H. H., C. Jones, and O. L. Rossolimo, eds. 1987. *Mammal collection management.* Lubbock, TX: Texas Tech University Press.

Grzywacz, C. M. 1995. Air quality monitoring. In *Storage of natural history collec-*

tions: A preventive conservation approach, eds. C. L. Rose, C. A. Hawks, and H. H. Genoways, 197–209. York, PA: Society for the Preservation of Natural History Collections.

Hatchfield, P. 1995. Wood and wood products. In *Storage of natural history collections: A preventive conservation approach,* eds. C. L. Rose, C. A. Hawks, and H. H. Genoways, 283–290. York, PA: Society for the Preservation of Natural History Collections.

Hoagland, K. E., ed. 1994. *Guidelines for institutional policies and planning in natural history collections.* Washington, DC: Association of Systematics Collections.

Honan, W. H. 1991. The museum insider who became a thief. *New York Times* (The Living Arts), December 19, 1–2.

Howie, F. M., ed. 1992. *The care and conservation of geological materials: Minerals, rocks, meteorites, and lunar finds.* Oxford, UK: Butterworth-Heinemann, Ltd.

Johnston, D. 1996. A professor helps to catch Smithsonian's curator-thief. *New York Times* (National), February 17, 1, 9.

Knell, S. J., ed. 1994. *Care of collections.* New York: Routledge.

Koelling, J. M. 2002. Digitizing your collection. *American Association for State and Local History, Technical Leaflet* 217:1–8.

Krebs, M. 1999. A strategy for preventive conservation training. *Museum International* 51(1):7–10.

Liston, D., ed. 1993. *Museum security and protection: A handbook for cultural heritage institutions.* New York: Routledge.

Malaro, M. C. 1998. *A legal primer on managing museum collections.* Washington, DC: Smithsonian Institution Press.

Moore, B. P., and S. L. Williams. 1995. Storage equipment. In *Storage of natural history collections: A preventive conservation approach*, eds. C. L. Rose, C. A. Hawks, and H. H. Genoways, 255–267. York, PA: Society for the Preservation of Natural History Collections.

Nichols, S. K., ed. 1989. *Organizing your museum: The essentials.* Washington, DC: Technical Information Service, American Association of Museums.

Nishimura, D. W. 1995. Film supports: Negatives, transparencies, microforms, and motion picture films. In *Storage of natural history collections: A preventive conservation approach*, eds. C. L. Rose, C. A. Hawks, and H. H. Genoways, 365–393. York, PA: Society for the Preservation of Natural History Collections.

Norris, D. H. 1995. Historic and contemporary photographic prints. In *Storage of natural history collections: A preventive conservation approach,* eds. C. L. Rose, C. A. Hawks, and H. H. Genoways, 355–363. York, PA: Society for the Preservation of Natural History Collections.

Nugent, W. R. 1995. Compact discs and other digital optical discs. In *Storage of natural history collections: A preventive conservation approach*, eds. C. L. Rose, C. A. Hawks, and H. H. Genoways, 401–408. York, PA: Society for the Preservation of Natural History Collections.

Phelan, M. E. 1994. *Museum law*. Evanston, IL: Kalos Kapp Press.

Porter, D. R., III. 1985. *Current thoughts on collections policy*. Nashville, TN: Technical Reports, American Association for State and Local History.

Professional Practices Committee, RC-AAM, S. Hanna, Chair. 1991. Statement of practice for borrowing and lending. *Registrar* 8(2):3–10.

Reibel, D. B. 1997. *Registration methods for the small museum*. 3rd ed. Walnut Creek, CA: AltaMira Press.

Rose, C. L., and A. R. de Torres, eds. 1992. *Storage of natural history collections: Ideas and practical solutions*. Pittsburgh, PA: Society for the Preservation of Natural History Collections.

Sandwith, H., and S. Stainton. 1991. *The National Trust manual of housekeeping*. Rev. ed. London, UK: Penguin Books.

Schultz, A. W., ed. 1992. *Caring for your collections*. New York: Harry N. Abrams, Inc.

Simmons, J. E. 1995. Storage in fluid preservatives. In *Storage of natural history collections: A preventive conservation approach*, eds. C. L. Rose, C. A. Hawks, and H. H. Genoways, 161–186. York, PA: Society for the Preservation of Natural History Collections.

Spiess, K., and P. Spiess. 1990. Museum collection. In *The museum: A reference guide,* ed. M. S. Shapiro, 141–166. New York: Greenwood Press.

Stovel, H. 1998. *Risk preparedness: A management manual for world cultural heritage*. Rome, Italy: International Centre for the Study of the Preservation and Restoration of Cultural Property.

Thompson, J. M. A., ed. 1992. *Manual of curatorship: A guide to museum practice.* 2nd ed. Oxford, UK: Butterworth-Heineman, Ltd.

Thomson, G. 1986. *The museum environment.* 2nd ed. Oxford, UK: Butterworth-Heineman, Ltd.

van der Reyden, D. 1995. Paper documents. In *Storage of natural history collections: A preventive conservation approach,* eds. C. L. Rose, C. A. Hawks, and H. H. Genoways, 327–353. York, PA: Society for the Preservation of Natural History Collections.

von Endt, D. W., W. D. Erhardt, and W. R. Hopwood. 1995. Evaluating materials used for constructing storage cases. In *Storage of natural history collections: A preventive conservation approach,* eds. C. L. Rose, C. A. Hawks, and H. H. Genoways, 269–282. York, PA: Society for the Preservation of Natural History Collections.

Weil, S. E., ed. 1997. *A deaccession reader.* Washington, DC: American Association of Museums.

Weintraub, S., and S. J. Wolf. 1995. Environmental monitoring. In *Storage of natural history collections: A preventive conservation approach,* eds. C. L. Rose, C. A. Hawks, and H. H. Genoways, 187–196. York, PA: Society for the Preservation of Natural History Collections.

Zorich, D. M. 1999. *Introduction to managing digital assets: Options for cultural and educational organizations.* Los Angeles, CA: Getty Trust Publications.

Chapter 9

Ambrose, T., and C. Paine. 1993. *Museum basics.* New York: Routledge Press.

Ball, C., A. Yardley-Jones, and B. Walsh. 2001. *Help!: A survivor's guide to emergency preparedness.* Edmonton, Alberta: Museums Alberta.

Becker, F. 1990. *The total workplace: Facilities management and the elastic organization.* New York: Van Nostrand Reinhold.

Born, C. 2001. Lecture presented as part of session, "Service sensibility—Now that you have it, how do you keep it?" AAM Annual Meeting, St. Louis, MO, May 8.

Borun, M., and R. Korn, eds. 1999. *Introduction to museum evaluation.* Washington, DC: American Association of Museums.

Brown, D. W. 1996. *Facility maintenance: The manager's practical guide and handbook.* New York: American Management Association.

Burcaw, G. E. 1997. *Introduction to museum work.* Walnut Creek, CA: AltaMira Press.

Butcher-Younghans, S. 1993. *Historic house museums: A practical handbook for their care, preservation, and management.* New York: Oxford University.

Canadian Conservation Institute. 1995. *Emergency preparedness for cultural institutions: Introduction.* Ottawa: Canadian Conservation Institute Notes 14/1:1–2.

Candee, M., and R. Casagrande, eds. 1993. *PREP: Planning for response and emergency preparedness.* Austin, TX: Texas Association of Museums.

Cassar, M. 1995. *Environmental management: Guidelines for museums and galleries.* New York: Routledge.

Cotts, D. G. 1999. *The facility management handbook.* 2nd ed. New York: American Management Association.

Edson, G., and D. Dean. 1994. *The handbook for museums.* New York: Routledge.

Edwards, S. R., B. M. Bell, and M. E. King, eds. 1981. *Pest control in museums.* Lawrence, KS: Association of Systematics Collections.

Faulk, W. 1993. Are you ready when disaster strikes? *History News* 48:4–11.

Florian, M.-L. 1997. *Heritage eaters: Insects and fungi in heritage collections.* London: James & James, Ltd.

Hargraves, R. 2002. *Cataclysm and challenge: Impact of September 11, 2001, on our nation's cultural heritage.* Washington, DC: Heritage Preservation, Inc.

Haskins, S. M. 1996. *How to save your stuff from disaster.* Santa Barbara, CA: Preservation Help Publications.

Hatchfield, P. 1995. Wood and wood products. In *Storage of natural history collections: A preventive conservation approach,* eds. C. L. Rose, C. A. Hawks, and H. H. Genoways, 283–290. York, PA: Society for the Preservation of Natural History Collections.

Hillberry, J. D. 1995. Architectural design considerations. In *Storage of natural history collections: A preventive conservation approach,* eds. C. L. Rose, C. A. Hawks, and H. H. Genoways, 103–122. York, PA: Society for the Preservation of Natural History Collections.

Jacobs, J. F. 1995. Pest monitoring case study. In *Storage of natural history collections: A preventive conservation approach,* eds. C. L. Rose, C. A. Hawks, and H. H. Genoways, 221–232. York, PA: Society for the Preservation of Natural History Collections.

Jessup, W. C. 1995. Pest management. In *Storage of natural history collections: A preventive conservation approach,* eds. C. L. Rose, C. A. Hawks, and H. H. Genoways, 211–220. York, PA: Society for the Preservation of Natural History Collections.

Kahn, M. 1995. Disaster prevention and planning: Part II. *Local History Notebook* 11:i–iv.

Keller, S. R., and D. R. Wilson. 1995. Security systems. In *Storage of natural history collections: A preventive conservation approach,* eds. C. L. Rose, C. A. Hawks, and H. H. Genoways, 51–56. York, PA: Society for the Preservation of Natural History Collections.

Lewis, R. H. 1976. *Manual for museums.* Washington, DC: National Park Service, U.S. Department of the Interior.

Linnie, J. M. 1996. Integrated pest management: A proposed strategy for natural history museums. *Museum Management and Curatorship* 15:133–143.

Liston, D., ed. 1993. *Museum security and protection: A handbook for cultural heritage institutions.* New York: Routledge.

Lord, B., and G. D. Lord, eds. 1983. *Planning our museums.* Ottawa, Ontario, Canada: National Museums of Canada.

Makos, K. A., and E. C. Dietrich. 1995. Health and environmental safety. In *Storage of natural history collections: A preventive conservation approach,* eds.

C. L. Rose, C. A. Hawks, and H. H. Genoways, 233–252. York, PA: Society for the Preservation of Natural History Collections.

McLean, K. 1993. *Planning for people in museum exhibitions.* Washington, DC: Association of Science-Technology Centers.

National Park Service. 1990. *Biological infestations. Museum handbook part 1.* Washington, DC: National Park Service, U. S. Department of the Interior.

Nelson, C. L. 1991. *Protecting the past from natural disasters.* Washington, DC: The Preservation Press, National Trust for Historic Preservation.

Olkowski, W., H. Olkowski, and S. Daar. 1988. "What is IPM?" *Common Sense Pest Control* 3:9–16.

Parker, A. C. 1966. *A manual for history museums.* New York: AMS Press, Inc.

Phelan, M. E. 1994. *Museum law.* Evanston, IL: Kalos Kapp Press.

Registrars Committee. 1998. *Revised standard facility report.* Washington, DC: Professional Practice Series, Technical Information Service, American Association of Museums.

Roberts, B. O. 1995. Emergency preparedness. In *Storage of natural history collections: A preventive conservation approach,* eds. C. L. Rose, C. A. Hawks, and H. H. Genoways, 81–99. York, PA: Society for the Preservation of Natural History Collections.

Ryan, V. M. 1995. *Integrated pest management.* Denver, CO: Rocky Mountain Conservation Center.

Sandwith, H., and S. Stainton. 1993. *The National Trust manual of housekeeping.* rev. ed. London: Penguin Books.

Schwarzer, M. 1999. Schizophrenic agora: Mission, market and the multi-tasking museum. *Museum News* 78(6):40–47.

Sebor, A. J. 1995. Heating, ventilating, and air-conditioning systems. In *Storage of natural history collections: A preventive conservation approach,* eds. C. L. Rose, C. A. Hawks, and H. H. Genoways, 135–146. York, PA: Society for the Preservation of Natural History Collections.

Strang, T. J. K. 1997. *Controlling insect pests with low temperature.* Ottawa: Canadian Conservation Institute Notes 3/3.

Vaughan, J. M. 1999. Focus on recovery: The Hermitage, the home of President Andrew Jackson and its tornado. *History News* 54(3):12–15.

Wilcox, U. V. 1995. Facility management. In *Storage of natural history collections: A preventive conservation approach,* eds. C. L. Rose, C. A. Hawks, and H. H. Genoways, 29–41. York, PA: Society for the Preservation of Natural History Collections.

Wilson, J. A. 1995. Fire protection. In *Storage of natural history collections: A preventive conservation approach,* eds. C. L. Rose, C. A. Hawks, and H. H.

Genoways, 57–79. York, PA: Society for the Preservation of Natural History Collections.
———. 1999. Protecting cultural heritage properties from fire. Technical Leaflet, American Association for State and Local History 206:1–8.
Zycherman, L. A., and J. R. Schrock. 1988. *A guide to museum pest control.* Washington, DC: Foundation of the American Institute for Conservation of Historic and Artistic Works and the Association of Systematics Collections.

Chapter 10

American Association of Museums. *Accreditation.* World Wide Web: http://www.aam-us/programs/accreditation/accredproginfo.cfm. Retrieved September 3, 2002.
American Association of Museums. 1978. Museum ethics. *Museum News* 56(4):21–30.
———. 1994. *Code of ethics for museums.* Washington, DC: American Association of Museums.
———. 2000. *Guidelines on Exhibiting Borrowed Objects.* World Wide Web: www.aam-us.org.
Andrei, M. A., and H. H. Genoways. 1997. Museum ethics. *Curator, The Museum Journal* 40:6–12.
Blum, D. E. 2001. Sketching out a plan for survival. *The Chronicle of Philanthropy,* March 8, 57–59.
Boyd, W. C. 1991. Museum accountability: Laws, rules, ethics, and accreditation. *Curator, The Museum Journal* 34:165–177.
British Museum. *Newsroom.* World Wide Web: http://www.thebritishmuseum.ac.uk/newsroom/current/universalmuseums.html. Retrieved December 15, 2002.
Carey, T. 1978. Bringing museum ethics into focus. *Artnews* 77:93–97.
Davies, S. 1994. A sense of purpose: Rethinking museum values and strategies. In *Museum provision and professionalism,* ed. G. Kavanagh, 33–40. London: Routledge.
Edson, G., ed. 1997. *Museum ethics.* London: Routledge.
Edson, G., and D. Dean. 1994. *The handbook for museums.* London: Routledge.
Fray, P. Museums get tough on "trophy" returns. *The Age.* World Wide Web: http://www.theage.com.au/articles/2002/12/10/1039379835169.html. Retrieved December 16, 2002.
Friedman, A. J. 1994. Why did the 1991 Code of Ethics fail? *Curator, The Museum Journal* 37:9–11.

Genoways, H. H., and M. A. Andrei. 1997. Codes of professional museum conduct. *Curator, The Museum Journal* 40:86–92.

Grinnell, J. 1922. The museum conscience. *Museum Work* 4:62–63.

Gurian, E. H. 1999. The many meanings of objects in museums. *Dædalus,* Summer, 163–183.

Guthrie, K. M. 1996. *The New-York Historical Society: Lessons from one nonprofit's long struggle for survival.* San Francisco: Jossey-Bass, Inc.

Hoagland, K. E., ed. 1994. *Guidelines for institutional policies and planning in natural history collections.* Washington, DC: Association of Systematics Collections.

Independent Sector. 1994. Obedience to the unenforceable. In *Writing a museum code of ethics.* 2nd ed., 113–133. Washington, DC: American Association of Museums.

Janes, R. R. 1997. *Museums and the paradox of change: A case study in urgent adaptation.* Calgary, Alberta: Glenbow Museum.

Kainz, H. P. 1988. *Ethics in context.* London: The Macmillan Press Ltd.

Kolb, C. E. M. 1999. *Developing an ethics program: A case study for nonprofit organizations.* Washington, DC: National Center for Nonprofit Boards.

Lovin, R. W. 1994. What is ethics? In *Writing a museum code of ethics.* 2nd ed., 15–20. Washington, DC: American Association of Museums.

Macdonald, R. R. 1991. Developing a code of ethics for museums. *Curator, The Museum Journal* 34:178–186.

———. 1992. Ethics: Constructing a code. *Museum News* 71:62–65.

———. 1994. A question of ethics. *Curator, The Museum Journal* 37:6–9.

———. 1995. Collections, cash cows, and ethics. *Museum News* 74:42–43.

———. 1996. Museum ethics: The essence of professionalism. In *Museums: A place to work,* eds. J. R. Glaser and A. A. Zenetou, 35–40. London: Routledge.

Madison, H. L. 1994. Tentative code of museum ethics. In *Museum provision and professionalism,* ed. G. Kavanagh, 265–270. London: Routledge.

McCord, J. 1993. Vatican art draws record crowd. *Omaha World Herald,* August 25, 37–38.

Noble, J. V. 1970. Museum manifesto. *Museum News* 48(8):16–20.

Phelan, M. E. 1994. *Museum law.* Evanston, IL: Kalos Kapp Press.

Rosenbaum, L. 1995. New-York Historical Society sells New York heritage. *Wall Street Journal,* January 19.

Rosso, H. A. 1991. *Achieving excellence in fund raising.* San Francisco: Jossey-Bass, Inc.

Singer, P. 1994. *Ethics.* Oxford: Oxford University Press.

Skramstad, H. K., Jr. 1993. Excellent inequities. *Museum News* 72(1):50–51.

Swain, P. P. 1994. Development of a code of ethics: Museum of Science, Boston, MA. In *Writing a museum code of ethics.* 2nd ed., 21–27. Washington, DC: American Association of Museums.

Taylor, R. L. 1990. *Museum accreditation: A handbook for the institution.* Washington, DC: American Association of Museums.

Terence, I., trans. 1985. *The Nichomachean ethics by Aristotle.* Indianapolis, IN: Hacket Publishing Co., Inc.

Ullberg, A. D., and P. Ullberg. 1981. *Museum trusteeship.* Washington, DC: American Association of Museums.

Vogel, C. 1996. A museum's fortunes rise by $31 million at an auction. *New York Times*, November 14, B1, B4.

Weil, S. E. 1983. *Beauty and the beasts.* Washington, DC: Smithsonian Institution Press.

———. 1990. *Rethinking the museum.* Washington, DC: Smithsonian Institution Press.

———. 1992. The deaccession cookie jar. *Museum News* 71(6):54–55, 63.

———. 1995. *A cabinet of curiosities.* Washington, DC: Smithsonian Institution Press.

Wilson, D. M. 1982. Public interest versus conservation. *Museum* 34(1):65–67.

Chapter 11

Adams, G.D. 2000. Make your museum an expert on its customers. *History News* 55(2):15–19.

Atkins, J. T. 2001. Lecture presented in "Friend raising and collaboration: Museum tools for advocacy." AAM annual meeting, St. Louis, MO, May 8.

American Association of Museums. 1999. *America's museums: Building community communications kit.* Washington, DC: American Association of Museums.

———. 2002. *Mastering civic engagement: A challenge to museums.* Washington, DC: American Association of Museums.

Bangs, D. 1992. *Creating customers.* Dover, NH: Upstart Publishing Company.

Bonk, K., H. Griggs, and E. Tynes. 1999. *The Jossey-Bass guide to strategic communications for nonprofits.* San Francisco: Jossey-Bass, Inc.

Boone, L. E., and D. L. Kurtz. 1993. *Contemporary marketing plus.* 8th ed. Orlando, FL: The Dryden Press.

Booth, M., and Associates. 1995. *Promoting issues and ideas: A guide to public relations for nonprofit organizations.* New York: The Foundation Center.

REFERENCES

Drucker, P. F. 1974. *Management: Tasks, responsibilities, practices.* New York: HarperCollins.

Harris, T. L. 1991. *The marketer's guide to public relations.* New York: Wiley.

Herbig, P. A. 1998. *Handbook of cross-cultural marketing.* New York and London: The International Business Press.

Herron, D. 1997. Promotion, publicity, and PR. In *Marketing nonprofit programs and services,* 147–167. San Francisco: Jossey-Bass, Inc.

Humphreys, J. M. The multicultural economy 2002: Minority buying power in the new century. *Georgia Business and Economic Conditions* 62(2). World Wide Web: http://www.selig.uga.edu/forecast/GBEC/GBEC022Q.pdf. Retrieved November 26, 2002.

Ingenthorn, M. K. 2000. Creating your marketing plan: First know your audience. *History News* 55(2):20–23.

Kawashima, N. 1998. Knowing the public: A review of museum marketing literature and research. *Museum Management and Curatorship* 17:21–39.

Kotler, P. 1997. *Marketing management: Analysis, planning, implementation and control.* 9th ed. Upper Saddle River, NJ: Prentice Hall.

Kotler, P., and A. Andreasen. 1991. Managing public relations. In *Strategic marketing for nonprofit organizations,* 569–591. Englewood Cliffs, NJ: Prentice Hall.

Kotler, N. G., and P. Kotler. 1998. *Museum strategy and marketing: Designing missions, building audiences, generating revenue and resources.* San Francisco: Jossey-Bass, Inc.

Levy, S. J. 1980. Arts consumers and aesthetic attributes. In *Marketing the arts,* eds. M. P. Mokwa, W. M. Dawson, and E. A. Prieve, 29–45. New York: Praeger Publishers.

London, D. 2001. Lecture presented as part of "All the bells and whistles: Your website as a powerful marketing tool." AAM Annual Meeting, St. Louis, MO, May 7.

Long, J. S. 1999. Partnerships in disaster response: A national perspective. *History News* 54(3):6–11.

Lovelock, C. H., and C. B. Weinberg. 1978. Contrasting private and public sector marketing. In *Readings in public and nonprofit marketing,* eds. C. H. Lovelock and C. B. Weinberg, 27–32. Palo Alto, CA: The Scientific Press, USA.

Luther, W. 1992. Public relations. In *The marketing plan,* 110–116. New York: American Management Association.

Mason, D. 1996. Building a cohesive organization. In *Leading and managing the expressive dimension,* 128–156. San Francisco: Jossey-Bass, Inc.

Mathews, A. W. 2002. Entertainment companies aim to thrill museum throngs. *Wall Street Journal,* November 25, B1, B5.

Mellon Bank Corporation. 1985. *Discover total resources: A guide for nonprofits.* Pittsburgh, PA: Community Affairs Division, Mellon Bank Corporation.

Mokwa, M. P., W. M. Dawson, and E. A. Prieve. 1980. Promotion policy making. In *Marketing the arts,* eds. M. P. Mokwa, W. M. Dawson, and E. A. Prieve, 230–239. New York: Praegar Publishers.

Mokwa, M. P., K. Nakamoto, and B. M. Enis. 1980. Marketing management and the arts. In *Marketing the arts,* eds. M. P. Mokwa, W. M. Dawson, and E. A. Prieve, 14–28. New York: Praeger Publishers.

Peake, J. 1980. *Public relations in business.* New York: Harper and Row Publishers.

Peniston, W. A. 1999. *The new museum: Selected writings by John Cotton Dana.* Washington, DC: American Association of Museums.

Robinson, C. 2000. Create compelling programs before you market. *History News* 55(2):6–8.

Runyard, S., and Y. French. 1999. *The marketing and public relations handbook for museums, galleries and heritage attractions.* Walnut Creek, CA: AltaMira Press.

Saffir, L., and J. Tarrant. 1993. *Power public relations: How to get PR to work for you.* Chicago: NTC Business Books.

Searles, P. D. 1980. Marketing principles and the arts. In *Marketing the arts,* eds. M. P. Mokwa, W. Dawson, and E. A. Prieve, 65–69. New York: Praeger Publishers.

Stern, G. J. 1990. *Marketing workbook for nonprofit organizations.* St. Paul, MN: Amherst H. Wilder Foundation.

Strang, R. A., and J. Gutman. 1980. Promotion policy making in the arts. In *Marketing the arts,* eds. M. P. Mokwa, W. Dawson, and E. A. Prieve, 225–239. New York: Praeger Publishers.

Chapter 12

Adamchick, K. 1993. Museum magnet schools. *Museum News* 72(1):42–44.

Alexander, E. P. 1996. *Museums in motion: An introduction to the history and functions of museums.* Walnut Creek, CA: AltaMira Press.

American Association of Museums. 1992. *Excellence and equity: Education and the public dimension of museums.* Washington, DC: American Association of Museums.

Balzar, J. 2001. And the next item up for bids: The Smithsonian. *Los Angeles Times,* June 6 (Reprinted in *Lincoln Journal-Star,* June 17, p. 5D).

REFERENCES

Bannerman, C., and A. Kendall. 1981. *Museums magic & children: Youth education in museums.* Washington, DC: Association of Science-Technology Centers.

Beard, R. 1999. Building museums that last. *History News* 54(3):17–20, 22–23.

Bearman, D., and J. Trant, eds. 1999. *Museums and the web 1999.* Pittsburgh, PA: Archives and Museum Informatics.

Bedno, J., and E. Bedno. 1999. Museum exhibitions: Past imperfect, future tense. *Museum News* 78(5):39–43, 59–61.

Belcher, M. 1991. *Exhibitions in museums.* Washington, DC: Smithsonian Institution Press.

Bergmann, E. 1992. Exhibits: A proposal for guidelines. In *The audience in exhibition development* (Course proceedings from a training program developed by the Office of Museum Programs, Smithsonian Institution), 81–83. Washington, DC: American Association of Museums.

Blackmon, C. P., T. K. LaMaster, L. C. Roberts, and B. Serrell. 1988. *Open conversations: Strategies for professional development in museums.* Chicago, IL: Field Museum of Natural History.

Borg, W. R. 1981. *Applying educational research: A practical guide for teachers.* New York: Longman Inc.

Braden, D., and G. W. Overhiser, eds. 2000. Old collections, new audiences: Decorative arts and the visitor experience for the 21st century. Dearborn, MI: Henry Ford Museum and Greenfield Village.

Carr, D. 1999. The need for the museum. *Museum News* 78(2):31–35, 56–57.

Chambers, M. 1999. Critiquing exhibition criticism. *Museum News* 78(5):31, 33, 35, 37, 65.

Cornell, J. B. 1979. *Sharing nature with children: A parents' and teachers' nature awareness guidebook.* Nevada City, CA: Ananda Publications.

Crane, V., ed. 1994. *Informal science learning: What the research says about television, science museums, and community-based projects.* Dedham, MA: Research Communications, Ltd.

Csikszentmihályi, M., and K. Hermanson. 1995. Intrinsic motivation in museums: What makes visitors want to learn? *Museum News* 74(3):34–37, 59–60, 62.

Davis, J., and H. Gardner. 1993. Open windows, open doors. *Museum News* 72(1):34–37, 57–58.

Dean, D. 1994. *Museum exhibition: Theory and practice.* New York: Routledge.

Diamond, J. 1999. *Practical evaluation guide: Tools for museums and other informal educational settings.* Walnut Creek, CA: AltaMira Press.

Dow, P. B. 1993. Teaching with objects: No fault learning? *Social Studies* 84:230–231.

Edson, G., and D. Dean. 1994. *The handbook for museums.* New York: Routledge.

Eisner, E. W., and S. M. Dobbs. 1988. Silent pedagogy: How museums help visitors experience exhibitions. *Art Education* 41(4):6–15.

Falk, J. H. 1999. Museums as institutions for personal learning. *Dædalus* 128(3):259–275.

Falk, J. H., and L. D. Dierking. 1992. *The museum experience.* Washington, DC: Whalesback Books.

———. 2000. *Learning from museums: Visitor experiences and the making of meaning.* Walnut Creek, CA: AltaMira.

Fleming, L., and B. Peyton. 1986. *Project WILD.* Boulder, CO: Western Regional Environmental Education Council.

Friedman, A. J. 1991. Evaluation and museum management. In *Try it! Improving exhibits through formative evaluation,* eds. S. Taylor and B. Serrell, 76–86. Flushing Meadows, Corona Park, NY: New York Hall of Science.

Garfield, D. 1993. Michael Spock. *Museum News* 72(6):34–35, 58–60.

Giese, R. N., J. K. Davis-Dorsey, and J. A. Gutierrez, Jr. 1993. Evaluating the experience. *Museum News* 72(1):46–47, 59.

Gilborn, C. A. 1991. The director's role in exhibition and educational interpretation. In *Leadership for the future,* ed. B. F. Tolles, Jr., 71–82. Nashville, TN: American Association for State and Local History.

Henderson, A., and S. Watts. 2000. Learning how they learn: The family in the museum. *Museum News* 79(6):40–45, 67.

Johnson, N. B. 2000. Tracking the virtual visitor: A report from the National Gallery of Art. *Museum News* 79(2):42, 43–45, 67–71.

Jones, J. P. 1995. Communicating and learning in Gallery 33: Evidence from a visitor study. In *Museum, media, message,* ed. E. Hooper-Greenhill, 260–275. New York: Routledge.

Kotler, N. G., and P. Kotler. 1998. *Museum strategy and marketing: Designing missions, building audiences, generating revenue and resources.* San Francisco: Jossey-Bass, Inc.

LeBlanc, S. 1999. The slender golden thread, 100 years strong. *Museum News* 78(6):49–55, 63.

Lewis, W. J. 1991. *Interpreting for park visitors.* Yorktown, VA: East Acorn Press, Eastern National Park and Monument Association.

Lord, R. 2000. Quid pro show: Museums that take corporate shillings risk looking like corporate shills. *Pittsburgh City Paper,* December 27.

Lusaka, J. 2000. Digital visionary: George F. MacDonald and the world's first museum of the Internet century. *Museum News* 79(2):34–39, 41, 72–74.

MacDonald, S. 1995. Changing our minds: Planning a responsive museum service. In *Museum, media, message,* ed. E. Hooper-Greenhill, 165–174. New York: Routledge.

Mager, R. F. 1984. *Preparing instructional objectives.* Belmont, CA: Pitman Learning, Inc.

Malaro, M. C. 1985. *A legal primer on managing museum collections.* Washington, DC: Smithsonian Institution Press.

McLean, K. 1993. *Planning for people in museum exhibitions.* Washington DC: Association of Science-Technology Centers.

Miles, R. S. 1988. *The design of educational exhibits.* London and Boston: Allen and Unwin.

National Science Foundation. 1998. *Elementary, secondary, and informal education program announcement and guidelines.* Washington, DC: National Science Foundation.

Neuborne, E. 1997. This exhibit is brought to you by. . . . *Business Week* November 10(3552):91, 94.

Nichols, S. K., ed. 1989. *Organizing your museum: The essentials.* Washington, DC: American Association of Museums, Technical Information Service.

O'Donnell, S. C. 1995. The New York City museum school: A learning process. *Museum News* 74(3):38–41, 64, 66, 68.

Patton, M. Q. 1987. *How to use qualitative methods in evaluation.* Newbury Park, CA: Sage Publications, Inc.

Perrot, P. 1992. Profit and museums 1. In *Museums 2000: Politics, people, professionals and profit,* ed. P. J. Boylan, 148–168. New York: Routledge.

Pitman, B. 1993. Excellence and equity: Moving forward. *Museum News* 72(1):48–49, 60.

Prakash, M. S., and S. S. Shaman. 1988. Museum programs: Public escapism or education for public responsibility? *Art Education* 41(4):16–24, 41–43.

Said, T. 1999. America's promise and a place for museums. *Museum News* 78(3):40–43, 45, 56–57.

Skolnik, R. 1992. Arts & cultural organizations seek increased private support as public funding dwindles. *Public Relations Journal* 48(2):18–21.

Smithsonian. Guidelines for accessible exhibition design. World Wide Web: http://www.si.edu/access/exdesign/start.htm.

Spodek, B., O. N. Saracho, and M. D. Davis. 1987. *Foundations of early childhood education.* Englewood Cliffs, NJ: Prentice-Hall, Inc.

Teather, J. L. 1990. Professionalism and the museum. In *The museum: A reference guide,* eds. M. S. Shapiro and L. W. Kemp, 299–328. New York: Greenwood Press.

Tilden, F. 1977. *Interpreting our heritage.* 3rd ed. Chapel Hill, NC: University of North Carolina Press.

Watkins, C. A. 1998. Unnatural history museums. *Museum News* 77(4):31, 67.
Weil, S. E. 1990. *Rethinking the museum and other meditations.* Washington, DC: Smithsonian Institution Press.
———. 1999. From being about something to being for somebody: The ongoing transformation of the American museum. *Dædalus* 128(3):229–258.
Williams, B. L. 1996. An examination of art museum education practices since 1984. *Studies in Art Education* 38(1):34–49.
Williams, P. B. 1992. Professional standards for museum educators. In *Patterns in practice,* 60–65. Washington DC: Museum Education Roundtable.
Yellis, K. A. 1990. Museum education. In *The museum: A reference guide,* eds. M. S. Shapiro and L. W. Kemp, 167–198. New York: Greenwood Press.
Zeller, T. 1985. Museum education and school art: Different ends and different means. *Art Education* 38(3):6–10.

Chapter 13

Abercrombie, J. 1993. Where to go for advice and information about ADA. *The Public Garden,* July, 31–33.
Americans with Disabilities Act. 1990. *U.S. Code.* Title 42, chapter 126, sections 12101–12213.
Association of Science-Technology Centers. n.d. World Wide Web: http://www.astc.org/resource/access/index.htm.
Boyd, T. H., and J. Haas. 1992. The Native American Graves Protection and Repatriation Act: Prospects for new partnerships between museums and Native American groups. *Arizona State Law Journal* 24:253–282.
Briggs, G. 1993. Building access to friendships and gardens. *The Public Garden,* July, 24–27.
Brown, C. K. 1992. The museum's role in a multicultural society. In Patterns in Practice. *Journal of Museum Education, Roundtable Reports,* 3–8.
Buck, R. A., and J. A. Gilmore, eds. 1998. *The new museum registration methods.* Washington, DC: American Association of Museums.
Burcaw, G. E. 1997. *Introduction to museum work.* 3rd ed. Walnut Creek, CA: AltaMira Press.
Committee on Education and Labor, U.S. House of Representatives. 1990. *Legislative history of Public Law 101–336—The Americans with Disabilities Act.* Vol. 1 of 3. Washington, DC: U. S. Government Printing Office.
Disability Rights Education and Defense Fund. 1994. *Explanation of the Americans with Disabilities Act of 1990.* Washington, DC: U.S. Government Printing Office.

REFERENCES

Dongoske, K. E. 1996. The Native American Graves Protection and Repatriation Act: A new beginning, not the end, for osteological analysis—a Hopi perspective. *American Indian Quarterly* 20:287–296.

Echo-Hawk, W. 1992. The Native American Graves Protection and Repatriation Act: A legislative history. *Arizona State Law Journal* 24:74–76.

Evan Terry Associates, PC. 1993. *Americans with Disabilities Act facilities compliance: A practical guide.* New York: John Wiley & Sons, Inc.

Ferguson, T. J., R. Anyon, and E. J. Ladd. 1996. Repatriation at the Pueblo of Zuni: Diverse solutions to complex problems. *American Indian Quarterly* 20:251–273.

Ferguson, T. J., E. J. Ladd, and W. L. Merrill. 1993. The return of the Ahayuida: Lessons for repatriation from Zuni Pueblo and the Smithsonian Institution. *Current Anthropology* 34:523–551.

Green, T. J., V. D. Green, and J. C. Rose. 1996. NAGPRA is forever: Osteology and the repatriation of skeletons. *Annual Review of Anthropology* 25:81–103.

Hill, R. 1979. Indians and museums: A plea for cooperation. *Council of Museums Anthropology Newsletter* 2:22–23.

Horse Capture, G. P. 1991. Survival of culture. *Museum News* 70(1):49–51.

Hutter, M. J. 2000. *An overview of intellectual property.* Albany, NY: Albany Law School, Institute of Legal Studies.

Kent, A., and H. Lancour, eds. 1972. *Copyright, current viewpoints on history, laws, legislation.* New York and London: R. R. Bowker Company.

Killheffer, R. K. J. 1995. Reburying the past: Controversy over Native American artifacts and remains. *Omni* 17(9):30–36.

Lind, R. C., R. M. Jarvis, and M. E. Phelan. 2002. *Art and museum law: Cases and materials.* Durham, NC: Carolina Academic Press.

Majewski, J. 1993. Accessibility for people with disabilities: Razing the problems. *The Public Garden,* July, 8–9.

Malaro, M. C. 1998. *A legal primer on managing museum collections.* 2nd ed. Washington, DC: Smithsonian Institution Press.

McManamon, F., and L. V. Nordby. 1991. Implementing the Native American Graves Protection and Repatriation Act. In *Technical Information Service's forum: Native American collections and repatriation,* 60–82. Washington, DC: American Association of Museums.

Miller, P. L. 1989. Putting your house in order: More accountability equals less liability. In *Organizing your museum,* ed. S. K. Nichols, 147–148. Washington, DC: American Association of Museums.

Monroe, D. L., and W. Echo-Hawk. 1991. Deft deliberations. *Museum News* 70(4):55–58.

National Parks Conservation Association. n.d. World Wide Web: http://www.npca.org/cultural_diversity/diversity and http://www.npca.org/.

Native American Graves Protection and Repatriation Act (NAGPRA). U.S. Code. Title 25, chapter 32, sections 3001–3013, Native American graves protection and repatriation, 2001.

Nimmer, M. B. 1979. *Cases and material on copyright and other aspects of laws pertaining to literary, musical, and artistic works.* St. Paul, MN: West Publishing Company.

Phelan, M. E. 1994. *Museum law.* Evanston, IL: Kalos Kapp Press.

Platt, G., Jr. 1991. The repatriation law ends one journey—but opens a new road. *Museum News* 70(1):91.

President's Committee on Employment of People with Disabilities. 1993. Americans with Disabilities Act: Focus on key provisions. Leaflet.

Quick, A. n.d. *The Americans with Disabilities Act: A framework for action and decisions required under key section of Title III of the ADA.* Omaha, NE: Borens-Tate Consulting Group, Inc.

Rehabilitation Act of 1973. U.S. Code. Title 29, chapter 16, sections 701–797.

Sackler, E. 1992. Three voices for repatriation. *Museum News* 71(5):58–61.

Salmen, J. P. S. 1998. *Everyone's welcome: The Americans with Disabilities Act and museums.* Washington, DC: American Association of Museums.

Shapiro, M. S., and B. I. Miller. 2000. Copyright in the digital age. *Museum News* 79(1):36–45, 66–67.

Tabah, A. 1993. Native American collections and repatriation. In *Technical Information Service's forum: Native American collections and repatriation,* 5. Washington, DC: American Association of Museums.

Teichman, J. L., P. G. Powers, and G. C. Hartman, Jr. 1989. Collection objects of uncertain status: indefinite loans, deposits, and undocumented objects—what are the museum's alternatives? In *Organizing your museum,* ed. S. K. Nichols, 61–64. Washington, DC: American Association of Museums.

Thompson, R. H. 1991. Dealing with the past and looking to the future. *Museum News* 70(1):37–40.

Ullberg, A. D., and R. C. Lind, Jr. 1989. Consider the potential liability of failing to conserve collections. *Museum News* 68(1):32–33.

Ullberg, A. D., and P. Ullberg. 1981. *Museum trusteeship.* Washington, DC: American Association of Museums.

UNESCO. n.d. *The ABC of copyright.* Paris, France: United Nations Educational, Scientific, and Cultural Organization.

U.S. Department of Justice: Civil Rights Division: Disability Rights Section. 1996. *Americans with Disabilities Act.* Washington, DC: U.S. Government Printing Office.

U.S. Department of Justice: Civil Rights Division: Disability Rights Section. 1997. *Commonly asked questions about the Americans with Disabilities Act and law enforcement.* Washington, DC: U.S. Government Printing Office.

U.S. Equal Opportunity Commission and the U.S. Department of Justice. 1992. *Americans with Disabilities Act handbook.* Washington, DC: U.S. Government Printing Office.

U.S. Public Law 101–601; 25 U.S.C.A. 3003(b)(1)(c).

Wilkoff, W. L., and L. W. Abed. 1994. *Practicing universal design: An interpretation of the ADA.* New York: Van Nostrand Reinhold.

Williams, P. B. 1989. American Association of Museum Standing Professional Committee on Education. *Journal of Museum Education* 14(3):11–13.

Wolf, T. 1999. *Managing a nonprofit organization in the twenty-first century.* New York: Simon & Schuster.

Zimmerman, L. J. 1996. Epilogue: A new and different archaeology? *American Indian Quarterly* 20:297–307.

Chapter 14

Alexander, E. P. 1983. *Museum masters.* Nashville, TN: American Association for State and Local History.

———. 1997. *The museum in America: Innovators and pioneers.* Walnut Creek, CA: AltaMira Press.

Ames, M. 1986. *Museums, the public, and anthropology: A study in the anthropology of anthropology.* New Delhi, India: Naurang Rai Concept Publishing Company.

Bal, M. 1996. *Double exposure: The subject of cultural analysis.* New York: Routledge.

Banner, L. W. 1994. Three stages of development. In *Gender perspectives: Essays on women in museums,* eds. J. R. Glaser and A. A. Zenetou, 39–46. Washington, DC, and London: Smithsonian Institution Press.

Boylan, P., ed. 1992. *Museums 2000: Politics, people, professionals, and profit.* London: Routledge.

Carnegie, E. 1992. Case study: Working with women's groups. In *Developing museum exhibitions for lifetime learning,* ed. G. Durbin, 173–175. London: The Stationery Office for the Group for Education, Museums and Galleries Commission.

Cortés, C. E. 2000. *The children are watching: How the media teach about diversity.* New York: Teachers College Press.

Cove, J. J. 1995. *What the bones say.* Ottawa, Ontario: Carleton University Press.

Coxall, H. 1997. Speaking other voices. In *Cultural diversity: Developing museum audience in Britain,* ed. E. Hooper-Greenhill, 99–115. London: Leicester University Press.

Engelhardt, T. 1996. Fifty years under a cloud. In *Multiculturalism,* ed. R. Long, 112–121. New York: H. W. Wilson.

Etzowitz, H., C. Kemelgor, M. Neuschatz, and B. Uzzi. 1994. Barriers to women in academic science and engineering. In *Who will do science? Educating the next generation.* Baltimore: Johns Hopkins University Press.

Gordon, M. 1994. An inside view. In *Gender perspectives: Essays on women in museums,* eds. J. R. Glaser and A. A. Zenetou, 108–112. Washington, DC: Smithsonian Institution Press.

Greenfield, J. 1989. *The return of cultural treasures.* Cambridge, UK: Cambridge University Press.

Harris, N. 1995. Museums and controversy: Some introductory reflections. *Journal of American History* 82:1102–1110.

Hooper-Greenhill, E. 1994. *Museums and their visitors.* London: Routledge.

———. 1997. *Cultural diversity: Developing museum audience in Britain.* London: Leicester University Press.

Horn, M. 1997. Through the glass darkly. *U.S. News and World Report* 122(20):54.

Hoving, T. 1993. *Making the mummies dance.* New York: Simon and Schuster.

Huyck, H. 1997. Placing women in the past. *Cultural Resource Management* 20(3):4–6.

Joppke, C., and S. Lukes. 1999. *Multicultural questions.* New York: Oxford.

Kelly, J. 2000. Nature, natives, and nations: Glorification and asymmetries in museum representation, Fiji and Hawaii. *Ethos* 65(2):95–126.

Kotler, N. G., and P. Kotler. 1998. *Museum strategy and marketing.* San Francisco: Jossey-Bass, Inc.

Kurin, R. 1997. *Reflections of a culture broker.* Washington, DC: Smithsonian Institution Press.

Landi, A. 1997. Museum-quality women: Obstacles facing women today who are seeking museum directorships. *ArtNews* 96(5):146–149.

Langley, A. 2002. Sons close cultish Hepburn museum. *The Guardian,* October 31.

Lewin, T. 2001. Women profit less than men in the nonprofit world, too. *New York Times,* June 3.

Messenger, P. M. 1989. *The ethics for collecting cultural property: Whose culture? Whose property?* Albuquerque: University of New Mexico Press.

REFERENCES

Moon, K. 1997. Raising our sites, integrating women's history into museums. *Cultural Resource Management* 20(3):32–34.

National Museum of Women in the Arts. 2002. *History of NMWA.* World Wide Web: http://www.mmwa.org/about/history.asp.

O'Donnell, S. C., D. Frankel, K. D. Southern, G. Becker, B. Franco, and K. H. Conwill. 1997. Women in museums: A progress report. *Museum News* 76(2):34–41.

Pandian, J. 1985. *Anthropology and the Western tradition.* Prospect Heights, IL: Waveland Press, Inc.

Paul, H. 1994. In preparation for the future. In *Gender perspectives: Essays on women in museums,* eds. J. R. Glaser and A. A. Zenetou, 115–124. Washington, DC: Smithsonian Institution Press.

Pearce, S. 1997. *Experiencing material culture in the Western world.* Leicester, UK: Cassell-Mansel.

Rice, D. 1993. The cross-cultural mediator. *Museum News* 72(1):38–41.

Said, E. 1978. *Orientalism.* New York: Pantheon Books.

Schank, R. C. 1991. *The connoisseur's guide to the mind.* New York: Summit Books.

Shannon, C. 2001. *A world made safe for differences.* Lanham, MD: Rowman and Littlefield Publishers, Inc.

Shohat, E. 2001. *Taking visions: Multicultural feminism in a transnational age.* Cambridge, MA: MIT Press.

Simpson, M. G. 1996. *Making representations: Museums in the post-colonial era.* New York: Routledge.

Sims, R. R., and R. F. Dennehy. 1993. *Diversity and differences in organizations: An agenda for answers and questions.* Westport, CT: Quorum Books.

Sullivan, R. 1994. Evaluating the ethics and consciences of museums. In *Gender perspectives: Essays on women in museums,* eds. J. R. Glaser and A. A. Zenetou, 100–107. Washington, DC: Smithsonian Institution Press.

Talbot, F. 1994. Balancing gender representation. In *Gender perspectives: Essays on women in museums,* eds. J. R. Glaser and A. A. Zenetou, 66–68. Washington, DC: Smithsonian Institution Press.

Tator, C., F. Henry, and W. Mattis. 1998. *Challenging racism in the arts: Case studies of controversy and conflict.* Toronto, Canada: University of Toronto Press.

Taylor, K. 1994. Pioneering efforts of early museum women. In *Gender perspectives: Essays on women in museums,* eds. J. R. Glaser and A. A. Zenetou, 11–27. Washington, DC: Smithsonian Institution Press.

Tucker, M. 1994. From theory to practice: Correcting inequalities. In *Gender per-*

spectives: Essays on women in museums, eds. J. R. Glaser and A. A. Zenetou, 51–54. Washington and London: Smithsonian Institution Press.

Weber, J. 1994. Changing roles and attitudes. In *Gender perspectives: Essays on women in museums,* eds. J. R. Glaser and A. A. Zenetou, 32–36. Washington, DC: Smithsonian Institution Press.

Wilson, D. 1989. *The British Museum: Purpose and politics.* London: British Museum Publications Ltd.

Chapter 15

Ackerson, A. W. 1998. New director! New directions? American Association for State and Local History, Technical Leaflet 203:1–8.

Adams, R., and T. J. Ritzenthaler. 1999. *Guide to museum studies and training in the United States, 1999–2000.* Washington, DC: Professional Practice Series, Technical Information Service, American Association of Museums.

American Association of Museums. 1999. *America's museums: Building community.* Washington, DC: American Association of Museums.

———. 2001. Museums and community update. Handout distributed at AAM annual meeting, May 7, St. Louis, MO.

Belasco, J. A., and J. Stead. 1999. Owning up to your work. *Perdido* 6(4):21–24.

Bennis, W. 1989. *Why leaders can't lead: The unconscious conspiracy continues.* San Francisco: Jossey-Bass, Inc.

Bennis, W., M. S. Gretchen, and T. G. Cummings, eds. 2001. *The future of leadership: Today's top leadership thinkers speak to tomorrow's leaders.* San Francisco: Jossey-Bass, Inc.

Besser, H. 1997. The changing role of photographic collections with the advent of digitization. In *The wired museum: Emerging technology and changing paradigms,* ed. K. Jones-Garmil, 115–127. Washington, DC: American Association of Museums.

Carr, D. 1999. The need for the museum. *Museum News* 78(2):31–32, 34–35, 56–57.

Clifton, D. O., and P. Nelson. 1992. *Soar with your strengths.* New York: Delacorte Press.

Davies, S. W. 1999. Visionary leadership and missionary zeal. In *Management in museums,* ed. K. Moore, 108–132. London and New Brunswick, NJ: The Athlone Press.

Drucker, P. F. 1996. Not enough generals were killed. In *The Leader of the future,* eds. F. Hesselbein, M. Goldsmith, and R. Beckhard, xi–xv. San Francisco: Jossey-Bass, Inc.

———. 1999. The future that has already happened. *Perdido* 6(4):17–19, 24.

Duckworth, W. D., H. H. Genoways, and C. L. Rose. 1993. *Preserving natural science collections: Chronicle of our environmental heritage.* Washington, DC: National Institute for the Conservation of Cultural Property.

Durel, J. 1998. A new director's first year. *History News* 53(4):18–20.

Edson, G., and D. Dean. 1994. *The handbook for museums.* London and New York: Routledge.

Farren, C., and B. L. Kaye. 1996. New skills for new leadership roles. In *The leader of the future,* eds. F. Hesselbein, M. Goldsmith, and R. Beckhard, 175–187. San Francisco: Jossey-Bass Publishers, Inc.

Fleming, D. 1999. Leadership. In *Management in museums,* ed. K. Moore, 93–117. London and New Brunswick, NJ: The Athlone Press.

Handy, C. 1996. The new language of organizing and its implications for leaders. In *The leader of the future,* eds. F. Hesselbein, M. Goldsmith, and R. Beckhard, 3–9. San Francisco: Jossey-Bass, Inc.

———. 1999. A proper education. *Perdido* 6(4):5–15.

Hecht, B., and R. Ramsey. 2002. *ManagingNonprofit.org: Dynamic management for the digital age.* New York: John Wiley & Sons.

Ioanid, A., and V. Bowman. 2001. Data and metadata: An overview of organization in searchable full-text databases. In *Creating web-accessible databases: Case studies for libraries, museums, and other nonprofits,* ed. J. M. Still, 143–156. Medford, NJ: Information Today, Inc.

Johnston, L. 1997. Imaging in museums: Issues in resource development. In *The wired museum: Emerging technology and changing paradigms,* ed. K. Jones-Garmil, 93–113. Washington, DC: American Association of Museums.

Jones-Garmil, K. 1997. Laying the foundation: Three decades of computer technology in the museum. In *The wired museum: Emerging technology and changing paradigms,* ed. K. Jones-Garmil, 35–62. Washington, DC: American Association of Museums.

Koelling, J. M. 2000. Revealing history: Another look at the Solomon D. Butcher photographs. *Nebraska History* 81:50–55.

———. 2002. Digitizing your collection. American Association for State and Local History, Technical Leaflet 217:1–8.

Kouzes, J. M., and B. Z. Posner. 1996. Seven lessons for leading the voyage to the future. In *The leader of the future,* eds. F. Hesselbein, M. Goldsmith, and R. Beckhard, 99–110. San Francisco: Jossey-Bass, Inc.

Leigh, A., and M. Maynard. 1996. *The perfect leader.* London: Arrow Business Books.

Levenson, J. A. 1998. Digital imaging and issues of authenticity in the art museum. In *The virtual and the real: Media in the museum,* ed. S. Thomas and A. Mintz, 89–101. Washington, DC: American Association of Museums.

London, D. 2001. Lecture presented as part of "All the bells and whistles: Your website as a powerful marketing tool." AAM Annual Meeting, May 7, St. Louis, MO.

McCauley, C. D., and M. W. Hughes. 1993. Leadership in human services: Key challenges and competencies. In *Governing, leading, and managing nonprofit organizations,* eds. D. R. Young, R. M. Hollister, V. A. Hodgkinson, and Associates, 155–169. San Francisco: Jossey-Bass, Inc.

Meléndez, S. E. 1996. An "outsider's" view of leadership. In *The leader of the future,* eds. F. Hesselbein, M. Goldsmith, and R. Beckhard, 293–302. San Francisco: Jossey-Bass, Inc.

Mintz, A. 1998. Media and museums: A museum perspective. In *The virtual and the real: Media in the museum,* ed. S. Thomas and A. Mintz, 19–34. Washington, DC: American Association of Museums.

Morrissey, K., and D. Worts. 1998. A place for the muses? Negotiating the role of technology in museums. In *The virtual and the real: Media in the museum,* ed. S. Thomas and A. Mintz, 147–171. Washington, DC: American Association of Museums.

Nanus, B., and S. M. Dobbs. 1999. *Leaders who make a difference: Essential strategies for meeting the nonprofit challenge.* San Francisco: Jossey-Bass, Inc.

Nicholson, C. 1995. Advisors to partners: Bridging the cultural gap. *History News* 50(4):10–13.

Perlin, R. R. 1998. Media, art museums, and distant audiences. In *The virtual and the real: Media in the museum,* ed. S. Thomas and A. Mintz, 73–87. Washington, DC: American Association of Museums.

Phillips, W. 1998. What it takes to lead into the next millennium. *History News* 53(4):28–29.

Powell, J. L. 1995. *Pathways to leadership.* San Francisco: Jossey-Bass, Inc.

Sayre, S. 1998. Assuring the successful integration of multimedia technology in an art museum environment. In *The virtual and the real: Media in the museum,* ed. S. Thomas and A. Mintz, 129–144. Washington, DC: American Association of Museums.

Schein, E. H. 1996. Leadership and organizational culture. In *The leader of the future,* eds. F. Hesselbein, M. Goldsmith, and R. Beckhard, 59–69. San Francisco: Jossey-Bass, Inc.

Schwarzer, M. 2001. *Graduate training in museum studies: What students need to know.* Washington, DC: American Association of Museums.

REFERENCES

Simerly, R. G. 1991. Seven critical issues for museum leaders. Unpublished manuscript, 23 pp.

Speck, V. H. 2001. Taking a database to the web: A case study. In *Creating web-accessible databases: Case studies for libraries, museums, and other nonprofits,* ed. J. M. Still, 87–101. Medford, NJ: Information Today, Inc.

Tolles, B. F., Jr., ed. 1991. *Leadership for the future.* Nashville, TN: American Association for State and Local History.

INDEX

ABOUT THE AUTHORS

Hugh H. Genoways, currently a professor at the University of Nebraska–Lincoln, holds an A.B. from Hastings College and a Ph.D. from the University of Kansas. He has been curator at the Museum of Texas Tech University, Lubbock, Texas, and at the Carnegie Museum of Natural History, Pittsburgh, Pennsylvania, and was director of the University of Nebraska State Museum from 1986 to 1994. He served on the organizing committee for the Museum Science Program at Texas Tech University and as the founding chair of the Museum Studies Program at the University of Nebraska–Lincoln from 1989 to 1995. He is now serving a second term as chair. Dr. Genoways was a founding member and president of the Nebraska Museums Association (1992–1994), and later he served as secretary. He received the association's first Recognition Award. He has also served on the boards of the Association for Systematics Collections and the National Institute for the Conservation of Cultural Property. Dr. Genoways has authored or edited many books and articles, primarily in the areas of mammalogy and museology.

Lynne M. Ireland holds a B.A. from Nebraska Wesleyan University and an M.A. from the Cooperstown Graduate Programs, State University College at Oneonta, New York. She also completed the J. Paul Getty Trust's Museum Management Institute. At the Nebraska State Historical Society she has held the positions of folklife/special projects coordinator, coordinator of museum programs and public relations, acting museum director of the Museum of Nebraska History, and associate director for museums and historic sites. Currently, Ms. Ireland is assistant director for program development. She is also an adjunct professor in the museum studies program of the University of Nebraska–Lincoln, having joined the department in 1992. She has served the Nebraska Museums Association as newsletter editor and as president (1996–1998). She is the author of a number of publications interpreting the history of food, including a chapter in the *Smithsonian Festival of American Folklife Cookbook*, and has written and produced a history radio spot series and coproduced short history programs for the Nebraska Educational Television network.

Breinigsville, PA USA
31 July 2010
242739BV00001B/2/P

9 780759 102941